Retail Marketing

Retail Marketing

Ogenyi Omar

FINANCIAL TIMES
PITMAN PUBLISHING

FINANCIAL TIMES

MANAGEMENT

LONDON · SAN FRANCISCO
KUALA LUMPUR · JOHANNESBURG

*Financial Times Management delivers the knowledge,
skills and understanding that enable students,
managers and organisations to achieve their ambitions,
whatever their needs, wherever they are.*

London Office:
128 Long Acre, London WC2E 9AN
Tel: +44 (0)171 447 2000
Fax: +44 (0)171 240 5771
Website: www.ftmanagement.com

An imprint of Pearson Education Limited

First published in Great Britain in 1999

ISBN 0 273 63859 9

British Library Cataloguing in Publication Data
A CIP catalogue record for this book can be obtained from the British Library

10 9 8 7 6 5 4 3 2 1

Typeset by Pantek Arts, Maidstone, Kent
Printed and bound in Great Britain by Redwood Books Ltd, Trowbridge

The Publishers' policy is to use paper manufactured from sustainable forests.

Contents

Preface

Retailers normally perform two essential functions. One is the satisfaction of consumer needs and wants; the other is the provision of outlets for production. These two functions are complementary and reciprocal. Goods produced have no value in themselves. It is only when they are made available to consumers who want them and are able and willing to buy them that they assume any value. Retail distribution therefore is the final function of production.

Most production takes place in quantities that far exceed the everyday wants of individual shoppers. Goods are produced in specialist factories throughout the UK and the world. Customers' needs may be few or occasional but they usually want a selection from which to choose. The retailer consequently is the intermediary who brings together production and consumption, both in a quantitative and a qualitative way. Retailers must know their markets in terms of supply, foreseeing future demand, and anticipating changes and trends; they also buy in wholesale quantities, hold stock and sell in individual amounts. Advising and assisting consumers, often providing extra services or amenities as well, is another important role of the retailer. The motive is to make a profit sufficient to repay the effort and investment.

Specifically, retail marketing as an activity in retail management has three important roles to play in the:

- identification and specification of particular market areas for individual retail organisations;
- management of retail marketing mix; and
- design and implementation of retail promotion, retail advertising, display and similar activities within the store and in the various media.

Once a retailer has decided to operate in a particular product market area, it becomes necessary to understand the patterns of demand and bases of consumer behaviour in the chosen field. The essence of retail marketing management at this stage is to identify a worthwhile target market in numerical terms which is not being adequately serviced at present and to which the retailer can respond with existing or potentially available resources.

Target readership

This book is primarily offered as both an introduction to retail marketing and a basic reference text, covering the functions and most types of retail organisation. Indeed, the breadth of coverage is designed so as to allow material to be selected to meet specific, individual needs across a wide spectrum of retail organisational situations. It also makes the basic assumption that you may not be currently involved directly in the retailing function itself, and may not previously have had any significant exposure to the theory or practice of retail marketing. The scope of this book enables its use as a reference source in even the most demanding of contexts and should equip students to meet most practical retail marketing requirements.

Although aimed at undergraduate-level courses in retail management, this book will also appeal to the young and ambitious retail decision makers who would like to do better than their competition; they realise the value of strategic decisions and strategy development as opposed to making decisions on a day-to-day basis. This book will also appeal to professional researchers and consultants, not because it has a heavy research orientation but rather because it raises research-related issues and imparts some new research findings.

Although many of this book's readers will not be expert practitioners of retailing, the author does not feel it is justifiable to take a superficial view of retail marketing. The book, therefore, delivers an in-depth treatment of the subject. It is further assumed that the reader has the intellectual capacity and curiosity to want to know in some detail what retail marketing is about. The content of the book is therefore deep enough to satisfy the most erudite of professional retailers.

In order to provide this breadth and depth of information without forcing the student to absorb too many pages of esoteric theory, some of the more advanced retailing elements are offered as reference materials. Those who wish to read further, may study at their leisure; the ordinary reader may skip to more practical material. Some of the content is designed to be particularly useful to those with interests in retail marketing generally, by highlighting and expanding upon the general skills which are the province of all retail managers.

Theory and practice

An attempt is made in this book to cover the most important theory and related practice in retail marketing discipline. Where possible, this broad coverage is supplemented by deeper level studies. This is because much of the understanding of retail marketing comes from an in-depth appreciation of individual techniques and the basic consumer needs that they address. As with all marketing education, theory alone will not make the student a qualified retail manager; for that the student will also need relevant practical retail marketing experience. However, this book should give the student a good feel for what retail marketing is about, and help the student to talk sensibly and productively to retailers in their own language.

This book also caters for those who may be practising retail managers and who are learning about the theory of retail marketing in their spare time. Such students have the great advantage of immersion in a real-life case study – the workings of the retail organisation in which they operate. The author has taken just such a pragmatic approach, developing this book in the light of practical experience with many thousands of students. A wide range of practical questions have been similarly developed, based on continuous reference to the practice of retail marketing within retail organisations. The questions are of varying degrees of complexity, ranging from the simplest of questions, requiring only straightforward answers, to those requiring the formulation of a complete retail marketing plan.

In line with its emphasis on practicality, the book offers the various theories only as tools to be used when applicable: as aids to understanding consumer needs and what satisfies them. It critically examines the theories in the context of what they may offer practising retail managers. Thus each subject is approached as if the students are practising retail managers. Whenever possible, it is suggested which of the various theories – these tools – may be appropriate for a given situation. However, it is emphasised that there are several tools which may be equally applicable to the situation, each of which offers a different framework for individual analysis. In this context, retail marketing as a discipline can provide few generalised principles or theories. The major contribution of retail marketing to retail management is in its approach to problem identification and likely solution prescription.

This view is supported throughout: the book is firmly rooted in retail marketing practice, with the theoretical base being used to provide a useful framework. However, as David Mercer appropriately explained, less than half a century after the arrival of marketing as a widely used practical tool of management, too many marketing theorists appear to be hankering after academic respectability and are beginning to adorn their work with, for example, esoteric mathematical approaches. However, the subject, as practised, remains as determinedly 'fuzzy' as it ever was. These contradictions are explained clearly throughout this book.

Retail marketing management practice is pragmatic and it is based upon what has been shown by experience to work rather than what theory would prescribe. Philip Kotler has observed that marketing people often say that marketing experience is the best teacher; and that planning and performing a diversity of marketing activities such as selling, pricing, advertising, and servicing help to create sound judgement about what will and what will not work.

The approach in this book is, therefore, more akin to what David Mercer referred to as 'an academic form of gardening'. The test, of course, is whether the application of any particular retail marketing tool works in the specific situation which faces the retailer, and whether it helps a retail manager in his or her managerial function. In most retail marketing problem-solving situations it will be obvious whether the apparently 'best choice' retail marketing tool is a success or failure.

An introduction to the structure of the book: aims and objectives

The aim of this book is to provide an introduction to the theory and practice of retail marketing, for both non-specialists and newcomers to the discipline. Thus, by the time you have completed the main chapters, you should:

■ appreciate why retail marketing is so important for retail organisations and what this means for their successful retail operations;

- understand the basic principles and main theories of retail marketing together with how retail management may apply these in practice;

- recognise the limitations of such theories and the practical remedies which may help retail managers overcome these limitations;

- be able to understand the language used by retailers and marketing practitioners and assess the merits of their recommendations in the retail marketing context;

- be able to apply relevant marketing concepts and techniques to the more general retail operations in the UK and elsewhere in the world.

One special attraction of retail marketing as an area of study is that it is a part of the working economy which affects almost everyone on a daily basis. In addition to this, the 1980s and early 1990s saw significant changes taking place in the way in which retail management is carried out throughout the world. Taking such changes into consideration, the retail marketing ideas developed in this book are based on the notion that effective retail marketing involves: planning, implementing, evaluating, and controlling the performance.

The book is comprised of 16 chapters. Chapter 1 presents an overview of retail marketing and the nature of its development. The first few chapters explore the external activities of retail marketing namely, the general retail marketing environment (Chapter 2) and specific aspects of consumer behaviour pertaining particularly to retail purchase behaviour (Chapter 3). Chapter 4 examines retail market segmentation and positioning.

Chapters 5, 6 and 7 bring external factors closer to the individual retail store. Whereas Chapter 5 explores store image, loyalty and patronage management, Chapter 6 examines the specific aspects of distribution and logistics. Chapter 7 expands on the foundation established in Chapters 5 and 6 by exploring retail location, feasibility and logistics. Similarly Chapter 8 expands on Chapter 5, specifically reviewing product selection, buying and merchandising management. Chapter 9 is, in part, a continuation of Chapter 8, concentrating on retailers' own-label branding.

Retailing mixes are retail management's tools for implementing the overall strategy and for fulfilling the store objectives. Chapters 10, 11 and 12 discuss these mix components: price mix, promotion mix, and service provision. Thus, these chapters deal with implementation of the planned strategy: Chapter 10 looks at retail pricing, Chapter 11 evaluates retail promotion and advertising, and Chapter 12 reviews retail services provision – each as part of the retail marketing mix.

Since effective retail marketing involves managing research information, Chapter 13 provides a paradigm for managing the research and information systems. This chapter on research and retail information management systems (RIMS) delves into establishing a general system in order to ascertain the degrees of success or failure in implementing retail marketing strategies. This leads on to Chapter 14 which brings together all the elements of the retail marketing mix in the context of planning and control. It explores the control element of the retail marketing plan, describing retail control functions for specific and general purposes. Since the existing literature perhaps places too much emphasis on financial controls, this chapter attempts to balance this by giving equal attention to non-financial controls.

Chapter 15 highlights some of the key areas of international retail marketing theory and practice, and bridges some significant gaps in the general understanding of international retail marketing management. Finally, Chapter 16 reviews the area of retail technology and electronic retailing, with emphasis on marketing via the Internet.

Most books on retailing contain a separate chapter on retailing research; this book does not. However, this does not mean the subject of retailing research is ignored; research topics and concepts are discussed throughout the book, with important research topics being handled as necessary within the most appropriate chapter.

The book reflects the author's many years of teaching, research, and consulting experience. Most of the exhibits relate to the author's field research and consulting activity. However, although some of the chapters reflect the author's extensive research knowledge, others pose questions and raise issues that need to be thought out and require further research in the future.

Ogenyi Ejye Omar
LCP School of Retail Studies
The London Institute
London, 1999

Acknowledgements

In acknowledging the contributions from so many people, I would like to state that nothing ever happens unless an effort is made. Then, with perseverance and a little bit of luck anything is possible. The writing of this book is the result of such effort. Although, I will always claim the sole authorship of this book, a lot of other people have helped to produce it. The book has therefore benefited from numerous suggestions from colleagues who participated and expressed opinions during the reviewing of the text proposal.

My special thanks are due to Dr Will Bridge, Head of College, London College of Printing for the encouragement he provided, and Peter Thompson, the Acting Dean of School of Retail Studies, for allowing the time to research and write the book. I would like to thank my very many friends and the staff of LCP School of Retail Studies, The London Institute for their help and co-operation in researching and writing the book. In particular, I am grateful to Anthony Kent, Alan Hirst, Audrey Kirby, and Dawn Lavelle for reading and reviewing the initial draft and for their assistance in pre-testing the drafted case studies in the classroom for suitability. I thank my many friends within and outside the London College of Printing, for the various ways in which they helped mainly through the exchange of ideas.

Special thanks are also due to Charles Blankson School of Marketing Kingston University Business School for reviewing the initial draft of the book. I am highly indebted to Gordon Dixon, of the Manchester Metropolitan University for all his efforts in reading through all the pieces of writings and in successfully directing and educating me through the various phases of writing the book. His suggestions greatly helped to direct my thoughts. Above all, his kindly and warm hearted friendliness is deeply appreciated.

I thank the very many number of students who took my retail marketing classes at the London Institute. Their comments, question, and classroom observations have improved my understanding of retail marketing as it should be taught. My sincere thanks to those who took part in reading and testing the case studies in the classroom for suitability before they are used in this book.

The staff at Financial Times Management played a special part in the writing of this book, and I thank Jane Powell for planning and suggesting the structure of the book. I am grateful to Michelle Graham for her encouragement and advice. More importantly I am grateful to both of them for their sense of order and organisation which kept the writing from getting out of hand and which helped to make the writing of the book a reality.

I wish to thank my wife, Odu Ogenyi, who did much of the secretarial work for the draft of this book. My sincere gratitude also goes to Kim Causac who assisted with some of the word processing work. I am ever grateful to God for giving me a special and wonderful family. I thank my children – Igyato, Oguma, Omar and Uduma for their love, affection, patience, and support which always are the instigating catalysts in all my undertakings. To them I dedicate this book.

1

The nature of retail marketing

LEARNING OBJECTIVES

After reading this chapter you should be able to:

- discuss the historical background to marketing and how it is used in the retail organisation;
- explain the meaning and functions of marketing as related to retailing;
- know the theory of retail institutional change and its relevance in retailing;
- evaluate the role of competition in retailing and compare retailers' use of competitive advantage;
- know the elements of retail marketing mix and establish the relationships between the variable elements.

In a highly competitive business environment, successful retail marketing actions are usually the result of good management information and the application of common sense. Similarly, the prosperous retail organisations are those that think ahead, making positive efforts to anticipate changes in the business environment. They are then able to develop an organisation capable of recognising and evaluating business opportunities ahead of their competitors. Although retail marketing techniques are still in the process of being developed, they are becoming increasingly scientific and technologically based.

Retail marketing influences our daily lives in our roles as consumers and shoppers. It encompasses a wide range of activities such as environmental analysis surrounding the retail industry; retail market research; consumer analysis; product planning; distribution planning; promotion planning; pricing planning; and retail marketing management. The role of retail marketing changes in each new retailing situation. The formal study of retail marketing requires an understanding of the definition of marketing, its importance, scope and functions, as well as the evolution of marketing and the marketing concept. Since retail marketing is the application of marketing concepts and philosophy relating to retail operation, a clear definition of marketing is a good base for better understanding.

The main focus of this chapter is on getting to grips with exactly what **marketing** is, particularly in relation to its application in retailing – retail marketing.

| Exhibit 1.1 | Match products/services to markets |

A retailer's products and/or services must be related to their target markets and attractive enough in performance and price for customers to buy. Customers are sometimes unaware of their wants and these have to be aroused by retail marketing communications. For instance, when cigarette lighters were not wanted – they were not a desired object in a smoker's mind – the advantages of a cigarette lighter over matches had to be demonstrated and a need created for them. This is the essence of retail marketing: developing products and services that will satisfy specific needs of customers and then supplying them at prices that will yield profits. Any retailer who pays insufficient attention to customers' needs and offers products developed in the factory rather than designed for the market will be outsold by competitors who are more aware of market needs.

The chapter comes to the simple but important conclusion that the focal point of retail marketing must be the customer, and the key activity the 'dialogue' between supplier, retailer and the customer.

Historical background to marketing

Kotler, a leading writer in marketing who traced the history of marketing, noted that 'marketing has been in existence for a number of millennia; ever since people first started to barter the surpluses they had accumulated. For most of that time, though, it has been seen as a peripheral activity; because, in subsistence economies, such surpluses represented a relatively small part of the total' (1997). After the Industrial Revolution made such surpluses more commonplace, the 'marketing' of these became the province of the salespeople, with their specialised skills.

Mercer (1996) suggests that the first academic discussions of 'marketing' can be traced back to the early twentieth century: to, for instance, the E.D. James's series of articles in *Mill Supplies* between 1911 and 1914. However, in the wider sphere of practical business management, it was only after 1955 that the newly fashionable advertising agencies began to redefine the discipline in a way which came close to the modern concept of marketing. The 1950s may be seen as the decade of advertising: the influence of the agencies peaked and their clients appointed advertising managers to control this newly discovered resource.

Indeed, it was arguably only at the beginning of the 1960s that marketing in its modern form, based upon a customer focus (in particular, making extensive use of market research to investigate customers' needs and wants), emerged on anything like the scale that we now witness. This decade represented the heyday of 'pure' marketing management – and of the few pioneers who became brand managers, at the pinnacle of a new profession. Almost all of these pioneers, however, practised techniques which had been learned by a practical apprenticeship rather than by the study of theory in the classroom (*see* McGoldrick, 1990).

The discipline matured in the 1970s as – led by Kotler's seminal text *Marketing Management*, first published in 1967 – the ideas which had developed from practical experience were codified. Marketing became a routine activity and an increasingly important function of management. In the 1980s, however, marketing lost much of its previous self-confidence, not least in terms of the new ideas being developed. Attention shifted to more aggressive techniques with a more immediate pay-back; including derivatives of those developed by Porter (1980); these, however, focused on short-term results and conveniently ignored the longer-term perspectives. It was clear that the formerly 'new' concept of marketing had become outdated and that the times demanded a strategic concept of marketing. A major evolution in the history of marketing thought thus shifted the focus from the customer or product to the firm's external environment.

In the early 1990s, the leading edge of marketing moved on, at least in part, to the service industries – particularly to retailing and financial services which were experiencing massive changes. Such rapid and significant changes tend to be major catalysts for extensive change throughout retail organisations.

Marketing in retail organisations

Historically, marketing is regarded as the concept of presenting goods which people want in the manner and place in which they are required, and therefore encompasses research and presentation, packaging, and so on. Its origin lies in the USA, where the total marketing concept was applied to production in the post-war years. In the UK the term has been rather loosely used in retailing, where the marketing manager and the merchandise manager may work hand in hand and their areas of work may be complementary or even interchangeable.

McGoldrick (1990) discussed marketing in retailing as having grown with the shift in power from the manufacturer to the retailer in the early 1980s, noting that this was the period when most own-label activities started to grow as part of retailers' two-pronged strategy to improve their profit margins and to differentiate themselves from competitors. As retailers' power within the marketing channel grew, they sought considerable, control over all aspects of the products they sell. This power has not always been translated into a truly coordinated marketing function. Many retailers have employed marketing tools without necessarily adopting an integrative and strategic approach to their marketing activities. Thus in retailing, implementation of the marketing concept appeared to be mostly at the firm's operational rather than strategic levels; for example, policies, such as customer service, refund policies, hours of operation, and other areas of tactical importance, seemed to be more affected by the marketing concept than were truly strategic levels of management. McGoldrick (1990) saw this problem as arising, to a large extent, from the lack of a strong marketing function within the retail organisation. However, some retail organisations have been '**marketing-led**' for many years – for example J. Sainsbury, Tesco, and Marks & Spencer.

The response of small to medium sized retail firms to the marketing challenge has often been simply to bestow the title 'marketing' upon an existing group or individual within the organisation. While this may serve to signal a new orientation, it is unlikely to unlock the full potential of the retail marketing approach. Evidence with respect to marketing within UK retail companies indicates that, in the majority of retail organisations, marketing shows the following five characteristics (McGoldrick, 1990):

1 The majority of marketing departments were established in the 1980s.

2 Most marketing departments are still small in size, although they are growing.

3 Marketing functions vary slightly between retail organisations, and by type of organisation.

4 The head of marketing is seen as having a higher status than other departmental heads.

5 Many retail organisations see themselves as marketing-oriented organisations.

Despite this evidence depicting a situation in which the marketing function is growing rapidly in size and status, marketing is still under-represented in many retail organisations in the UK and possibly elsewhere in Europe.

The meaning and functions of marketing

Marketing is a widely used term which is often misused and misunderstood. It has come to mean many things to many different people. According to Baker (1985), 'if you put the question "what is marketing?" to one hundred people in any city in Britain, you are likely to receive one hundred different answers with respect to what marketing means to them.' He observed that people who work in various departments in a retail operation – for example production, research and development, accounting and finance, retail and distribution, and sales – recognise that marketing plays some role in their organisation, but are not unanimous in their understanding of what marketing is.

People who work in the product development department may think that without the marketing department's 'exaggerated' demands for different types of products and services in a variety of colours and sizes, their department could get on with the job of producing and designing one product in the colour and shape that they can produce best. The management accountant may see the organisation as a financial system to create wealth through added value by meeting budgets and taking as few risks as possible, and will not encourage speculative research and development by marketing which will require substantial financial investment. Similarly, the finance department may resist plans to 'throw money away' on unquantifiable advertising or promotion initiated by marketing. The research and development (R&D) department may concentrate on how to take advantage of new technological developments. It may look upon research done by the marketing department as scientifically unfounded concerned soley with what customers want, and disruptive to its technical advances.

A retail and distribution department, having matched and satisfied the needs of their organisation to the historical customer base with well-planned routes serviced by traditional types and sizes of vehicles, may suddenly find itself back to square one simply because marketing research has identified a new sector or a more productive way of servicing their customers. It can be very inconvenient for the distribution department with a traditional set-up and consequently strongly resisted.

In a manufacturing firm, for instance, the sales department may see marketing as little more than production scheduling. To the salesforce, marketing may be the back room people – the theorists – who never venture out into the field and serve only to create havoc with journey cycle priorities. The marketing provision of new information about customers' needs and product requirements is also a problem for the salesforce. The allocation of time for new product lines seems to create problems for the salesforce who are already complaining of too much work in hand. They normally have to report back all relevant information concerning their customers, the market, and the products; and they do not think that retail marketing is making good use of this information.

Although the views of these people may differ, marketing tends to be the glue that holds together all of these different functions within the organisation, as is shown in Figure 1.1. It helps define the organisational goals and influences every part of the retail organisation in meeting them. One of the major functions of marketing is to identify consumer demand (obtaining demand); a second is to attempt to satisfy it (servicing demand), as shown in Figure 1.1. Marketing affects

Fig. 1.1 MARKETING FUNCTIONS AND ACTIVITIES

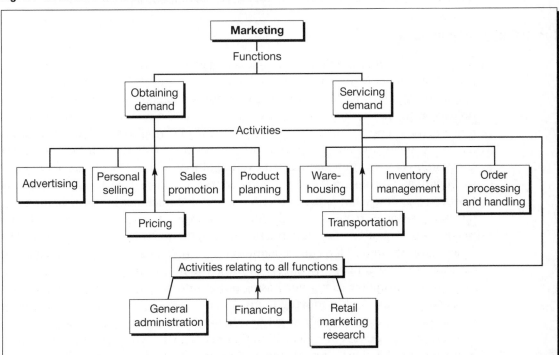

the appearance and price of the product, the area and method of distribution, the direction of research and development, the introduction of new technology, and so on. It does this through a constant flow of information and analysis about the market and customers' needs into the organisation. Kotler similarly stressed the important functions of marketing, noting that 'marketing helps to shape and create the market, by product development through technological innovations; and most notably by information it sends out from the organisation in the form of advertising and promotion. Thus, marketing aims may be defined as ensuring that all resources of the retail organisation meet and respond to customer requirements in the most profitable way' (1997).

The essence of retail marketing

The key aspect of marketing is an attitude of mind. It requires that, in taking 'marketing' decisions, the retail manager looks at the situation from the viewpoint of the customer. These decisions will thus be driven by what the customer needs and wants. Davies and Brooks (1989) emphasised much of what retail management does as being concerned with taking decisions which revolve around how the products or services of the retail organisation can be offered to match the customer's needs and wants. The most difficult part of retail marketing but the key to its success is the ability to adopt the customer's viewpoint. The lesson for retail management is to place the shoppers' needs and wants at the forefront of product/service delivery. A simple offer of normal courtesies to the shopper by the retailer will put his or her organisation ahead of competitors.

The definition of marketing

As stated earlier, many definitions of marketing exist with differing emphases on the process of marketing, the functional activities that constitute marketing, and the orientations of marketing. The **marketing concept** is the management orientation that holds that the key task of the organisation is to determine the needs and wants of target markets and to adapt the organisation to delivering the desired satisfactions more effectively and efficiently than its competitors. This is often held to be the cornerstone of marketing and has led to a definition of marketing being adopted by the main marketing professional body in the UK, The Chartered Institute of Marketing, as: 'the management process responsible for identifying, anticipating and satisfying customer requirements profitably'. However, to enable detail analysis and to answer the question of what marketing means, it may be necessary to expand The Chartered Institute of Marketing's definition to read: 'marketing is the management function which organises and directs all those business activities involved in assessing and converting consumer purchasing power into effective demand for a specific product or service, and in moving the product or service to the final consumer or user so as to achieve the profit target or other objectives set by a company'.

This is clearly a descriptive definition that needs an analytical explanation to help us understand the nature of marketing and its operational functions (*see* Table 1.1).

Table 1.1
MARKETING DEFINITION: OPERATIONAL FUNCTIONS AND ANALYTICAL EXPLANATION

Operational function	Analytical explanation
It is a management function	It is a part of that function which is concerned with the establishment and definition of objectives. It deals with the creation of the conditions under which it will be possible to achieve the objectives.
It organises and directs	It is a function which determines what shall be done, how it shall be done and when. It is not concerned soley with performance, and may not in fact be concerned with it at all, passing on actual performance to others, e.g. salespeople, advertising contractors, transport contractors, etc. But being concerned with organising and directing, marketing must necessarily also be concerned with controlling, monitoring and evaluating what has been done.
It has a function of assessing	It has a function of gathering and evaluating information in order to enable it better to organise and direct. This function of assessment covers all features of marketing research, that is market research, product research, distribution research, and promotion research.
It has a function of conversion	It has a function of creation and persuasion – it must create products or services which will be demanded, and it must inform and persuade those with purchasing power to exercise it.
It deals with consumer purchasing power	Marketing must, therefore, analyse what 'purchasing power' is in terms of the ability of the customer to purchase now. Consumer purchasing power may include money which they have now, either from current earnings or from savings, or money which they may have in the future.
It deals with consumers or users	It deals with real people in the real world. Unlike other academic disciplines such as economics, which must make assumptions in order to build models of the world and which, in consequence, have to make unreal assumptions about the potential behaviour of humans, marketing must deal with people as they are. Those of us involved in marketing cannot make the assumption that people will act rationally or objectively, but we can study the influences which will tend to make them act in a subjective or an irrational way. Behavioural sciences play, therefore, an important part in the study of marketing.
It deals with moving products to final consumer	It deals with the means by which, and the channels through which, the producer and consumer are brought together.
It achieves the profit target or other objectives set	It recognises that marketing, or any other business activity, does not operate in a vacuum. Marketing is not an end in itself, but exists to achieve the overall objectives of the organisation. It follows from this that the establishment of marketing objectives is dependent upon the establishment of overall organisation objectives. One cannot properly exist without the other and it is probably not too strong to suggest that, in the majority of cases, the overall organisation objectives must be stated in terms of a marketing objective.

The definition also recognises that the organisation may have objectives other than profit. This covers two categories: organisations which have no monetary profit objectives and for-profit organisations which have aims that are not profit motivated. This means that marketing applies with equal force to such organisations as government, local authorities, charities, and service organisations. It also means that even profit-oriented organisations may have overall objectives, the achievement of which may be non-profit making or even have the effect of reducing possible profitability. We have recognised that within any organisation which produces a product or service, it is the customer who holds the key to whether or not the enterprise will be economically successful. We have also determined that it is effective demand which is the key to economic success. Having looked at the meaning and functions of marketing, the next section reviews the structure of marketing and its role within the retail sector.

Retail institutional change

On a higher level, six theories or working hypotheses have attempted to explain retail institutional changes. They are the wheel of retailing; the dialectical process; retail life cycles; natural selection in retailing; the retail accordion theory (or general-specific-general process); and the Markin-Duncan adaptation theory (*see* Robertson, 1994).

The wheel of retailing

One of the best known theories of how retail institutions change is the wheel of retailing hypothesis proposed by McNair (1957). According to this theory, changes in retail institutions move in circle consisting of three phases: entry (innovation), trading up, and vulnerability. Figure 1.2 illustrates the three phases of McNair's retail cycle and how the repetition of these phases creates a pattern of continuous movement.

In the entry phase of the cycle (innovation), a new retail institution enters the market at the lower end of the shopping opportunity. Its **differential advantage** over existing competitors is its lower price. To offer lower prices, the institution controls its costs strictly by limiting store services, by locating at low rent sites, and often by lowering store standards and merchandise quality. To maintain its lower prices, the innovator sometimes sacrifices profit margins in comparison to those of its established competitors.

If the innovation succeeds, emulators copy it over time and increase the level of **competition**. In response to competitive pressure, the stores then add services and improve quality to create differential advantage. Higher merchandise prices usually accompany such store trading up (second phase). In other words, competition from within the strategic group forces the stores to move to the right along the shopping opportunity lines. This creates the opportunity for new institutions to enter at the lower end of the shopping opportunity line. In this way the cycle continues.

Fig. 1.2 CIRCLE OF THE WHEEL OF RETAILING

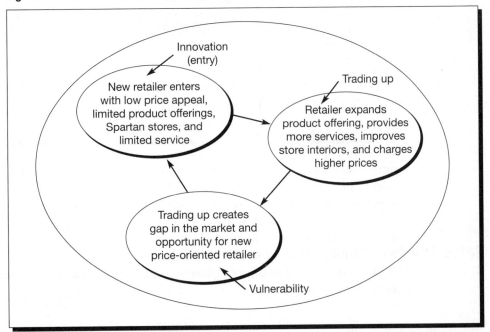

The wheel of retailing concept has been the subject of numerous studies. It is generally agreed that, although it cannot explain all retail changes, it does provide considerable insight into how low-end retail stores emerge and develop. The evolution of discount stores, catalogue showrooms, and warehouse clubs all seem to follow the pattern of the wheel. Prestige boutiques and speciality stores, however, are examples of some institutions that did not follow this model; they did not begin at the low end of the shopping opportunity line.

The dialectical process

The dialectical process is another model that describes the emergence and growth of retail institutions. It views retailing as an evolutionary system in which different retail institutions adapt to each other, in the process generating new retail formats. The central premise of the dialectical model is that 'when challenged by a competitor with a differential advantage, an established institution will adopt strategies and tactics in the direction of that advantage, thereby negating some of the innovators' attraction'. The new institution then modifies (*see* McGoldrick, 1990) its strategy to maintain its **competitive advantage**. These mutual adaptations gradually move the two retailers together in terms of merchandise offerings, service, and price.

The emergence of the discount department store is perhaps the best example of how the dialectical process works. As shown in Figure 1.3, department stores were traditionally located in the city centre areas and offered high levels of customer service. They also had relatively high prices and high margins. In the 1950s, discount stores emerged as a competitive force challenging department stores. The

Fig. 1.3 DIALECTICAL PROCESS

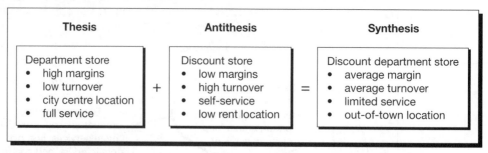

early discount stores were generally located out of town, had lower prices, and offered little or no customer services. In contrast to the department store, their managerial philosophy stressed lower margins to create greater merchandise turnover. As department stores and discount stores adapted to each other over time, discount department stores such as K mart in the USA evolved, blending the two opposing forces. Discount department stores combined the strengths of both department stores and discount stores and created a competitive position of their own (Walters and White, 1987).

Retail life cycles

The retail life cycle is a concept that describes the process of institutional change in retailing. This model states that retail institutions pass through a life cycle that can be divided into four stages: introduction, growth, maturity, and decline (*see* Figure 1.4). New types of retail institutions first appear at the introduction or innovation stage, as department stores did in the 1860s. Similarly, franchised fast-food outlets were at this stage of their life cycle in the 1950s and early 1960s. During this stage the new retail concept has a marked competitive advantage over conventional outlets. This advantage may be based on price, merchandise assortment, convenience, or a new approach to sales and promotion.

Fig. 1.4 RETAIL LIFE CYCLE

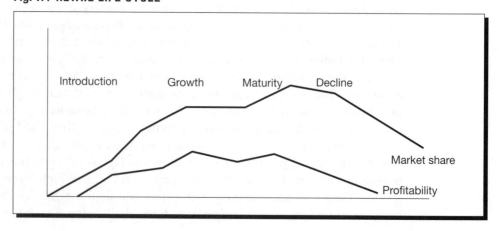

The competitive advantage propels the institution into the second stage of the life cycle, which is characterised by growth in both sales and profits. This stage is also marked by the emergence of new competitors who imitate the original concept. As competition increases, firms expand their chains geographically to reach new markets and increase sales. Between 1983 and 1985 in the UK, for example, large electronic retail chains such as Dixons, Tandy, and Comet expanded their network of outlets into a number of new markets to establish a dominant position in those markets. By expanding their own networks, these chains restricted new competitors from entering into this sector of retailing.

The stage of rapid growth is inevitably followed by one of maturity when the speed of market growth slows and sales start to stagnate. Currently chemists, sports stores, and electronic stores (PC World and Energy Centres, for example) seem to be in this stage of their life cycle. After growing rapidly during the first part of the 1980s, total sales at these stores have slowed down considerably. In the early 1980s, the consumer electronic market grew by more than 20 per cent a year; in contrast, there has been little or no growth in the 1990s. As growth slows, competitive rivalry intensifies as firms fight aggressively to maintain their share of the market. Consequently, profits start to decline during this stage of the life cycle.

The final stage is one of decline. Both sales and profits are low during this period. The lack of competitive advantage often leads to the total demise of the institution. However, failure can often be avoided by repositioning or by a reversal of environmental trends. Department stores, for example, got a new lease of life in the middle 1970s when many cities initiated urban regeneration projects to attract more shoppers to city centre areas.

Although one can never forecast the duration of an institutional life cycle with any certainty, considerable evidence suggests that life cycles are accelerating (Kotler, 1997), and the time taken for institutions to reach the mature stage is becoming shorter with each new kind of retail innovation. Whereas traditional department stores took approximately eighty years to reach maturity, later innovations such as home improvement centres and fast-food outlets matured in around fifteen years (Davies and Brooks, 1989). More recent innovations, such as off-price or cut-price retailers, may reach maturity even faster. The acceleration of the retail life cycle reflects increased competitive pressures in the retail industry and the rapid pace of environmental change; neither of these processes is expected to slow down in the future.

Natural selection in retailing

Charles Darwin's theory of the evolution of the species by the action of natural selection has been widely recognised as the survival of the fittest and this principle is being loosely applied to the business world. According to this working hypothesis, retail institutions may lose their relative position or disappear. The dilemma of the central business districts, the relative decline of department stores or disappearance of 'mama and papa' (corner) shops, are all a function of shifting environmental conditions (which are discussed in detail in Chapter 2); and this working hypothesis purports that no retail institution is sacred: safe from environmental changes or the threat of decline.

However there is a reverse – positive – side to this hypothesis: the fittest will survive. Clearly, those retail institutions that are keenly aware of their operating environment and which can also react without undue delay can both avoid the unfriendly elements in their environment and realise disproportionate gains from changes in the friendly elements. All of this suggests that the successful retail operation should keep all elements of the environment under regular scrutiny and be prepared to react quickly to both positive and negative environmental changes alike.

The retail accordion theory

The retail accordion theory (also known as the general-specific-general process) is based on the premise that the changing character of retail competition stems from strategies that alter the width (selection) of the **merchandise mix**. Historically, retail institutions have evolved from general stores, offering a wide variety of merchandise; these were superseded by the speciality stores, offering a limited variety of merchandise; which were followed by a move back to general-line stores; and so on. The term accordion is used to suggest the alternating expansion and contraction of the retailer's merchandise mix.

This working hypothesis maintains that retailing varies from general to specific to general again. For a period of time, consumers are predominantly served by general stores. Following that period, they are served by speciality stores and then again by the general store. This sequence of events continues. Thus, the retail system has undergone an era of an extremely wide variety offerings by retailers, followed by a period of great specialisation and then a return to a broad variety of merchandise offered. With the rehabilitation of city centres, the increasing energy crunch, and the growing emphasis on convenience, the specific end of the cycle may be recurring in the near future. The validity of this working hypothesis has not been tested further. However, with the emergence of boutiques and other highly specialised stores, there is some evidence to support the theory.

The Markin–Duncan adaptation theory

Markin and Duncan (1981) have adopted a Darwinian approach to the transformation of retail institutions, maintaining that retail institutions survive through adaptation. This approach posits the doctrine that functional processes or their transformation gain value only through survival. Thus, Markin and Duncan maintain that the retail institution emerges, adapts, survives, declines and disappears depending on how well it serves the market's needs. It becomes clear that retail institutions which cannot adapt to the pressures of the changing market environment are replaced by those that are more adaptable. This adaptation and accommodation point of view provides a strong explanation for the extreme diversity of the retailing sector, for the wide variation among retail institutions. An institution's functions are determined by its structure, which in turn is conditioned by market forces. When market forces change, institutions are put under pressure to accommodate and adapt or face failure.

When changes by individual firms in response to changes in market forces are followed by a large number of firms, then the structure of the retail sector is likely to be modified – which itself represents an **institutional change**. A series of social, technological and economic forces, for example, caused the emergence of supermarkets in food retailing. As supermarkets entered the food retailing market with their cash-and-carry, high-turnover, low-price and self-service practices, they caused a radical change in the appearance, location and management of retail food marketing.

According to the biological theory of adaptation discussed above, the fit will survive – at least for the present. This 'fitness' implies that the retailer's functions and services are deemed valuable by the marketing environment. However, managerial ignorance and lack of capital investment can cause retail institutions that are fit today to lose the ability to thrive or survive in the future. Many small retailers operate under severe capital shortages; they suffer from inertia, ignorance, and are typically too small to compete on the same terms as large establishments. In the face of changing market values, such a position may make many firms extremely vulnerable.

The role of competition

Retailing is more competitive than most other aspects of marketing because at the retail level **multidimensional** competition exists. Its multidimensional aspects could be attributed to its varying levels, with varying factors. Basically, five levels of retail competition can be identified (Samli, 1989; *see* Figure 1.5). The first level deals with the most specific aspects of retail competition: product and service, communication and physical distribution. The second level is related to the retail organisation and its horizontal competitors. Level three is the other retail organisations and the vertical competition. The fourth level deals with geographical dimensions which include store location and the complexity of the shopping environment. The fifth level explores the nature of the market in which retailers fight for their share of the market; this is the broadest of the five levels. A successful retailer must understand the varying nature of retail competition at each stage, and must respond to it both speedily and appropriately.

Dimensions of change in retail competition

Retail competition has been changing along spatial, institutional, and functional dimensions.

Fig. 1.5 MULTIDIMENSIONALITY OF RETAIL COMPETITION

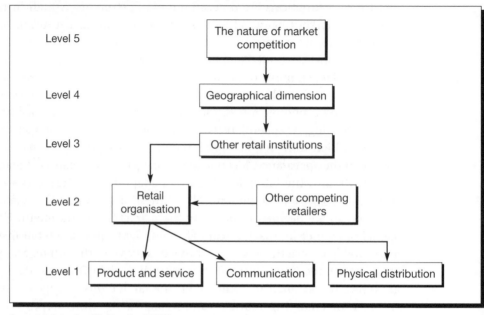

Source: Adapted and modified from Samli (1989).

Spatial dimension

This form of retail competition primarily implies that retailing has to follow population trends: as people move from the countryside to the city or vice versa, retailing must be able to do so too. The most specific aspect of spatial retail competition has been in the area of city centre versus out-of-town shopping. This competition has had a far-reaching impact on retailing structure and practice.

The institutional dimension

Institutional dimensions of retail competition are exhibited in numerous ways. Large corporate enterprises have pushed small retailers out of existence or have forced them to find new ways of functioning in order to survive. For a long time, multiple retailers captured ever larger proportions of the total retail business at the expense of small firms. So, for many years, department stores held the lion's share of total retail business. This situation continued until discount stores emerged (*see* discussion on the wheel of retailing above). Strong competition now exists between these two forms of retail business and the expected outcome is increased consumer service.

The functional dimension

This dimension of retail competition has taken two distinct paths: non-price competition and price competition. Non-price competition has led retailing to develop a multitude of functional practices that have made it easier and more pleasant for consumers to shop. Among these are special customer services, improved store layout and proper signs for making shopping easier, background music, wall-to-wall carpeting, special emphasis on certain brands, air conditioning, store-own brands and product lines, and distinctive merchandise mixes. All of these are components of the store image which in turn provides the competitive advantage the store is seeking to develop customer patronage. Price competition, on the other hand, implies that, rather than other features, the store tries to establish its competitive advantage by offering better prices than those of its competitors.

Intensity of competition usually means that product and/or service prices will be lower; larger firms will have less control over the prices they set; and the allocation of resources will be the most efficient. It is important for retail management to have a complete understanding of the level of competition in the retail industry, not least because of its impact on pricing. If a retailer has a major advantage over its competitors, this will certainly be reflected in its pricing. Competition similarly influences all other areas of retail marketing, strongly influencing the purchasing habits of the individual firms and guiding their expansion policies – particularly in relation to the location of new outlets.

Retail concentration

High concentration of retail competition could be attributed to **ease of entry** into retailing (it takes little capital to open a small store). An entrepreneur starting a retail business needs to invest considerably less money per worker than would be necessary in a manufacturing enterprise. The implication of the low entry costs in retailing are obvious. High profit in a retail enterprise almost immediately invites competition, resulting in **retail concentration**. Ease of entry constantly forces profits down, hence few firms are in a position to control prices in the market. Accordingly, concentration of sales among the large retail firms are considerably below that in most manufacturing industries. Acquisitions, mergers and takeovers in retailing continue to take place all over the world. As expected, most of the mergers in retailing occur among the largest retail organisations.

Exhibit 1.2	**Retail concentration in the food industry**

During the 1970s, a strategic change in direction by UK food retailers led to industry rationalisation, investment in modern technology, shift in production category, and business restructuring through acquisitions and diversification. Many small food producers were taken over or ceased to trade. The merger and the take-over activity was connected with the wish of large retailers to extend their product ranges to counter the growing concentration and the buying power of large multiples. Thus, by 1997, merger activity resulted in Britain having 20 of the 1000 largest food businesses in the world, ranked by turnover.

The activity within the retail industry since the mid-1980s has created an oligopolistic, diversified, multi-product and transactional industry. The growth in scale and concentration, as discussed by Omar (1992), may be attributed to the following factors:

1 The policies of the world's leading economies' (the G7 nations) financial systems help the expansion of large established firms rather than the growth of small firms.

2 The world's leading economies' health and safety regulations, and so on, are costly to comply with, which eliminates small firms and enables large ones to dominate the market.

3 The firm level economies of scale in, for example, purchasing, marketing, distribution, and research and development (R&D) encourage the growth of multiple firms by takeover rather than organic growth.

4 Amalgamation is used as a defensive measure to counter competitive pressure and declining market share against a background of slow market growth and excess production capacity in the leading global economies.

5 'Modern' and affluent consumers in Europe and north America are more willing to accept processed foods and other innovative products in comparison to consumers in the Asian and African markets, for example.

On the other hand, the growth in retail concentration could be ascribed to the competitive pressure generated by the expansion of supermarkets, the development of retailers' own-labels and the end of resale price maintenance (RPM). Galbraith's theory of 'countervailing power' that 'the long term trend towards concentration of industrial enterprise in the hands of a relatively few firms has brought into existence not only strong sellers, but also strong buyers. The two developed together, not in precise step but in such a manner that there can be no doubt that the one is in response to the other' (Galbraith, 1967), supports this view.

Competitive advantage (differentiation)

This means that a retailer has managed to differentiate itself from its competitors – it has found a way to standout from the crowd. The differential congruence through which competitive advantage is achieved also implies a positive balance between the store's image and the individual customer's self-image (*see* Chapter 5). Successful retail marketing management, therefore, aims to achieve differential congruence as a means of coping with the growing competition.

In its attempt to differentiate itself from its competitors, retail management can create a congruence between the store's **perceived image** and the customer's self-image. If successful, the store will achieve differential advantage made possible through **differential congruence**.

Exhibit 1.3 **Differential congruence at Marks & Spencer**

Marks & Spencer's shoppers, for instance, know what to expect from a Marks & Spencer store and they feel comfortable shopping there. An example of such comfort levels was demonstrated when Virginia Bottomley, the then Health Secretary in the British government, made special arrangements in January 1994 to do early morning shopping at Marks & Spencer.

All the current indicators reveal that differential congruence exists at Marks & Spencer. The same could be claimed for customers of Selfridges at the higher end of the socio-economic spectrum, and Woolworth's at the lower end of the socio-economic scale. Multiple retailers – and more specifically the successful ones – understand that they are unique and that their success is associated with shoppers' appreciation of this uniqueness.

Perfect and monopolistic competition

The movement from perfect competition to **monopolistic** competition by the retailers made a significant impact on the theory and practice of retail competition. The retail market can be described as the typical example of monopolistic competition where each retail organisation has certain unique features. A retailer may be unique in terms of its merchandise mix, its location, its prices, its store layout, or some other special feature. To the extent that a particular feature is appealing to the specific target market, the retailer claims **monopoly power**. Monopoly power implies a certain degree of store loyalty whereby the customer remains particularly attached to the store and does not tend to immediately switch stores even if the prices in their preferred store go up.

In so far as less than perfect competition is the realistic way of describing the working of the retail operations sector, every retailer has an opportunity to develop specific features which will create differential congruence and will thus give their organisation advantage over its competitors. In order to have the ability to use the opportunity to create competitive advantage, the retailer has to establish a degree of monopoly power, which will lead to survival and prosperity for the entire retail organisation. The ability to use the opportunity to create competitive advantage is indicative of good retail marketing management. The conditions that monopolistic competition imposes on retail organisations (*see* Samli, 1989) are:

- relative ease of entry
- relative ease of exit
- a less than perfectly **elastic demand** function
- less than perfect information for individual firms
- the possibility of acquiring additional information
- consumer behaviour being less than entirely rational.

Some consumers are, however, more informed and capable of making rational choices than others. Under the given conditions which reflect the reality of monopolistic competition, the individual retailer establishes differential congruence. The conditions of this differential congruence do not have to be purely factual. The ABC supermarket, for example, could claim it has a lower priced groceries and value for money own brands. This claim may not be factual, but special skills in advertising and promoting it could make it possible for ABC to establish an advantage over its competitors. In less than perfect competition, differential advantage may be based on real or imaginary features that retailers either have or claim to have. Even if the features claimed are not factually based, if the retailer can do an effective job of convincing its target markets, the ploy can be very successful. This implies an ability to create differential congruence and, therefore, advantage over competitors; and it is likely that such skills will not be equally or proportionately distributed among retail organisations.

The marketing mix management

Marketing mix is a term used to describe the various elements and methods required to formulate and execute marketing strategy. In its simplest form it may consist of the product, where it is sold (place), its price, its promotion (advertising), how it is sold, and the service elements included in the offering. Retail managers must determine the optimum mix of marketing activities and coordinate the elements of the mix. While many elements may make up a firm's retail marketing mix, the essential elements include: store location, merchandise assortments, **store ambience**, customer service, price, customer **communication**, personal selling, store image, and sales incentives (*see* Figure 1.6). The aim is for each store to have a distinct retail image in consumers' minds, emerging from its combination of the various elements of the retail marketing mix. The mix may vary greatly according to the type of market the retailer is in, the type of products to be marketed, or the current state of the business or marketplace.

Each element of the mix must be consistent with the others or the image will be confused. To attract upper-income customers for high-priced fashionable clothes, a store must create an inviting shopping atmosphere and an ambience that suits the merchandise. It would be inconsistent for such a store to be located next door to car dealers and scrap metal yards. The store must have well trained salespeople to help its customers, and to accept cheques and various credit cards. The store must properly orchestrate the elements of the retail marketing mix to create the desired image or brand (*see* Chapter 5). A store may compete on the basis of its unique combination of the elements of retail marketing mix – its **marketing orientation**. The integrated decisions reached among each of the competitive areas will collectively paint the store's image in the minds of the shoppers.

Fig. 1.6 THE ELEMENTS OF RETAIL MARKETING MIX

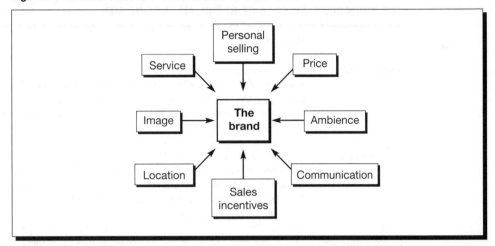

Consumers usually patronise the store which appears to be capable of most completely satisfying their needs. An appropriate retail marketing mix creates a retail personality that will generate seller–buyer trust, and **customer loyalty**, and goodwill. The importance of individual retail marketing mix elements is identified in Table 1.2.

The retailer must be sensitive to market demands and market opportunities, must understand customer buying motives and habits, and must become skilled in developing satisfactory relations with customers. Above all, 'the customer is king': the retailer's business and profits depend upon satisfying customers and thus ensuring their continuous patronage (as discussed in Chapter 5). The goods and services they want – when, how, and where they want them, and at the prices they are willing to pay – must be offered continuously.

Retailers who accept and practice this 'consumer is king' philosophy are said to be using the marketing concept – it is part of their **marketing philosophy**. Specifically, they accept customer needs and wants as the starting point for all their efforts. Consequently, they plan their merchandise assortments, the services they render, their physical facilities, and their personnel policies so as to meet these needs and wants. Everyone in the firm takes their 'marching orders' from the market. The successful retailer must learn the relationships involved in the elements of retail marketing mix, and will benefit generally from blending effective buying, judicious pricing, sound merchandising control, creative advertising and sales promotion, constructive salesmanship, an adequate store system, enlightened personnel administration, attractive customer services, and effective expense control. It is the efficient blending of these marketing activities that determines the retailer's retail marketing mix and its consequent successful management.

Table 1.2
THE VARIABLE ELEMENTS OF RETAIL MARKETING MIX

Elements	Related roles
Store location	This is usually a response to the convenience component of customer expectations. Shopping decisions are based upon ease of access, available parking space and travelling time. The amount of merchandise purchase (bulk) may depend on store proximity, especially when the customer travels by public transport.
Merchandise	The nature of merchandise the store offers may depend on the customer expectation and the store's perceived image of itself. The store's competitive advantage may develop through its merchandise assortment. All the other marketing variables are shaped by the nature of merchandise assortment offered by the store (see Figure 1.6).
Store ambience	This is the atmosphere or the 'experience' that the retailer wishes to convey. In-store ambience is clearly an important feature within the retail marketing mix and is essential to store positioning.
Customer service	The extent of customer service may depend upon the expectations of the shoppers. For some groups of customers, the range and depth of services offered by the store may be the key incentive to patronage and their continuous loyalty.
Price	Many consumers may see brand price as the signature of brand quality. In the absence of other variable marketing cues, price may be used as a surrogate to perceived quality and value for money. Thus, in the past, own-label marketing depended on price and value.
Communication	The role of customer communications is to make customers aware of the store's offerings and to integrate the important activities of merchandise display, internal signs, advertising and personal selling. A customer communications strategy which promises to deliver and fails because of a mismatch – the wrong assortment of merchandise and an inappropriate trading format – can seriously damage customer perception, loyalty and patronage.
Personal selling	Personal selling remains a very important element of the retail marketing mix in some sectors, especially where products are relatively complex, expensive and infrequently purchased. In predominantly self-service stores, well trained staff with high levels of product knowledge are a major asset; they help to guide shoppers in their brand selection.
Store image	Many retailers have developed particular images that they consider to be assets. Retailers need to know how the public see them because it is the favourable image perception that brings the shoppers to the store. Store patronage may depend on store image as well as other factors.
Sales incentives	Most retailers now offer store cards and loyalty schemes as an added inducement to patronise their store. These, and many more sales incentives, are used as part of the store's retail marketing mix to improve sales and profitability.

SUMMARY

The key components of this chapter, which are necessary for revision, may be summarised in terms of theory and practice. Retail marketing is a practical marketing discipline and managers have to be careful in their use of the many theories outlined in the chapter. The chapter points to many possible definitions of marketing, but most of them centre on the customer as the focal point of decision making. The 'transaction' between the supplier, the retailer and the customer is also described and emphasised.

The retail marketing mix refers to the various elements of retail marketing which are employed in retail marketing campaigns to create a favourable image of both the retailer and the product on offer in the perception of shoppers. This is a very simplistic framework; however, it can lead to distortion of the image if adopted without due care. In terms of organisational structure, retail marketing varies in its application depending upon the different circumstances within which it is practised. The main dimensions are the factors which lead to the differences in structure, product, and customers.

KEY TERMS		
communications	institutional change	monopolistic
competition	marketing	monopoly power
competitive advantage	marketing concept	multidimensional
customer loyalty	marketing-led	patronage
differential advantage	marketing mix	perceived image
differential congruence	marketing orientation	retail concentration
ease of entry	marketing philosophy	retail marketing
elastic demand	merchandise mix	store ambience

ASSIGNMENT

You work for an international menswear specialist firm which intends to establish a new store in the London area. The company has not regarded marketing as an important area of its international operation. However, you recognise the importance of marketing in contributing to the company's successful development.

Task

Using other international retailers which, in your opinion, have got their retail marketing right as examples, prepare a report for your company director describing what you understand by marketing orientation. Explain how your organisation could benefit from adopting a retail marketing philosophy of 'the customer is king' (that is, putting the customer at the forefront of its operation). Your report should be no longer than 1800 words.

REVISION QUESTIONS

1 What is the general accepted definition of marketing as put forward by the Chartered Institute of Marketing (CIM)?

2 How could the CIM definition of marketing be expanded, and why is such expansion necessary?

3 Despite the differences of opinion as to what marketing does, marketing tends to be the glue that holds together all the different functions within the retail organisation. Discuss.

4 Six working hypotheses could be used to explain retail institutional change. Briefly explain the concepts and the symbolic usefulness of each theory.

5 Basing your argument on the theory of retail competition, discuss the conditions imposed on retail organisations by monopolistic competition.

6 Mastering the process of trying to optimise the retail marketing mix still defies and frustrates most retail managers. Explain why personal guesswork and intuitions are used by managers most of the time.

7 The key aspects of marketing is an attitude of mind. Explain.

8 It is the effective blending of all the retail marketing activities within the retail organisation that determines the success of retail marketing management. Do you agree?

9 What do you understand by the term retail marketing as used in this chapter?

10 The growth in scale and concentration within retailing could be attributed to several factors. Discuss these factors.

CASE STUDY

Co-operative Society: Developing a strategic marketing philosophy

On 16 February 1997, the head of the Co-operative Wholesale Society (CWS) read that a tiny investment company wanted to make a £500 million offer for part of the CWS and Co-operative Retail Society (CRS), its sister organisation. The story was confirmed later that day when Lanica Trust issued a statement that it wished to discuss the possible purchase of certain non-food businesses of the societies. Lanica is an investment company headed by Andrew Regan who bought and later sold the CWS food-manufacturing arm. Regan had set up a company called Galileo as the vehicle for his offer to buy the Co-ops' businesses, such as its opticians, travel agents, garages and funeral activities. Traditionally, the Co-ops are run along principles enshrined in the co-operative ethos and supported in more than 150 years of trading.

After the war serious flaws began to emerge: competition increased and, for the first time in its history, the British co-operative movement stopped growing. The fragmented nature of the business meant its local operations found it impossible to compete with slicker nationally controlled organisations such as Marks & Spencer, Tesco, Safeway and Sainsbury. Gradually the societies started to merge their interests. Those unable to support themselves were rescued by neighbours and debts began to grow. The days when the Co-op made everything from boots to bicycles were disappearing from the British retailing scene.

By the late 1990s 'the Co-op' consisted of 51 Co-operative societies, which operate in 10 main product sectors: food retailing, non-food retailing, undertaking, travel, milk, chemists, garages, farming, banking and insurance. In each sector they face competition, sometimes from global companies with access to vast amounts of capital, and marketing and technological know-how. The CWS and CRS are the movement's two monoliths, with core businesses in food retailing. The smaller societies and individual members make up the ownership of the CWS. But consolidation has not been enough to hold off the big four grocers: Tesco, Sainsbury, Safeway and Asda. From their heyday, when Co-operative societies accounted for a quarter of all food spending in the country, they have slipped into tenth place just ahead of Somerfield.

Paradoxically, however, the Co-op seem to be in tune with the modern retailing environment. While Tesco and Sainsbury are only now moving into banking, the Co-op has offered financial services since 1872. The bank, part of CWS alongside the Co-operative Insurance Society (CIS), has most effectively marketed the movement's ethical stance and gained many new customers in recent years as a result. The managing directors at The Co-op Bank turned a loss of £5.9 million in 1993 into a profit of £36.7 million in 1997, representing a return of 22 per cent on average shareholders' funds. At CIS, total income has risen to more than £2 billion. Operating in the mass market, it has a customer base of 3.5 million homes and is second only to The Prudential Corporation.

The movement is open to the charge of underperformance and marketing inefficiency. Management duplication is rife and it operates an archaic structure. The CWS board, for instance, has 30 elected members – ranging from managers of local societies to teachers and social workers – who are ultimately responsible for assets management. The co-operative philosophy is flourishing in other parts of the world, such as Japan, Scandinavia and Spain, but in Britain the movement has so far failed to capitalise on its size, reach and related activities. CRS made profits of £26 million on sales of £1.4 billion; CWS profits were only £58.7 million in 1997 on sales of £3 billion – even taking into account £1.6 billion of inter-group sales, this is a small surplus.

Managers within The Co-op recognise it needs to change both its conceptual framework and its marketing philosophy to survive in the modern retail marketing environment. The company needs to realign its business activities, although that does not mean the company has to dissimulate. The question senior managers have to answer is 'How far and how fast can The Co-op change without sacrificing its beliefs, traditional marketing concept, and marketing objectives?'. Rationalisation has already begun. As the company was unable to justify its manufacturing capacity, three years ago the CWS took the decision to sell its factories and packaging businesses. Own-label products had become too small an activity

▶

to keep the factories busy and rival retailers were reluctant to take Co-op goods. After much deliberation, the board sold to Regan's Hobson group for £111 million. He closed several plants, raised profits and sold the remainder 18 months later for £120 million.

After many false starts the societies are talking about a merger. Four attempts to merge the CWS and the CRS have failed in the past but, approaching the end of the century, the talks now have an extra urgency. Each side has argued that there is a will to come together to create a single brand with a streamlined structure and combined sales of £4.4 billion (a strategic marketing collaboration). In 1995 the CRS, which complements the CWS geographically, even launched a manifesto called 'the time is right'. Apparently, however, it was not the right time for such a move. Relations grew acrimoniously after such attempts failed. Since then the CWS has created a purchasing alliance – Co-operative Retail Trading Group (CRTG) – representing 16 societies or 60 per cent of purchases. The CRS has organised a rival consortium of independent co-operatives (CIC), representing five societies, and has set about modernising its organisation under a programme called 'towards 2000'. Both organisations recognise the benefits of strategic collaboration (pooling resources). While buying is only one dimension of the strategic marketing operations, personnel and technology could also benefit from the centralisation of all activities, including own-label marketing.

BRITAIN'S CO-OPERATIVES BY SALES VALUES, ACTIVITIES, AND MARKET SHARE

Society	Retail sales (£m)	Activity	Market share (%)
CWS	2177	Banking	3.0
CRS	1686	Farms	4.2
Midlands	631	Food	7.0
United Norwest	624	Funerals	25.0
Yorkshire	283	Garages	2.5
Anglia Regional	260	Household goods	1.6
Ipswich and Norwich	229	Insurance	9.8
Oxford, Swindon and Glos.	209	Milk	14.5
Portsea Island	199	Optical and chemists	5.5
Lincoln	170	Travel agents	15.0

Source: Co-operative Annual Report, 1997

Questions for discussion

1 What do you consider to be the problems facing the co-operative movement in Britain with regard to its marketing concept?

2 What marketing direction could you suggest for CWS and CRS for future development?

REFERENCES

Baker, J.M. (1985) *Marketing Strategy and Management*. London: Macmillan.

Davies, G. and Brooks, J. (1989) *Positioning Strategy in Retailing*. London: Paul Chapman.

Galbraith, J.K. (1967) *The New Industrial State*. Harmondsworth: Penguin.

Kotler, P. (1997) *Marketing Management: Analysis, Planning, Control*. 9th edn. New Jersey: Prentice-Hall.

McGoldrick, P. (1990) *Retail Marketing*. 2nd edn. London: McGraw-Hill.

McNair, M.P. (1957) 'Significant trends and developments in the postwar period', in Smith, A.B. (ed.) *Competitive Distribution in a Free High-Level Economy and the Implications for the University*, University of Pittsburgh Press, pp. 1–25.

Markin, G. and Duncan, J. (1981) 'Retailing strategies', *The Economic Bulletin*, Summer: 20.

Mercer, D. (1996) *Marketing*, 2nd edn. Oxford: Blackwell.

Omar, O.E. (1992) 'Grocery shopping behaviour and retailers' own-label food brands', PhD thesis, Department of Retailing and Marketing. The Manchester Metropolitan University, UK.

Porter, M.E. (1980) *Competitive Strategy*. New York: The Free Press.

Robertson, T. (1994) 'New development in marketing: a European perspective', *European Management Journal*, 12(4): 16–27.

Samli, C.A. (1989) *Retail Marketing Strategy: Planning, Implementation, and Control*. Connecticut: Quorum Books.

Walters, D. and White, D. (1987) Retail Marketing Management. London: Macmillan.

2

The retail marketing environment

LEARNING OBJECTIVES

After reading this chapter you should be able to:

- describe the retail marketing environment and how it affects the retailer's ability to provide satisfactory services;

- understand how environmental factors affect retail marketing mix management;

- explain how changes in the retail environment affect a retailer's marketing decisions;

- keep track of the main changes occurring in the political, cultural, economic, and technological environments;

- discuss the retail marketing environment in the context of European retail marketing management.

The environment in which retailers operate is dynamic and the pattern of consumer demand within such an environment changes constantly. In order to develop reliable strategies upon which retail marketing decisions are based, retailers must monitor changes in the retail environment to identify trends that might affect their ability to compete effectively. They must, therefore, respond to changes in a manner that protects the performance of their organisations.

This chapter examines the need for retail firms to be aware of trends in the consumer, economic, technological, and legal environments that affect retail firms. These forces interact to define the macro environment in which all retailers operate, domestically and internationally. This chapter demonstrates how changes in these factors create opportunities and pose threats to retail marketing management.

The need for retail establishments

Retailing exists in many forms and in order to survive retailers have developed efficient distribution systems to meet differing consumer demands. One justification for the existence of retailers is that they provide the consumer with the opportunity to make transactions conveniently.

Fig. 2.1 HOW RETAILERS CREATE VALUE FOR CUSTOMERS

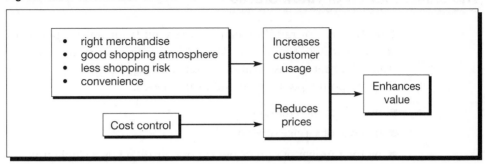

Retailers collect together many different items that the consumer can purchase in one location and in one transaction, thereby providing consumers with 'place convenience'. Similarly, by offering the right merchandise at the right price and in a convenience place, retailers create value – with the intention of satisfying their customers (*see* Figure 2.1). Although manufacturers may be located many miles from the consumer's residence, retailers and other **marketing intermediaries** help bridge this geographical gap by providing local outlets. This process of buying goods from suppliers to sell to consumers is known as distribution; the methods and means used are the channels of distribution (discussed in Chapter 6 of this book).

The retailer also performs a useful function by helping other intermediaries (middlemen) break the large-volume shipments from producers into smaller units that consumers can use most efficiently. The necessity for this 'breaking of bulk' is illustrated by the supermarket, which receives 'case lots' of fresh produce but sells small quantities to meet individual consumers' needs. Similarly, raw materials may be sorted before manufacturing, transformed into consumer products, and shipped to a warehouse where they are stored until needed. The retailer then orders the products in different styles, sizes and colours, and they are then displayed so that the consumer will know of their availability and can purchase the merchandise in the form and at the place and time desired.

Retailers function as a source of information for both manufacturers and consumers. Moreover, retailers, the mass media and other consumers are the main sources of product and/or service information available to consumers. In many cases, cooperative advertising programmes between a manufacturer and a retailer (or retailers) are used to provide consumers with information. The growth of the **consumer movement** has placed more emphasis upon the presentation of factual information by retailers and retail advertisements. Another phase of the information transmission process provided by retailers is the feedback of consumer preference and reactions to manufacturing firms, which is needed if production firms are to respond to changes in consumer demand. Retailers communicate consumer information to manufacturers by their order levels, buyers' comments, refund levels on inferior merchandise, and the like. All of these marketing functions must be performed if the desired goods and services are to reach the consumer at a convenient place and time and in the quantities demanded. Individual retailers survive and grow if they perform these functions efficiently.

The classification of retail stores

The structure of retailing can be analysed from several points of view, but this chapter confines the discussion to the classification systems used to describe retail stores. Five retail classification systems are used to describe retailing from alternative viewpoints (*see* Berman and Evans, 1995):

- by type of merchandise;
- by level of service offered;
- by the number of outlets owned or controlled by a single firm;
- by relative emphasis on price;
- by the number and nature of surrounding stores – that is, by location.

By merchandise offered

This classification groups retail establishments according to the types of merchandise offered for sale. A varied offering of different types of products to meet a wide range of consumer needs would be classed, on one end of a scale, as a 'general store' (Bolen, 1988). Many large-scale retailers such as Safeway, Asda, and so on offer 'one-stop shopping' which is reminiscent of the traditional general store. Admittedly, the variety of goods has been significantly expanded, but so have consumer demands. At the other end of the spectrum are 'speciality stores', which stock a narrow range of merchandise and appeal to a specific segment of the market. Shoe shops, fruit and vegetable shops, and travel agencies all exhibit a narrow line or assortment of merchandise and service. Their competitive advantage lies in their depth of assortment. Most of Europe, in the late 1990s, is experiencing a significant increase in the number of speciality stores because the consumer has more money available for increasingly differentiated needs. Paradoxically, general stores that offer place convenience are also growing to meet the needs of individuals who prefer to save time and energy by shopping closer to home. Shoppers seem to be shopping for everyday needs in general stores, yet expressing a desire for individuality by patronising speciality shops.

By service offered

The survival of a retail firm may depend upon the services it is able to offer to consumers. Many consumers throughout the world appear to be willing to spend more of their **disposable income** on the purchase of services for shelter and household operations, arrangement of travel and holidays, medical care, education, etc. Thus, the product offered for sale tends to be a product–service mixture that is likely to yield satisfaction to the consumer.

In general stores, the consumer expects little or no service beyond credit. Conversely, in speciality stores the potential customer expects to be greeted and professionally assisted in his or her purchase decision. Thus, the breadth of merchandise is inversely related to the amount of service provided. Department stores, having made a point of recognising the differing needs of various consumer groups, provide both minimum-service 'bargain basements' and upper floors that stress boutique or speciality shops (Euromonitor, 1995). Considerable personal and customer services are also provided.

By number of outlets

Another method of classifying retail activity is by the number of outlets owned by a retail organisation. 'Chain store' refers to the common ownership of multiple units. Such chains of stores have grown because of the economies of scale that can be effected through more efficient advertising exposure and the centralised buying of goods. All units within the chain generally exhibit uniform architectural design, pricing and availability of credit. Such firms as J. Sainsbury, Tesco and the other multiple retailers attempt to centralise all their purchasing and credit operations so that consistent process and credit policies are presented to customers throughout the country. Independent grocery chains (such as Spar, Londis, and so on) often attempt to accomplish similar objectives with regard to price, product assortment and store decor.

Another aspect of classification by number of outlets is the catalogue store. Catalogue stores attempt to establish a presence in a local or rural community. They rely on central store stocks, and swift and efficient merchandise interchange and delivery to meet customers' need. This practice makes it unnecessary for such stores to carry duplicate or complete assortments of merchandise, thus limiting excessive fixed overheads due to warehousing costs. Recent renewed consumer interest in catalogue sales, if not discouraged by costly and ineffective delivery systems, may reduce the need for large numbers of outlets while still producing additional sales revenue.

By relative emphasis on price

A close relationship exists between classifying a store according to merchandise diversity and according to relative emphasis on price. There are no 'free services'. Every activity performed by a retailer costs money that must be recouped either by lowering costs or by higher prices charged to the consumer. Thus it could be found that retail firms that emphasise relatively lower prices either perform fewer customer services than their competitors or use a variable mark-up strategy to achieve 'higher than normal' mark-up on non-comparable or luxury items. Retailers tend to differentiate themselves on the basis of initial mark-up on the products they offer; in short, retail organisations can generally be categorised by their relative emphasis on mark-ups, which results in varying price lines and price images in the minds of consumers.

By nature of location

Under the conventional classification system it is possible to group retail establishments according to the number and nature of store location. Historically, retailers have gathered together at convenient points of travel: early retail settlements were usually placed at the convergence of rivers, land trails or transport intersections. This same tendency can be observed in the modern era: in every central business district, regional shopping centre, community shopping centre, high street shopping centre, airport, and bus or train station.

It is important to note that certain types of retail stores require more 'aggregate convenience' than others to grow. Here again the product becomes important when viewed in the light of consumer shopping habits. For example, when consumers want to do comparative shopping for clothing, they may frequent a local shopping centre because the city centre containing the 'main' stores, no longer has complete assortments or depth of stock. Many small retailers offer products to shoppers as they travel by car to the major chain and department stores in the shopping centre. Similarly, it is quite common for shopping centre clusters to contain supermarkets, pharmacies, hardware shops, and petrol service stations because they complement each other's product assortments and are convenient for customers. If properly located, marketed and managed, these complementary stores should succeed as a collective unit.

The general retail marketing environment

Every retail organisation is affected by environmental forces which can be segmented into the internal (micro) environment, the external (macro) environment, and the proximate environment. They combine to shape the activities of the retail organisation by playing a constraining role, limiting the success of the retailer, and by playing a positive and lively role, providing opportunities for growth. These environmental forces are shown in Figure 2.2. The figure emphasises the pivotal position of the customer. It can also be observed that the nature of products and/or services provided by the retailer is influenced by these environmental factors. The success of a retail organisation within its environment is determined largely by how well it adjusts to the constraints and opportunities presented by these environmental factors.

These individual factors may be seen as a subsystem of the general retailing environment. Retail marketing management is concerned with anticipating and reacting to perceived changes occurring outside the retail organisation itself. This external environment is usually referred to as the **macro environment**. The term 'general retailing environment' is used here to mean all factors and forces that have an impact – positive or negative – upon retail marketing management's ability to conduct its activities successfully. This includes interdepartmental factors and influences that hinder or create business opportunities, as well as the roles of the employees, the unions, shareholders, and the local community – these elements are generally termed the **micro environment** or internal environment.

Fig. 2.2 THE GENERAL RETAIL ENVIRONMENT

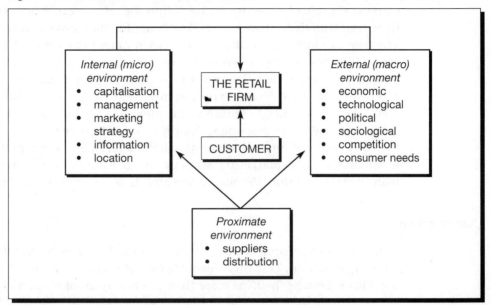

Retail organisations exist in order to fulfil the needs of the environmental niche in which they operate at a particular time and place; a retail marketing operation is no different. A successful retailing enterprise has to be dynamic and able to change in response to shifts in the general business environment: what is needed is rapid reaction to the stimuli that signify the need for change.

Internal (micro) environment

The retail marketing department has to work in cooperation with other functional departments within the retail organisation. For example, retail marketing research may be used to identify a 'gap' in an existing market that the retailer could commercially exploit. In order to produce services that may fill such a gap, the retail marketing department will have to call upon the services of other functions such as the finance, merchandising, and legal departments. Retail marketing tasks cannot be accomplished in isolation; the cooperation of other departments is required. When considering the overall retailing environment in which retail marketing operates, it is important to appreciate that although the retail marketing function is the mechanism by which the retail organisation adapts to changes in external conditions, it has to take into account internal factors. Decisions made about retail marketing functions affect the performance of other departments and vice versa. When addressing environmental problems facing the retail marketing department, the degree of conflict and cooperation inherent in the interaction between the functional areas needs to be carefully examined.

In producing the retail marketing plan (*see* Chapter 14), retail managers must consider the role of the other groups within the retail organisation: employees and their representatives, shareholders, and other functional systems within the firm. These groups form the retailer's micro environment (*see* Figure 2.2). Retail managers must make decisions within the overall plans made by top management. In general, retail marketing plans must be approved by top management before they can be implemented. Retail managers must also work closely with other departments, as stated earlier, to ensure a unanimously agreed strategic plan. Apart from these departmental relationships, five key factors will have significant influence on the consistency of internal environmental management: capitalisation, management dimensions, marketing strategy, retail information systems and their management, and store location. These aspects are briefly explained below.

Capitalisation

This is a common problem in retailing, particularly among small and medium retail organisations. Less than adequate capital investment typically leads to failure. This is because, perhaps more than in other types of business, if large profits are to be made in retailing, large sums of money need to be invested. Many small marginal retail operations are under-capitalised and, as a result, are likely to be located in undesirable sites and have inadequate stocks (Galbraith, 1977). They barely use promotion, and their stores lack the necessary internal attractiveness or appeal. At the other end, multiple retailers are able to control and dominate market position due to their efficient capital management.

Retail management

Once retail marketing strategies have been decided upon, the management must select a retail marketing mix that will convey the desired price–service image. Goals and objectives must be set, stating what the retailer wants to achieve. Retail management must also ensure that the firm's positioning is consistent with how it wants to be perceived. Strategies must explain how the firm will achieve its goals, objectives, and desired strategic position. Efficiency must be ensured within the whole retail organisation so that departmental conflict may be avoided. One of the major reasons for poor management is the relative freedom of entry into the retail sector, allied with the dream of being one's own boss. As a result, freedom of exit also comes into play, and inexperienced and unprepared owner-managers mismanage and eventually fail – a large percentage within the first two years. On the whole, however, a well-planned retail set up is likely to be managed efficiently.

Marketing strategy

In designing their marketing strategies, retailers must consider the **competitive environment** in which they operate. The competitive environment is shaped by the interactive process that results as retailers seek ways to satisfy customers more effectively than their competitors. The marketing decisions made by an individual firm influence consumer response in the marketplace, and they also affect the marketing strategies of their competitors. It is worth noting here that a poor marketing strategy may, in fact, be a non-existent marketing strategy. It is this interaction among the marketing strategies that creates competitive rivalry and shapes the competitive environment. It is important, therefore, clearly to understand how retail stores compete with each other and how their marketing strategies interact.

Regardless of its size and type, the retail organisation must have an effective marketing strategy; only when the firm has a good marketing strategy is it in a position to ensure survival.

Retail information management

A well-developed decision support system includes market intelligence – information informally collected by store managers, buyers and salespeople. This type of information is based mostly on in-store observations and conversations with customers. Structured research information may be used and could give a retailer a competitive edge over their main rivals. In contrast, inadequate market intelligence particularly in small retailing, has been a proverbial problem. The retailer, especially the small retailer, makes decisions on the basis of experience and hunches. Retail information based on research is almost non-existent; even when information is available, small retailers typically do not know how to use it. As a result, decisions relating to marketing strategy taken by small retailers are often not based on factual information, which increases the probability of making poor decisions.

Exhibit 2.1 **Managing retail market information**

A downturn in the economic environment caught Hong Kong retailers unprepared. As retailers were scrabbling to respond to collapsing sales, Dickson Concepts, the territory's biggest home-grown luxury retailers, used inside market information to limit its sales decline. The organisation, which also has several outlets in Taiwan, moved several of its high-priced items to Taiwan where the impact of the market decline was minimal. Dickson Concepts has, therefore, benefited from its efficient information system and prompt management response.

Retail location strategy

In a mobile world, competitiveness depends heavily on location. However, a revolution is taking place in the way companies choose to deploy resources, and the old ways of thinking no longer apply. Competitive pressures mean that locations chosen by retailers will, more than ever before, have a decisive impact on how well they perform. A customer's decision to visit a particular store involves complex decision making, using criteria such as location, price, convenience, selection or store reputation. Proximity and convenience of store location may significantly influence shopping loyalty and must be carefully managed. On the other hand, location has an irreversible, negative impact on the well-being of the retail organisation. Since traffic is the backbone of retailing, a location that does not have the necessary traffic to or around it does not provide the retail organisation with a high probability of success. In addition, though some locations are poor from the outset, others can become poor over time. For instance, a city centre may become old and dilapidated; consequently, locations that were fashionable and popular may become shabby and undesirable. This process naturally causes many retail business failures and is eventually reflected in retail population patterns.

External (macro) environment

External environmental factors are those influencing factors that retailers are not directly able to control but which they will have to bear in mind during operation. It is usually the uncontrollable factors in the external macro environment that are the most important sources of both opportunities and threats to the retail organisation. The term macro environment, as used here, denotes all forces and agencies external to the retail organisation itself. Some of these external forces may be closer to the organisation than others. Some of the major interacting systems making up the retailer's external environment (Berman and Evans, 1995), as shown in Figure 2.3, are discussed briefly in the following sections.

Fig. 2.3 THE CHANGING EXTERNAL ENVIRONMENTAL SYSTEMS

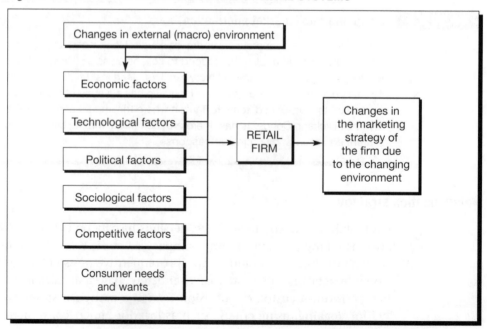

Economic factors

Economic conditions affect retail population in at least two ways: the development of the business cycle and the cost of doing business based on specific economic requirements. The development of the retail life cycle has a profound impact on retail business failures and their discontinuance. Most of the business failures and business discontinuance are retailing businesses. The same relationships, therefore, prevail between business cycles and the retail sector. Research has shown that business failures increase during recessions and decrease during booms. In a less than perfectly competitive economic system, since it is not possible to guarantee that those who fail are inefficient, the increased failure rate does not imply any improvement in the efficient of the retail sector. However, regardless of the efficiency factor, retail establishments fail or discontinue at substantial rates. Thus, many retailers disappear, and others appear as the economy experiences ups and downs.

Retailers' costs of doing business have gone up steadily. These increases can be attributed to a number of economic factors, including: rental costs, labour costs, costs of the larger inventories necessary for effective competition in the modern retail industry and costs of developing and maintaining a modern store. Modern retailers find themselves obligated to run stores in good locations with all the features that appeal to their targeted market segments. Many retailers, particularly small retailers, do not own their building and their land and thus rent them, often from absentee landlords who seldom care about the retailer's well-being. So, despite other economic pressures, rental costs have been going up steadily irrespective of income.

As retailing has become more sophisticated and demanding, labour costs have also risen. The unionisation of retail employees has proven especially costly to the retail sector. Almost by definition, modern retailers have to carry larger inventories with greater depth and breadth than ever before. One reason why inventories have expanded is that the average consumer is using a greater variety of products. In the context of retail service, modern retailers are being forced to offer a wide variety of services such as a liberal returns policy, credit, free delivery, packaging, and free information. Many of them have had to develop an elaborate internal layout so that customers can find their way around the store. Air conditioning, background music, modern displays and show windows are all part of the total image-building process.

Technological factors

Technology refers to the development and use of machinery, products and processes. Many technological advances are beyond the control of individual firms; for example, no firm has been able to develop a cure for the common cold. Small retailers face additional difficulties in that they are often unable to afford the latest technological advances, for example those in physical distribution management. As organisations head towards the end of the twentieth century, they must realise the need for improved technology in order to remain competitive in domestic and foreign markets and to minimise the impact of resource shortages. Oil, clean air, clean water, and skilled craftspeople are among the declining resources that must be re-channelled (*see* Drucker, 1970).

Changes in technology not only affect the products manufacturers produce and sell but also the way that they sell them. Most particularly the influence of computerisation and the development of sophisticated data capture facilities have led to improved efficiency for marketing organisations. In the retail industry, for example, the introduction of electronic point-of-sale (EPOS) equipment has provided retailers with detailed information on sales which allows for extremely efficient stock control systems, price change procedures, and up-to-the-minute sales and stock reports.

Exhibit 2.2	**Use of technology speeds up intelligence gathering**

Both producers and retailers are now more able to take advantage of technology to gain a competitive advantage through the speed of marketing intelligence gathering. Technology is already reducing the lead time needed to respond quickly to changing customer needs and minimising any delays in the supply of goods and services. To be successful, retail organisations are going to have to use technology to stay ahead of competitors.

Food and commodity manufacturers such as Heinz, Unilever and many others, have well-constructed retail marketing intelligence systems that rapidly inform relevant departments in different parts of their organisation of any new product developments and launches. With new technology, retailers are also likely to be served by better retail marketing intelligence systems.

Political factors

The political climate is an important determinant of retail population. Three considerations touching on the political climate are taxation, small business assistance, and the general sentiment toward business.

Taxation and related practices, such as licensing or fees charged to practice, are all significant in terms of encouraging businesses to enter the market. A substantial increase in fees to practice in a city centre location, for instance, may determine whether a retail organisation remains in the same location, relocates or discontinues. In addition, some administrations – both local and national – have used tax credit incentives to stimulate business. Such practices encourage many small businesses and particularly small retailers to enter or to remain in the market.

Small business assistance can also have a strong effect on the shape and size of the retail population. Small business assistance may be government instigated, government operated or privately encouraged; typically, all three processes take place simultaneously. When financial advice and guidance are available for small businesses – in a pro-business atmosphere – their number increases and their share of the market does not decline as quickly as it would have otherwise done. Anti-retail business sentiment, in addition to punitive taxation and lack of business assistance, could cause hardship to business in general and for retailing in particular. Anti-business sentiment could lead to anything from anti-business legislation (including excessive regulation) to loss of good managerial talent to non-business sectors.

It is not possible to isolate the impact of any one of the external factors discussed so far. Many of them function simultaneously and/or in conjunction with others. It must be reiterated that the aforementioned factors do not represent an exhaustive list; other factors could have a significant bearing on retail population. It has been stated, for instance, that when Liverpool's dockers went on a prolonged strike many businesses in Merseyside went under.

Exhibit 2.3	**Volatile economic and political conditions**

For many retail organisations, both domestic and international political considerations are of prime concern – especially for retailers involved directly in international operations. Many global retailers have joint ventures or subsidiaries all over the world. In many countries, particularly those where the domestic politics and economic situation is less stable than in the UK (as in many African, Asian and South American countries), retail operation is much more difficult to plan and control. In many African countries, for example, political change is often sought by force (military takeover), rather than through the democratic process.

Retailers operating in volatile conditions have to monitor the local political situation very carefully. In general, however, whatever industry the retailing firm is involved in, changes in the political and legal environments at both the domestic and international levels can affect the company's operations.

Sociological factors

Sociological factors may be categorised as the movement of people and the characteristics of peoples. The British and Europeans in general, tend to move around freely; it has been estimated, for example, that one-fifth of all Europeans move every year. Movement has been varied: from rural to urban and from urban to suburban areas. Similarly, the population centre has been moving towards the prosperous nations of Europe. Another trend, particularly marked in the UK, is the movement from north to south. In all of these cases, if retailing does not or cannot follow the population movement, it cannot succeed. In the past, studies have indicated a high correlation between the number of enterprises and population size. Although no recent data are available in this particular area, it would seem fair to assume that there would be no significant difference between past and present relationships.

Competitive factors

Retail **competition** has been changing on many fronts three of which are spatial, institutional and functional. Spatial dimensions of retailing competition imply primarily that retailing has to follow population. As people move from urban to suburban areas or from the countryside to the city, retailing must be able to follow. The most specific aspect of spatial retail competition has been seen in the area of city centre versus out-of-town shopping. This competition has had a far-reaching impact on retailing structure and practice, changing the very landscape of the retail industry.

Institutional dimensions of retail competition are depicted in numerous ways, some of which are discussed later in this chapter (*see* Retail marketing implications). Large enterprises have pushed small retailers out of existence or have forced them to find new ways of functioning in order to survive. The small retail sector struggled to stay in business, seeking out niche target markets and aiming to fulfil their needs, while the corporate entity continued to appear stronger in terms of ability to survive. For a long time multiple retailers continued to capture ever larger proportions of total retail business at the expense of small firms, with department stores winning a large percentage of total retail trade. This situation continued until discount stores emerged (*see* discussion on the wheel of retailing, Chapter 1). The strong competition between these two types of shop is expected to result in better service for the consumer.

Retail competition has taken two basic forms: non-price competition and price competition. Non-price competition has led retailing to develop multitudinous functional practices that have made it easier and more pleasant to shop and buy in retail organisations, including: special customer services, well-designed store layout and proper signs for making shopping easier, background music, and so on. All of these enhancing features are components of the store image which, in turn, is translated into the competitive advantage the retail store is seeking. Price competition, on the other hand, implies that the store is aiming to establish its competitive advantage by offering better prices than those of its competitors rather than by offering service-oriented advantages.

Consumer needs and wants

Changing consumer needs are reflected in changing consumption patterns. There are several reasons why consumption patterns have changed, including economic conditions, education, lifestyles, leisure time activities, and changing values. During the late-1980s and early 1990s economic conditions have had a significant impact on consumption patterns (Worthington and Britton, 1994):

1 Due to high levels of inflation, consumers' discretionary income was reduced. As a result, the purchase of necessities was emphasised – for example, food, medicine, and children's wear – at the expense of non-essentials such as gift items, entertainment, eating out, and so on. Some retail businesses involved in the latter sectors, therefore, suffered either losses or low sales volume.

2 As a result of high unemployment levels among some segments of British society, often concentrated in particular geographical areas, **income** became relatively low. In response, retailing concentrated even more specifically on basics in the areas where these people lived.

The average level of education in the UK, and in Europe in general, has increased. More people are entering higher education than ever before and this change has resulted in a corresponding shift in consumption patterns. Studies have shown that higher levels of education have switched the emphasis to housing, entertainment and food rather than on motor cars and clothing. Similarly, higher education means higher personal income, which would also have a direct impact on consumption patterns. Lifestyles in terms of activities, interests and opinions (AIO) are changing, reflecting changes in consumption patterns. A cosmopolitan lifestyle, for example, reflects specific consumption patterns that specify certain needs.

Western Europeans have more leisure time than ever before, and this has increased demand for certain types of leisure and entertainment activities. Expenditure on sporting goods, hobby-related products and other recreation-related activities have had a significant impact on changing consumption patterns.

When British values changed during the period of the Thatcher Government (most noticeably during the 1980s), significant changes in consumption patterns were observed. During that time British people became more aware of body weight, more 'do-it-yourself' types, more informal, more time conscious, and, hence, perhaps more efficient and less work-oriented. As a result of these changes in values, long-established products lost their market position and more products hit the market which could be assembled at home, such as toys and DIY products. Healthy foods and green products were in high demand, whereas linen table cloths, cloth napkins, and other formal products faced a substantial decline in demand. More efficient products became more popular, for example, jet planes as opposed to propeller planes. All of these changes in consumer needs have added up to changes in consumption patterns. As consumption patterns have changed, some aspects of retailing have gained power at the expense of others (*see* Jones and Simmons, 1990).

The proximate retail environment

There are elements in the external environment which are closer to the operation of a retail organisation than others, for example, their suppliers, distributors and even competitors. These 'closer' external forces are often collectively referred to as the retailer's proximate macro environment to distinguish them from the wider external forces found, for instance, in the legal, cultural, economic and technological sub-environments. The proximate macro environment consists of people, organisations and forces within the retailer's immediate external environment; some of the relevant factors affecting a retailer include suppliers, distributors and customers. These factors collectively may have a significant effect upon the retail marketing function within an organisation.

ᴛᴇ suppliers

Suppliers are firms and individuals who provide the resources needed by the retail organisation to produce goods and services. For example, large retailers such as Marks & Spencer Plc purchase clothing and other textile products from a wide range of suppliers which have a variety of business forms; one supplier, Gent Plc, which supplies only Marks & Spencer, is a public company. Many suppliers to large retailers supply finished goods rather than intermediate goods – product components. Supplier developments can seriously affect retailing and retail managers need to watch out for any difficulties that may have an impact on their business, for instance upward price trends of their key inputs. Rising supply costs may force price increases that can harm the retailer's sales volume. Retail managers must also watch supply availability (supply shortages, strikes, and other events which can lose sales in the short run and damage customer goodwill in the long run). Unexpected developments in the supplier environment can have immediate and potentially serious effects on the retailer's business operations. Thus retail marketing management, by means of its intelligence system, should continually monitor changes and potential changes in the supplier environment – possibly having contingency plans ready to deal with potentially adverse economic developments.

Physical distribution firms

Physical distribution firms help the retail organisation to stock and move products from manufacturers to their destinations (retail stores). Warehousing companies store and protect the products before they are moved to their next or final destination. Transport firms include nationwide railway networks, airlines, shipping firms, road haulage firms and others that specialise in moving goods from one location to another. A retail organisation must decide on the best ways to store and move the goods, taking into consideration such factors as cost, delivery, safety and speed.

The customers

Retailers need to study their customer markets closely, and understand the needs and concerns of consumers.

Exhibit 2.4	**The effects on the market of consumer environmental concerns**

The concern for environmental issues have caused consumers to think more critically about the origins, content and manufacturing processes of the products they buy. Consumers want products made with the minimum of pollution and want the reassurance, where necessary, that they come from renewable resources. Many paper products now carry notices stating that they are made from wood from managed forests that are replanted after harvesting. Similarly, consumers are also demanding that unnecessary packaging is eliminated. The Body Shop has built its entire retail marketing approach on these consumer concerns. It emphasises that the ingredients of its products are as natural as possible and that the packaging is recyclable.

Although a retailing firm has control over the selection of a target market, it cannot control the characteristics of the population. Retailers can react to but not control these consumer characteristics (age, marital status, occupation, income, education, race, and place and type of residence). For instance, Heinz could develop baby foods acceptable to the mothers, but it could not stop the decline in the birth rate; thus, to continue its successful growing strategy, it must expand into other products and services. A retailer can operate in five types of customer markets (Berman and Evans, 1995):

■ *consumer markets* – individuals and households that buy goods and services for personal consumption;

■ *industrial markets* – organisations that buy goods and services for further processing or for use in their production process;

■ *resale markets* – organisations that buy goods and/or services for the purpose of reselling them at a profit;

■ *government markets* – government agencies that buy goods and services in order to provide public services;

■ *international markets* – export buyers, including consumers, producers, resellers and overseas governments.

Each of the above market segments has special characteristics that call for careful study by retailers. Retailers must understand the interpersonal influences on consumer behaviour. This is particularly important because the purchases that consumers make are affected by family, friends, religion, level of education, standards of performance, taboos, customs, and other factors that shape culture and society. Consumer groups and organisations constantly speak out on behalf of consumers at public hearings and shareholder meetings, and express consumers' views to the media. In the UK, *WHICH* is one of many magazines that publish consumer surveys revealing shoppers' reactions to and experiences with different products. Consumers may also form efficient **pressure groups** to lobby on their behalf. To avoid negative consequences brought on by active consumer groups, retail organisations must communicate with consumers, anticipate problems, respond to complaints, and generally ensure customer satisfaction through the efficiency of their operations.

European retail marketing environment

The nature of retailing changes dramatically as European economies develop (Harris and McDonald, 1994). Among other things, there is a huge expansion in the product range, with branding becoming an important sales factor. Developments such as these combine to make marketing a crucial element of retailing in developed economies. No longer is it sufficient to source many goods locally; for example, in grocery retailing, out-of-season fruits must be imported from, say, Africa or South America, and retail marketing management has assumed a growing importance in ensuring customer requirements are met.

The above observations are especially true of the UK and many countries in Western Europe. However, there are European countries such as Portugal and Greece where mass retailing has yet to become established. This makes it essential to qualify generalisations about retail marketing within the European Union (EU). So, while in grocery retailing there are large supermarket chains run by companies such as Ahold in The Netherlands and Tengelmann in Germany, no direct counterparts exist in parts of southern Europe (Alexanda, 1995). The pace of development of retailing is clearly linked to income growth: as the population of a country becomes richer it purchases more goods and services. It is, therefore, important to realise that within the EU there are major disparities in incomes.

Of course, disparities in income tend to overstate the differences in purchasing power between countries; low-income countries often have low prices for, say, accommodation and services, which makes their population less poor than might first appear to be the case. Political initiatives within the EU, such as completion of the Single European Market (SEM) and the planned creation of a single currency (European Monetary Union, EMU) are certain to make the economic characteristics of EU countries less dissimilar than they are at present. Similarly, business initiatives such as moving production from high-cost countries to low-cost countries could well mean, over the long term, that income differences will be reduced. Retail marketing within the EU seems likely to become less differentiated than it is now. However, it is important not to attribute convergence in consumer taste solely to the completion of the SEM. Most retailers in the European environment have tended to opt for one of four choices for further business development (Alexander, 1995):

1 Retail diversification in the home market, which involves selling new product ranges as well as the established ones.

2 Non-retail activities – where new business is sought in unfamiliar sectors. A good example is the Burton Group, which has diversified from retailing into property and financial services.

3 Improving supply chain efficiency in order to gain a competitive edge over retail rivals. Many UK companies have chosen this route.

4 Internationalisation of retail operations – where the same or a similar retail format is introduced into other countries.

The future structure of retailing within the EU is, therefore, crucially linked to regulation which affects development in the retail sector. Regulation which acts to inhibit the activities of the multiples is mainly of two kinds. First, there is regulation which is contained within the planning controls exercised by local governments. It is common to most countries of the EU that planning permission is required to erect new buildings or change the use of existing ones. Planning controls have had a major impact on the number of hypermarkets and superstores built in some countries because suitable greenfield sites are so rarely made available for development.

| Exhibit 2.5 | **Planning restrictions on greenfield sites in Europe** |

In the UK it has proved very difficult to obtain sites in the 'green belt' around London because this land has effectively been set aside for amenity purposes. However, the green belt continues to be eyed jealously by developers, who see considerable potential for hypermarket development in such close proximity to large population centres.

French multiple retailers face similar restrictions but, on the whole, multiple retailers in both France and the UK have had considerable success in developing sites for supermarkets (and hypermarkets in the case of France), although not always being able to build quite where they wanted to. In Belgium, however, where the high population density makes land scarce, the problems of expansion for the multiples have been altogether more severe.

A second form of control on retail development is to restrict the entry of new commercial enterprises into the retail market. This was the purpose of Law 426 which was introduced in Italy. In effect, Law 426 has fossilised the structure of the Italian retail market; it remains fragmented and characterised by independent retailers (EC Commission, 1989). Change may result as a consequence of retail deregulation: the rapid expansion of multiple retailers in Denmark took place only after the repeal of a law which restricted the number of retail outlets that could be owned by any one retailer in a particular area. Similarly, the retail multiples may develop in Italy if Law 426 were to be repealed, but their prospects remain uncertain. There is some feeling that Italian consumers will continue to show a strong preference for using independent retailers, despite the best efforts of the multiples to win business. There is a clear conflict of interest between the large retail chains (such as Sainsbury, Tesco, Aldi and Netto) and the small retailers, with the large out-of-town sites – whether they be supermarkets or hypermarkets – trying to attract and dominate a core sector of the European retail market.

It is only recently that voluntary organisations have begun to confederate across the European Union (EU) to lobby collectively and to reform discriminatory practices. It is unlikely that small and large retailers will have the same retail marketing problems, either domestically or across Europe, and small retailers are in need of representation. Benetton is a good example of a small franchise operation in the north of England which has unique everyday retail marketing problems. Makro's expansion outlines how the German–Dutch wholesaler came into operation and became a major supplier on a world basis. It also touches upon the latest trend in retailing as the cost discount store. The growth of The Body Shop demonstrates how a business may be developed from a small scale operation into a global company, and continue to reflect the flair and vision of its founders (*see* Case Study on p. 48). Using technology a retailer can become a market leader, but only by being innovative and establishing effective retail marketing strategic alliances.

Environmental forecasting

Retail sales have increased because of increases in both population and per capita sales. Despite the declining birth rate, the UK population is not expected to stop growing until around the year 2020. In addition, family incomes are expected to increase substantially. Market analysts believe that this increase in income will upgrade the demand for quality and speciality merchandise, better customer service, and more skilled retail personnel. Increasingly limited natural resources may cause an even greater demand for skilled repair services and services such as leasing.

A sharp expansion of government controls over business is likely to result in (anti-monopoly antitrust) actions, limitations on corporate growth, and environmental regulations. Retail industry forecasters foresee an increase in the price of most goods to cover the cost of proper disposal (part of the green, 'polluter pays' principle). Most retailers believe that this cost will result in a price increase paid by the consumer, and do not believe that the added cost will be paid for by a reduction in retail profit margins.

Increased leisure time is another factor forecasted and it is believed that it will result in 24-hour opening, 365 days a year for many retail outlets. This would result in higher in-store labour costs. On the other hand, the market for leisure merchandise is also expected to expand. The increase in women who work outside the home is another factor that would encourage the extension of store opening hours. Almost half (49 per cent) of all women in the 20–60 age group were employed in 1997 and this trend is expected to increase over the next decade. The expansion in the number of working women will enhance sales of women's fashions, and convenience goods and services.

New advances in technology are expected to have an important effect on the retailing structure. In the early years of the new millenium better in-store use of computerised information will reverse the present trend for tactical decisions to be centralised in chain store operations. Cable television is currently revolutionising promotion and sales methods and is expected to be in 50 per cent of UK households early into the twenty-first century. It is designed for consumers to use in ordering merchandise that has been displayed on their television set. Apart from cable television and catalogue stores, discount houses, direct mail, and telephone selling are likely to offer the most growth opportunities in the near future. Technological improvements can ease retailing constraints by:

■ reducing the cost of handling merchandise and servicing shoppers;
■ providing a wider variety of goods and services;
■ providing a greater knowledge of consumer needs and the retailers' operations;
■ improving communications to consumers and employees.

In view of the possible decline of convenience stores (such as supermarkets) and the rise, in their place, of large-scale warehouses offering direct delivery to homes, added to the predicted increase in the importance of certain speciality stores, only six reasons may be found as to why consumers would prefer going to a shop to make their purchases rather than having the shopping delivered to their homes – with virtually no investment of shopping time and money for transport, parking, etc.:

1 A few stores are able to provide that sense of belonging that causes shoppers to talk about 'our store'.

2 Some kinds of shopping provide immediate gratification, for instance, the buying of clothes and certain home furnishings.

3 The store will offer more choices to the shopper.

4 The difficulty of deciding what merchandise will be needed may often be solved by a quick trip to the store to procure the item as soon as the need for it arises.

5 There is less uncertainty or psychological pain, because merchandise of questionable quality or appropriateness can be personally scrutinised: tomatoes can be pinched and the fat in the steaks shrewdly evaluated.

6 Customers to save money. So long as store operation and transport is cheaper than home delivery, many shoppers will invest the time and energy to make the trip.

Changes in consumer values may lead to tomorrow's shoppers searching mostly for immediate gratification. They may avoid the time and energy investments needed for shopping at stores. The increasing concentration of population, the proliferation of cars, limited fuel supplies, and the growing affluence of our society are likely to stimulate non-store shopping, even if in-store shopping could offer moderate savings in money terms.

Retail marketing implications

Retailers have been slow to recognise the changes discussed earlier and slower to adapt their retail marketing strategy to them. This may be due in part to most retail managers being in a salary band and social class where fewer changes have taken place and they have, therefore, failed to notice the changes in their customers' needs. A growing tide of criticism has been levelled at retail organisations in a variety of forms. It has been expressed that retail marketing has:

■ abused and misused the powers of persuasion at its disposal, and has been guilty of deceiving the customer in many cases;

■ placed too great an emphasis upon material goals (profit, and sales volume) and too little upon the non-material and **social values**;

■ forced the pace of technological change with little consideration of its impact and possible side effects;

■ been slow to respond to the public interest and the changing aspirations of society;

■ often failed to live up to its promises, and retailers who thought that retail marketing practitioners could – in some magical way – solve all their problems have been sadly disillusioned.

Every retail manager should have a general knowledge of how environmental influences affect the growth and development – or the demise – of retail institutions. While the retailer may not be able to control these influences, they may have an opportunity to influence certain outcomes that will ensure the survival of their organisation.

Shift in marketing application

Most retailers believe that trends are now developing that will exert a considerable impact upon future retail operations. The problem has been that retailers have too often paid only lip service to retail marketing. It has been seen as one of those quick 'cure alls' which the retail industry grabs at just because it is fashionable. Properly applied, the main benefits of the application of the retail marketing concept may be seen as:

- reduced risk – based on systematic market research and the evaluation of data to aid decision making;
- better planning as a result of early identification of market opportunities;
- greater competitiveness based on marketing skill in the face of narrowing technological differences.

But the power of retail marketing has often been abused and debased by those who have viewed it only as some form of magic art. The retail marketing concept requires the retailer to be customer oriented (*see* Chapter 1). The retail marketing concept should be based on 'customer concern': a positive effort by the retailer to make the customer the focus of all retail marketing decisions and to provide service that delivers genuine consumer values. The problem is, however, that business is profit oriented, and many of the things that need to be done can only be done at the expense of profits. Here lies the root of the present profit–service dilemma; as yet, there is no real answer to this. It is not suggested that businesses should not plan to make profits but that they may have to plan to make satisfactory levels of profit within a set of constraints. These constraints may be either voluntary or imposed upon them. As far as retail marketing is concerned, however, it does mean that the needs and desires of customers – not only for physical things but for the whole range of satisfactions including the environment – must be placed at the centre of the enterprise more firmly than ever before.

SUMMARY

Every retail organisation must start with the retail marketing environment in searching for opportunities and monitoring threats. The retail marketing environment consists of all the factors and forces that affect the retailer's ability to transact effective retailing with the target market. The retailer's retail marketing environment can be divided into the micro environment, the macro environment and the proximate environment. The micro environment consists of the internal environment (the retailer's several departments) which has an impact on the retail management decision-making process. The retailer's macro environment consists of major forces that shape opportunities and pose threats to retail organisation (economic, political and legal, technological and culture). The proximate environment also consists of the retail marketing channel organisations that cooperate to create value (the suppliers, distributors, consumers and the intermediaries).

The entire retail marketing environment joins forces to create retailing opportunities or pose business threats. Environmental factors can significantly affect the growth and development of selected retail institutions. Successful retailers anticipate such events and forecast their impact on their operations; they can thus take innovative or adaptive proaction instead of some form of defensive reaction.

KEY TERMS		
competition	macro environment	retail marketing
competitive environment	marketing intermediaries	environment
consumer movement	micro environment	social values
disposable income	monopoly	technology
environmental forecasting	physical distribution	
income	pressure groups	

ASSIGNMENT

Research conducted among British consumers suggests that they are less concerned with systems and order than was the case in the past. There appears to be a growing acceptance that it is perfectly alright to give in to moods and occasions. Such changing social values could result in fewer shopping lists and more impulse purchases. Write an essay discussing how changes in social values of this nature could influence not only marketing strategy but other environmental variables (1000 to 1500 words).

REVISION QUESTIONS

1 Retailing exists in many forms because each form is part of the most efficient distribution system currently available to meet differing consumer demands. Discuss the forms of UK retailing.

2 The 'natural selection' or 'survival of the fittest' concept maintains that the retail institution that most effectively adapts to its environment is the one most likely to survive and grow. Comment on this statement.

3 The general retail marketing environment is made up of a number of separate but inter-related factors. What are these factors and how do they interrelate?

4 What are the internal or micro environmental factors, and how could these affect retail marketing planning?

5 The main factors making up the retailer's macro environment fall into four categories. Identify these categories and discuss them briefly, with the aid of examples.

6 Suggest reasons for why social and cultural factors may be the most difficult for retailers to evaluate.

7 Most UK retailers believe that trends are now developing that will exert a considerable impact upon future retail operations. What are these trends?

8 Many European retailers tend to opt for one of four strategic choices for further business development. Briefly evaluate these choices, with examples.

9 Discuss the environmental implications for retail marketing management for retailers in the UK.

10 Discuss how you think technology will affect the development of retail marketing within Europe in the near future.

CASE STUDY

The Body Shop: an environmentally friendly retailer

Based in London, The Body Shop puts environmental concerns at its core and in the process finds its way to the green in customers' pockets. This natural cosmetics store strives to meet its dual goals of environmental correctness, and social action and change. Its skin and haircare stores display literature on ozone depletion next to sunscreens and fill their windows with information on issues like global warming. The company opposes testing on animals, helps Third World economies through its 'trade, not aid' mission, contributes to rainforest preservation efforts, is active in women's issues, and sets an example for recycling. The Body Shop participates in 'save the whales' rallies, advocates for other endangered species (a line of its children's bath products, for example, comes with informative storybooks about various endangered animals), and supports the development of alternative energy sources. Every employee is assigned to spend half a day each week on activist work. Customers get discounts if they bring their old bottles back to the store for recycling. In 1988 the chain collected over a million signatures in Britain on a petition asking Brazil's president to save the rainforests. The Body Shop practices a tell-all policy that provides complete information on all of its products, including natural emollients such as peppermint foot lotion, sandalwood shaving cream, and banana shampoo. Cards on every counter tell customers about the ingredients and centuries-old history of some lotions; leaflets offer tips about natural skin and haircare. Getting on the company 'soapbox', the retailer provides explanations of why it is against animal testing for cosmetics, campaigns to increase the membership of Amnesty International, and promotes its 'voter invigoration project' by registering voters and displaying such pro-democracy pro-vote slogans as 'register your hope and do not let the future happen without you – register to vote'.

These efforts are not ancillary to The Body Shop brand; they are an integral part of it. The vision is carried right throughout customers' in-store experiences. Enter a branch of The Body Shop, and you are greeted by a assistant who not only wears a The Body Shop T-shirt bearing a social message but also believes in the company's causes, values and products. Displayed among the store's goods and tester samples are posters and colourful handouts (printed on recycled paper) that provide information about the products, about social causes the company supports, and about how customers can get involved in rallies, social-cause advocacy groups, and the like.

Compare The Body Shop's brand identity with those of its competitors. Most skin care and cosmetic lines are indistinguishable, focusing on similar product attributes and 'health and beauty' promises. Their customers are not involved with even their favourite brands – except to make a transaction or to receive a broadcast-style advertising message. Clearly, The Body Shop has transformed the skin care and cosmetics experience into something more than it has ever been.

It is probable that The Body Shop did not deliberately seek to pursue an alternative brand-building method instead of mass-media advertising. Instead, it was blessed with liabilities (lack of funds) that encouraged creativity. Although, not every retailer is 'blessed' with such liabilities, the lessons The Body Shop learned are valuable and transferable. Similarly, developing a set of alternative approaches to brand building is not easy, especially for retailers who have relied on media promotion as the cornerstone of their brand-building efforts. But with dedication and commitment from senior managers, building-brands without the mass media could be a worthwhile investment. The Body Shop's success has attracted several imitators. Some of them are jumping on the natural and aromatic bandwagon, profiting from the public perception – amplified by the efforts of The Body Shop, that something natural is better, healthier and more socially correct.

Questions for discussion

1 The success of The Body Shop in the natural cosmetics market may attract imitators. If you are the manager of one of these shops, where else will you take your store within the cosmetics retail marketing environment?

2 Why do you think The Body Shop has succeeded in a sector considered by many to be difficult?

REFERENCES

Alexander, N. (1995) 'UK retailers' motive for operating in the single European market', *International Review of Retail, Distribution and Consumer Research*, 5(4): 22–41.

Berman, B. and Evans, J.R. (1995) *Retail Management: A Strategic Approach*. New York: Macmillan.

Bolen, W.H. (1988) *Contemporary Retailing*. 3rd edn. Englewood Cliffs, New Jersey: Prentice-Hall International.

Drucker, P. (1970) *Technology, Management, and Society*. London: Heinemann.

Euromonitor (1995) *Retail Trade in the United Kingdom*. London: Euromonitor.

Galbraith, J.K. (1977) *The Age of Uncertainty*. London: Andre Deutsch.

Harris, P. and McDonald, F. (1994) *European Business and Marketing: Strategic Issues*. London: Paul Chapman.

Jones, K. and Simmons, J. (1990) *The Retail Environment*. London: Routledge.

Worthington, I. and Britton, C. (1994) *The Business Environment*. London: Financial Times Pitman Publishing.

3

Consumer behaviour and retail marketing strategy development

LEARNING OBJECTIVES	After reading this chapter you should be able to:

After reading this chapter you should be able to:

- understand the basic model of consumer behaviour;
- describe the consumer information processing approach to the study of consumer behaviour;
- evaluate the consumer decision-making process and know the factors that influence it;
- explain the concept of consumer decision making and understand the theory of motivation;
- gain insight into cognitive activities such as perception, attitude change and learning;
- recognise the influence of personality on consumer choice behaviour;
- understand the risks involved in choosing between alternatives.

In order to increase the probability of success, retailers must understand **consumer behaviour**. Consumer behaviour may be defined as the process that underlies an individual's decision of what, when, where, how, and from whom to purchase goods and services. Consumer behaviour models – and the research that supports and contributes to their construction – have enjoyed much popularity during the 1980s and 1990s. Increased emphasis on the marketing concept and simultaneously, the strengthening voices of dissident consumers have helped to accelerate consumer-related research. However, this research was only partially extended into retail marketing and retailing-related areas. Thus, retailing has been deprived of an ever-accumulating knowledge about consumer behaviour.

Purchase behaviour at the retail level is a complex phenomenon with multiple phases and dimensions. Any attempt to systematise and organise information relating to purchase behaviour would be welcomed by retailers, as it allows them to adjust to different components of the market differently – enabling retail managers to be selective and to concentrate on market segments that offer them the best opportunities.

Adopting the customer's viewpoint is the essence of good retail marketing. This chapter, therefore, focuses on the customer and the way shoppers behave while shopping. In particular, it is about **consumer decision making**: about how shoppers

Fig. 3.1 BASIC INFLUENCING FACTORS IN THE SHOPPING PROCESS

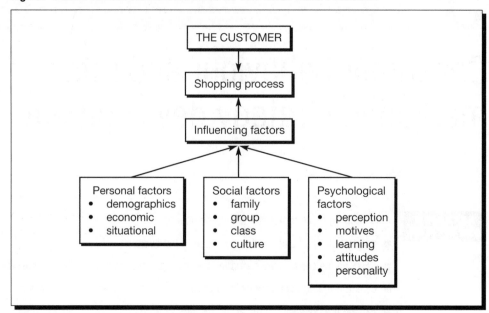

make buying decisions; what the processes are (awareness, trial and repeat, for instance) and what the factors which influence them (traditional or cultural) may be. *See* Figure 3.1 for a simple outline structure of the basic factors influencing the shopping process.

Once more it has to be stressed that each individual product or service evokes a specific, and possibly unique, response from its set of customers. Indeed, each shopping situation is unique: a uniqueness which retailers do exploit through face-to-face contacts with shoppers. Both large multiples and small independent retailers need to understand what their customers' specific needs and wants are. It is possible to vary the shopping decision-making process from an almost intuitive reaction to shopping for food, to a complex process in the case of consumer durables. This complexity of shopping process should be kept in mind when dealing with choice theory. The choice theory provides a theoretical framework and justification for much of retail marketing, particularly in the area of the design of retail advertising strategies. Since the mid-1980s, choice theory has been a major focus of research, in the hope that one or more simple models may be found, by which all subsequent retail marketing concepts could be explained.

The shopping behavioural process

The first question to ask is: 'How do customers make their shopping decisions?'. This question is more difficult to answer than is generally expected. Shoppers do not come to each buying decision with conveniently blank minds and then rationally consider the options. According to economic theory, often the only significant variable to be considered is the price. But how a customer comes to his or her purchase decision is a much more complex process than the theoretical assumptions would indicate. It may include the following elements: shopping experience, shopper's **lifestyle**, point of sale, retail promotion and/or price. In reality, the shopping decision-making process is an extended, complex and often confused one. Even in the apparently simple case of buying a tin of baked beans, a shopper in a supermarket, faced by the large number of competing brands, may have a number of factors in mind, such as those discussed below (*see also* Figure 3.2):

Elements in the purchase decision process

Shopping experience

The shoppers will probably have tried a number of brands and decided that some are acceptable and others are not. They may have had bad experiences with a particular brand or may have found one to be particularly good. Alternatively, shoppers may simply have become bored with the taste of the brand to which they have been loyal for some time. Experience is a much undervalued factor, particularly by those advertising agencies that believe 'creative marketing' is all it takes to sell the brand. Most shoppers will usually take practical experience into account over any other factors. If the shopper does not like the brand, no amount of retail advertising – no matter how creative – will succeed in selling it.

The shopper's lifestyle

Apart from the 'physical' experience of the product, the prospective shoppers may also demand that it conforms to their 'lifestyle'. Thus, some shoppers may positively seek out tins of Heinz baked beans because these match their emotional needs to be seen as caring parents who feed their children on the best brands available on the market. On the other hand, a few may deliberately buy the own-label brand, either because it is cheaper in price (representing value for money) or because they perceive own-label to be the same quality at lower price.

Fig. 3.2 BASIC VARIABLES IN SHOPPING DECISION MAKING

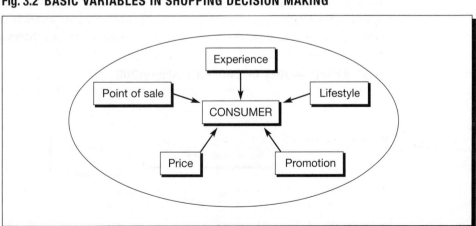

Retail promotion

Although few shoppers will admit it, retail advertising they have seen over the preceding weeks will, to an extent, have shaped their views – at least that is the fervent hope of the retailer. The most influential 'promotion', according to McGoldrick (1990) however, is word of mouth recommendation – that is, one that has come by way of a friend, an 'opinion leader', or the family.

The price of the item

Faced with the choices available, the shopper may compare the value for money of alternative brands. Price is a major factor in own-label marketing, and shoppers are known to have bought own-label because it is seen as better value for money (*see* Omar, 1994). On the other hand, price plays other roles in shoppers' decisions; for example, in fashion marketing price is usually seen as a surrogate to perceived quality.

Point of sale

At the point of sale, the shopper will be limited to the brands on offer (unless he or she decides to go to another supermarket). It is at this time that the shopper will also be confronted with the display at the point of sale. This display reflects the supermarket's own contribution, which is in turn influenced by the buying patterns of its other customers. Which of these factors (shopping experience, lifestyle, retail promotion, price and point of sale), if any, will eventually swing the balance depends upon the individual shopper, the product or any one of a number of other influences. What happens is usually not clear, least of all to the shoppers themselves. As a result there are several theoretical models of the shopping decision-making process. The following sections examine some of the simpler models, which should clarify the process; as Howard (1989) observed, more complex models too often contribute more layers of confusion.

Basic models of shopping behaviour

In the case of those products that are purchased frequently and used repeatedly, the simplest model breaks the process down into three stages: awareness, trial, and repeat purchase (*see* Figure 3.3). This is a very simple model, and as such does apply fairly generally. Its lessons are that retailers cannot obtain repeat purchases, even from loyal

Fig. 3.3 SIMPLE MODEL OF SHOPPING BEHAVIOUR

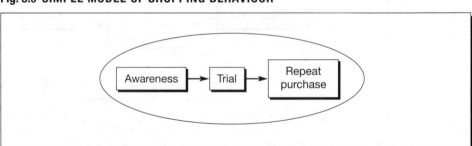

shoppers, without going through the stages of building awareness and then obtaining trial use, which has to be successful. It is a pattern that applies to all repeat purchase products and services – and to industrial products just as much as to groceries.

Although this simple theory is typically concerned with, and limited to, repeat purchases it is rarely taken any further, to look at the series of transactions that such repeat purchasing implies. The shoppers' growing experience over a number of such transactions is often the determining factor in their future shopping behaviour. All the succeeding transactions are interdependent, and the overall decision-making process may accordingly be as complex as that in any industrial buying process.

In the case of durable goods, such as electric cookers for households or grinding machine tools for firms, it is not realistically possible to indulge in 'trial' (or in repeat buying over anything other than very extended periods), although the experience of one purchase, such as a cooker, may be extended to a similar purchase such as an electric heater. In these situations, therefore, the typical consumer will seek reassurance from other sources. The industrial buyer may seek 'reference customers' to check whether their trial has been satisfactory. In consumer markets the prospective shopper (even with the protection offered by guarantees) may have to resort to relying on the 'reputation' of the retailer, reports in consumer magazines (such as *Which*), and word of mouth experiences of friends and acquaintances.

Kotler (1997) favours a slightly more complex five-stage model, placing more emphasis on the earlier stages:

- problem recognition;
- information search;
- evaluation of alternatives;
- purchase decision;
- **post purchase** behaviour.

This assumes that the shopper is rational and is following a rational shopping decision-making process – an assumption that may not be justified in practice. Once more, though, it does give some insight into how retailers may exert influence at each of the five stages.

Problem recognition

The buying process starts with the buyer's recognition of a need. That recognition may be internally generated, or externally influenced by environmental factors in general or suppliers' promotional stimuli in particular. It should be noted that a great deal may be done even in terms of external environmental influences – from recognising them to acting to steer them in directions most favourable to the retailer's own needs.

Information search

For most products and services the consumer will obtain **information** passively: absorbing messages from the media, both advertising and editorial, and from friends and contacts – often subconsciously. For some particularly important decisions, however, the information search will be proactive. The consumer will discuss the matter with friends and 'experts', and will seek out information from sources such as consumer magazines. In the 'information search' stage the retailer must, in both of the above cases, make certain that suitable information, usually in the form of carefully planned advertising, is available to the shoppers.

Evaluation of alternatives

For most products or services there are likely to be a number of competing brands in the market, ranging from internationally distributed brands, such as Coca-Cola, down to those that can only be obtained in a few local shops. The process of choosing between these can be represented as the result of a number of 'filtering' processes, some of which are under the consumer's control and some under the retailer's; *see* Table 3.1 for a detailed listing.

Table 3.1
EVALUATION OF ALTERNATIVE CHOICES

Filtering process	*Control*
Availability	The first consideration is whether the consumer has access to the product or service. This is mainly under the control of manufacturers and their distribution chains, which is why they put so much emphasis on obtaining high levels of distribution. How far the consumer is prepared to venture in search of a difficult-to-obtain product is, of course, dependent upon the characteristics of the market. The tin of beans may have to be on the specific supermarket shelf just when needed. On the other hand, some consumers will wait several months and travel hundreds of miles to see a musical concert.
Awareness	If the shopper is not aware of the brand, it will not be on the shopping list. Again, awareness is to a large degree in the control of the retailer and/or the supplier, and reflects the amount spent and the success of the promotional strategy.
Suitability	Not all brands will be identical (except in pure commodity markets), at least in terms of how the various suppliers have presented them. Some of them will clearly be more suitable, at least in the consumer's eyes, while some will seem definitely unsuitable. The retailer may, for instance, use 'segmentation' (discussed in Chapter 4) as a means of targeting the brand on a specific segment of the market. This device matches the brand specification to the needs of that segment, so it is seen to be more suitable to that target market – but this probably also makes it less suitable to buyers in other segments of the market.
Consumer choice	It is perhaps at this stage that the shopper's choice is asserted, to select from the brands that remain after the previous filtering stages. The shopper is not totally at the mercy of the advertiser; and will make brand choice on the basis of whatever reasons are seen as necessary. To the shopper at that time the choice is absolutely rational and the brand best meets the perceived needs.

Purchase decision

Howard described one model of the consumer's decision-making process (CDM) in terms of matching chosen attributes to appropriate products or services:

> The process is seen as one in which the consumer first decides exactly which attributes are important. At the same time building a picture, in terms of these attributes, for each of the brands. The consumer then matches these lists against those of competing brands, taking account somehow of the varying importance of the attributes and the various degrees of match or mismatch (1989).

But these 'attributes' are not just the physical features beloved of suppliers; they include not only price, but also a wide range of attitudinal factors. CDM is discussed in detail in the following section.

Consumer decision making (CDM)

The previous sections looked at the theory and a number of factors that may have an impact on consumer shopping behaviour. However, these factors do not act in isolation; they all interrelate. The most relevant of all these models for retail marketing management is Howard's Consumer Decision Model (CDM), reproduced here (Figure 3.4) in a simplified form. Originally developed for financial services, it has been modified for general supermarket shopping decisions.

The CDM is defined as a model made up of six interrelated components (variables), as shown in Figure 3.4: information (F), brand recognition (B), attitude (A), confidence (C), intention (I), and purchase (P). Of these six, the three central

Fig. 3.4 CONSUMER DECISION MODEL (CDM)

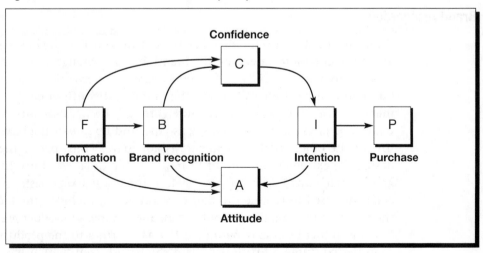

Source: Adapted from Howard (1989).

components – brand recognition (B), attitude toward the brand (A), and confidence in judging the brand (C) – make up the buyer's **brand image** and can be thought of as the ABCs of consumer behaviour. The interrelationship of the six components is shown graphically in Figure 3.4.

Information (facts)

Information or 'facts' (F) has to be defined with care, as a massive amount of research indicates (*see* Omar, 1994). First, as a stimulus, it is some physical event that one or more of the buyer's five senses (seeing, hearing, smelling, touching, and tasting) are exposed to, either voluntarily or involuntarily. Typically, brochures, newspapers, radio, television, and word of mouth are sources of information for the shopper. Sight and hearing are the two major sense organs by which the customer absorbs the information. But in food, taste and smell are generally important (Omar, 1994). Touch is highly significant for partially sighted and blind people, but the belief is that retail marketing management has yet to use that sense fully among the sighted.

The concern is much more with the percept than with the **input stimuli**. The percept is defined as that which the shopper perceives from being exposed to the stimulus. Since the retailer's interest is in the percept, information (F) is defined as the percept that is caused by the stimulus. The standard measure of the consumer's **perception** (F) is recall.

Facts of various kinds and from varied sources are often critically important to the consumer when making a purchase decision. As the CDM shows, information (F) causes the shopper to recognise the brand (B), to evaluate it in terms of their needs, which is **attitude** (A), and to create in his or her mind a level of confidence (C) or certainty of how well it can be judged whether the brand will yield satisfactory or unsatisfactory results.

Brand recognition

Brand recognition (B) is defined as the extent to which the buyer knows enough about the criteria to categorise the brand, but not enough to evaluate and distinguish it from other brands in its product category. Recognition helps consumers to build both an attitude (A) toward the brand and **confidence** (C) in their judgement of it (*see* direction of arrows in Figure 3.4). Recognition attributes of a brand tend to be physical: the colour, size, shape, and texture of the box. A simple outline of the object with a little data is adequate. Thus, packaging and product design are extremely important. A new 'Classic Cola' was introduced to the UK grocery market by J. Sainsbury in 1994. In the test market questionnaire, the characteristics used to represent brand recognition (B) included the kind of package, the colour of the can, the size of the can, and manner of product presentation.

Brand recognition may be thought of as referring to the product's form rather than the consumer's attitude toward the brand itself, which has to do with its function – namely, what the product does to cause the buyer to like or dislike it. This distinction is basic, since form and function can perform markedly different roles in the shopper's thinking. However, a consumer needs information about both form and function to be able to categorise a brand in a product class. Equally important, these physical attributes are a major reason why marketing a product and marketing a service, such as a health service, pose different problems. Increasingly the physical attributes of a service are being emphasised in practice. There has also been some attention to trademarks and related ideas though they have not yet been studied in depth. Practitioners are, at least, intuitively aware of them. That is why service companies sometimes outfit their employees in standard uniforms – as a substitute for the physical product.

Brand image is the total picture of the brand in the shopper's mind and is made up of all three elements: brand recognition, attitude toward the brand, and confidence in judging the quality of the brand. These could be referred to as the ABCs of retail marketing. The concept of brand recognition is not widely recognised in practice at present, but it will become more so as its role in consumer thinking is better understood. Recently, however, product designers have been talking about 'visual clues' and product 'semantics'; and advertisers have been using 'semiotics', which deals with signs, symbols, and their functions in communicating with consumers.

Attitude

Attitude (A) toward the brand, the second part of brand image, is defined as the extent to which the shopper expects the brand to yield satisfaction of a particular need. To the extent the shopper does, it spurs the intention to buy the brand. Attitude is probably the most basic and widely accepted concept throughout the social sciences; it is as pervasive to the social sciences as the concept of the atom is to the natural sciences. Great progress has been made since the late 1970s in understanding the nature of attitude and its relation to behaviour, both in retail marketing and the basic social sciences. The discussion here, however, is only an overview to build upon in developing a coherent theory of consumer buying processes.

Attitude measurement

Attitude can be measured in at least two ways: unidimensionally and multidimensionally. Unidimensional attitude is when the buyer is asked: 'Will you please rate brand X on a 1 to 5 scale, where (5) is favourable and (1) unfavourable'. To that question, the buyer has a single or unidimensional answer – any one of five numbers. A **multidimensional measurement**, often called an 'expectancy value' measure, has several stages. First, the researcher asks a pilot group of shoppers to tell him or her the attributes or benefits by which they evaluate a brand in this product class. Benefit is defined as a characteristic of the product or service that the consumer values either positively or negatively. Then each shopper in the regular sample is asked to rate the relative importance of these benefits. Next, the shopper is asked to rate how well the brand performs on each of the more important of these benefits. The benefits can be either negative or positive; for example, price is usually rated as negative by the shoppers.

With this kind of measurement one brand's high rating on a certain benefit offsets or compensates for its low rating on another benefit in the consumer's mind, and this is called the 'linear compensatory rule'. For example, the buyer may like the style of one car but finds the price too high; however, the positive style compensates for the negative price. The retailer takes each of the shopper's answers and multiplies the ratings on the importance of each benefit by the ratings on the amount of each benefit the shopper perceives in the brand. These products are then added together to produce the 'attitude' variable in the CDM (*see* Table 3.2). This is the multidimensional measure of the buyer's attitude toward the brand.

Table 3.2 gives a multidimensional measure of the shopper's attitude toward the grocery shopping process. In the first column are the shopper's benefits: brand quality; value for money; price; and taste. The second column is how important each of these benefits is to the shopper on a 1 to 7 scale in evaluating any brand of grocery. The third column contains a particular shopper's ratings of the specific grocery brand, on these benefits. The two ratings for each benefit are multiplied together and the product inserted in the fourth column. These products are then summed to give a measure of 'attitude'. The multidimensional measure is altogether more useful than the unidimensional measure – as a guide to assessing consumer shopping processes and behaviour, and for other similar uses. In addition, devoting funds to improving the more important benefits provides a better pay-off than does pouring money into the less important benefits. The multidimensional measure is also a guide to designing the promotional message and deciding the optimum amount of promotional expenditure.

Table 3.2
MULTIDIMENSIONAL MEASURE OF ATTITUDE TOWARD GROCERY SHOPPING

Benefits	Importance	Performance	Output
Brand quality	6.14	6	36.8
Value for money	6.10	4	24.4
Price	6.00	4	24.0
Taste	5.98	3	17.9
		Attitude =	103.1

Confidence in judgement

Confidence is the third element in the shopper's image of a brand. It is defined as the shopper's degree of certainty that this evaluative judgement of a brand is correct. The shopper's confidence in a particular brand is increased when their thinking is reinforced by repeated reminders from the retailers and from peers that other shoppers like it, that it is distinct from other brands, and that the information is consistent with what the shopper already knows about the brand. In turn, confidence leads to intention to buy (*see* Figure 3.4) by removing the hesitancy to act caused by uncertainty.

It may seem strange that increasing the consumer's confidence (C) necessarily increases the intention to buy (I). It could be argued that if the attitude (A) toward the brand is low then the shopper does not care for it and increasing the confidence (C) would merely be adding to the shopper's belief that it is a poor brand. This should decrease the intention to buy it, contrary to what the model indicates. The reason confidence (C) affects intention (I) favourably is because when confidence (C) is low the shopper 'looks' for information. There is substantial evidence, much of it unpublished, that a positive relationship holds between confidence (C) and intention (I). Also, attitude affects confidence to some extent, but this relationship is complex and is not shown in Figure 3.4.

Although shown as three separate elements making up brand image, brand recognition, attitude towards a brand, and a buyer's confidence in the judgement of the brand are all intimately interrelated. Brand recognition forms a mental foundation, or 'chunk' in the memory, upon which the other two components of brand image build. Thus, B causes both A and C in Figure 3.4. Technically, B is an eidetic image, which means that it can be seen in the shopper's mind's eye in vivid detail. The sharper it is, the more effective it will be in affecting attitude and confidence and, therefore, in influencing behaviour indirectly.

Attitude also helps determine into which product category the shopper will group the brand. For example, if the petrol consumption of a car is rated favourably (that is, having low petrol consumption), the car is more likely to be grouped as a sub-compact car. Attitude also aids brand recognition in distinguishing a particular brand from other brands in its category. Likewise confidence, which is the result of information and built on brand recognition, adds strength to the brand image. A successful retailer helps shoppers to group a brand into the appropriate category and to distinguish it from other brands in that category. Unless shoppers can put a new brand into a category, they are unlikely to buy it. If the retailer's information is not clear enough, the store could lose a prospective shopper who is too busy to expend the time and effort required to learn about the product category.

Intention

Intention (I) to buy is defined as a mental state that reflects the shopper's plan to buy some specified number of units of a particular brand in some specified time period. It is useful for the retailer to understand the shopper's intention. If the retailer surveys the consumers, a feel for the typical consumer's current intentions could be assessed. Simultaneously, the retailer can tap other elements of the customer's thinking: F, B, A and C. Consequently, since the retailer finds out intention to buy at that time, he or she can measure the effects of B, A and C on I – and thus measure, indirectly, the effect of B, A and C on P. This works well for frequently purchased products, but for infrequently purchased items some problems may arise because of the time lag between when intention is measured and when the purchase is executed.

In addition, events in the shopper's life other than information may affect the intention, and these too can be fed into intention if desired. The retailer is often able to identify these events and thus estimate their future effects on intention and indirectly upon purchase. For example, a consumer's expectations about future income can strongly shape the intention to buy a house. Again, as seen in Figure 3.4, attitude and confidence affect intention; intention in turn affects purchase.

Purchase

To the retailer, purchase (P) is obviously the most important variable in the entire system. It represents the pay-off – or lack of it – for retail marketing expenditures. In the shopper's decision process, purchase is defined as when the buyer has paid for a brand or has made some financial commitment to buy some specified product during some specified time period. It is caused by intention to buy. Measurement of purchase (P) is relatively simple: the customer did or did not buy, or make a financial commitment to buy, during a certain time period. Depending upon the frequency of purchase, it is sometimes useful to distinguish between the decision to purchase and the act of purchase. Such models may help theorists to understand and explain consumer behaviour better, but it can be more difficult to put the knowledge to practical use.

Strategy development and influencing factors

It is arguable that in taking their final decision, and indeed throughout the whole process, customers are influenced by a wide range of factors and not just those relating to the obvious features of the product. Examples of the factors most generally discussed by retail marketing theorists include: age and lifestyle, situational influences, psychological factors and social factors.

Age and lifestyle

The demands of individuals and families vary over time. Mercer (1996) identified a number of stages in an adult's life, each of which has characteristic patterns of earning and consumption:

1 Bachelor stage – young, single people not living at home.
2 Newly married couples – young, no children.
3 Full nest I – youngest child under six.
4 Full nest II – youngest child six or over.

5 Full nest III – older married couples with dependent children.

6 Empty nest I – older married couples, not retired, no children living at home.

7 Empty nest II – older married couples, retired, no children living at home.

8 Solitary survivor I – in labour force.

9 Solitary survivor II – retired.

These stages may have important implications for retail marketing strategies. Stage 1 individuals, for example, are recreation-oriented and hence are prospective customers for providers of entertainment. Those in stage 2 have high joint incomes and tend to spend them; among this group are the so-called yuppies beloved of the suppliers of luxury goods. In stage 3 are the typical first-time house buyers (who at the same time also buy all the other durable and household goods that become part of a home). Those in stages 3 and 4 are often the target of the mass consumer advertisers; they represent the archetypal housewife with a family to feed. By stage 5 the pattern of buying may have become more selective as income increases. Those in stages 6 and 7 are once more able to spend on luxuries, although of a different type. Finally stages 8 and 9 pose different support requirements. Clearly, each retail organisation will target those age groups that are most relevant to its product or service. In the financial sector, organisations selling insurance, for example, will probably ignore stages 1 and 2 to concentrate on stage 3.

The demography of these age groups is not static, and there are peaks and troughs. Most notable, in the late twentieth century, was the 'baby boom' of the 1960s which was reversed in the 1970s, when there was a comparable drop in birth rates. These changes had significant marketing impacts. Retailers are understandably attracted by a booming retail market, not least because this allows more opportunities for new brands. A falling market is more difficult to enter, with the existing brands very much on the defensive. Thus, in the 1960s suppliers to the baby market had a field day; in the UK, the Mothercare retail chain blossomed. By the early 1980s, however, the number of babies born per year had fallen by a third or more and Mothercare's performance looked less dynamic. On the other hand, the boom babies were then reaching their twenties – many becoming yuppies or young parents – with a consequential benefit to manufacturers of luxury goods for this age group and the builders of 'starter homes'. In the early 1990s, retailers were already starting to look to the over-50s, the 'empty nest' stage, for the next big boom in spending.

Situational influence

Situational factors are the external circumstances or conditions that exist when a shopper is making a purchase decision. These factors can influence the shopper at any stage of the buying decision process and may cause the individual to shorten, lengthen or terminate the process. For example, a change in situation may arise which causes a shopper to lengthen or terminate the buying decision process. A consumer, for instance, who is considering taking an exotic safari holiday and is laid off from work during the stage of evaluating alternatives may decide to reject the purchase entirely.

The effects of situational factors can be felt throughout the buying decision process in a variety of ways. Uncertainty about a partner's health may sway a consumer against making a new car purchase. On the other hand, a conviction that the supply of a particular product is limited may impel a person to buy it while it is available. In Nigeria, for example, consumers have purchased and hoarded petrol, food products and even toilet tissue when these products were believed to be in short supply. These and other situational factors can change rapidly; their influence on purchase decisions is generally as sudden as it is short lived.

Psychological factors

These factors operating within individuals determine, in part, people's behaviour in general terms and thus influence their behaviour as consumers. A number of **psychological factors** are also proposed: from the widely reported teachings of Freud, through to Herzberg's discussion of 'dissatisfiers' (characteristics of a product that will veto its purchase for a given customer) and 'satisfiers' (which will positively persuade the customer to choose the product). In the context of retail marketing, however, perhaps the most widely quoted approach is that of Abraham Maslow (1954), who developed a hierarchy of 'needs', ranging from the most essential, immediate physical needs to the most luxuriously inessential (*see* Figure 3.5). Maslow's contention was that the individual addresses the most urgent needs first, starting with the physiological needs. But as each is satisfied, and the lower-level physical needs are (at least among the affluent) soon satiated, attention switches to the next higher level, resulting ultimately in achievement of the level of self-actualisation. It is argued that retailers are increasingly required to address their attentions to the two highest levels. It is also contended that even in the early years of the twenty-first century retailers may have to concentrate almost exclusively on the needs for self-actualisation.

Fig. 3.5 MASLOW'S HIERARCHY OF NEEDS

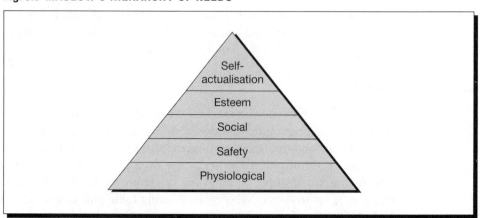

Source: Maslow (1954).

Cognitive dissonance

There is one more interesting effect on consumer behaviour to be found immediately after a purchase has been made; this was predicted by Leon Festinger in 1957, as his **cognitive dissonance** theory. The theory states that, where there were dissonant elements in the original decision to buy (the negative aspects of the product purchased, and the positive elements of the alternatives not purchased), there would, post purchase, be tension in the consumer's mind. Festinger's prediction was that buyers would read promotional material even more avidly after purchase than before in order to justify their decisions and to displace the dissonant elements by concentrating on those aspects of the promotion that stressed the good points of the product purchased. However, later work has not tended to be very supportive. Nevertheless, there is an implication for retailers that they need to recognise the role of retail promotion in general and of retail advertising in particular, in the post-purchase period as well as in the build-up to the sale. Other primary psychological influences on consumer behaviour include: perceptions, motives, learning, attitudes, and personality. Although these psychological factors operate internally, it is apparent that they are very much affected by social forces external to the individual.

Perception

Different people perceive the same thing at the same time in different ways. Similarly, the same individual at different times may perceive the same item in a number of ways. Perception is the process of selecting, organising and interpreting information inputs to produce meaning. Information inputs are the sensations received through sight, taste, hearing, smell and touch. Each time we see an advertisement, watch television, visit the shops or use a product, we receive information inputs. This information thus influences our decisions whether to buy or not.

Motives

A motive is an internal energy-giving force that directs a person's activities towards satisfying a need or achieving a goal. Motivation is the set of mechanisms for controlling movement towards goals. A shopper's actions at any time are affected by a set of motives rather than by just one. Each shopper's motives are unique and, at a single point in time, some motives in the set have priority. However, the priorities of motives vary from one occasion to another. Motivation also affects the direction and intensity of behaviour. Individuals must choose which goals to pursue at a particular time.

Learning

Learning refers to changes in a person's behaviour caused by information and experience. The consequences of behaviour strongly influence the learning process. Behaviour that results in satisfying consequences tends to be repeated. For

| Exhibit 3.1 | **Understanding patronage motives** |

Motives influencing where a person purchases products on a regular basis are called patronage motives. A shopper may use a particular shop because of such patronage motives as price, service, location, honesty, product variety or friendliness of sales-people. To capitalise on patronage motives, retailers should try to determine why regular customers patronise a store and then emphasise these characteristics in the store's marketing mix.

Useful lessons may also be learned by studying and understanding people's reasons for patronising competing brands or outlets.

example, when a consumer buys a box of Bird's Eye Fish Fingers and enjoys them, he or she is more likely to buy the same brand next time. In fact, the individual will probably continue to purchase that brand until it no longer provides satisfaction. But when the effects of the behaviour are no longer satisfying, the person will perhaps switch to a different brand or start eating an alternative frozen food, such as chicken nuggets, instead.

When making purchasing decisions, shoppers have to process information. Individuals have differing abilities in this regard. When shopping for a computer, for instance, a computer technician who has experience with computers may be able to read, comprehend and synthesise the considerable quantities of information found in the technical brochures for various competing brands. On the other hand, a person with limited abilities with computers may be incapable of performing this task and will have to rely on information obtained from advertisements or from the sales representative of a particular brand.

Attitudes

An attitude refers to an individual's enduring evaluation, feelings and behavioural tendencies towards an object or activity. The objects or acts towards which we have attitudes may be tangible or intangible, living or non-living. Some attitudes relate to things that have a major impact on our lives, while others are less important. For example, we have attitudes towards relationships, culture and politics, just as we do towards reading and sports (*see* the discussion of attitude in the section on consumer decision making, CDM, above).

Personality

Personality includes all the internal traits and behaviours that make a person unique. Each person's unique personality arises from both heredity and personal experiences (nature and nurture). Personalities are typically described as having one or more characteristics, such as compulsion, ambition, gregariousness, dogmatism, authoritarianism, introversion, extroversion, aggression, and competitiveness. Marketing researchers attempt to find relationships among such characteristics and buying behaviour. Although few links between several personality characteristics and buyer behaviour have been determined, the results of many studies have been inconclusive. However, retailers are convinced that a shopper's personality does influence the types and brands of products purchased. The type of clothing or cars that people buy, as well as the way their hair is styled and the leisure activities they engage in, may reflect one or more personality characteristics.

Social factors

The forces that other people exert on buying behaviour are called social factors. These factors can be grouped into major areas including: family, social classes, culture, sub-cultures, and reference groups.

Family influence

All of us occupy positions within groups, organisations and institutions. Associated with each position is a role – a set of actions and activities that a person in a particular position is supposed to perform, based on the expectations of both the individual and surrounding people. Because people occupy numerous positions, they also have many roles. For example, one man may perform the roles of father, husband, grandfather, son, machine tool operator, part-time youth club organiser and member of the local rambling association. Thus there will be several sets of expectations placed on each person's behaviour.

An individual's roles influence both general behaviour and buying behaviour. The demands of a person's many roles may be inconsistent and confusing. To illustrate, assume that a man is thinking about buying a boat. While he wants a boat for fishing, his children want one suitable for water skiing. His wife wants him to delay the boat purchase until next year. A colleague at work insists that he should buy a particular brand known for high performance. Thus an individual's buying behaviour may be partially affected by the input and opinions of family and friends.

Social classes

Within all societies, people rank others into higher or lower positions of respect. This ranking results in social classes. A social class is an open group of individuals who have similar social rank. A class is referred to as 'open' because people can move into and out of it. The criteria for grouping people into classes vary from one society to another. In the UK, as in other Western countries, many factors are taken into account including: occupation, education, income, wealth, race, ethnic group and possessions. In the former Soviet Union, on the other hand, wealth and income are less important in determining social class than education and occupation; for example, although Russian doctors and scientists do not make a great deal of money, they are highly valued in Russian society. A person who is ranking someone does not necessarily apply all of a society's criteria. The number and importance of the factors chosen depend on the characteristics of the individual being ranked and the values of the person who is doing the ranking. For example, one individual may particularly respect status within a church or religious sect, while another may regard it as having little relevance.

The traditional main focus for retail advertising has been that of social class (O'Brien and Ford, 1988). This, although it revolves around occupation (usually that of the head of the household), is based on more than just income groups alone. It used to be assumed that the upper classes were the first to try new products, which then trickled down (the name of the theory) to the lower classes. Historically, there may have been some justification for this: the refrigerator, the washing machine, the car, canned baked beans and the telephone were all adopted first by the higher social classes. Recently, however, as affluence has become more widespread, the process has become much less clear. The new 'opinion leaders' now come from within the same social class. The class groupings which have been traditionally used by the advertising agencies are shown in Table 3.3. This approach has been reported to be of decreasing value in recent decades. Whereas in the late 1950s, when these groupings were first widely used, the numbers in each of the main categories (C, D and E) group in total (although now usually split to give C1 and C2) forms such a large sector that it dominates the whole classification system and offers less in terms of usable concentration of retail marketing effort. In addition, increased affluence has meant that consumers have developed tastes that are based on other aspects of their lifestyles. Class-related behaviour appears to have decreased significantly in terms of purchasing patterns. There is also a political will in the UK to strive to produce a society that is ever-closer to a classless one.

Culture

The overall **culture** is another increasingly important factor. It is most noticeable in terms of nations; the Mediterranean way of life, in the sun, may be quite different from the Nordic lifestyle, in the cold. The culture of the UK is seen to be riddled with persisting class-consciousness; but, as was pointed out above, cultures change – and much of marketing has yet to recognise this fact.

Table 3.3
CLASS GROUPINGS

		Percentage (%)
AB	Managerial and professional	20
C1	Supervisory and clerical	19
C2	Skilled manual	29
DE	Unskilled manual and unemployed	32

Source: The UK National Readership Survey, 1994.

Within the overall culture there will be smaller subculture groupings, which have their own distinctive values. These are perhaps most obvious in ethnic or religious groupings, which attract their own specialist suppliers. But they may also be as diverse as 'yuppies' in the major financial centres or football supporters, each of which groups holds a very strong set of cultural values – and each of which may be targeted by specialist retailers, supplying Porsche cars or team football strips.

Reference groups

Within these cultures and subcultures, there is a powerful force at work – peer pressure – requiring members to conform to the overall norm of the group. These 'reference groups' are sometimes referred to as 'membership groups' when the individual is formally a member of, for example, a football club, a political party or a trade union. Individuals may also have 'aspiration groups' (social cliques, such as yuppies) to which they would like to belong. They may also recognise 'dissociate groups' with which they would not wish to associate (for example, wine drinkers may go to great lengths to avoid being associated with those they see as 'lager louts').

Much of the marketing research industry still uses class and age as the main discriminators. Since the mid-1980s, however, increasing affluence has resulted in spending patterns that may now vary quite considerably, even within the same age and class groups – they now reflect individual lifestyles. A number of lifestyle classifications have been proposed by researchers, including the following:

1 *Activities, Interests, Opinions (AIO)* – this approach seeks through usually long questionnaire such as those proposed by Joseph Plummer, to measure respondents' positions on a number of dimensions spread across some predetermined categories as well as the demographic groupings. Based on their responses, the interviewees are then allocated, using sophisticated computer analysis techniques, to the appropriate AIO (lifestyle) groups.

2 *Value Lifestyles (VALS)* – this system was developed using similar groupings. It was developed by drawing up four main categories subdivided into nine lifestyles, again based on:

   – need-driven groups – 'survivors' and 'sustainers';
   – outer-directed groups – 'belongers', 'emulators' and 'achievers';
   – inner-directed groups – 'I-am-me', 'experientials' and 'societally conscious';
   – combined outer – and inner-directed groups – 'integrated'.

According to this framework, the outer-directed groups – 'belongers' (conventional, conservative, and so on) and 'achievers' (leaders who make things happen, and so on) – account for two-thirds of the US population. Thus *The Times* newspaper, to take a UK example, might expect to target 'achievers', and possibly to address a larger total market segment than the *Guardian*, which may be looking to the 'societally conscious' (inner-directed groups) for its most ardent supporters. Less widely reported is that the VALS typology also suggests that there is a possible progression within the lifestyles – from 'survivors' through to 'integrated'. There are probably two alternative routes for this progression the traditional path – the outer-directed developmental path; and the contemporary path – the inner-directed developmental path.

The customer franchise

One of the most positive ways of consolidating the consumer as the most important focus of the retail organisation is to look on this relationship as a prime asset of the business – one that has been built up by a series of retail marketing investments over the years. As with any other asset, this investment can be expected to bring returns over subsequent years. But, also like any other asset, it has to be protected. This 'asset' is often referred to as the 'customer franchise'. At one extreme, it may be derived from the individual relationship developed face-to-face by the retailer; at the other, it is the cumulative image held by the consumer resulting from long exposure to a number of retail advertising campaigns.

In some markets the customer franchise may be so strong as to be exclusive, in effect giving the retailer a monopoly with those customers. For example, high street banks can be reasonably confident that, once they have recruited a customer as a teenager, generally the recruit will remain loyal to them for the rest of his or her life.

The franchise may be much wider than this. Consumers may regularly switch brands for variety, but may still retain a positive image of the brand, which will swing the balance when their next purchase decision is taken. The franchise may thus still have a value (upon which the retailer can build), even if the current purchasing decision goes against it; a later decision may, once again, be in the retailer's favour. The customer franchise is, therefore, a very tangible asset in terms of its potential effect on sales, even if it is intangible in every other respect.

The customer franchise is based, however, on an accumulation of impacts over time. Unfortunately, too many retailers fail to recognise the importance and long-term nature of this investment. They treat each new retail advertising campaign as if it could be taken in isolation, no matter how well or badly it meshes with previous messages that have been delivered to the consumer. The evidence is that consumers do not view retail advertising and promotion campaigns as isolated from each other. Instead they incorporate it into their existing image – 'to good or bad' effect, depending upon how well the new retail advertising campaign complements the old (*see* Chapter 11).

SUMMARY

An understanding of consumers' needs and motives is an essential prerequisite of a successful retail marketing strategy. The identification and satisfaction of consumer needs is one of the most fundamental principles of retail marketing; without this focus, strategic planning can easily become dominated by the actions of competitors or internal influences.

The extended typology of motives underlying the shopping activity represents an important development from the view of shopping as simply a process of economic exchange. Many consumers do not overtly acknowledge these personal and social motives, preferring to justify their shopping behaviour in more rational terms. Much research work has, therefore, failed to detect the strength of these factors within the consumer's patronage decision process. Most retailers would claim to be customer-oriented and may also point to their constant interface with shoppers as being indicative of an understanding of consumer needs. Although much insight could be gained through the interaction between customers and staff, in reality, the full potential is rarely realised. A deeper understanding of how consumers decide where and how to shop is important and retailers should strive to reach it.

KEY TERMS	attitude	consumer decision making	multidimensional measure
	brand image	culture	perception
	brand recognition	fact	post purchase
	cognitive dissonance	information	psychological factors
	confidence	input stimuli	purchase behaviour
	consumer behaviour	lifestyle	situational factors

ASSIGNMENT

After years of declining market share, unsuccessful advertising campaigns, management upheaval, and finally a takeover by Grand Metropolitan Plc, Burger King Corporation wanted to change consumers' perceptions of the company and their attitudes towards it. Burger King altered its marketing mix to stem its declining market share and to change its image by relating the Burger King experience to consumers' self-concepts. Breaking away from fast-food marketing's traditional focus on price and treatment of their products as 'commodities', Burger King developed a new advertising campaign designed to set it apart from competitors and its own troubled past.

Task

Write an essay (not more than 1800 words) suggesting reasons why you think Burger King's new marketing strategy will or will not work.

REVISION QUESTIONS

1 Adopting the customer's viewpoint is the essence of good retail marketing. Briefly explain this statement.

2 Consumer behaviour theory is a simplified, abstract representation of reality. Discuss.

3 Briefly discuss the essential characteristics of a good theory.

4 Within the overall culture there will be smaller subculture groupings which have their own distinctive values. What use are these distinctive subgroup values to retailers?

5 An understanding of consumers' needs and motives is an essential prerequisite of successful retail marketing strategy. Discuss.

6 How could the customer franchise be related to customer usage and brand loyalty?

7 How could the two models of lifestyle be compared with the various psychological approaches?

8 Of what retail marketing value are consumer behavioural models to the retail organisation?

9 Outline the basic principles of the multi-attribute attitude model. What are the main limitations of this concept as a good model of the consumer's patronage decision?

10 What is the basis of the VALS classification system? Explain how you could use this system in grouping consumers with similar interests in a product.

CASE STUDY

Restoring consumer confidence in British beef

The impact of bovine spongiform encephalopathy (BSE), commonly known as 'mad cow disease', on consumer confidence in meat is the rationale behind the formation of Assured British Meat (ABM), an independent organisation that is to run a nationwide consumer safety assurance scheme, embracing all supply chain elements. The ABM's umbrella function embraces assured animal feed supplies, individual farm assurance schemes, livestock transport, abattoirs, processing plants, catering butchers, and retail outlets. The remit recognises that a chain is only as strong as its weakest link.

The total ABM initiative concentrates on food safety issues. It is a consumer reassurance scheme, not a quality assurance scheme. Thus from the ABM point of view, there should be no competition between retailers on food safety. Meat variations should be confined to meat quality issues and all of the functions joining together under the ABM umbrella – including 22 000 farmers who are current members – have agreed to this aspect.

While consumers need not concern themselves with the intricacies of breeding animals for beef production, they can take comfort from the fact than an increasing proportion of their beef is now coming from animals bred specifically for this purpose. This is in comparison to pre-BSE beef production, when 60 per cent of total beef supplies were derived directly and indirectly from stock bred primarily for milk production. This stock included surplus pure-bred male calves from the dairy herd (the majority are now slaughtered at birth), and older cows and bulls from both dairy and beef herds, culled at the end of their working life. Since the BSE scare began (22 March 1996), regulations have been introduced:

cattle for the beef market must be no more than 30 months of age, with all older stock being sent for incineration. The resulting rise in the quality of beef has been substantial.

Breeders are also adopting improved and proven methods which guarantee that required qualities – including reduced fat content and more lean meat in the carcass – are passed from parent to offspring. This is achieved through the ability to rate animals for a variety of measured traits and compile an estimated breeding value (EBV). Components include weight at birth, at 200 and 400 days old, muscle score, and fat depth recorded by ultrasonic scanning of the live animal. Statistical analysis of these and other qualities carried by animals in the breeding population, allow geneticists to compile multi-trait EBVs for bulls and cows.

Those with high ratings can then be selected to pass their qualities on to the next generation. Such methods are a major advance on traditional breeding methods by which farmers mated good looking animals together in the expectation that like would beget like. The results from mating stock with no recorded and analysed evidence of their breeding worth, purely on eyeball appraisal, led to more disappointment than success. Modern breeding methods developed with MLC support, and now offered to the industry, are removing the mystery and disappointment from beef breeding and production down on the farm.

Despite the trauma of low prices for finished stock, and the savage BSE culling programme coupled with a disposal scheme for surplus calves, one favourable result is that it has removed animals of inferior beef conformation and quality from the system. Thus, the young finished animals now coming on to the market are of superb eating quality. Enhanced quality is also being reinforced by traceability of the product through independently audited schemes, epitomised by the national Farm Assured British Beef and Lamb scheme (FABBL) and its Scottish and Welsh equivalents. Supermarkets are not only insisting on traceability, but launching their own producer club variations on the basic formula.

Producers are obliged to subscribe to the extra cost of the farm assurance scheme at a time when many are losing money on beef production. The extra costs are just about bearable for producers who are doing an efficient and carefully costed job already but others are suffering badly. However, it must not be ignored that most other industries are subjected to similar disciplines. Independently audited production and traceability standards, enshrined in FABBL, are also part of the farmers' 'due diligence' obligations under the 1990 Food Safety Act, so there is no escape.

The National Farmers Union (NFU) is solidly behind all farm assurance schemes but they are very concerned that separate initiatives by the leading chain stores do not confuse the issue. The farmers union believe that the concept of an overall Assured British Meat scheme, setting agreed standards and embracing meat production from conception on the farm to consumption on the plate, is the best way forward.

▶

Questions for discussion

1 How difficult do you think it will be to change consumer perceptions about British beef?

2 Do you think the new breeding innovations introduced and the BSE culling programme are enough to change consumer attitudes and improve beef consumption rate?

3 What other ways could you suggest for changing consumer attitudes to and perceptions of British beef?

REFERENCES

Howard, J.A. (1989), *Consumer Behaviour in Marketing Strategy*. Englewood Cliffs, NJ: Prentice-Hall.

Kotler, P. (1997) *Marketing Management: Analysis, Planning, Implementation and Control*. Englewood Cliffs, NJ: Prentice-Hall.

McGoldrick, P. (1990) *Retail Marketing*. London: McGraw-Hill.

Maslow, A. (1954) *Motivation and Personality*. New York: Harper & Row.

Mercer, D. (1996) *Marketing*. 2nd edn. Oxford: Blackwell.

O'Brien, S. and Ford, R. (1988) 'Can we at last say goodbye to social class?' Paper presented to the 31st Annual Conference of the Market Research Society.

Omar, O.E. (1994) 'Comparative product testing for own-label marketing', *International Journal of Retail & Distribution Management*, 22(2): 12–17.

Plummer, J.J. (1974) 'The concept and applications of the lifestyle segmentations', *Journal of Marketing*, 38 (Winter) 21–8.

4

Retail market segmentation and positioning

LEARNING OBJECTIVES

After reading this chapter, you should:

- understand the meaning and definition of a retail market;
- recognise various consumer groupings and their specific needs;
- recognise how retail organisations group consumers together for the purpose of serving them efficiently;
- understand brand and segment targeting decisions;
- recognise and understand retail strategies for brand positioning.

Appreciation of the influence of groups upon shopping behaviour and the falling level of success of the standardised products have led manufacturers to introduce different features into their products, though they have not always understood the theory behind the action. Quality, style and image permit products to be offered to different parts of what had previously appeared to be a single market. The interface between the consumer and the retailer is the **retail market**. The 'position' in that retail market chosen by the retailer for the product or service – against the 'map' of **consumer** needs – defines all the retail marketing actions thereafter. Whether decided formally or by default, it is at the heart of retail marketing operation.

The initial stage, however, may be to 'segment' the market itself: to choose a smaller part on which to concentrate resources and gain control over the competition. However, the segment has to be viable, and sophisticated retail marketing research is needed to optimise the 'segment'. **Market segmentation** is an approach to marketing which appreciates that the total market for a product type is not a homogeneous whole (Doyle and Sharma, 1977). Within the whole there may exist groups which are homogeneous to the extent that certain variables which are significant in relation to the product are the same within the group.

Positioning, or targeting, then places the product or service in the optimal position, mapped against the competitors, on the 'dimension' which is most critical to the consumers. The focus for this activity is often a 'brand'; alternative branding policies are investigated in Chapter 9. Branding, combined with positioning, usually offers the most sophisticated and powerful application of retail marketing principles.

The main foci of this chapter are market segmentation and market positioning (targeting). The entire discussion is centred on and related to the retail market and the grouping of customers according to their needs and wants. Instead of directly answering questions relating to segmentation or lack of it, this chapter presents an inductive approach involving a detailed discussion of a series of theories that have attempted to identify different market segments to which separate retail organisations have been catering.

The retail market

A market is where the product or service is delivered to the buyer by the seller and profits are generated. On the other hand, it can be defined in terms of the product or service (where 'market' describes all the buyers and sellers for that product or service – the car market, the money market, and so on). This is the framework favoured by many economists. The market may also be defined geographically or demographically. Here, it is most appropriate to define a retail market in terms of consumers with money to spend. That, however, excludes people who, although they may like the product or service, have no money to pay for it. These poor people do not, therefore, represent a viable market for the product or service. Thus, the key for the retailer, should be to define the retail market in terms of the customer (shoppers). Kotler (1997) sees buyers (actual and potential) as constituting the market, whereas sellers constitute the industry, and his definition is: 'a market consists of all the potential customers sharing a particular need or want who might be willing and able to engage in exchange to satisfy that need or want'.

It is important that the differences between segments should be significant and meaningful; the usefulness of groups is increased where there is a maximisation of differences between segments rather than within a segment. This means that there are a number of significant variables relating to the product which can also be found concentrated in a group.

The retail market is, thus, a group of shoppers; but, in many practical respects, it is still defined in the short term by what retailers have to offer. After all, shoppers cannot make their wishes known if there is no suitable product on offer (Omar, 1996). In the long term, however, it is the shoppers who will decide what the retail market really is – by their buying patterns. They set the boundaries and, by their purchases, choose what products or services will remain in the market. Inevitably, to understand the market the retailer must understand the customer. This is done through market research (discussed in detail in Chapter 13) and research provides the cornerstone of effective retail marketing. Remember that the basis of sound retail marketing practice is the ability to identify with the customer or client and to be able to adopt the shopper's point of view.

Customer dimensions

In a normal retail marketing environment, retailers will generally see markets in terms of where their business is in these markets. This means that they often look at the markets specifically in terms of their own existing customers and potential customers. In many retail markets it may seem an easy task to define who the customers are: they are simply the buyers of the brand on offer. But the dividing line is often not so clear. Where do those who have now switched to another brand lie? Where do you put very loyal users who have most recently bought another brand, just for a temporary change? How do you categorise a consumer of a particular durable, when their last purchase might have been half a decade ago? The questions go on. In the public sector, for instance, the boundaries may be even more blurred: unemployment benefit is paid to those out of work, but is intended just as much to support their dependants.

Users

In some instances the person who buys the product may not be the person who uses it; thus, users are not always the same as purchasers. It may be the children in the family who actually consume the cornflakes; and they will usually make their brand preferences very well known – and their preference may be for a certain brand because they want to collect the free gifts in the packets. The difference is most noticeable in the case of newspapers and magazines, where readership figures (the number of those who read a given issue, as determined by market research surveys) can be much higher than figures for circulation (the number of copies actually sold, from special audits of the publishers' own accounts).

Prospects

The term **prospects** is most often used in personal selling where the transaction is a face-to-face selling opportunity; 'potential customers' is often the term used in mass retail markets, but the meaning is the same – those individuals in the retail market who are not the retailer's customers. Again, however, the boundaries are not quite so clear. Are lapsed customers to be included? Is everyone in the market a prospect? Should only those who are likely to buy the particular brand be included? The concept of 'prospects' may sometimes be just as applicable in the public sector as in retailing. A government will undertake extensive advertising campaigns because as few as fifty per cent of those entitled to family benefits actually claim them. The government is, in this case, attempting to convert prospects into customers. In practice, however, these are seen as broad categories, so the fine distinctions raised as questions above do not normally pose critical limitations. The important fact is that some of the individuals in the market buy the retailer's brand and some do not. The measure of this difference is often given by **brand penetration**.

Brand penetration

This is the proportion of individuals in the market who are users of the specific brand or service, as determined by the numbers who claim to be users in response to market research (Martinson, 1995). In the non-profit sector it can often be used just as effectively: for example, a measure of the number of clients receiving help as a proportion of the total population who might need the service. The measure of 'penetration', however, does not allow for the rate of usage or purchase by different individual shoppers. The most commonly used measure in retail marketing context, therefore, is **market share**.

Market share

This is the share of overall market sales taken by each brand. In the fast moving consumer goods (FMCG) sector this is usually measured by audit research on panels of retail outlets, such as that undertaken by A.C. Nielsen. It represents consumer purchases and necessary usage, although the distinction is usually not important. The share can be quoted in terms of volume (the brand has a 10 per cent share of the total number of units sold) or value (at the same time the brand took 15 per cent of the total amount of money being paid out for such products, since it was a higher priced brand).

Exhibit 4.1   **Measuring market share: volume versus value**

This difference can sometimes be dramatic. In computer retailing, Amstrad claimed at one time to have achieved the same market share as IBM, which was then the market leader in the personal computer (PC) market. This was true, but it was in terms of volume. In terms of value, Amstrad had less than a third of IBM's market share and was actually in fifth position in the market.

The measure of share and the concept of prospects are important because they delineate the extra business that a retailer may reasonably look for, and where it could be obtained from. On the other hand, the evidence in many retail markets is that most business comes from repeat purchasing by existing customers.

The Pareto effect

There may be 'heavy' and 'light' brand users within a market, the former being much more important to both the retailer and the manufacturer. At the end of the nineteenth century, for instance, Pareto noted that the bulk of the wealth in Italy was in the hands of 10 per cent of the population. This principle has since been adopted by business management in general and enshrined as a very valuable rule of thumb. The principle is known as the Pareto 80:20 Rule, and can be applied to a wide range of situations in retail markets.

It applies to groupings of shoppers' choice and preference for a brand in a retail store. In the industrial sales field the top 20 per cent of customers will often account for 80 per cent of sales. It also applies to groupings of products, where there is an extended product list; the best-selling 20 per cent of products will often take 80 per cent of the volume or value of overall sales. The importance of the principle is that it highlights the need for most manufacturers and retailers, often against their natural inclinations, to concentrate their efforts on the most important customers and products. In other words, retailers should concentrate their efforts on the profitable segments of the market.

Retail market segmentation

In time, retailers realised that neither their customers nor their trade areas were homogeneous. The realisation that their trade areas comprised of several heterogeneous sub-markets within which there was homogeneity of needs, motives, and so on prompted some retailers to attempt to employ the market segmentation strategy.

Exhibit 4.2	Market segmentation on the high street

Retailers may begin by identifying variable segments with a goal to adjust the supply to heterogeneous demand. They will normally view the market as one of varied customers and try to offer a select market mix to satisfy specific needs. Many of the speciality stores can be shown to be examples of segmentation in retailing. Laura Ashley, Boots the chemist, and Mothercare are all examples of speciality retail chains that appeal to carefully defined market segments.

Some department stores also appeal to particular segments of the market: Miss Selfridges, Littlewoods and Marks & Spencer are examples. Similarly, while Harrods, for example, may be aiming at the upper class, Marks & Spencer may be aiming at the upper middle class and Mothercare at the lower middle class mothers. Although some of these companies may not have planned their retail marketing in this way, they still appeal primarily to these segments.

At best, the evolution of marketing strategy development for retailing is still in the segmentation stage. Accordingly, the most significant contrast between the manufacturers' and retailers' evolution exists at the positioning stage. It is here that we see that retail evolution is incomplete. Although segmentation is necessary for differential congruence, its practice is still not sufficiently advanced (Samli, 1989). Segmentation must produce congruence between the store image and the consumer's self-image. Both retailers and manufacturers tend to define markets quite broadly, in terms of the physical characteristics which are important to their operations. The result is that these larger markets often contain groups of customers with quite different needs and wants, each of which represents a different 'segment', with different characteristics in terms of its consumers. Manufacturers and retailers need to find a way to reach these differentiated consumers. This process is called **target marketing**, because the supplier and the retailer carefully 'target' a specific group of customers.

Basis for segmentation

Although marketing literature suggests that it was John Robinson and Edward Chamberlain who made important contributions in bringing imperfect market systems into focus as more realistic models for studying consumer groups, it was sociologists like Lloyd Warner who provided a workable path for marketing strategists. Lloyd Warner and very many other researchers analysed the **heterogeneous markets** in terms of Index of Status Characteristics (ISC) and divided them into five socio-economic categories. Following this pattern, the specific consumption behaviour of each group was studied. These studies paved the way for what has come to be known as market segmentation, perhaps because segments were more tangible and easy to identify. Early attempts to segment the market were based on demographic characteristics. In addition to ISCs, age, sex, income distribution, geographic location, educational and occupational background, and stage in the life cycle, are all used as bases for segmentation (*see* Table 4.1). Indeed, any one of these **segmentation variables**, or a combination of them, have been very useful tools in reaching many marketing decisions.

Marketing literature tends to assert that demographics are not the best way of looking at consumers (Samli, 1976), suggesting that consumers should be scrutinised for important differences in attitudes, motivations, values, usage patterns and aesthetic preferences. This may be necessary because we are not dealing with different types of people, but with differences in people's values. The concept of compulsives or punitiveness could be used as factors to segment the market. This may be possible because a man who drives an expensive car may prefer cheap whisky, or a woman who shops at Harrods (a London-based high class department store) may wish to have dinner occasionally at her local restaurant. The reaction of different consumer groups to changes in prices may be used to group them into distinguishable segments. Many multiple retailers normally use price and quality relationships in segmenting the market for their own-label brands. In recent years, more creative and perhaps functional techniques of segmentation have emerged; among these, benefit segmentation stands out. Proponents of this technique maintain that different groups of consumers derive different benefits from the use of a product, service or store. Thus, the degree of benefit becomes the key criterion by which different segments in the market can be identified. If the consumers of certain products or customers of certain retail establishments are to be analysed and categorised after the information is recieved, segmentation will be more realistic. Table 4.1 illustrates some of the most important bases for retail segmentation and gives examples for each segmentation criterion.

Table 4.1
BASIS FOR RETAIL SEGMENTATION

Segmentation criteria	Examples of use
Demographics	
Age	Teenage market, elderly market
Income	High-income market; low-income market
Education and occupation	Highly educated sophisticates
Sex	Male or female consumers
Sociological	
Subcultures	Yuppies, Wasps
Racial differences	Blacks, Orientals
Behavioural	
Psychographics	Extroverted yuppies or narcissistic jocks
Life cycle	Empty-nesters, young married couples
Lifestyles	Jet setters
Innovativeness	People who try products early
Store loyalty	
Heavy users	Those people who buy products often
Regulars	Those who come to the store regularly
Benefit	
Direct benefit	Satisfaction from the store or products directly
Indirect benefit	
Greater versus lesser benefit	Satisfaction delayed as in gifts, health foods
	Those who experience greatly improved health from attending a health spa
Geography	
Distances	Those who live nearby versus those who live far away
Reputation of the location	
Urban versus rural	Fashionable area
	Those who live in the country

Demographic segmentation

The examples presented in Table 4.1 make these criteria rather self-explanatory, but it may be observed that consumers of certain products share similar characteristics. To the extent that these characteristics can be detected and measured, segmentation is achieved. For instance if it is found that, on average, Volvo car owners are between the ages of 35 and 55, belong to the upper socio-economic category and are achievers, it may be possible to develop, change, or continue the marketing strategy for Volvo accordingly. All aspects of market potential: pricing, promotion, product characteristics, and distribution can be planned along similar lines.

In speciality stores, the demographic and behavioural characteristics of the immediate customers appear to be of great significance since they are determinable and somewhat quantifiable. Although some degree of heterogeneity always exists in retail markets, a high-status speciality clothing store such as Tie Rack appeals primarily to an identifiable and quantifiable group of customers (Omar and Kent, 1996). This quantification lends itself more readily to demographic and behavioural criteria. In such cases, it is more important to determine the segments most suitable for that retail outlet. On this premise, an attempt could be made to combine a number of variables under the title of segmentation index.

Exhibit 4.3 | **Segmentation and carpeting retailers**

Consumers will usually make four basic decisions when shopping, for example, for carpeting: the style they like best, the colour and texture best suited to the home; the best quality; and the price that can best be afforded. Where speciality stores are competitively pressured by department and discount stores, the speciality carpet store has to convince the prospective consumer that its store is the place where all four of these basic decisions can be made effectively. Discount carpeting stores, on the other hand, emphasise price and bargain aspects, which they expect to be of prime importance to buyers. These approaches are designed to appeal to different consumer groups and, hence, to enable each store to survive and prosper.

Segmentation by price and quality

The early Amstrad computers were clearly aimed at a market which could not afford the IBM and Compaq machines, which were then up to ten times the price of an Amstrad machine. The value of discovering such separate segments, each with rather different characteristics, is that they allow producers to offer products that address the needs of just one segment, and hence are not in direct competition with the overall market leaders.

Exhibit 4.4 | **Segmenting the computer market**

A review of the personal computer (PC) market shows how segmentation works. The overall PC market is often loosely defined in terms of being self-contained computers which are used by one person. However, a number of alternative criteria may be employed. Segments within this market can be defined in terms of the physical hardware: the Intel range of chips, the Motorola series of chips, and the Apple range of chips. Personal computers can also be defined in terms of use: those in homes and used mainly for games; those used at home mainly for word processing, those used as integral parts of other systems (e.g. some retail systems or process control applications); those used in office systems (the main IBM compatible market); those used as desktop publishing systems – a segment very effectively exploited by Apple; and those in the computer aided design (CAD) segment – developed by Compaq, etc.

Again in terms of price segmentation, while IBM offers a comprehensive range with almost universal applicability, Amstrad specifically targeted the price-sensitive segment, and Apple the desktop publishing segment. Despite their aggressive posturing, both companies are actually avoiding head-on confrontation with IBM – and by concentrating on their specific target segment, they can offer users in that segment a better match to their needs.

Although the concept of segmentation is classically described in terms of products, it can be just as applicable to services. In the car market, there are dealers who provide support for private car owners and those who specialise in supporting the large company fleet market – each being totally different segments of the overall motor car market.

Behavioural segmentation

One focus for segmentation may be consumer behaviour – so called **behavioural segmentation**. In this context, the influences on the consumer provide one set of starting points. Kotler (1997) distinguishes between consumer inherent characteristics and consumer product-related 'approaches' grouping them as shown below.

Inherent characteristics	*Product-related responses*
1 Geographical	1 Occasions (when used)
2 Demographic	2 Benefits
3 Psychographic	3 Usage (including heavy or light)
	4 Attitudes (including loyalty)

Consumer inherent characteristics categories reflect 'who buys' the brand; while the consumer product-related response category is generally based on 'what brand is bought'. If the emphasis is on the retailer's point of view, this can be expanded to include elements of the retail marketing mix. It is likely that shoppers may genuinely believe that a disinfectant bought in a plastic bottle from a supermarket, for instance, belongs to a different segment of the retail market from one in a glass bottle bought from a chemist. On the other hand, consumers may actually be making the choice on totally different grounds: it offers particularly gentle protection for the baby in the family, for instance. It is in the best interest of retailers or manufacturers to know what the true reasons for consumers' choice of brands because the promotional message often determines how the product is seen by the consumer, and what it is seen as being.

In practice the picture may be much more complex, with the truly meaningful segments being based on intangible benefits which only the consumer sees, or based on natural consumer groupings that have their roots in far more deep-seated social processes. In some consumer markets, 'factor analysis' and 'cluster analysis' may be required to identify what the key segments are.

Cross-elasticity of demand

In order to reduce confusion and demonstrate the validity of the segments eventually chosen by the retailer, the Henley Centre for Forecasting used **cross-elasticity of demand** as a measure of the separation of segments. If a reduction in price of one group of products has no effect on the demand for another group of products, it is reasoned that the two ranges of products lie in two independent segments. This concept is derived from economics and is quite simply defined as:

$$\frac{\text{Proportionate change in quantity of product X}}{\text{Proportionate change in price of product Y}}$$

The effect here will be different if Y is a substitute for X. For example, in the case of margarine versus butter, the result will be a positive cross-elasticity. This means that the sales of margarine will increase if the price of butter increases. On the other hand, if Y is a complement (say, bread versus butter), then the cross-elasticity will be negative, since the sales of X will decrease with an increase in the price of Y. In practice this can become a very sophisticated technique.

Segmentation by benefits

Using much more productive to relate segmentation to the specific characteristics of the market for the product or service. Different customers, or groups of customers, look for different combinations of benefits; and it is these groupings of benefits which then define the segments. Using these differences, retailers can target them they sell and position these where they most clearly meet the needs of the consumers in that segment.

Exhibit 4.5	Segmenting by benefits in the computer market

In order to meet the needs of publishing companies and their market requirements, Apple provided graphics-oriented hardware and software which offered the benefit of very easy typesetting to users in the ordinary office environment. This segment was then told about it with particularly effective television advertising. In contrast Atari offered very sophisticated screen-handling hardware which is ideal for the fast-moving images demanded by computer games.

The toothpaste market (*see* Table 4.2) shows that the benefits which people are seeking in consuming a given product are the basic reasons for the existence of true market segments. Experience with this approach has shown that benefits sought by consumers determine their behaviour much more accurately than do demographic characteristics or volume of consumption. In supporting Haley's views, Omar (1996) argued that each retail market segment is identified by the benefits it is seeking. It is the total configuration of benefits which differentiates one segment from another, rather than the fact that one segment is seeking one particular benefit and another

Table 4.2
BENEFIT SEGMENTATION OF THE TOOTHPASTE MARKET

	Sensory segment	Sociable segment	Worrier segment	Independent segment
Principal benefits sought	Product appearance, flavour	Brightness of teeth	Decay prevention	Price
Demographic strength	Children	Teens young people	Large families	Men
Special behavioural characteristics	Users of spearmint flavour	Smokers	Heavy users	Heavy users
Brands highly favoured	Colgate Stripe	Macleans Plus white	Crest	Any
Life style	Hedonistic	Active	Conservative	Value oriented

Source: Haley (1968), 'Benefit segmentation: a decision-oriented research tool,' *Journal of Marketing,* 32(3): 30–35.

a quite different benefit. Individual benefits are likely to have appeal for several consumer segments and most people would like as many benefits as possible Omar (1996). The relative importance they attach to individual benefits can differ and may be used as an effective lever in segmenting retail markets.

Segmentation by consumption profile

In recent times, a number of research agencies have started to characterise consumer segments in terms of the buying choices of the consumers in them. Thus they are characterised by their purchases of a range of key products and, in particular, by the range of media they are exposed to (newspapers, radio, magazines, etc.) and television programmes they watch. These data may be provided in some depth by Target Group Index (TGI) surveys or in less (but still adequate) depth by less wide-ranging surveys. Whatever the set of key products chosen, the profile as described in terms of the bundle of brands purchased is supposed to be more meaningful to retailers than the relatively esoteric categories offered by lifestyles.

Segment viability

There is a pure, customer-oriented, marketing reason behind segmentation. By designing products or services which are narrowly targeted on the needs of one specific segment, it may be possible to offer those consumers the best match to their needs. In practice, however, retailers usually target segments rather than the overall market because this allows them to concentrate their resources on a limited group of consumers, so that the brand can be made to dominate that segment – and gain the benefits of being segment leader. Retail marketing strategies adopted by brand leaders such as Coca-Cola reflects this sort of benefit segmentation. To be viable, a segment has generally to meet a number of broad criteria such as the size of the segment; the identity of the segment; the relevance of the segment; and the retailer's access to the segment. A brief explanation of each of these factors is necessary for clarity.

Size of the segment

The first question to be asked is simply whether the segment is substantial enough to justify attention, and will there be enough volume generated to provide an adequate profit? Segmentation, at least in the short term, is a process that is largely under the control of the retailer; it might be possible to find an increasing number of ever smaller segments which could be targeted separately. In general, however, it is best to choose the smallest number of segments, and hence the largest average size, which still allows the resources to be concentrated and head-on competition with the market leaders avoided.

In part, the viable size will be defined in terms of the retailer's cost structures. In terms of manufacturing, the car market is heavily segmented. For example Ford targets a wide range of separate segments, but even the smallest of these (sharing the same assembly line as others) has to be worth some tens of thousands of cars a year simply to earn its place on that assembly line. On the other hand the Mini Metro, with its custom hand-building, can very effectively target a segment which is worth just a few hundred cars a year.

Identity of the segment

Wilson *et al.* (1993) have noted that the segment has to have characteristics which will enable it to be separately identified (and measured by market research) by producers, retailers and consumers. In the car market there is, for example, an identifiable segment for small cars, a segment against which Renault targets the Clio, Peugeot the 205, and so on. Within this segment, and across the larger car segments as well, there is a segment for higher-performance cars against which Renault, for example, targets the Alpine brand.

Segmental relevance

The basis for segmentation must be relevant to the important characteristics of the product or service – it must be 'actionable'. For example, the type of pet owned will be highly relevant in the pet food market, but will rarely be so in the car market. While this may seem obvious, much retail marketing is still undertaken (mistakenly) on the basis of overall population characteristics rather than those directly relating to the specific brands or service. Thus, for example, in many markets the tacit segmentation has been made in terms of social class: yet the major manufacturers' segmentation of the car market, to give one example, no longer follows these lines – for obvious reasons listed above.

Gaining access to the segment

The retailer must be able to gain access to the segment that has been found. If tapping that segment is too difficult and consequently expensive, clearly it will not be viable. Imagine that a small segment of the general low-priced car market exists which could be met by a small manufacturer using hand-building techniques. However, if the consumers within that segment are diffused evenly throughout the population, the car manufacturer may face difficulties on two levels:

1 Manufacturers may have difficulties in obtaining national distribution on low volumes. Setting up a separate dealership network, to provide the maintenance facilities, would be almost impossible (even some of the smaller existing manufacturers in the UK for instance, such as Peugeot and Fiat, have incomplete networks).

2 There may be problems in finding the means of delivering the promotional message to the potential buyers.

All of these criteria are equally applicable to the segmentation available in the non-profit sector. If the criteria can be met, segmentation is a very effective marketing device. It can allow even the smaller retail organisations to obtain leading positions in their respective segments ('niche' marketing) and gain some of the control this offers. It is worth repeating that the most productive bases for segmentation are those which relate to the consumers' own groupings in the market and not to artificially imposed retailers' segmentations. In any case, it must be remembered that segmentation is concerned only with dividing customers or prospects (and not products or services) into the segments to which they belong.

Types of segments

There is wide range of detailed actions which could be suggested by the results of a segmentation analysis. Of this range of likely actions, only the four main strategies (single segment, customised marketing, multiple segment, and **cross segment**; *see* Table 4.3) which may be adopted by retailers are briefly discussed here. Other segmentation strategies such as **mass marketing**, including differentiated and undifferentiated strategies, are discussed under brand management and presentation in Chapter 9. It is sufficient here to say that the focus of **differentiation** strategy is 'branding'.

The product is given a 'character' – an 'image' – almost like a personality. This is based first of all on a name (the brand), but then are added the other factors affecting image, including the packaging and advertising. An attempt is being made to make the brand its own separate market, so that shoppers buy Heinz baked beans rather than Tesco's baked beans. This sometimes succeeds to the extent that brands such as Kleenex (tissues), Hoover (vacuum cleaner) and Biro (ballpoint pen) become generic terms for the items themselves. The firm's branding strategy is to make its products different from its competitors in such a way that customers can be convinced that they are superior. This may be done by making the product physically different or by making the way in which customers perceive the product

Table 4.3
TYPES OF MARKET SEGEMENTS

Type of segment	Segmentation process
Single segment	Concentrate on one segment, and position the product firmly within that segment (sometimes described as 'niche' marketing). This is a very effective form of marketing, especially for small retail organisations, since it concentrates resources into a very sharply focused campaign. It is perhaps more risky, because there is a likelihood of the 'niche' disappearing from the market due to changes in lifestyle or in environment. On the other hand, it is considerably less risky than spreading resources too thinly across a number of segments.
Customised marketing	In recent years, the increased variety demanded and flexible manufacturing methods have combined to allow for ever narrower segments or niches. The outcome has been that even some 'mass merchandising' can now provide individually customised products to some degree. With the use of 'precision marketing' techniques, the retailer is now able to 'talk to' the customer and deliver a 'product' specifically designed for an individual.
Multiple segment	This method addresses several major segments with one brand, or launches several brands each targeted against different segments. This latter strategy is adopted, for example, by Nestlé, which has brands to meet the 'ground coffee', 'continental' and 'decaffeinated' segments, as well as the main brand itself which – in line with the former strategy – spans a number of segments. This technique may also be adopted by a retail organisation which ultimately intends to achieve full coverage, but may approach this by invading the market segment by segment.
Cross segment	A company may specialise in a particular type of product which covers a number of segments (grocers selling fashion items), for instance.They may have a band of devoted customers who recognise the specialised expertise embodied by the company. This is a particularly relevant and successful strategy in the industrial area. A more sophisticated approach would be based upon deliberately targeting across segments which have similar characteristics, such as similar production technologies.

different (by psychological or emotional differences). These factors can be achieved by: packaging differences, having a range of sizes, shape, qualities, gimmicks, after-sales service provision, promotional activity, and so on. These factors are usually linked to at least one of the other differences. In monopolistic competition promotion is very often the main form of competition.

Positioning strategy

The retail organisation will start with a specific position aiming at specific competitors. It attempts to take away a good share of the market from a well-established competitor. In a specific well-defined market, a new retail store may position itself so that it will take advantage of the best market with the least competition.

The retailer views the market as if there were some crucial differences between his or her loyal customers and the immediate competitor's loyal customers. The retailer segments the market and differentiates the marketing mix. However, the mix is not only different but also better for the segment which the retailer is aiming to take away from the key competitor. Figure 4.1 distinguishes the four different retail marketing strategies and presents a comparative summary.

Fig. 4.1 HOW DIFFERENT RETAIL STRATEGISTS COMPETE OVER TIME

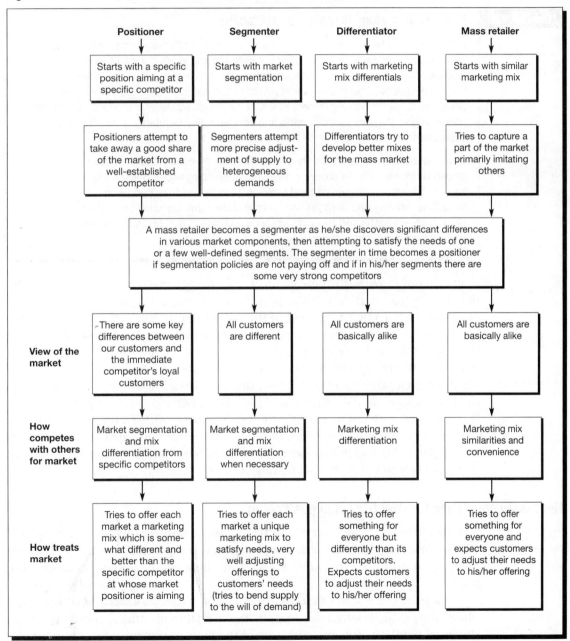

Market positioning is necessary for differential congruence but is not sufficient. Successful positioning implies successful segmentation and successful congruence between the store image and the customer's self-image. The current need to apply the positioning strategy in the retail situation is very real due to changes within the retail environment. The 'historical' position occupied by already established retailers may erode as those changes (shift in population; new values; new economic realities; continued competition) take place.

Exhibit 4.6	**Positioning strategy to maintain profitability**

Positioning may be pivotal to the department store's profitability because it can be considered to be the main determinant of both the shopper's choice of store (the revenue function) and the way management allocated resources (the cost function). Shoppers choose among competing stores on the basis of how those stores are perceived to perform along dimensions that the shoppers deem important. An effective positioning strategy employs a marketing approach that profitably distinguishes the department store from its competitors along these dimensions.

Industrial observers have said that Kwik Save, a UK-based discount food retailer, closed down many of its stores in 1997 because of improper positioning. Kwik Save had continued to maintain its food retailing activities as they had been for years. In the meantime, society had kept on changing and the retail competition had continued, but along different paths and more rigorous than before. Changes in the retailing environment necessitate reconsideration of the strategy.

In order to move with these changes and still achieve basic objectives, retailers may find it necessary to use the positioning strategy. The key to effective retail positioning is selecting a segment of the market that is not particularly well served in terms of its specific requirements. It is likely that more and more retailers will turn to positioning strategy as competitive pressures mount. Retail positioning may be most appropriate for those retailers located in the maturity stage of the retail life cycle. One retail institution that is believed to occupy this stage is the high street supermarket; they face new forms of competition and must reassess their **market position** as Exhibit 4.6 demonstrated. Although retail positioning strategy is theoretically attractive, effective retail positioning appears to be possible only if particular conditions exist. The retailer who does not meet these requirements is likely to fail in the positioning attempt.

Necessary conditions for effective retail positioning

Five conditions are necessary for effective retail positioning and these include: retailer's market position, market opportunities, competition, resources, and communication (Samli, 1976). Table 4.4 lays out these conditions and corresponding positioning actions.

The retailer must then think over these 'maps' to decide exactly what the 'battle plans' should be, taking into account the available resources, competition and shoppers' profile. This is probably one of the most important set of decisions that

Table 4.4
CONDITIONS FOR EFFECTIVE POSITIONING

Conditions	Effective positioning action
Market position	Retailer's market positioning is considered an attractive strategy for the non-dominant firm. For non-dominant retailers, it is a viable alternative to the leader. The leading retailer in a given market has little to gain from positioning against the second or third place entrants and at the same time may have a great deal to lose. On the other hand, a second or third place retailer has much to gain and little to lose, relative to the number one retailer.
Opportunities	The positioning firm must be aware of market opportunities. The retailer should audit its current position, and ask itself how favourably consumers view that position and whether that position is likely to be effective in the future. Understanding market opportunities requires the forecasting of shopping and competitive trends in market segments relative to the store's present position and future objectives. Since this condition applies, positioning cannot be effectively performed without some form of marketing research.
Competition	The positioning retail firm must be able to assess its position relative to that of the competition. The firm's primary concern is how its own products and services are viewed *vis-à-vis* those of its competitors. Perhaps the most accurate assessment of the retailer's position comes from identifying what image consumers have of that store and competing stores. Retailers should not have difficulty in meeting this condition since considerable literature has been developed concerning the retail store image.
Resources	The positioning retailer must have the resources needed to perform the strategy. These resources may include personnel, finance, store location, and quality merchandise. The retailer can only make claims that are within the 'comparison boundaries' possessed by the consumer. For example, it seems unreasonable for Kwik Save to attempt the same type of positioning strategy by comparing its stores to those of Tesco. A retail store cannot position itself as being something it is not.
Communication	Effective positioning requires that retailers are able effectively to communicate with their markets. A retailer's positioning strategy will be ineffective unless they plan and execute a promotional campaign that accurately conveys the desired position. The promotional effort must clearly show the consumer what the retailer has to offer relative to the competition. The advertising programme, therefore, is crucial as it actually establishes the retailer's position in the consumer's mind.

many retailers have to make. The intellectual effort which needs to be committed to this process cannot, therefore be underestimated.

Product positioning

There is sometimes confusion between 'segmentation' and 'positioning', and indeed the two processes often overlap. The key difference is that segmentation applies to the market, to the customers (or occasionally 'product') who are clustered into the 'natural' segments which occur in that market, whereas positioning relates to the product or service, and to what the retailer can do with these products or services, to best 'position' them against these segments (Martinson, 1995).

A further complication is that positioning can sometimes be divorced from segmentation. The retailer can choose dimensions on which to position the brand that are not derived from research, but are of the retailer's own choosing. Such positioning can be applied (to differentiate a brand, for instance) even when segmentation is not found to be viable. Further confusion can arise when the process is associated with 'product differentiation'. The practical positioning of products or services so that they are recognisably different from their competitors is important. This is measured in terms of their positions on the 'product space' – the 'map' of competitive brand positions against the dimensions which matter to the consumer. The most effective segmentation of a retail market is usually based on sets of characteristics that are specific to that retail market. The spread of users across these characteristics may, however, differ quite significantly.

Both the homogeneous example (where all the users have similar, closely grouped, preferences, for example, a commodity such as sugar) and the diffused example (where they have requirements evenly spread across the spectrum) tend to specify treatment of the retail market as one single entity – but for very different reasons. Segmentation is not relevant unless competitors in a diffused retail market have left part of it uncovered. It is in the 'clustered' market, which is often encountered in practice, where segmentation can be most successfully used. Ideally, a retailer would choose to place the product exactly in the centre of the cluster that he or she is aiming for.

Another approach, where the clusters may be too small to justify a segmentation policy or the retailer simply wants to have a more general brand which can be correspondingly larger, is to launch the product or service so that it is equidistant from several clusters that the retailer wishes to serve. In this case, though not matching the needs of any one group exactly, the product may be close to meeting those of several groups. However, such positioning may be vulnerable to attack from competitors who may position a rival brand precisely on one of the clusters.

Actual product positioning maps will of course be more complex, involving a number of dimensions, and drawn with less certainty as to where the boundaries may lie. But they do offer a very immediate picture of where potential may lie, and which products and services are best placed to tap it. They offer a sound basis for reposition-

| **Exhibit 4.7** | **Drawing the map** |

Conventionally, product positioning (product space) maps are drawn with their axes dividing the plot into four quadrants. This is because most of the parameters upon which they are based typically range from 'high' to 'low' or from plus (+) to minus (–), with the average or zero position in the centre. This is best shown graphically; Figure 4.2 is a typical example. The value of each product's (or service's) sales as well as that of each cluster of consumers, is conventionally represented by the area of the related circle. In Figure 4.2, there are just two clusters of consumers: one buying mainly on the basis of price and accepting the lower quality that this policy entails; another, buying on the basis of quality and prepared to pay extra. Against these segments there are just two main brands (A and B), each associated with a cluster or segment. There is also a smaller brand (C), associated with cluster 1, offering an even higher quality alternative but at an even higher price.

ing existing products or launching a complementary new product. They match the requirements of the specific clusters on which they are targeted. In Exhibit 4.7, Brand C may be content to remain a niche product. Alternatively, the positioning map shows that if it were reduced in price slightly and were backed by sufficient promotion it might become a very competitive contender for Brand A's market share.

It is possible, at least in theory, to use promotion to move the consumer ideal closer to the brand rather than the other way round. This technique is much favoured by 'conviction retailers'. Equally, the launch of a really innovative new product, such as the compact disc audio player, may change the dimensions of the whole retail market. Such approaches, however, while very effective indeed when they succeed, are very difficult to achieve.

Positioning over time

So far the discussion has been centred on the positions at a particular point in time (the current position). However, if the positioning research is carried out regularly, over a period of time the map may also show that these positions are changing, hopefully in line with the strategy being pursued. Going back to Exhibit 4.7 and the suggestion following that Brand C may compete for Brand A's market share, a longer-term map – for example – show Brand C's strategy and its effects on Brand A and that segment of the market. It may be seen that Brand C has moved only slightly, in line with strategy; however, in doing so it has improved its competitive position significantly, helped by the fact that Brand A's competitive response – also reducing price – has moved it away from the ideal.

Fig. 4.2 PRODUCT SPACE AND CONSUMER CLUSTER MAP

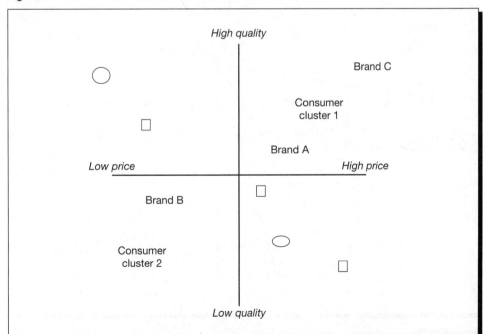

Multidimensional maps

There are alternative graphical approaches to the static positioning map. For example, to try to produce just one diagram which contains all the information which would otherwise be contained in the various dimensions requiring a number of separate maps, a computerised plotting compression technique is used. As it is most often used, this initially plots the brands, say, against the two dimensions shown to be most significant. On this it then overlays vectors from the origin, showing the other, less important, dimensions. The direction of these vectors is calculated so that the relative displacement of the brands from each of them reflects its position against them on the original two-dimensional map (*see* Figure 4.3). In Figure 4.3 the unmarked horizontal dimension contrasts 'taste' on the left with 'premium price' on the right, and the also unmarked vertical dimension plots relative lightness (moving from 'light' to 'heavy', top to bottom). Budweiser is seen

Fig. 4.3 MULTIPLE DISCRIMINATE ANALYSIS OF BEER BRANDS

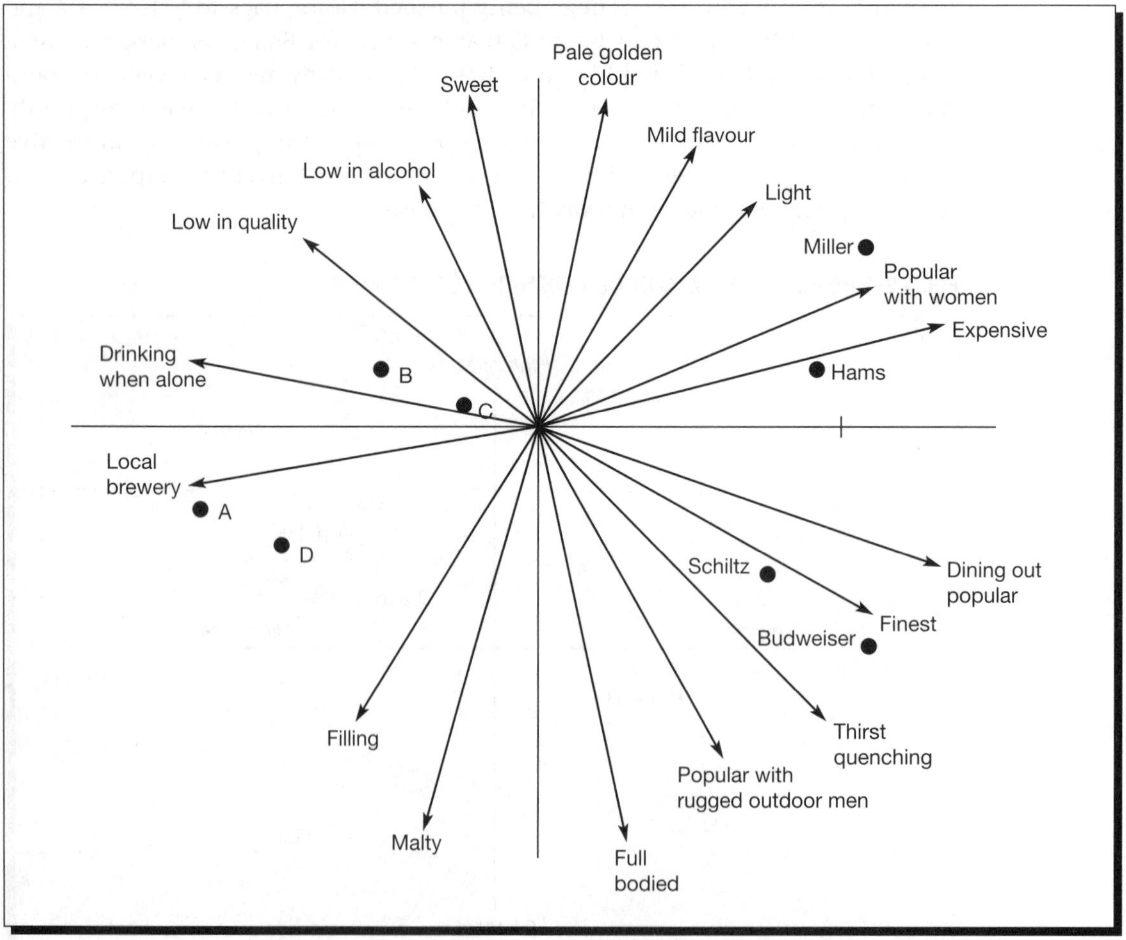

Source: Johnson (1971).

as being 'finest' since this vector is positioned relatively close to them; on the same basis, Miller is especially popular with women.

This type of representation offers a useful shorthand, which is easier for retail managers to digest. On the other hand, if the retail manager is capable of digesting the contents of the three or four separate two-dimensional plots, then these should offer even a better picture. The one key point to remember, however, is that the dimensions of these brand positioning maps must be those that are important to the consumer. Such knowledge can be worth a great deal of money to the retailer who is able to use it optimally to position the brand where it becomes most attractive to the market segment on which it is targeted.

Fig. 4.4 DISTRIBUTION OF IDEAL POINTS IN THE PRODUCT SPACE

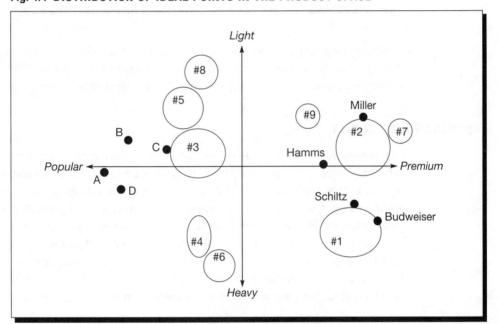

Target marketing

Targeting is centred upon the decision about which segment(s) a retailer decides to select for its sales and marketing efforts. Target marketing, in other words, is where the retailer identifies market segments, selects one or more of them, and develops products and marketing mixes tailored to each. Marketing segmentation reveals the firm's market segment opportunities. The firm then has to evaluate the various segments, and decide how many and which ones to target. In evaluating different market segments, a company must look at three factors: segment size and growth, segment attractiveness, and the company's objectives and resources.

Exhibit 4.8 | **Using target marketing to focus on marketing opportunities**

Coca-Cola now produces soft drinks for the sugared-cola segment (Coca-Cola Classic and Cherry Coke), the diet segment (Diet Coke and Tab), the no-caffeine segment (Caffeine Free Coke), and the non-cola segment (Minute Maid sodas). The trend in the late 1990s indicates that many firms are moving away from mass marketing and product-variety marketing and moving towards target marketing.

Target marketing can help retailers to find their marketing opportunities more efficiently. They can develop the right product for each target market and adjust their prices, distribution channels, and advertising effectively to reach the market targeted. Instead of scattering their marketing efforts, they can focus on the buyers who have the greater purchase interest.

Market targeting activity should make an effort to select the segments which best meet the needs of the organisation. This involves consideration of the available resources as well as the consumer segments and the relative competitive positions.

Segment size and growth

The company must first collect and analyse data on current segment sales, growth rates and expected profitability for various segments. It will be interested only in segments that have the right size and growth characteristics. Some companies will want to target segments with large current sales, a high growth rate and a high profit margin. However, the largest, fastest-growing segments are not always the most attractive ones for every company. Smaller companies may find that they lack the skills and resources needed to serve the larger segments or that these segments are too competitive. Such companies may select segments that are smaller and less attractive generally, but are potentially more profitable for them.

Segment structural attractiveness

A segment may have desirable size and growth and still not offer attractive profits. The retailer must examine several major structural factors that affect a segment's long-term attractiveness. For example, a segment is less attractive if it already contains many strong and aggressive competitors; the existence of many actual or potential substitute products may limit prices and profits that can be earned in a segment. The relative power of buyers also affects segment attractiveness; if the buyers in a segment (as in the UK grocery sector) possess strong bargaining power relative to sellers, they will try to force prices down, demand more quality or services, and set competitors against one another – all at the expense of sellers' profitability. A segment may be less attractive if it contains powerful suppliers who can control prices (BT in telecommunications) or reduce the quality or quantity of ordered goods and services. Suppliers tend to be powerful when they are large and concentrated, when few substitutes exist, or when the supplied product is an important, even vital, input.

The retailer's objectives and resources

Even if a segment has the right size and growth and is structurally attractive, retailers must consider their objectives and resources in relation to that segment. Some attractive segments may be quickly dismissed because they do not blend with the retailer's long-term objectives. Although such segments may be tempting in themselves, they might divert the retailer's attention away from their main goals. The segment may also be rejected if it is a poor choice from an environmental, political, or social responsibility viewpoint.

Generally, if a segment fits the company's objectives, the company then must decide whether it possesses the skills and resources needed to succeed in that segment. If the company lacks the strengths needed to compete successfully in a segment and cannot readily obtain them, it should not enter the segment. Even if the company possesses the required strengths, it needs to employ skills and resources superior to those of the competition in order to win out in a market segment. The company should enter segments only where it can offer superior value and gain advantages over competitors. It is after successful segmentation and targeting that the company may seek to position itself within the chosen segment(s) of the market.

SUMMARY

In this chapter, the roles of market segmentation and customer analysis have been explored. The chapter has demonstrated that market segmentation offers the retail organisation an opportunity to obtain a much more detailed understanding of both existing and potential customer groups. The analysis suggested includes the examination of attitudes as well as behaviour before, during, and after the shopping process.

Segmentation is less clear-cut for retailers than for producers of specific products for specific markets. As a result, in order to understand the degree of segmentation that a retailer has been able to accomplish, a concept of retail market segmentation is introduced. This is necessary to determine and distinguish the core market from the fringe market in retailing. If the core market is not large enough, the retailer may have to emphasise the fringe markets.

It is worth noting that market segmentation, as a strategy, is perhaps one of the most commonly used approaches. The need to spend a fair amount of time and effort on market segmentation analysis is a fact of retail marketing life and this chapter outlines some approaches to this analysis. However, it should be remembered that the justification for individual retailers spending money on this type of market analysis is one of benefits versus costs, that is, the analysis must be useful in terms of enhancing business returns without being prohibitively costly.

KEY TERMS

behavioural segmentation	demographic segmentation	Pareto effect
benefit segmentation	differentiation	perceptual map
brand monopoly	heterogeneous market	positioning
brand penetration	market position	product position
consumer	market segmentation	prospects
counter segmentation	market share	retail market
cross elasticity	mass marketing	segmentation variables
cross-segment	multidimensional maps	target marketing

ASSIGNMENT

You have learned in this chapter that consumers could be segmented (grouped together) in various ways for the purpose of serving them collectively.

Task

Write an essay of not more than 2000 words in length, and with the aid of examples, explaining why retailers should concern themselves with the market segmentation process.

REVISION QUESTIONS

1 A market is where the product or service is delivered to the buyer by the seller and profit is generated. Which other ways could you define a retail market?

2 In a normal retail marketing environment, retailers will see markets in relation to their positions within them. Explain.

3 Several segmentation strategies have been discussed in this chapter. Of what particular use is benefit segmentation strategy?

4 In order to demonstrate the validity of the segment, cross-elasticity of demand could be used as measure for separating segments. With the help of suitable examples, describe this process.

5 A market segment viability is determined by a number of broad criteria. Discuss.

6 Market positioning strategy is necessary for differential congruence but is not sufficient on its own. Why?

7 Which of the segmentation policies dealt with in this chapter would you recommend to a grocery retailer operating throughout the UK?

8 Market targeting helps retailers to concentrate on profitable market segments. Discuss this statement.

9 What problems, if any, are there in defining what is or what are the retailer's suitable market segment(s)?

10 The personal computer (PC) market could be segmented for example by type of use. Comment.

CASE STUDY

Segementing the children's market

Children's pestering power is greater than ever before, and parents are increasingly more likely to succumb to the demands of their offspring. Both manufacturers and retailers have now taken notice of the expansion of this market segment. Safeway successfully introduced the child characters Harry, Molly and Joe into its advertising campaign to highlight the child-friendly focus of its stores and product-lines. Children's influence over parental spending on the weekly shopping has increased substantially since the 1970s; consequently, the range of products targeted at children has also substantially increased.

Demographically, there were over eleven million children in the age range of between birth and 14 years in the UK in 1996, despite the country's declining birth rate (Office of National Statistics, 1996). More pertinent, however, are social trends: changes in parents' attitudes towards child rearing. It seems that most parents are spending more on their children and allowing them greater influence over household expenditure. Working mothers have increased family affluence and are more inclined to give children what they want. Single parent (one parent with one or more children) and one-child households (a couple with only one child living at home) are rising, increasing the potential for indulgence. There is a broad shift in eating patterns, with less formal family mealtimes, a general increase in the use and range of convenience foods, and a substantial growth in the sale of lunch box snacks.

CHILDREN'S PESTER POWER

Items	Percentage of housewives agreeing that children influence purchase	Equivalent value of that influence in money (£)
Toys	73	512.00 m
Breakfast cereals	73	291.27 m
Clothes (children's)	70	1.87 bn
Soft drinks	60	1.48 bn
Day-to-day meals	54	12.96 bn
Holidays	44	3.29 bn
Computer	33	1.56 bn
Restaurants	30	1.04 bn
TV/hi-fi	22	58.00 m
House	22	6.27 bn
Car	17	1.64 bn
Totals		31.49 bn

Source: Saatchi and Saatchi (1997) 'Kid Connection'.

Advertising agency Saatchi and Saatchi, in research conducted among housewives with children up to the age of 15, estimates that children influence over £31 billion worth of UK adult spending annually. The key grocery sectors the

▶

research highlighted were: breakfast cereals, where children's influence over purchase is rated at 73 per cent; soft drinks at 60 per cent; and day-to-day meals at 54 per cent. Similarly, Wall's (research agency) annual pocket money survey regarded children's direct purchasing power as significant, with an average weekly pocket money of £2.33. But as children get older and wiser, their pester power becomes more strategically inclined. At a young age, children are usually indiscriminate, wanting everything from cereals, to chocolate to alphabet pasta and so on. As they get older, experience tells them they will not get everything they ask for so they target their pestering – focusing on what they really want. By the time they reach their teens, they have become quite manipulative, trying to get parents to buy what they consider essential items – such as the latest deodorant – so they can maximise their pocket money. Targeting this market is not easy, particularly as products invariably have to appeal both to parents and to children, but in different ways.

The key to successful segmentation in the children's product market is to understand what is relevant to children on a personal level, and this varies according to age. Children could be classified into four approximate age groups:

Age classification	Age group (year)
Nursery	0–5
Playground	4–7
Street corner	7–11
Underground	11–14

However, age boundaries are becoming less defined, with children becoming more sophisticated at an increasingly younger age. This is often due to the influence of older siblings. Successful product development and marketing depends on focusing on specific aspects which appeal to each age group, while also taking into account the differing levels of parental involvement in the purchases. At all ages, there must be an appropriate level of parental involvement, a positive one which enables children to buy into the brand of their choice. For example, 'Mr Matey' bubble bath may be more attractive to young children than The Body Shop's 'Animals in Danger' bath foam since bright packaging and bubble bath that changes colour are more interesting to the average five-year-old than the ethical issues confronted by The Body Shop. Similarly, 'Kinder Surprises' may be more sought after than 'Milky Ways' probably because a Kinder Surprise offers intrigue and excitement.

With the vast amount of research into this market, some elements of what constitutes universal appeal to children have become well established. This understanding is most apparent in the collectable items and character merchandising markets.

Questions for discussion

1 Discuss how the children's market could be segmented for better targeting by UK grocery retailers.

2 The key to successful segmentation in the children's product market is to understand what is relevant to children on a personal level. Discuss the implications of this for varied parental involvement.

REFERENCES

Doyle, P. and Sharma, A. (1977) 'A Model for Strategic Positioning in Retailing', Conference Proceedings, American Marketing Association, Chicago, 10–14.

Haley, R.I. (1968) 'Benefit segmentation: a decision-oriented research tool', *Journal of Marketing*, 32(3): 30–5.

Johnson, R.M. (1971) 'Market Separatism: a strategic management tool'. *Journal of Marketing Research*, 8(1): 13–18.

Kotler, P. (1997) *Marketing Management*. 8th edn. Englewood Cliffs, NJ: Prentice-Hall.

Martinson, R. (1995) 'The role of brands in European marketing', *Journal of Brand Management*, 2(4): 213–18.

Office of National Statistics (1996) 'Birth rate'. London: ONS.

Omar, O.E. (1996) 'Grocery purchase behaviour for national and own label brands', *The Services Industries Journal*, 16(1): 58–66.

Omar, O.E. and Kent, A. (1996) 'Manufacturers' food brands: assessment of marketing opportunities in the UK supermarkets', *Journal of Brand Management*, 3(5): 327–36.

Samli, C.A (1976) 'Segmentation Index and a store image in retail and service establishments', Proceedings of ESOMAR seminar 29, on *Research that Works for Today's Marketing Problems*, Lucerne (November), 2–5.

Samli, C.A. (1989) *Retail Marketing Strategy: Planning, Implementation and Control*. New York: Quorum Books.

Wilson, R., Gilligan, C. and Pearson, D. (1993) *Strategic Marketing Management: Planning, Implementation and Control*. London: Butterworth/Heinemann.

5

Store image, loyalty and patronage management

LEARNING OBJECTIVES

After reading this chapter you should be able to:

- understand the meaning and explain the summation of all the attributes of a store as perceived by the shopper;

- describe the beneficial outcomes when the store image is adequately managed within the retail organisation;

- recognise that differential advantage gives life to a retail organisation and could be achieved by finding a positive match between the store image and the shopper's self-image;

- explain the reasons why people shop and recognise that patronage motives are those which encourage consumers to shop at one store in preference to other stores;

- discuss store loyalty as a behavioural response expressed over time by consumers in making shopping decisions and in selecting one store in preference to others.

A store's image is a product of its marketing strategy. The type of customer a store attracts, the way it differentiates itself from others in the market, as well as the store's location, merchandise, atmosphere, pricing policy, advertising and service policies, all influence **store image.** Every retailer must periodically monitor its image; only in this way can it know how it is positioned relative to competitors in consumers' minds. For example, a store that wants to differentiate itself on the basis of high-quality service must ascertain how customers rate its service relative to that of the competition, in order to ensure that its image is consistent with its strategy. Since the image is a representation of the store in consumers' minds, systematic research to measure store image is necessary.

The battle to gain customers and, more importantly, their loyalty is intensifying as the major retailers continue to position themselves as the main point of contact for shoppers. So, rather than being Kellogg's or Weetabix brand buyers, we are becoming a nation of Tesco supporters or Asda fans. Given this competitive retail environment, retailers are now vying for the consumer's attention and – more importantly – for the consumer's loyalty, paying more attention to providing **loy-**

alty schemes. Such a remarkable shift to loyalty-building activity has been made possible because the cost of recruiting each consumer into a loyalty scheme has fallen substantially. Similarly, the cost of capturing, managing and manipulating data has fallen substantially in real terms since the early 1970s. But, any loyalty scheme must be driven by a database to ensure that it adds a significant new element rather than being simply another promotional activity.

The store has many personal and impersonal aspects that distinguish it from other stores – aspects which, in turn, produce many tangible and intangible stimuli. Store image not only distinguishes the store from all other stores, but also provides the basis for **competitive advantage.** Since the image is very important to the well-being of the store, its management becomes a focal point within the larger retail management strategy. This chapter deals with the definition, dimensions and management of store image. It reviews the motives for store patronage and suggests reasons for store loyalty.

The concepts and definitions of store image

Martineau (1958) made one of the earliest attempts to analyse the concept of image and to measure it. He described store image as 'the way in which the store is defined in the shopper's mind' and, in analysing the components of store image, proposed two components:

1 The **functional qualities** of a store. This component includes such elements as assortment of product offerings, store layout, store location, price–value relationships, and other such qualities that the consumer can somewhat objectively compare to competitors.

2 The **psychological attributes.** These refer to the consumer's perception of the store attributes, such as friendliness and helpfulness of store personnel or attractiveness of decor.

Both of Martineau's phrases imply the existence of multiple descriptors to which a 'goodness' to 'badness' rating can be attached. Although he did not discuss the interaction between the two or even a possible casual relationship, Martineau set the stage for a number of subsequent definitions of store image and numerous research attempts to measure the concept of image.

Oxenfeldt (1975) following the functional qualities and psychological attributes dichotomy of Martineau, discussed 'a combination of factual and **emotional material** which constitute the store image'. This viewpoint stressed that many customers will hold factually based opinions about a store and feel certain ways toward it. The general consensus of academic researchers is that store image may have many dimensions (McGoldrick, 1990) including merchandise, service, facilities, convenience, atmosphere, promotion, and satisfaction offered.

Store image is the summation of all the attributes of a store as perceived by the shoppers through their experience of that store. It is the store's 'personality' as it is seen by different publics. This personality is made up of physical attributes, character, and skill qualities. When shoppers enter a store they want the store's displays and departments to tell them what the store is like. The image that the store is attempting to project must be close enough to the reality that it will be immediately obvious. The store must, therefore, deliberately project an image through personal and impersonal communicators – through a combination of the tangible and intangible.

In the simplest sense, the store image is the way the store says *'this is what I am'*. The greater the discrepancy between the store's claims regarding its image and consumers' perception of it, the less effective the image management activity of that store. It is also important to discuss what is meant by 'different publics'. All retail stores deal with different publics, including loyal customers, irregular customers, loyal customers of competitors, the rest of the community, store management itself, and competing managers. Of course, the image perceived by loyal customers is quite different from the image of those who dislike the store. The retailer must be able to project a particular image and, over time, manipulate it to make the store more appealing to the intended customers or to target market segments. Thus, image management is a very important aspect of strategic retail marketing.

Store image management

If properly conducted, store image studies increase the likelihood of retail marketing success. Theoretically, developing and maintaining favourable images within selected market segments can lead to increased sales and profitability. Accordingly, a retailer's repeat business is considered to be a function of the image that shoppers have of the store.

Store loyalty may be closely related to store image. The image of the store may sometimes be more important to the shopper than the image of the merchandise bought. Based on human nature and our **image perception**, a living-room carpet bought from a high prestige store may well have a more favourable product image than the same carpet bought from a low prestige store. The shopper's evaluation of products purchased is influenced by knowledge of where they were purchased. Thus, a high image ranking of a store may be valued by shoppers and seen as reducing the risk inherent in the product purchase situation.

The implication here is that store image may be used as a surrogate indicator of product quality. Samli (1989) found that a store's reputation (or image) is very important in attracting particular market segments to that store. The store image may also be used as a surrogate indicator of a store's success; managing the store well, is managing its image successfully. The store image management may include the following steps:

1 Examine the current store image.

2 Examine the competing store image.

3 Design and implement the image change.

4 Assess the change in store image.

5 Determine the impact in terms of store patronage.

These factors are discussed in some detail below.

The examination of the current store image

Store image management begins with understanding the present image. In order to gain this understanding, the current image must be defined. Its salient image dimensions and their relative power must also be defined. The importance of this assessment must be emphasised: unless the retailer is keenly aware of the present store image and its salient characteristics, it will be impossible to manipulate it. The relative weights of these salient characteristics will indicate better directions and offer more viable alternatives for the modification of the current image.

Examine competing store images

Store image salience and valence cannot be assessed without a comparison with other store images.

Exhibit 5.1	Comparing store images

If Store A wants to upgrade its image and position itself against Store B, it must understand the strengths and weaknesses of Store B's image in comparison to its own. It then becomes possible to determine where the emphasis should be placed if Store A is successfully to position itself in relation to Store B.

Research may indicate that Store B has an image of good quality at reasonable prices, attractive store layouts and good locations, among other image features. If Store A discovers that its image indicates low price and medium quality, relatively unattractive store layouts and somewhat questionable locations, it becomes clear where the company must focus its improvement efforts. It is important to find out what features of image are below par for Store A and it is at least equally important for retailers to know the relative importance of these factors within the total image projection.

At whatever level of retail operations, dynamic comparative retail image research is a necessity. Unlike static studies which analyse image characteristics at a given point in time, dynamic comparative retail image studies focus on a retail marketing strategy change. Retail management must attempt to change store mix variables. When such retail marketing changes are implemented, shoppers must perceive the image change efforts in exactly the way management intended. However, this perception cannot be measured in isolation; it must be assessed *vis-à-vis* other changes and developments in the retail marketing environment. By comparing consumers' reactions to strategy change with management's intent, it is also possible to achieve a successful and timely direct evaluation strategy. The implication here is that image is a dynamic concept. Retailers involved in image management must undertake a comparative analysis before and after attempts have been made to manipulate a store's image.

Designing and implementing image change

Once the store image is assessed, it is easy to identify the store's strengths and weaknesses. Laura Ashley, for instance, may be known for its product variety, quality and reliability, but may not be admired for its location, atmosphere or helpful salespeople. It is necessary to consider the importance of image dimensions within the particular market segments. If, again, Laura Ashley is dealing primarily with upper and lower middle-class markets, and if these classes emphasise price and salespeople's expertise, then Laura Ashley is likely to be in trouble. In a situation such as this, a retailer would be failing to emphasise the image components that are particularly important to its target markets. It is clear that a major step toward managing image and implementing image change would be to design the retail marketing mix so that it projects the image required to attract the target market segment. Special care must be taken to make sure that the intended image and the perceived image are not too far apart; the closer these two are, the more efficient the image projection efforts.

Assess the change in store image

Once the new image becomes a reality, the changes between the previous and present images must be examined. Image-related research data must, therefore, be obtained for both the before and the after situations. The data must be comparable – that is, be based on similar standards or criteria – and be of acceptable validity and reliability. Once the previous and present images are compared, it becomes obvious whether the image improvements are paying off. If the difference between the present and previous images is in the direction that was agreed on before the new image was developed, then efforts have been successful to a greater or lesser degree. Continuing with the earlier example of Laura Ashley: after having found out that the company has been dealing primarily with the upper and lower middle class, and that price and the expertise of their salespeople are less than par, let us assume they have made a concerted effort to rectify the situation. The question, of course, is not only knowing whether or not the efforts in changing the image have been successful, but also how successful they have been. The direction and intensity of the change from the earlier image measurement must therefore be identified.

Determine the impact in terms of retail success

In the final analysis, the image is important because, indirectly, it indicates the degree of success. However, the real success is in the way the market performance of the retail store has changed. Market performance indicating retail marketing success is measured in four different ways (Stephenson, 1979).

1 Changes in sales volume and market share.

2 The change (if any) in the degree of store loyalty.

3 The outreach of the retail establishment, through its attempts to change its image, is assessed by examining whether or not new customers are coming to the store and whether or not they develop a certain degree of commitment to the store.

4 The profitability of the store.

If as a result of the efforts to achieve a new image the profitability of the store improves, it can be inferred that the image management efforts have been successful. This success reflects the way the store image has been managed and changed to suit the image perception of the customers.

Matching store image with shopper's self-image

Differential advantage gives life to a retail organisation and could be achieved by finding a positive balance between the store image and individual shopper's **self-image**. Samli (1989) identified the match (congruence) between the store image and individual self-image as taking four different forms (**self-congruity**, **ideal congruity**, **social congruity**, and **ideal social congruity**). It is very likely that consumers will shop in a store they regard as a store with a 'good image'. A good image appears to be one which differentiates the store from its competitors or which positions it close to the general view of the ideal retailer in a given sector. Companies such as Marks & Spencer in the department stores sector and Tesco in food retailing have managed to combine both approaches, being at the same time close to the ideal and differentiated from competition.

Shoppers differentiate one store from another by the images they each project. The simplest approach to such image projection is likely to be based solely on price and/or quality.

In previous chapters a good deal of evidence is presented to confirm the view that it is not enough simply to evolve a coherent image for a retailer, that image must be different from others on offer in the marketplace. John Lewis', for example, succeeded by moving away from Debenhams; Asda suffered because Tesco

---

Exhibit 5.2 **Store image based on price**

Kwik Save offers an excellent example of price-led retailing to the point where price advantage is not only its main corporate platform, it is also its main image factor. MFI, the furniture retailer, offers a similar example of a genuine price-led strategy being successful because it has a real economic advantage to base the strategy upon.

moved closer to their position in the market. All German department stores, most British menswear retailers in the early 1980s, and the larger DIY retailers suffered from a lack of differentiation and have since readjusted their retail marketing policies to reflect the images they want to portray. Among electrical retailers there seemed to be a need to move away from mere price promotion as few appeared to have sufficient economic advantage to sustain a price-led strategy in the long term. There are several other examples of image-led options.

Ideal image

One obvious and important point to emerge from all the image studies is the value of what had to be a hypothetical 'ideal' store in each retail sector. The position of the ideal store acts as a reference point in each model but the fact that some image factors can be included in the ideal and that some are more useful in segmenting the market needs further comment.

Taking food retailing as an example, the composition of the factors describing the ideal store have changed over time: both 'value for money' and 'good for fresh foods' joined the ideal during the 1980s. Organic food (healthy element) joined the ideal factor during the 1990s in response to a series of high profile food scares, for example those concerning salmonella and bovine spongiform encephalopathy (BSE). Most consumers had come to expect high standards to be delivered in these new areas of concern so these factors would have to be offered by all mainstream food retailers. Ideal factors do not, therefore, offer the retailer any basis for differentiation other than the choice of being placing their store closest to the customer ideal or possibly by deliberately differentiating from market segments. The first is no easy task to achieve given that all retailers will have to encompass some of the ideal factors to be able to compete at all in the sector. The second is a dangerous approach to take given that being placed too far from the ideal, which is after all the average view of what constitutes 'a good place to shop', will limit the size of the market segment that can be appealed to.

Exhibit 5.3 | **Differentiating on concepts at a distance from the ideal image**

Kendals, for instance, was well differentiated in the department store model during the 1980s. However, this was achieved by being associated with concepts that were some distance from the ideal and which may have appeal to only a minority of consumers.

Self-perception affects store loyalty through the activation and operation of the self-consistency motive. In contrast, ideal congruity affects store loyalty through the mediation of the self-esteem motive. The self-consistency motive refers to an individual's need to act in ways that are consistent with their self-perceptions; to do otherwise would cause dissonance (a psychological discomfort which threatens to invalidate an individual's beliefs about him or herself). A number of researchers have repeatedly addressed the psychological dynamics of this motive. An early study by Martineau (1958) indicated that the upper middle-class family shopped at speciality stores for their public appearance clothes, and hence its members were motivated by self-consistency motives. If the members of the family were to shop exclusively, say, in second-hand shops, they would all be quite frustrated knowing and feeling they were not in their element, that there was a mismatch between their self-perceptions and their views about second-hand clothes shops. The self-esteem motive, on the other hand, refers to an individual's need to act in ways that are instrumental in achieving goals that maintain and/or increase positive self-regard. This motive is extremely important and is a focal point of study in clinical psychology, for instance.

In the positive self-congruity condition, the shopper would be motivated to approach a store that would satisfy both self-esteem and self-consistency needs. For example, the view 'this store seems to have an image of high social class' (store image) can match the shopper's **self-image** that they are 'a classy person' (high self-congruity). If these personality attributes are positively valued by the individual then there is high ideal congruity. By patronising the store, this shopper would be able to maintain their **ideal self-image** (satisfaction of self-esteem needs) and simultaneously reinforce self-consistency needs (high level of **store loyalty**). The focal point of retail marketing strategy is to achieve high 'self' and 'ideal' relationships. This is called positive self-congruity, which implies differential advantage. Under the negative self-congruity condition, shoppers would experience conflict with regard to the store: in one way it would frustrate their self-esteem need; in another way it would satisfy their self-consistency need. Under the negative self-

---

Exhibit 5.4 | **Negative and positive self-congruity condition**

In a negative self-congruity condition the following may apply. 'I believe that the people who typically patronise Marks & Spencer are conservative' (store image); this condition is matched by, 'I am conservative' (**high self-congruity**) but 'I don't like being conservative' (low ideal congruity). In this situation, shoppers would not be motivated to maintain a state that they view in a negative light, since this would cause a fall in self-esteem. However, a shopper in such a case would be acting consistently with his or her conservative actual self-image to satisfy the self-consistency need. The result is a motivational state reflecting conflict (moderate level of store loyalty).

Under a positive self-incongruity condition the situation is reversed, but the motivational outcome remains the same. Here, a shopper will also experience a conflict between the self-esteem and self-consistency motives. On the one hand, patronage of Marks & Spencer would satisfy the self-esteem need but would frustrate the self-consistency need. For instance a store with a 'low' image may match the shopper's ideal self-image ('I like to be ordinary'), causing high ideal congruity. However, the shopper might not presently see themselves that way ('I am not ordinary') – **low self-congruity.** Patronising the store would, therefore, help the shopper attain the ideal self-image of being 'ordinary' (satisfying the self-esteem motive), but doing so would threaten the person's self-image as 'not the ordinary type' (frustrate the self-consistency motive). Store loyalty reflects this conflict toward the store (moderate level of store loyalty).

incongruity condition, the shopper would optimally be motivated to avoid the store, since patronage of the store would frustrate both self-esteem and self-consistency needs.

Reasons for shopping

Motives (predispositions to behave in a specific way) give direction to needs and identify objectives for achievement. One of the most influential theories of human needs has been that of Maslow, which was initially developed in the 1940s. He suggested a hierarchy of needs, from the most basic or primitive through to the most civilised or mature: physiological needs; safety needs; belonging or social needs; esteem needs; and self-actualisation needs. Maslow's theory suggests that people seek to progress through this hierarchy; as needs at one level are satisfied, desire for those at the next level tends to take over. Inevitably the theory has been criticised, mainly due to lack of empirical support for the number of categories or the hierarchical order.

Most studies of shoppers' motivations have tended to emphasise the need for the actual products or, alternatively, the reasons for selecting one store or shopping centre as opposed to others. Tauber (1972) made a notable departure from previous patronage research by asking the most basic question, 'Why do people shop?'. He encouraged strategists and researchers to address their attention to the primary motivations that determine the shopping activity, rather than simply to assume that the need to purchase products is the only – or even the main – reason for shopping. Tauber hypothesised that 'peoples' motives for shopping are a function of many variables, some of which are unrelated to the actual buying of products. It is maintained that an understanding of the shopping motives requires the consideration of satisfactions which shopping activities provide, as well as the utility obtained from the merchandise that may be purchased'. Based upon in-depth interviews with both male and female shoppers, Tauber suggested several types of personal motive for shopping, classified as follows:

1 **Role playing** – shopping may be a learned and expected behaviour pattern which, for some, becomes an integral part of their role.

2 Diversion – shopping may provide a break from the daily routine, be seen as a form of recreation; it can provide a diversionary pastime for individuals or free entertainment for the family.

3 **Self-gratification** – the shopping trip may represent an antidote to loneliness or boredom; the act of purchasing may be an attempt to alleviate depression.

4 Learning about new trends – many people enjoy shopping as an opportunity to see new things and get new ideas.

5 Physical activity – the exercise provided by shopping is an attraction to some, especially those whose work and travel modes provide little opportunity for exercise.

6 **Sensory stimulation** – the shopping environment can provide many forms of stimulation through light, colours, sounds, scents and the tactile pleasures of handling the products.

In addition to these personal motives, a number of social motives were also proposed:

1 Social experiences outside the home – like the traditional market, the shopping area can provide the opportunity for social interaction, meeting friends or simply 'people-watching'.

2 Communication with others having a similar interest – hobby, sports and even DIY shops provide the opportunity for interaction with staff and customers with similar interests.

3 Peer group attraction – using a particular store may reflect a desire to be among the group to which one chooses or aspires to belong; this may be particularly significant in the patronising of high-status stores (such as Harrods) or 'trend' stores.

4 Status and authority – these may be conferred by the way stores seek to serve the customer. Especially when contemplating high-cost comparison purchases some shoppers enjoy being 'waited on' while in the store.

5 Pleasure of bargaining – some shoppers derive satisfaction from the process of haggling or from shopping around to obtain the best bargains.

This extended typology of motives underlying the shopping activity represents an important development from the view of shopping as simply a process of economic exchange. Many consumers do not overtly acknowledge these personal and social motives, preferring to justify their shopping behaviour in more 'rational' terms. Many surveys have, therefore, failed to detect the strength of these factors within the consumer's patronage decision process. Omar's study (1992) which examined shopping within the context of leisure activities, revealed that many consider shopping for clothes to be fun, creative, active, social and/or a form of relaxation. Food shopping was regarded by most as an essential chore but also by many as an obligation undertaken for the family – possibly a form of role-playing (Omar 1992). These shopping activities are by no means stable and permanent; they change with lifestyle and habits. Therefore, constant research must be undertaken in order to provide guidelines in designing the competitive retail marketing mix.

Store choice and patronage management

Patronage motives are those which encourage consumers to shop at one store rather than another. Of course, patronage motives are a primary concern of every retailer and they are constantly seeking ways in which they can increase the store's number of customers (patronage). All the elements of the retail marketing mix are focused upon inducing consumers to come to the store and browse, thereby increasing the opportunities for consumers to see goods or services they wish to buy. Since consumers are attracted or repelled by certain retail stores because of their personality or image, it is important that the retailer develop a store image which will appeal to the targeted customers and encourage them to 'patronise' the store.

Consumers are often motivated to patronise a retail store because of its location; it is not unusual for a store's location either to attract or repel a customer. The growth in planned regional shopping centres has done much to attract consumers to certain retail stores. But on closer investigation, it becomes clear that planned regional shopping centres attract only particular types and kinds of retail stores. A discount retailer, for instance, will not normally be located in a regional shopping centre; they prefer to be located somewhere on the outskirts of an area where rents are lower. The outskirts of a trading area usually suffer from a 'lower' consumer image, however, a discount retailer is not concerned about this down-market perception because the consumer expects this type of store image. In fact, if a discount retailer were located in an expensive or exclusive shopping area, it is possible that many economy-minded customers would not patronise that store because the image would be wrong – they would be suspicious that bargains would be few.

Other patronage motives include the merchandise and service mix that the store makes available to customers. Some consumers will patronise a certain retail store because of its vast range and assortment of goods. Other consumers will patronise a particular store because they offer a full line of customer services (such as delivery, gift wrapping, credit, installation, and liberal return policies). This is why some retailers stress 'service and selection' rather than price in the hope of attracting those customers to whom service and selection are important issues.

Another patronage motive which often ranks high in the consumer's mind is the reputation of the retailer. A retailer develops a reputation – for good or ill – from the manner in which they conduct business with customers. Once customers find a retailer they trust, they are very likely to return again and again to that same retailer. Generally, it takes a long time for a retailer to build a relationship of respect and trust between their business and their clients, but if all business transactions are geared toward developing a reputation for fair business practices, a store's patronage will increase. Word-of-mouth advertising may be seen as inexpensive promotion, however, it can only be bought by paying constant attention to the needs of customers. It can be invaluable in enhancing the store's image but, of course, it can also work the other way.

Store choice determinants

Consumer diversity becomes most apparent when we examine store choice and patronage motives (the consumer's reasons for selecting various stores), since those motives vary not only between consumers but within each individual customer – from time to time and depending on the items being purchased. The same individual who rushes to the nearest convenience food store for a box of matches may go to an out-of-town shopping centre for a different item, to a self-service supermarket for purchasing weekly supplies of food, or to a chemist for health and beauty aids. One useful classification (*see* Davies and Brooks, 1989) divides shoppers into:

- economical shoppers who want to obtain the best value for the time and money invested in shopping;
- personal shoppers who want considerable attention and personal interaction;
- ethical shoppers who feel an obligation to patronise a particular group of stores, such as small or local retailers;
- apathetic shoppers who are disinterested in the whole process.

Store reputation, merchandise price/value relationships, merchandise quality, store atmosphere, convenience, parking facilities, personal selling, credit facilities, and other such factors normally influence customer evaluation of stores. Retailers should consider these and other aspects of consumers' store selection criteria in deciding on store location, interior layout, merchandise selection, store services and other retail marketing policies.

Exhibit 5.5	**Shopping – a necessary chore for some, fun for others**

The efficiency-oriented economical shoppers mentioned above want to control the time spent shopping and often plan purchases in advance. In addition to attractive prices, they like stores with predictable assortments, easy access to the goods and fast service. In contrast, personal shoppers want to 'kill time', browse leisurely, and chat at length with the sales staff. Some customers enjoy store restaurants and shopping centre entertainment, while others are totally uninterested.

Store selection criteria

The desire to reach clear understanding of why consumers patronise one store and not another has made this question a major topic for retail marketing research. As retailers have become more quick to respond to the actions of competitors, retail formats in some sectors (such as food retailing) have tended to converge. In these situations, the precise components of the patronage decision become increasingly difficult to identify and separate. There is considerable evidence that store selection criteria tend to be situation-specific and that they tend to shift over time (Omar, 1990). A shift towards quality, choice and convenience as major criteria is implied, and is accompanied by a reduced emphasis upon low prices.

Care must always be taken when making generalisations about customers' selection criteria; for example, in Birmingham (UK) prices were indicated to be the primary factor, whereas in Amsterdam (The Netherlands) it appeared to be 'shopping environment' (Omar, 1992). Some of these contrasts can be attributed to major differences in population densities, geographical dispersion and standards of living. In addition, these studies were carried out up to four years apart, and there were also some differences between the methodologies used. But the results do provide a warning of the dangers of generalising shopping motives across national boundaries or even within relatively confined geographical areas. Shoppers' motivations to use a specific store are also in part a function of their motives for patronising the shopping centre within which the store lies, and vice versa. The viability of major shopping centres is usually dependent upon the developer's ability to attract major 'anchor tenants', such as department/variety stores or a superstore. Although these are usually assumed to be the main magnets to the centre, customers are actually often drawn there by the availability of smaller, specialist stores. In some cases no specific shop or group of shops provide the main attraction, with customers being motivated by the sheer choice of stores or characteristics of the centre itself. The motivational structure of a multi-store shopping trip is likely to be very different from that of a single store trip, making it inappropriate to generalise about customers' patronage motives across dissimilar location types.

It is fairly obvious that different criteria will dominate in the selection of stores within different sectors. Omar (1992) obtained ratings of the importance of 30 attributes in the selection of grocery and department stores. Table 5.1 summarises the ten attributes that were rated as most important in each case. In that particular study, 'dependable products' received the highest importance ratings in both cases and six other attributes appear in both listings. Only in the case of the department stores do the 'risk reduction' attributes of returns/exchange policies emerge as important in their store choice process.

Table 5.1
ATTRIBUTE IMPORTANCE IN STORE SELECTION

Attributes	Grocery store (rank)	Department store (rank)
Dependable products	2	1
Store is clean	3	10
Easy to find items you want	4	5
Fast checkouts	4	6
High-quality product	5	4
High value for money	6	3
Fully stocked	8	2
Helpful store personnel	8	7
Easy to move through store	9	1
Adequate number of personnel	10	–
Fair on repair service	2	2
Easy to return purchases	–	8
Easy to exchange purchases	–	9

Key: 1 = Low; 10 = High

Source: Derived from Omar (1992), p. 44.

The perceived risks associated with the products to be purchased clearly influence patronage motives and behaviour. Similarly, the propensity to shop around is closely related to the level of perceived risk in the purchase. Thus, the reduction of this risk through the selling of known brands at reasonable prices, tends to give catalogue showrooms a distinct advantage over some of their competitors. Over many years, Marks & Spencer have successfully reduced perceived risks through its well-known product reliability and returns policies.

Figure 5.1 is a helpful aid to understanding the elements, their sequence, and the factors affecting the store choice process. Although less elaborate than some of the general consumer behaviour models, it points to the many household characteristics that influence both perceptions of attributes and the importance attached to these attributes. It also establishes the important distinction between the store decision and the brand choice decision. Efforts to influence store choice effectively and then to maximise sales within the store represent related but different elements of retail marketing strategy, a distinction that many models fail to convey. Figure 5.1 also stresses the important intervening role of attitude between the marketing mix variables and the store choice decision.

Fig. 5.1 SEQUENCE OF FACTORS AFFECTING STORE CHOICE

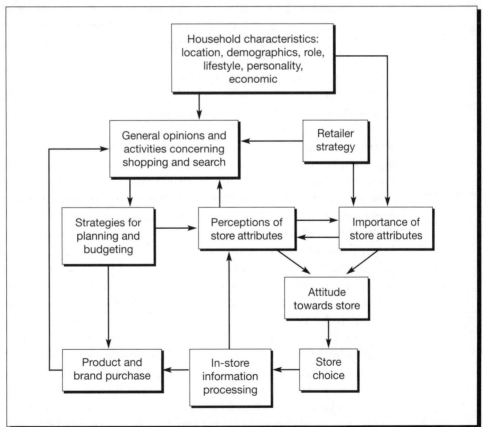

Store loyalty management

Retailers work to create and maintain a desirable level of loyalty toward their stores from the target market. Store loyalty could be defined as a biased behavioural response, expressed over time by some decision-making unit, with respect to one or more alternative stores out of a set of such stores, and as a function of psychological process (Tauber, 1972). In other words, consistent repurchase by itself may not be a sufficient indicator of loyalty; some form of psychological commitment on the part of the customer is also a necessary ingredient of true store loyalty. Probably, the frequency of patronage and recentness of store visits are sufficient indicators in the measurement of store loyalty.

Self-perception

The personality images associated with the individual self (self-perceptions) and others (person-perception) are cognitive schema that are organised at higher levels in the cognitive hierarchy (Sirgy, 1985). The cognitive schema that are high on this hierarchy are referred to as **abstract schema** and those that are low on the same hierarchy are referred to as **concrete schema.** Abstract schema are more accessible and become easily activated under conditions of high familiarity. The allocation of cognitive processing or effort necessary for abstract schema is minimal in relation to that required for concrete schema. Once an abstract schema is activated and processed, the same schema can be subjected to a decomposition procedure in which less abstract and more concrete schema are generated from the more abstract ones.

This social cognition theory can, therefore, be used to explain the relationship between self-image and product image match against functional store image evaluation, and store loyalty. The self-image and product image match variable involves abstract schema that become activated and processed at a less conscious level. This may then be followed by the decomposition process during which specific functional store image attributes are generated and subsequently evaluated. The overall evaluation of the store's functional attributes may, in turn, determine store loyalty behaviour. Thus, a positive relationship could be expected between ideal social congruity and functional store image evaluation and store loyalty.

With respect to the theoretical justification of the interrelationship of socio-economic status, area loyalty, shopping complex loyalty and store loyalty, it has been demonstrated that lower socio-economic consumers may express more loyalty to specific in-town shopping complexes than higher socio-economic consumers do (Lindquist, 1975). That is, lower socio-economic consumers cannot afford to 'out shop' and, therefore, are more restricted in terms of geographical mobility (many have no access to cars, public transport is poor and/or expensive, and so on). This proposition is also supported by social class theory. People in a higher social class exhibit greater social mobility than those from a lower social class. It is very likely, therefore, that a negative relationship between socio-economic status and shopping centre loyalty may be exhibited (Omar, 1992).

Shopping centre loyalty may also be determined by **area loyalty.** This is simply due to the containment variation. Those who express high loyalty to a specific geographical region (for example, a city centre) may also express loyalty to a specific shopping centre. The same argument can be applied to the relationship between shopping centre loyalty and loyalty to a specific store within that shopping centre facility.

Managing the loyalty schemes

Store loyalty indicates the differential advantage or the monopoly power of that store. If retailers could determine the nature and degree of loyalty, they could attempt to develop better retail strategies to increase or maintain satisfactory levels of sales. Fashion retailers enthusiastically embraced a wide range of loyalty programmes in Europe during the early 1990s. However, as the concept becomes more and more widespread – almost blanket-like in its coverage – almost the differentiation that such schemes provide between retailers is gradually lost. The question is, if every retailer is offering a loyalty scheme, what can a retailer do next to stand out from the crowd.

A common sleight of hand, both within and outside the loyalty scheme 'arena', is for retailers to offer discounts and special deals for their customers. In the same way that widespread discounting within stores can damage retail brand image, loyalty programmes offered by all the retailers in the same sector are counter-productive. Many loyalty schemes tend to set a dubious precedent. The retailer's loyalty to the customer should come from offering them a product they like, at a price they are happy and willing to pay; retailers should be very wary of any inducement over and above the merchandise. For example, if price is the key, the implication is that loyalty cards could start a more sophisticated round of the mark-down wars which held the high street stores to ransom in the late 1980s and early 1990s. Thus, if all retailers set up a loyalty scheme, it could become a zero sum game, with levels of competition reverting to price, service, quality and style. The danger is that incentive-led loyalty schemes are destined to inspire loyalty to the incentives, rather than loyalty to the company providing the offers; indeed, they tend to reward promiscuous retailing behaviour rather than loyalty. Customers may sign up solely for the discounts, with no greater loyalty to the company, and there is no evidence to suggest that loyalty schemes encourage the customers to use the store more.

Store loyalty factors

Store loyalty is the single most important factor in retail marketing success and store longevity. Without loyalty toward the retail organisation, the competitive advantage for which retail management is striving does not exist and the store is likely to be unsuccessful. Store loyalty is a function of customer satisfaction with the retail store. Several factors underlie customer satisfaction (*see* Figure 5.2) and any one or any combination of them can result in store loyalty. In an effort to determine the degree of store loyalty, a basic assessment of loyalty needs to be established. A number of variables can be used for that purpose including:

- the total volume purchased in the store;
- the frequency with which the store has been visited;

Fig. 5.2 THE ELEMENTS OF CUSTOMER SATISFACTION LEADING TO STORE LOYALTY

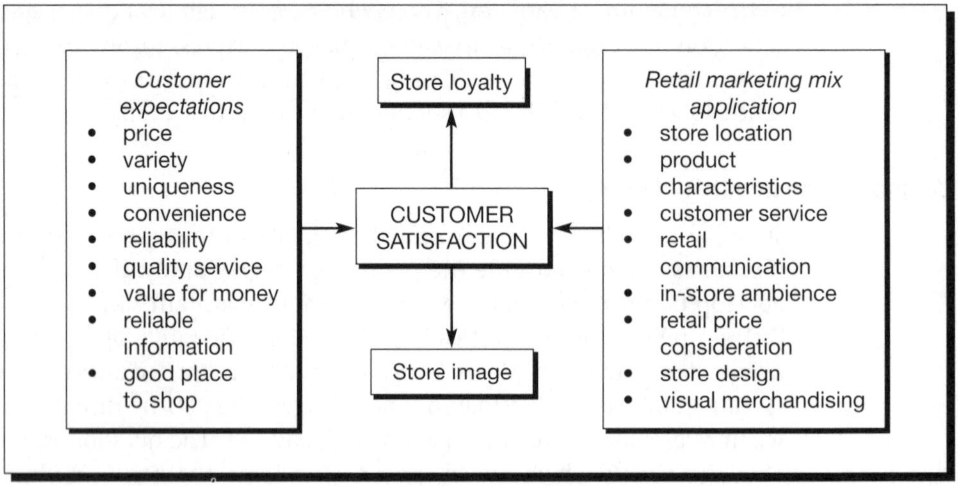

- the number of stores visited before the customer goes back to the store;

- the proportion of total purchases that has taken place in that store;

- whether the customers go back to the store;

- whether customers would recommend it to their friends;

- to what extent the individual is willing to go back to the same store whenever the need arises.

The criteria for a choice of any of these store loyalty variables may vary with the store type.

In all cases, whether the customer would go back to the store or would recommend the store to others are good criteria for the measurement of store loyalty. Two or more of these criteria may be used; however, it is important to note that there are no research findings showing which criteria or what combination of them should be used for store loyalty management. Figure 5.2 implies that customer satisfaction will be maximised when the retail marketing mix elements are coordinated to meet the expectations of the target customer group.

| **Exhibit 5.6** | **Assessing store loyalty – effective criteria vary according to store type** |

If the store is primarily a major product line shop selling items such as groceries or clothing, the total volume purchased in the store or the proportion of total purchases that took place in that store may be the best criteria for assessing store loyalty. However, for a department store or a large discount store where a large variety of products are sold, the frequency with which the store has been visited or the number of stores visited before the customer goes back to the store are better criteria.

Store management implications

Among the issues that need to be resolved or carefully looked into is the question of whether self-image and store image congruity causally affects store image evaluations. Store image evaluations may influence the matching process. A shopper, for example, may be familiar only with the store range of product prices. Based on this functional store image attribute, the shopper may infer the stereotypical or symbolic image associated with the store and not vice versa. It is also not clear whether either or both self-image and store image match and functional store image evaluations causally determine store loyalty. According to self-perception theory, it is conceivable that both functional and **symbolic store images** have been determined by attributing the causes of one's shopping behaviour to those symbolic and/or functional store images. These causal attributions may have accounted for subjects' responses to the store loyalty measures.

It is obvious that other unforeseen factors should be included in the model to prevent unnecessary speculation. These factors may include loyalty to specific brands which a store might not carry (**brand loyalty**) and the extent to which the store is new or has been in the market for some time (store life cycle). The managerial implications are that the retail manager must know how consumers perceive the functional as well as the symbolic characteristics of the store. This knowledge can be obtained through research on store image. Those functional store image characteristics found to be poorly evaluated by the majority of consumers should provide the basis for retail strategy development. These strategies should be developed to change consumers' image of the store and, therefore, increase store patronage and store loyalty.

Retail managers must also realise that symbolic images of the store (which most retailers pay hardly any attention to) play a significant role in store patronage and loyalty behaviours. The retailer is, therefore, also advised to gather information about how consumers see the store in personality terms. Is the store a friendly store? Is it a formal store or a classy store? In addition, retailers should know something about how consumers see themselves. If the personality of the store seems to coincide with the personality of most of the target customers, then the retailer can rest assured that the battle is half won. If the retailer finds that most of the target customers have personality images that are at odds with those propagated by the store, then it is time for action. Through various promotional efforts, the retailer should be able to change those symbolic store images to bring them more into line with those of target customers. This is essential since the effects of the match between self-image and store image, as demonstrated in this chapter, affect strongly how customers perceive the functional store attributes.

SUMMARY

Each store must specify in a well-formulated marketing strategy how it will compete in the marketplace and attract customers to its outlets. Development of the marketing strategy takes place in five major steps: customer analysis to identify potential market segments; selecting the target market; identifying how the firm will create a sustainable differential advantage in the marketplace; planning retail mix elements; and assessing store image. Consumers differ in terms of their tastes, preferences, and the way they perceive value from the shopping experience. These differences create the potential for dividing the market into several relatively homogenous customer groups. The total market can thus be viewed as comprising a number of smaller market segments. Retailers commonly describe segments based on consumer demographic, socio-economic, and lifestyle characteristics. Consumption patterns and shopping behaviour have been found to be strongly related to these factors.

Once it has identified segments, a retailer must choose one or more of them as its target market. To select the target market, each segment's market potential and competition level must be analysed. Market grids are often used to summarise this information and identify potential market opportunities. To differentiate, the retailer must set up a retail marketing mix of location, merchandise, shopping atmosphere, price, advertising, customer service, personal selling, and sales promotion. The elements of the retail marketing mix must be consistent with customer expectations, competitors' actions, and each other. A store's image is a perception of the retail organisation in shoppers' minds. The image is based partly on the functional qualities of the store and partly on psychological attributes.

KEY TERMS

abstract schema	ideal congruity	self-congruity
area loyalty	ideal self-image	self-gratification
brand loyalty	ideal social congruity	self-image
competitive advantage	image perception	sensory stimulation
concrete schema	low self-congruity	social congruity
emotional material	loyalty scheme	store image
functional qualities	psychological attributes	store loyalty
high self-congruity	role playing	symbolic store image

ASSIGNMENT

The battle to gain customers and, more importantly, their loyalty is intensifying as the major retailers continue to position themselves as the main point of contact for shoppers. So, rather than being a Kellogg's brand buyer, we are instead becoming a nation of Tesco supporters or Asda fans. You do not need a crystal ball to predict this trend, as the competition between brands, own-label, and discount supermarkets continue to converge on the market. Given this contentious environment, retailers are now vying for the consumers' attention and, more importantly, for consumers' loyalty.

Task

You are required to analyse the issues surrounding the steady rise in the attention paid to customer loyalty, and account for how retailers may meet the rising costs of recruiting new customers. Your essay must be between 1500 and 2000 words.

REVISION QUESTIONS

1 Image may be defined in several ways. What do you consider to be the meaning of the term 'store image'?

2 Store loyalty may be closely related to store image. Discuss.

3 A 'good' image appears to be one which differentiates the store from its competitors or one which positions it close to the general view of the ideal retailer in a given sector. Explain this statement with the aid of suitable examples.

4 Account for the notion that the image perceived by the loyal customers to a store may be significantly different from the image of those who dislike the same store.

5 A positive match between the store image and the customer's self-image is more likely to result in retail marketing advantage. Explain.

6 Explain why you think people shop.

7 John and Anita (both 26 years old) are planning to get married within the next six months. Show how their choice of a store from which to purchase a wedding dress may be influenced by the perceived risks of buying a wedding dress.

8 There is considerable evidence that store selection criteria tend to be situation-specific and that they tend to shift over time. What factors would you consider to be key to store selection criteria?

9 Store loyalty schemes are used to indicate the differential advantage or the monopoly power. How could fashion retailers use loyalty schemes to draw customers into their stores?

10 Retailers normally work to create and maintain a desirable level of store loyalty towards their stores from target markets. What do you understand by the term 'store loyalty', and how might retailers create and maintain it?

CASE STUDY

Persil Funfit Programme – how to handle customer loyalty

The Persil Funfit scheme is a nationwide health initiative to promote and encourage fun and fitness among children. The objectives are to draw customers away from the function or benefit of the product and perceive the brand as a participant in the 'caring 1990s'. As well as providing teaching material for schools, together with the badges and certificates to reward improvement, Persil Funfit also offer an on-pack offer with points to be redeemed by schools and playgroups for sports equipment (via handling house, Granby Marketing Services (Granby)).

A mailing list database of 30 000 primary schools was purchased and augmented through liaison with the pre-school playgroup association (PPA). Subsequently, a mailing with reply mechanism was actioned to introduce the scheme. The database is considered extremely valuable as it holds detailed data on numerous schools, and leisure clubs and organisations across the nation.

On registering for the scheme, organisations and schools receive a resource pack containing national curriculum resources pointers, programmes of exercises, plans, posters and charts to monitor progress and an order form for additional charts and badges. Once orders are received, either via the post or telephone, they are despatched.

Three different packs are supplied: pre-school groups and nurseries (3–5–year-olds), non-school pack gym clubs and primary schools (5–11–year-olds). The primary schools pack contains resource material to assist teachers in meeting the requirements of the National Curriculum. Endorsement for the scheme is supplied by the PPA, British Amateur Gymnastics Association (BAGA) and the British Council for Physical Education (BCPE). Various Members of Parliament (MPs) have also pledged their support for the scheme.

A dedicated team of teleoperators were assigned to customer care liaison, an umbrella term which included fielding calls, offering advice and information on the scheme, making outbound calls where necessary and taking orders. Almost 85 per cent of primary schools mailed have requested packs and 68 per cent of pre-school groups.

Questions for discussion

1 The Persil Funfit programme is regarded as very successful. Discuss why you think this programme achieved such a high consumer response.

2 Discuss why the Persil Funfit scheme pursued a caring objective rather than a functional objective and/or benefit objectives.

REFERENCES

Davies, G. and Brooks, J.M. (1989) *Positioning Strategy in Retailing*. London: Paul Chapman. p. 280.

Lindquist, J.D. (1975) 'Meaning of image: a survey of empirical and hypothetical evidence', *Journal of Retailing* 50(4): 29–38.

McGoldrick, P. (1990) *Retail Marketing*. London: McGraw-Hill.

Martineau, P. (1958) *Motivation in Advertising*. New York: McGraw-Hill. p. 175.

May, E.G. (1975) 'Practical applications of recent retail image research', *Journal of Retailing*, (Winter): 15–20.

Omar, O.E. (1992) 'Grocery shopping behaviour and retailer's own-label food brands', PhD thesis, Dept of Retailing and Marketing, Manchester Metropolitan University, UK.

Oxenfeldt, A.R. (1975) 'Developing a favourable price-quality image', *Journal of Retailing*, 50(4): 8–14.

Samli, A.C. (1989) *Retail Marketing Strategy: Planning, Implementation, and Control*. New York: Quorum Books. pp. 195–201.

Sirgy, M.J. (1985) 'Using self-congruity and ideal congruity to predict purchase behaviour', *Journal of Business Research*, 13 (June): 195–206.

Stephenson, Ronald P. (1979) 'Identifying determinants of retail patronage', *Journal of Marketing*, 33 (July) 57–60.

Tauber, E.M. (1972) 'Why do people shop?', *Journal of Marketing*, 36(4): 46–9.

6

Retail distribution and logistics management

LEARNING OBJECTIVES

After reading this chapter, you should be able to:

- understand how physical distribution activities are integrated into retail marketing channels and retailers' overall distribution strategies;

- understand the concept and nature of retail marketing channels;

- examine the structure and function of the channel system;

- understand how inventory management is conducted to develop and maintain an adequate assortment of products for target markets;

- gain insight into retailer logistics management which combines physical distribution management with the allied concept of material management into a single system.

The concept of supply chain management has evolved from two earlier ideas, **physical distribution management** (PDM) and **logistics management**. PDM evolved from the realisation that the physical movement of goods could be better coordinated by seeing stock management, warehousing, order processing and delivery as related rather than separate activities. The idea seems simple enough but the problems caused by the lack of coordination of these activities can still be seen in most industries. Also, some stock is necessary in most businesses, and selling out of stock is a major issue in retail marketing. A lost sale is bad enough but a lost customer because a competitor can manage its **supply chain** more efficiently is far worse. Suppliers who cannot guarantee availability risk prejudicing their relationships with retailers.

PDM is a term used to 'describe integrated operations concerned with the movement and storage of finished products'. However, in the context of retail marketing PDM largely refers to the interface between manufacturer and retailer. Often this interface involves separate transport firms and sometimes a wholesaler; where there is a wholesaler between manufacturer and retailer, there may be two entirely separate PDM systems. But in general, PDM is essentially about the management of finished goods. It assumes a guaranteed supply of such finished goods at the factory gate. It becomes clear that PDM on its own is not enough to ensure good supply management or to reduce stock to its bare minimum. What happens within a factory and to the raw materials before they reach the factory is clearly relevant to whether or not finished goods appear on time at the factory gate.

| Exhibit 6.1 | **Marketing practice** |

Distribution involves activities that make products available to customers when and where they want to purchase them. It is sometimes referred to as the 'place' element in the marketing mix. Choosing which channels of distribution to use is a major decision in the development of retail marketing strategies.

Changes in the manner in which products are distributed have a major impact on consumers. The move by multiple retailers, for instance, to sell petrol from sites adjacent to their supermarkets has affected the European petrol market in a number of ways. It has reduced petrol prices and increased promotional activity which are damaging to the supplier's profit margins and, ultimately, to their bottom line. In the long term this may force small suppliers of petrol out of the market, thus reducing consumer choice.

In addition to the major element of distribution, this chapter covers what seem to be very diverse elements, including channel decisions, channel management, customer support and **retail logistics**. There may be some shared logic between these various aspects of moving the goods or services between various levels of supplier and the final consumer. However, this chapter looks at each of these functional elements individually, taking their close relationships into consideration. The exact nature of the channels and distribution methods to be used is a fundamental strategic decision for any retail organisation. The **logistics** of distribution represent a specialised, but important function of management, ranging from data processing through inventory management to 'make or buy'. As this is a specialised subject, it is explored only briefly in this chapter.

The distribution channels

Frequently there is a chain of intermediaries, each passing the product down the chain to the next organisation, before it finally reaches the consumer. This process is known as the distribution chain. Each of the elements in these chains will have their own specific needs which the manufacturer must take into account, along with those of the all-important consumers. Channels of distribution may develop when many exchanges take place between producers and consumers (Lambert and Stock, 1993). The extent to which a channel of distribution creates an efficient flow of products from the manufacturer to the consumer is a major concern of both manufacturing and retail management. For instance, manufacturers depend on the distribution channel for such functions as selling, transportation, warehousing, and physical handling of goods and services (*see also* Figure 6.1). Consequently, the manufacturer's objective is to obtain optimum performance of these functions at minimum total cost.

In order to market its products successfully, a manufacturer must select the appropriate channel structure, choose the intermediaries to be used, establish policies regarding channel members, and devise information and control systems to ensure that performance objectives are met. Likewise, wholesalers and retailers must select manufacturers' products in a way that will provide the best assortment for their customers and lead to the desired profitability for themselves. The management must monitor and evaluate the performance of the distribution channel regularly. When performance goals are not met, management must evaluate possible channel alternatives and implement changes.

The meaning of distribution channel

The term **channel of distribution** has its origins in the French word for canal. This suggests a path that goods take as they flow from producers to consumers. In this sense, the channel of distribution is defined by the organisations or individuals along the route from producer to consumer. Since the beginning and ending points of the route must be included, both manufacturer and consumer are always members of the channel of distribution. However, there may be intermediate stops along the way. Several marketing institutions have developed to facilitate the flow of the physical product, or title to the product, from the manufacturer to the consumer. Organisations that serve as marketing intermediaries specialising in distribution rather than production are external to the manufacturing organisation. When

Fig. 6.1 CHANNEL FUNCTIONS

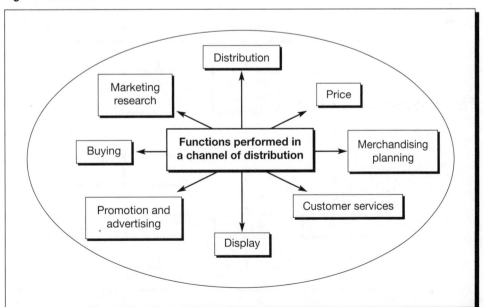

these intermediaries join with a manufacturer in a loose coalition to engage in exploiting joint opportunities, a channel of distribution is formed. A channel of distribution may, therefore, be defined as 'the collection of organisation units, either internal or external to the manufacturer, which performs the functions involved in product marketing' (Moore, 1991). The marketing functions are wide-ranging; they include buying, selling, transporting, storing, grading, financing, bearing market risk, and providing marketing information (*see* Figure 6.1). Thus, any organisational unit, institution or agency that performs one or more of these marketing functions is a member of the channel of distribution.

Channel structure

The structure of a distribution channel is determined by which marketing functions are performed by specific organisations. In a 'normal' distribution channel, a wholesaler is now mainly used to extend **distribution** to the large number of small retailers. Figure 6.2 describes the alternative routes for the provision of the performing arts. In general, channel structure could be described as:

- *conventional or free-flow*. This is the usual, widely recognised, channel with a range of middlemen passing the goods on to the end-user.
- *single transaction*. A temporary channel may be set up for one transaction – for example, the sale of property or a specific civil engineering project.
- *a vertical marketing system* (VMS). In this form, the elements of distribution are integrated.

Fig. 6.2 THE MARKETING CHANNELS FOR THE PERFORMING ARTS

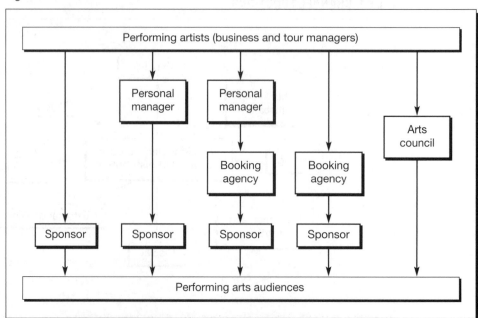

There is no 'best' channel structure for all firms producing similar products. Management must determine a channel structure within the framework of the firm's corporate and marketing objectives, its operating philosophy, strengths and weaknesses, infrastructure, manufacturing facilities, and warehouses. If the firm has targeted multiple market segments, management may have to develop multiple channels to service these markets efficiently. Unigate Dairies, for instance, sells a major proportion of its milk products through the major retailers, uses distributors and door-to-door home delivery for its milk brands, and also sell direct to the wholesalers. Marketing channels could, therefore, be said to develop because intermediaries (wholesalers and retailers) make the marketing process more efficient by reducing the number of market contacts. The use of an intermediary may reduce some or all of the following costs elements:

- selling costs – because fewer market contacts are required;
- transportation costs – because intermediaries may result in fewer but larger volume shipments;
- inventory carrying costs – if the intermediary takes ownership;
- storage costs;
- order processing costs;
- accounts receivable or bad debts – if the intermediary takes ownership;
- customer service costs.

From these cost elements, channel structure may be viewed as a function of product life cycle, logistics systems, and effective communication networks (Ellram and Cooper, 1990).

Bucklin's theory of channel structure

The most detailed theory of channel structure was developed by Bucklin in 1966. He bases his theory on the economic relationships among distributive institutions and agencies. Bucklin stated that 'the purpose of the channel is to provide consumers with the desired combination of its outputs (lot size, delivery time, and market decentralisation) at minimal cost. Consumers, therefore, are able to determine channel structure by purchasing combinations of service outputs' (1966). Bucklin concluded that functions will be shifted from one channel member to another in order to achieve the most efficient and effective channel structure. Given a desired level of output by the consumer and comparative conditions, channel institutions will arrange their functional tasks in such a way as to minimise total channel costs. This shift of specific functions may lead to addition or deletion of channel members. Bucklin's theory is based on the concepts of **postponement** and **speculation**.

Postponement

Costs can be reduced in two ways: by postponing changes in the form and identity of a product to the last possible point in the marketing process, and postponing inventory location to the last possible point in time, since risk and uncertainty costs increase as the product becomes more differentiated.

Manufacturers can use postponement to shift the risk of owning goods from one channel member to another. That is, a manufacturer may refuse to produce until it receives firm orders; a retailer may postpone owning inventories by purchasing from suppliers who offer the fastest delivery or by purchasing only when a sale has been made; and consumers may postpone ownership by waiting until they need a product immediately and so buying from retail outlets where they trust that products are kept in stock. Postponement results in savings because it moves differentiation nearer to the time of purchase, when it is easier to forecast demand. This reduces risk and uncertainty costs. **Logistics** costs are also reduced by sorting products in large lots, in relatively undifferentiated states.

Speculation

Speculation is the converse of postponement. The principles of speculation hold that changes in form, and the movement of goods to forward inventories, should be made at the earliest possible time in a marketing process in order to reduce the costs of the marketing system. That is, a channel institution assumes risk rather than shifting it. Speculation can reduce retail marketing costs through the economies of large-scale production; the placement of large orders, which reduces the costs of order processing and transportation; the reduction of stockouts and their associated costs; and the reduction of uncertainty.

Exhibit 6.2	**BT's successful use of postponement and speculation concepts**

To reduce the need for speculative inventories, many firms are exploring the strategies of time-based competition. British Telecommunications plc, for instance, is now able to manufacture products in about half the time it took just three years ago. Inventory and overheads have dropped, while quality has improved. Overall customer satisfaction has steadily improved. Postponement and speculation concepts have enabled BT to understand channel structures and their evolution.

The existence of speculative inventories may result in an indirect channel if the intermediary can perform the inventory risk-taking function at a lower cost than the manufacturer. Freight forwarders and agents who do not take title may reduce logistics costs in more direct channels of distribution where non-speculative inventories are present.

Channel decisions

Which channel to use is a major decision for most organisations. The most likely factors to be taken into account in such a decision are (*see* Mercer, 1996):

1 *Overall strategy* – the characteristics of the channel must be in line with the overall requirements of the marketing strategy.

2 *Product (or service)* – the characteristics of the product itself will play a part. For example, if a product needs to be kept refrigerated, then a specialised and appropriate distribution chain will be required.

3 *Consumer location* – where the end-users themselves are located will also have an influence.

4 *Cost* – the comparative cost of the alternative channels will be a relevant factor in the channel decision.

Flows in the channel of distribution

Typical channels of distribution and their functions are illustrated in Figures 6.2 and 6.3. Figure 6.3 shows the distribution channels of a grocery products manufacturer that sells its products to wholesalers, chain stores, co-operatives and the military. This figure illustrates the product flow and information flow that takes

Fig. 6.3 DISTRIBUTION CHANNEL FOR A GROCERY PRODUCTS MANUFACTURER

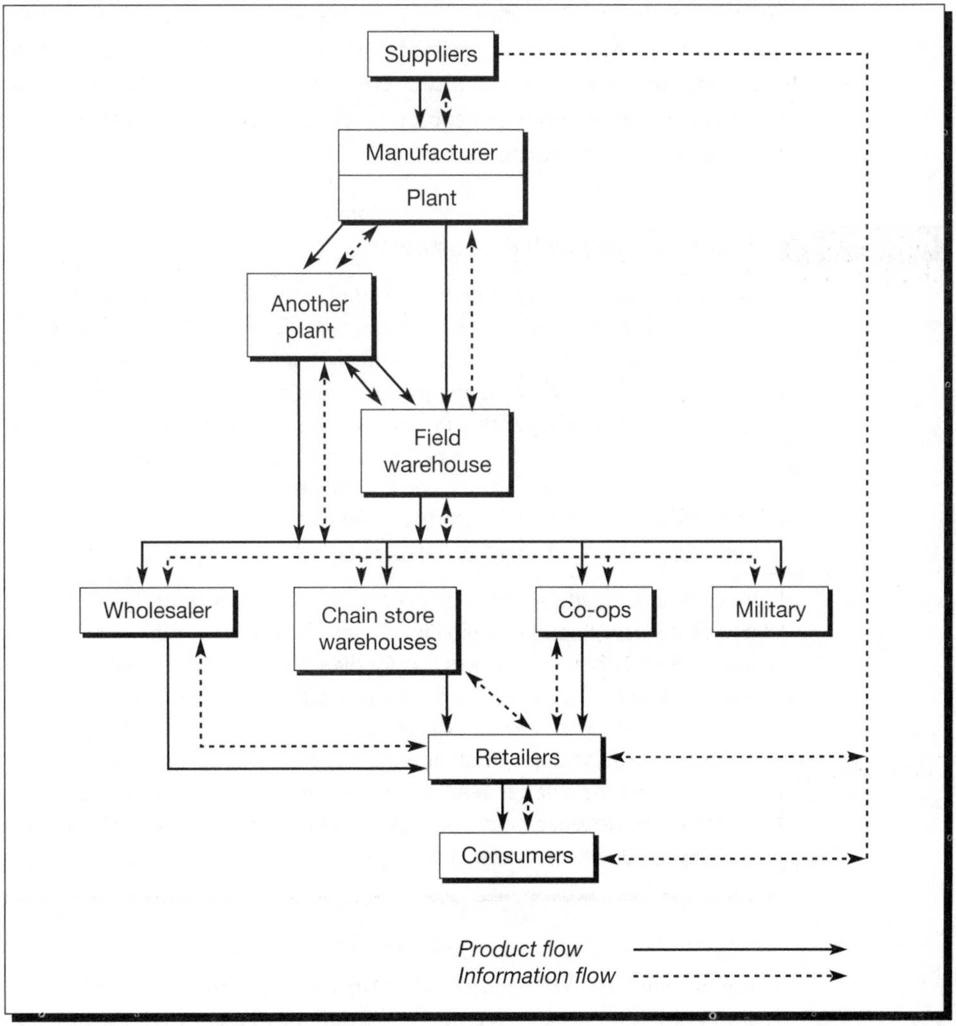

Source: Adapted from Lambert and Stock (1993), p. 83.

place in each channel. It may be remembered that product flow takes place only after information flow is initiated (*see* Figure 6.3). In addition to product and information flows, payments for the merchandise and promotional materials also move through the system.

The manufacturer may send salespeople to call on wholesalers and retailers, reach them by telephone using an internal telesalesforce, or use some combination of these approaches. Sales data and market research data also flow from customers to the manufacturer. Such data help the manufacturer determine whether its products are selling, to whom they are selling, and possibly why they are selling. Other types of information continually flowing between channel members include the quantity of inventory at each point in the channel, future production runs, service requirements, and delivery schedules.

In order to maximise profitability the manufacturer wants wholesalers and retailers to hold large inventories. Similarly, wholesalers and retailers want to shift responsibility to other channel members. The quality and speed of the information flows determine inventory size at each level of the channel. In many cases manufacturers need to include a direct communication link between the consumer and the firm, because product problems often do not become apparent until the product is in the hands of the end-user.

Exhibit 6.3 | **Communicating with the customer**

Given no direct method of communicating with the manufacturer, the consumer may take a course of action that is costly to the manufacturer as well as to other users. The unhappy consumer may, for instance, tell a government agency, a regulatory body or a consumer advocacy group about the product problem. This could prompt costly government regulation or even result in a direct reprimand, monetary or otherwise, for the firm. Consumers are also likely to share their dissatisfaction with friends, neighbours and family; such unfavourable word-of-mouth advertising may hurt sales. The consumer may also write to the manufacturer. However, letter writing takes time and effort – perhaps explaining why it is the least likely course of action.

In addition to all these potential problems, the defective product may cause serious and costly liabilities that could significantly alter the manufacturer's future success in the marketplace. If consumers have a direct and convenient way to communicate with the firm, there is less potential for large liabilities; the system can provide the firm with early warning of product defects, advertising and promotion problems, and of difficulties relating to product (or replacement parts) availability. A formal consumer response department can alert the manufacturer of a need to recall a product early – before major liabilities occur. Just as inventory acts as a buffer throughout the channel, so does considered communication.

Management must coordinate the firm's logistics strategy with the other components of the marketing mix to implement successfully the overall marketing strategy. In some cases, existing channels of distribution may dictate what types of products the firm sells, and how it prices and promotes them. Northern Foods and Procter & Gamble, for example, make excellent products that are well advertised and competitively priced. One of the most important factors that separates these companies from their smaller competitors, however, is the size and effectiveness of their distribution channels. Generally, management expects new products to be compatible with current distribution channels.

The physical flow of products (logistics channel) and the legal exchange of ownership (transaction channel) must both take place for the channel of distribution to be successful. However, these do not need to occur simultaneously: a product may change ownership without physically moving, and it may be transported from one location to another without changing ownership. Since transaction channel activities are not directly related to physical movement, there is no reason for both to occur at the same time.

Channel design and considerations

The role of channel members

The manufacturer, wholesaler or retailer may lead the channel design process, depending on the relative market power, financial strength, and availability of desired channel members.

The manufacturer's perspective

A manufacturer has market power when customers demand its product. When consumers demand a manufacturer's brand, retailers and consequently wholesalers are anxious to market its existing and new products because such products are profitable. However, a small manufacturer of a little-known brand may find it difficult to attract channel members either for its existing products or for new product offerings. Such a manufacturer lacks market power when entering channel negotiations. Financial resources determine a manufacturer's ability to perform marketing functions independently or internally; small manufacturers generally do not have the resources to distribute directly to retailers and must rely on wholesalers. Furthermore, in some locations suitable middlemen may not be available in every line of trade.

In industrial markets, when deciding between a direct or indirect channel of distribution, the manufacturer must consider the customer and the customer's needs, the product line, the size of the geographical area to be covered, the number of customers, the nature of the selling job, and the projected profitability of each option. For a small manufacturer with geographically dispersed customers, the cost of a direct channel may well be prohibitive. Firms in this situation include some manufacturers of electrical supplies, and small hand and machine tools. Even the manufacturer of a full line of products who has geographically concentrated customers may find direct channels less profitable than indirect channels for some products and some customers. Many pharmaceutical companies have increased their use of wholesalers, even in concentrated market areas, because of the high customer service levels required in the sector.

The wholesaler's power

Wholesalers make possible the efficient provision of possession, time and place utility. Wholesalers are economically justified because they improve distribution efficiency by 'breaking bulk', building assortments of goods, and providing financing for retailers or industrial customers. Wholesalers' market power is greatest when retailers order a range of various manufacturers' products in small amounts, or when the manufacturers involved have limited financial resources. For some products, such as electrical appliances and some lines of jewellery and fashion apparel, per-unit prices and margins may be large enough to enable the manufacturer to sell directly to retailers, even when the number of items sold to each retailer is small. But manufacturers of low-value or low-margin items such as cigarettes and some food items may find it profitable to sell only through wholesalers, though each retailer may order in relatively large quantities.

Wholesalers' and distributors' financial strength determines the number of marketing functions they can perform. Each function represents a profit opportunity as well as an associated risk and cost. The presence or absence of other firms offering comparable services influences the market power of individual wholesalers. Traditionally wholesalers have been regional in scope though this is changing; in some industries, like pharmaceuticals, wholesaler mergers have occurred.

The retailer's influence

Retailers exist in the channel of distribution where they provide convenient product assortment, availability, price, and image within the geographical market served. The degree of customer preference (loyalty due to customer service and price/value performance) that a retailer enjoys in a specific area directly affects its ability to negotiate channel relationships. The retailer's financial capability and size also determine its degree of influence over other channel members. Retailers' market power is discussed in Chapter 2 at length.

Types of distribution

There are basically three types of distribution that can be used to make products available to consumers: intensive distribution, exclusive distribution, and selective distribution.

Intensive distribution

In this distribution system, the product is sold to as many appropriate retailers or wholesalers as possible. Intensive distribution is appropriate for products such as chewing gum, chocolate bars, soft drinks, bread, film and cigarettes, where the primary factor influencing the purchase decision is convenience. All of these items fall into the convenience goods/convenience stores category in the product patronage matrix (Table 6.1). Industrial products that may require intensive distribution include pencils, paper clips, transparent tape, file folders, typing paper, transparency masters, screws and nails.

Exclusive distribution

When a single outlet is given an exclusive franchise to sell the specific product in a geographic area, the arrangement is referred to as exclusive distribution. Products such as speciality cars, some major appliances, some brands of furniture, and certain lines of clothing that enjoy a high degree of brand loyalty are likely to be distributed on an exclusive basis. This is particularly true if the consumer is willing to overcome the inconvenience of travelling some distance to obtain the product. Exclusive distribution is generally undertaken when the manufacturer requires a more aggressive selling approach on the part of the wholesaler or retailer, or when channel control is important.

Exclusive distribution may enhance the product's image and enable the firm to charge higher retail prices. The speciality goods/speciality store combination is the ultimate form of exclusive distribution. However, management sometimes chooses exclusive dealing for shopping goods, such as certain brands or lines of clothing, shoes, or stereo equipment, if sales to speciality stores or shopping stores enhance the product's image and provide sufficient margins to retailers. Sometimes

Table 6.1
CHANNEL MEMBERS BASED ON CONSUMER BUYING BEHAVIOUR

Categorisation of stores	Categorisation of products		
	Convenience goods	Shopping goods	Speciality goods
Convenience stores	Consumer buys the most readily available brand of product at the most accessible store	Consumer selects product from the assortment carried by the closest store	Consumer purchases favourite brand from the closest store that has the item in stock
Shopping stores	Consumer is indifferent to the brand of product but shops among different stores for better service and/or lower prices	Consumer compares brands and retail stores	Consumer has a strong preference for a particular brand but compares stores for the best service and/or price
Speciality stores	Consumer prefers a specific store but is indifferent to the brand of product	Consumer prefers a certain store but examines the store's assortment for the best buy	Consumer has a strong preference for a particular store and for a specific brand

Source: Adapted from Louis P. Bucklin (1963) 'Retail strategy and the classification of consumer goods', *Journal of Marketing* (January): 53–4.

manufacturers use multiple brands in order to offer exclusive distribution to more than one retailer. Exclusive distribution occurs more frequently at the wholesale level than at the retail level.

Selective distribution

In this system, the number of outlets that may carry a product is limited, but not to the extent of exclusive dealing. Shopping goods firms with established reputations commonly employ selective distribution, but this set-up is also used by new companies or for new products as a means of gaining distribution. By carefully selecting wholesalers and/or retailers, the manufacturer can concentrate on potentially profitable accounts and develop solid working relationships to ensure that the product is properly merchandised. The producer may also restrict the number of retail outlets if the product requires specialised servicing or sales support.

Selective distribution may be used for products such as clothing, domestic appliances, televisions, stereo equipment, home furnishings, and sports equipment. In general, exclusive distribution lends itself to direct channels (manufacturer to retailer), while intensive distribution is more likely to involve indirect channels with two or more intermediaries. With customer requirements and the type of distribution determined, management must select channel institutions. The increased use of scrambled merchandising – that is, non-traditional channels of distribution – has made this task somewhat more difficult. Grocery stores for example, have added non-grocery products like pots and pans, children's toys, hardware items, and books in order to improve margins and profitability. Some of the larger supermarkets even sell television sets and other large goods to maintain and improve the bottom line.

Control over the channel

A firm may have to exercise some control over other channel members to ensure product quality and/or post-purchase services. The need for control stems from management's desire to protect the firm's long-term profitability.

Exhibit 6.4	**Controlling distribution to control long-term profitability**

A manufacturer of premium confectionery products achieves national distribution through a chain of company-owned retail outlets and selected department stores, chemists, and speciality outlets. The marketing manager said the company does not sell to wholesalers because it wishes to avoid the mass market, fearing a loss of control over margins and product quality. If the manufacturer sold the product to a wholesaler, it could not prevent the wholesaler from selling to retailers such as Tesco or Sainsbury. Retailers would undoubtedly discount this nationally recognised brand, thus jeopardising the very profitable company stores and other channels of distribution that rely on the substantial margins allowed by premium prices.

Product characteristics

In addition to market coverage objectives, product characteristics are a major consideration in channel design. Nine product characteristics should be analysed by the channel designer, as shown in Table 6.2.

Table 6.2
ANALYSIS OF PRODUCT CHARACTERISTICS

Product characteristics	Evaluative analysis
The product's value	Products with a high per-unit cost require a large inventory investment. Consequently, manufacturers with limited resources usually shift some of the burden by using intermediaries. In general, intensive distribution is used for low-value products.
The technicality of the product	Technical products include such items as home computers, highly priced stereo components, expensive cameras and video equipment, imported sports cars, and a multitude of industrial products. Generally, direct channels and selective or exclusive distribution policies are used for these kinds of products.
The degree of market acceptance	New products with little market acceptance and low brand identification require aggressive selling at each level of the channel. If middlemen are reluctant to support the line, the manufacturer may have to employ 'missionary salespeople' or 'detail people' to promote the line to various channel members.
The degree of substitutability	When brand loyalty is low, product substitution is likely and intensive distribution is required. Firms place a premium on point of purchase displays in high-traffic areas. To gain support from wholesalers and/or retailers, the producer may offer higher than normal margins for shopping and speciality goods. Selective or exclusive distribution makes product support easier.
The product's bulk	Generally, low-value, high-weight products are restricted to markets close to the point of production. These products often require special material-handling skills. With less bulky products – low weight and small sized – more units can be transported by road, rail or container, thereby reducing the per-unit cost of transportation.
The product's perishability	This refers to physical deterioration or to product obsolescence caused by changing buying patterns or technological change. Perishable products are usually sold on a direct basis in order to move them through the channel more quickly and, therefore, reduce the potential for inventory loss.
The degree of market concentration	When the market is concentrated in a geographical area, direct channels may be the most effective and efficient method of distribution. When markets are widely dispersed, however, specialised intermediaries are necessary; they can capitalise on the efficiencies associated with moving larger quantities.
Seasonality	Seasonality requires out-of-season storage. Manufacturers must invest in warehouses or provide incentives to intermediaries so that they perform the storage function. Manufacturers may offer a seasonal discount to wholesalers or retailers who agree to take early delivery.
The width and depth of the product line	The width and depth of a supplier's product line influence channel design. A manufacturer of products with low per-unit values may use intensive distribution with direct sales if the product line is broad enough to result in a relatively large average sales volume.

Customer service objectives

Customer service represents the 'place' component of the marketing mix. Customer service can be used to differentiate the product or influence the market price – if customers are willing to pay more for better service. In addition, the channel of distribution selected determines the costs of providing a specified level of customer service. Customer service is a complex subject and is usually measured in terms of: the level of product availability, the speed and consistency of the customer's order cycle, and the communication that takes place between seller and customer. Management should establish customer service levels only after carefully studying customer needs. The most important measure of customer service is inventory availability within a specified order cycle time. Availability is usually expressed in terms of:

■ the number of items out of stock compared to the total number of items in inventory;

■ the items shipped as a percentage of the number of items ordered;

■ the value of items shipped as a percentage of the value of items ordered;

■ the number of orders shipped completed as a percentage of total orders received.

The first measure of availability is deficient unless products are categorised based on profit contribution, otherwise a stockout on a fast-moving item would be treated the same as a stockout on a slow-moving item. The weakness of the second measure is its failure to recognise products' importance to the customer. Furthermore, some products have higher contribution margins than others and losing sales of one of these will have a greater impact on corporate profits. The third measure, based on the value of items ordered, is somewhat better than the first two measures but still does not eliminate their weaknesses. The fourth measure is most likely to reflect the customer's view of customer service. The best measure of customer service reflects the product's importance to the customer and the customer's importance to the company.

Profitability

The profitability of various channels of distribution is the major criterion in channel design. The frameworks for judging alternative channel structures on the basis of estimated cost and revenue analysis vary slightly between firms. Management can use market research to format revenue estimates for each alternative channel structure (*see* Figure 6.4). It must estimate variable manufacturing costs for various levels of activity, and variable marketing and logistics costs, such as sales commissions, transpiration, warehousing, and order processing, along with accounts receivable. Management should apply the corporate cost of money to accounts receivable as indicated in Figure 6.4. It should also add, to each channel, alternative assignable non-variable costs incurred for each segment – including expenses like bad debts, sales promotion, salaries and inventory carrying costs. Finally, management should use the corporate opportunity cost of money as a charge for all other assets

Fig. 6.4 COST TRADE-OFFS REQUIRED IN A LOGISTICS SYSTEM

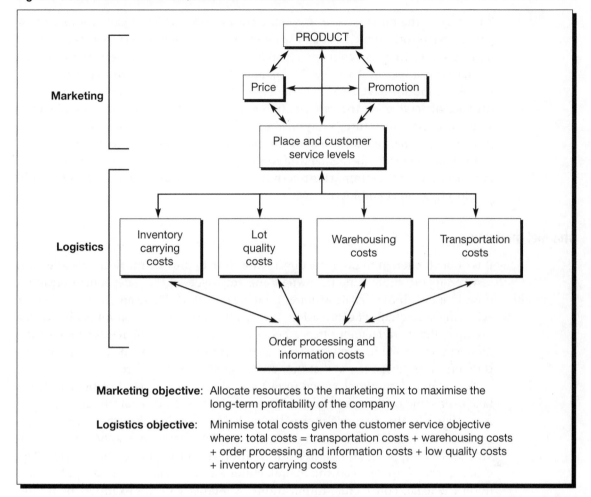

Marketing objective: Allocate resources to the marketing mix to maximise the long-term profitability of the company

Logistics objective: Minimise total costs given the customer service objective where: total costs = transportation costs + warehousing costs + order processing and information costs + low quality costs + inventory carrying costs

required by each channel structure alternative. The size of the net segment margin will determine which structure alternative is the best option from the standpoint of financial performance. This information, combined with estimates of future growth for each structural alternative, permits the channel designer to select the most desirable alternative. The cost and revenue analysis can be used to measure channel structure and channel member performance.

Channel management

If the manufacturer has any aspirations to be market oriented, their work should be extended to managing all the processes involved in the distribution chain, until the product or service arrives with end-user. This may involve a number of decisions on the part of the manufacturer; these are discussed below.

Membership management

To a degree, the manufacturer has some control over which organisations participate in the distribution chain and what the structure of that channel might be. At one extreme, in mass consumer goods markets where members of the chain merely offer a logistical service, the manufacturer's main concern may be to maximise distribution levels so that the largest number of outlets possible stock the product or service. At the other extreme, for example, where retailers take over some of the manufacturer's responsibility for supporting sophisticated technical products, the manufacturer may be primarily concerned about the quality of the individual retailer. In such circumstances in particular, the choice of channel members becomes a very important activity; it is almost as though they are being employed as direct employees.

Channel motivation

It is difficult enough to motivate direct employees to provide the necessary sales and service support; motivating the owners and employees of the independent organisations in a distribution chain requires even greater effort. There are many devices for achieving such **channel motivation**. Perhaps the most usual is a form of bribery: for example, the manufacturer offers a better margin, to tempt the retailer to push the product rather than its competitors; or a competition is set up, open only to the distributors' sales personnel, so that they are tempted to push the product.

The retail organisations which form the various links in the distribution chains take over some of the manufacturer's responsibilities. In general, the retailers' primary value to the manufacturer is the wider distribution that they offer, which increases the overall penetration of the brand. These retailers also hold stock, provide service support, and gather information useful to the manufacturers. The exact relationship between the manufacturer and the retailer will depend in part upon the legal, contractual implications. A retailer will, for example, be totally independent of the manufacturer, whereas an agent will act on behalf of that manufacturer – typically operating under the same terms and conditions. In return for these services, retailers receive payments:

1 Trade discounts – these are standard discounts, usually of a fixed percentage, offered to a channel member. However, the percentage may vary according to the category in which the manufacturer places the retailer.

2 **Quantity discount** – a quantity discount has the advantage that it offers an incentive for all the retailers to try to sell the maximum volume, and hence trade-up to higher discount levels.

3 Promotional discount – the manufacturer may also attempt to 'push' the product or service by offering promotional discounts, in the belief that these will persuade the retailer to substitute the brand being prompted for another, the end-user often accepting what is in stock. Alternatively, the intention may be to

persuade the retailer to overstock, thereby creating stock pressure, which, in turn, may force the retailer to give the brand extra display space.

4 Cash discount – most manufacturers normally offer retailers terms which require payment within 30 days. This is of considerable value to some retailers who have managed to reduce some of their stockholdings to less than five days. The extra 25 days' credit can, in effect, be used as a free loan. However, the manufacturer may wish to provide a cash incentive for retailers, or wholesalers, to pay earlier – usually a reduction of 1 to 2.5 per cent for payment within seven days.

Vertical and horizontal marketing

Both **vertical marketing** and **horizontal marketing** (relatively recent developments), integrate the channel, with manufacturers, wholesalers and retailers working in one unified system. This may arise because one member of the chain owns the other elements (often called 'corporate systems integration'). A supplier owning its own retail outlets is called **forward integration**. It is perhaps more likely that a retailer will own its own suppliers, this being **backward integration**. For example, MFI, the furniture retailer, owns Hygena, which makes its kitchen and bedroom units. Similarly, Marks & Spencer owns St Michaels' which produces its brand products. Integration may also be by franchise such as that offered by McDonald's hamburgers, Kwik Kopy print shops and Benetton clothes; or it may be achieved by simple cooperation as in the way that Marks & Spencer cooperates with its fashion suppliers (other than St Michael).

Alternative approaches are 'contractual systems', often led by a wholesale or retail co-operative, and 'administered marketing systems' where one dominant member of the distribution chain uses its position to coordinate the other members' activities. This has traditionally been the form led by manufacturers. Vertical integration is a strategy which is best pursued at the mature stage of the market (or product). At earlier stages it can actually reduce profits. It is arguable that vertical integration also diverts attention from the real business of the organisation. Suppliers rarely excel in retail operations and, in theory, retailers should focus on their sales outlets rather than on manufacturing facilities. The most successful retail operator in the UK, Marks & Spencer, very deliberately provides considerable amounts of technical assistance to its suppliers, but does not own them.

Horizontal marketing is a rather less frequent example of new approaches to channels and is where two or more non-competing organisations agree on a joint venture – a joint marketing operation – because it is beyond the capacity of each individual organisation alone. In general, though, this is unlikely to be justified by marketing synergy alone.

In conclusion, while the discussions so far has been about channel of distribution management in its general forms, the following sections discuss exclusively retailer logistics management in a European context.

Retailer logistics management

Logistics may be described as 'the process of strategically managing the movement and storage of materials, parts and finished inventory from suppliers, through the firm and on to customers'. Logistics combines physical distribution management (PDM) with the allied concept of materials management into a single system.

There are potential benefits in retailers seeing the flow of materials and the counter-flow of information as a single system, though the system cuts across the work of a number of departments inside the retail organisation. Transport and warehousing as individual activities have become elevated from their relatively unknown status to integral parts of logistics operations. The leading edge logistics departments could be seen to contribute to the strategic planning of their companies, as the need to coordinate what had always been significant parts of the business became apparent. With this came a change in focus for logistics management, away from cost saving, although this is still important, and towards a focus on better service, reduced **order cycle** times, and greater responsiveness to customers' needs. The structural changes in retailing (discussed in Chapter 1) have had a profound effect on the physical movement of merchandise. Individual companies or stores have become larger and have centralised their buying. Wholesalers have almost disappeared from the main retail sectors in Britain because larger retailers are dealing directly with suppliers.

During the early 1960s and until the end of the 1980s, most deliveries in Britain were made by manufacturers or wholesalers directly to retailers' premises. Today the norm is for delivery to be made to a retailer's own or controlled central warehouse. So instead of a wholesaler delivering an assortment of merchandise to the retailer, the retailer has replaced this role with its own warehousing and transportation. It is unlikely that multiple retailers could have secured their market share growth without the economic and operational benefits of centralised distribution. However, the advantages to the retailer do not stem from replacing the manufacturer's delivery system as much as from reducing stock levels, reducing the need for delivery procedures at store level, and freeing up storage space in retail outlets that can be converted to selling space. Other benefits stemming from better control may including fewer stockouts and lower shrinkage.

Retailers do not always adopt the same strategies for centralising distribution even within the same retail sector, but some generalisations can be made. There could be a differentiation made between pre-distribution and post-distribution philosophies (*see* Cooper *et al.*, 1993). With a **pre-distribution system** merchandise is sent directly to the store, based on the arrangement with the supplier when the merchandise is ordered, thus circumventing the multiple retailer's centralised system. Such an approach may be logical for both perishable items and slower-moving lines. For the majority of products in a country such as the UK, where distances between major population centres are relatively small, **post-distribution** is the norm. The post-distribution route reduces store deliveries from 60 a day on average in grocery retailing to 12 or less (Mercer, 1996). Own-label and imported products also tend to move via the retailer's system.

Innovation in retail logistics

Most sectors of retailing in Europe can provide at least one example of excellence in **retail logistics**. In clothing, Benetton has used innovative approaches to logistics to develop and sustain its position as a leading fashion retailer. In furniture retailing, Ikea would have been unable to expand from its Swedish home market without a good grasp of the importance of logistics in developing new business.

MINI-CASE ▪ **The importance of retail logistics**

At the conceptual level, logistics has a similar importance for all kinds of retail organisation. Considerable importance must be attached to the quality of logistics services. Delivery of products to stores must be reliable and the availability of the best selling lines must always be assured; considerations of this kind are central to the success of every retailer. Despite this shared importance, some retail sectors are ahead of others in their innovative approach to logistics. One sector which has consistently led with new ideas is grocery retailing, particularly in European countries where the multiples dominate the sector. France and the UK are now emerging as the leading innovators in grocery retailing, whereas Italy remains characterised by independent retailing (largely due to legislative conditions) and German retailers tend towards conservatism. French retailers pioneered the hypermarket concept and successfully introduced this form of retailing into Spain during the 1990s.

Grocery retailing in the UK has developed along different lines from those in France. Hypermarkets are less common, not least as a result of planning restrictions on large, out-of-town retail development. Instead, grocery retailing is based more on supermarkets and superstores, many sites being in urban high streets. The key to innovation in the UK grocery retailing has been fierce competition between multiples. It is interesting to draw parallels with Japanese manufacturing, in which major companies – especially in the cars and electronics markets – are locked in fierce competition with rivals in the domestic marketplace. Competition of this kind has been an important factor in promoting retail innovation (Stern and El-Ansary, 1982). This is true of UK grocery retailers in the field of logistics, where it is widely used as a competitive marketing weapon.

There are three key areas of innovation in retail logistics in the European retailing including the contracting out to specialist companies of those logistics activities, such as transport and storage, which are not part of the core retail business; the use of **information technology** (IT) to maintain better control over the supply chain; and the better use of **sales space** in retail outlets by eliminating storage space. It must be recognised that these particular innovations will not necessarily transfer in an unmodified form to retail outlets other than supermarkets. In hypermarkets, for example, storage space must often be adjacent to the sales space because, in provincial France, there is no scope for serving several hypermarkets from a separate distribution centre used for storage.

Contracting out logistics activites

How retailers organise and manage their own distribution systems varies. Some retailers insist on organising the collection of stock from their suppliers (Ellram, 1991). Some own transport and warehousing systems but many contract this function out to third parties. Such contracts vary greatly in their scope but can be very comprehensive, with some including custom-built premises, incorporation of the retailer's order processing, vehicles painted in the retailer's corporate colours, specialist racking and much more (Cooper *et al.*, 1993). Contracting out releases a retailer's capital and allows it to focus on its core business of retailing (Stern and El-Ansary, 1982). The third party operator can often achieve economies by such practices as back-loading for other companies or by combining its entire operations to make the best use of its transport fleet (Sussams, 1991). A third party operation does, however, introduce another company and another organisation into the supply chain. Having absorbed the wholesaler's role, many retailers are now recreating it – or something akin to it – in their third party relationships with transportation operators.

Quick response systems can be seen as a further innovation that helps retailers to concentrate on their core business. The benefits of electronic data interchange (EDI) and coordinated physical distribution are gradually being realised; they are capable of reducing inventory and improving customer service at the same time.

MINI-CASE | **Cooperating with suppliers to influence technical innovation**

Coles Myer represents 20 per cent of the Australian retail market. Its department store group, Grace Bros, operates a central distribution system and saw the value of cooperating with its suppliers of items such as electrical appliances and furniture, simultaneously to reduce stockholding and improve service to customers (Ellram, 1991). Grace Bros provides its suppliers with a 12-month sales forecast, which is updated every month. Suppliers commit to a two-day lead time for all products and have to hold the appropriate levels of stock in their system. Merchandise is called off from any sales made each day for delivery into Grace Bros's warehouse during the second day following the order. Grace Bros deliver to the customer the next day. 'Cooperation and trust' are cited as critical elements in making the system work.

Similar projects will work in other retail sectors, where sales and the turnover of stock need to be improved markedly. These may, in turn, lead to higher margins and greater returns on assets. Most North American retailers appear to be adopting quick response (Lambert and Stock, 1993). Co-ordination is required throughout the supply chain. Forecasting by retailers and manufacturers needs to be as precise as possible. Flexibility is needed at all stages in manufacture but, above all, the supply chain needs to work as one system.

Information Technology (IT)

The importance of IT in retail logistics cannot be underestimated. Spectacular advances in computer technology have made IT a key component of logistics planning in the retail industry. A major contribution of IT in logistics is that it increases transparency within the supply chain. At one time, the established way of discovering the amount of any given product held in a retail store was by physically counting it. For any particular product line, staff would have to count the items that were left on shelves and those held in the storeroom before they could judge whether a replenishment order was necessary. Within this routine the main uncertainty was the amount of stock on the shelves, since paperwork records could at usually be relied upon to determine stock levels in the storeroom. But the rate at which customers took products off supermarket shelves was uncertain due to poor monitoring – in turn due to the physical nature of stocktaking.

The introduction of electronic point of sale (EPOS) systems completely changed both how retailers check quantities at the store and how they re-order supplies. As customers pass through checkouts at supermarkets, light pens or bar code readers are now widely used to identify the products purchased. Whereas once the checkout operator had to enter the price of an individual item into a cash register, the EPOS system is used to check the price of the item and automatically add it to the total of other goods purchased by the shopper. At the end of the transaction, the customer receipt is printed out to include descriptions of the goods bought, together with the prices of the individual items.

This is very helpful for the customer, not least because the time through the checkout is reduced by the automatic identification of purchased items using the EPOS system. But the benefit for the retailer is even greater: there is an immediate registration within the EPOS system of goods sold. These data can then be quickly compared (electronically) with data for goods delivered to the store, and it is possible to have an immediate and up-to-date understanding of stocks held at the store for any given product line.

Exhibit 6.5	**Using EPOS and JIT**

Since upgrading their EPOS system, Argos, the UK catalogue retailer, no longer uses paperwork as the basis for recording deliveries to its stores. Instead, vehicle drivers hand in floppy diskettes at the store when making a delivery so that incoming goods can be entered into the store computer terminal without the data having to be keyed in. This procedure both reduces error and saves time. Using an EPOS system in association with just-in-time (JIT) delivery can eliminate waste and reduces the risk of oversupply of products to each Argos shop relative to demand at that particular store.

Similarly Boots, the UK chemist with over 40 000 product lines, used an EPOS system in association with JIT to eliminate oversupply to its stores.

The freshness of food products such as meat and fish, as well as vegetables, can be prolonged during transit by the use of vehicles with controlled environments – again contributing to longer shelf life. In this case, IT is combined with food handling technology to bring fresh food to shoppers and save losses through shrinkage for the retailer. IT can also be used to provide better measures of retail marketing performance. By capturing data at the checkout, EPOS enables the retailer to calculate a whole range of performance indicators relating to retail marketing including sales by item, slow or fast moving products, sales by location, product returns and inventory analysis. Retailers may be able to improve the marketing effort by having better sales information derived from the above sources. Other examples of the benefit of such information are the same as discussed above.

Sales space maximisation

Most retailers will be united in the belief that retail outlets are for sales, rather than storage. But many retailers feel they are forced to retain storage areas at retail outlets for fear of running out of essential product lines. If the shelves are empty, they can be filled by a short visit to the storeroom at the back of the shop; for many retailers this is preferable to the uncertainty of waiting for deliveries from a supplier. However, keeping products in store at the shop has a number of important disadvantages. Most important of all is that it reduces the sales area and hence the revenue-earning potential of a given retail outlet. In a competitive retail environment, this can be a very serious consideration. A second factor is that keeping products in the shop's storeroom is expensive. Once the retailer has taken delivery the business has to finance the cost of keeping the products, even before they are ready to go on sale. This is clearly bad for both cash-flow and profitability. But what is the solution, given the fear of not having products available for sale?

Unaffiliated independent retailers have little option other than to keep products in reserve at their shops, unless their suppliers (often including wholesalers and cash-and-carry outlets) provide a first-class delivery service at an acceptable cost – a condition which is quite rare. The unaffiliated independent retailer could keep products in store elsewhere – say, in a lock-up – where the rental cost of floor space will be less than for a shop. But shelf-filling is inconvenient if products are stored at a remote location; this represents a cost to be weighed against possible savings.

The prospect of eliminating storerooms at shops is better for an affiliated independent retailer if, say, the voluntary group to which the retail business belongs is prepared to innovate in logistics. Essentially what is required is a frequent delivery service from the voluntary group acting as wholesaler. Daily deliveries may have to replace deliveries every, say, two or three days. Furthermore, support will have to be forthcoming from other independent retailers affiliated to the same voluntary group to ensure sufficient volumes for economic delivery on a more frequent basis.

Overall, the multiple retailers have the best prospect of eliminating storage space at shops and, indeed, many of them have done just that. In some cases, however, the opportunity to do so may have come about as a consequence of first following other priorities. In Japan, for example, regional distribution centres (RDCs) were established in the first instance as a way to discipline deliveries to shops by suppliers. In effect, each RDC acted as a consolidation point for supplier delivery to a number of shops. Later developments were the contracting out of distribution services, followed by the centralisation of all storage at the RDC. So, in effect, the elimination of storage areas at supermarkets came about because the multiple retailers had already established RDCs as part of the supply chain to supermarkets. In Europe and the US there has been a substantial move by the multiple retailers towards the use of RDCs; the process is usually referred to as 'centralisation', reflecting the pivotal role of RDCs in management of the retail supply chain.

Clearly many UK retailers, including Sainsbury, Mothercare, Boots, Asda and Argos, have found the benefits of centralisation impossible to resist. They tend to be using 'logistical competency to gain competitive advantage'. Given the pivotal role of inventory in promoting the centralisation concept, retailers have also recognised that inventory is the focal asset of business.

The skill of retailers in logistics innovation is well documented in the literature. Sainsbury, pioneer of the RDC concept, now has around 25 distribution centres strategically located throughout the UK and responsible for handling over 7 million cases (85 per cent of the volume) each week to an estimated 296 supermarkets. Then there is Argos, whose efficient distribution enables it to achieve around 95 per cent level of product availability on a product range of almost 4000 throughout the year – at all of its 250 catalogue showroom outlets. Quite an efficiency record!

SUMMARY

This chapter showed that the distribution channel plays an integral part in a firm's marketing strategy; indicated the types of channel structures that are used; the factors that influence channel design, evolution, and performance; and how communication can improve the efficiency and effectiveness of distribution channels. A problem for both the supplier and the retailer is how open they should be with each other over their internal information. A retailer would like to be sure that its suppliers are holding adequate stock, but the supplier is also serving other retailers who might need the same stock. The supplier would like to know its level of sale in the retailer's outlets to make its own judgements on replenishment. The potential is there for a retailer to have access to the stock position of a number of alternative suppliers and to use information for example, on excessively high stocks to renegotiate prices. Whichever method is adopted within any one supply chain will depend upon the competitive posture of that supply chain to others. If the chain is supplying to and buying from only other members of the same chain, total integration of data systems would appear logical and low risk. Totally different styles of trading relationships will exist, and the level of transparency between suppliers and retailers systems will be a key issue.

backward integration	logistics management	quick response system
channel of distribution	order cycle	retail logistics
channel motivation	physical distribution	sales space
distribution	management	speculation
forward integration	post-distribution	supply chain
horizontal marketing	postponement	vertical marketing
information technology	pre-distribution system	
just-in-time	quantity discount	

ASSIGNMENT

Investment in technology has helped to control inventory, drive stock levels down and improve stock turn. Stock control in the retail sector has intensified the burden on suppliers, which are forced either to keep the stock or to develop more efficient production methods to reduce the amount of stock sitting on their premises and tying up their cash. The introduction of electronic point of sale (EPOS) systems completely changes how retailers both check quantities at the store and re-order new supplies. The whole thrust of EPOS and just-in-time delivery is to keep down stocks in the retail sector and put the onus back on the suppliers.

Task

With the aid of suitable examples, discuss the benefits of EPOS system for a chosen grocery retailer. Your essay should be between 1500 and 2000 words in length.

REVISION QUESTIONS

1   Define channels of distribution and comment on why they develop.

2   Explain, using relevant examples, how a firm could use postponement and speculation in the channel of distribution.

3   Explain the concept of structural separation and its implications for channel design.

4   Bucklin's theory of distribution channel structure helps retailers understand channel structure and predicts structural change. Discuss.

5   The patronage motives of potential customer segments must be determined in order to select intermediaries who can perform the selling function most effectively. Explain this statement.

6   What steps are employed in the successful channel design process?

7   In addition to market coverage objectives, what product characteristics are considered in a channel design?

8   There are basically three types of distribution that can be used to make products available to end-users. Briefly discuss them and suggest reasons why intensive distribution may be more difficult to control.

9   There are three key areas of innovation in retail logistics in UK grocery retailing. Discuss these areas with examples which illustrate your understanding.

10   The importance of information technology (IT) in retail logistics cannot be underestimated. Discuss contrast this statement.

CASE STUDY

European Monetary Union (EMU) – implications for supply chain management

A supply chain is a core process within a retail business; no matter what products are being delivered and distributed, it's vital that retail organisations are able to exploit information technology (IT) to create the most cost-effective and flexible supply chain.

A flexible supply chain is particularly important when more organisations are operating across Europe and/or globally. To compete in an ever more competitive retail industry, retailers need to reduce the cost of doing business and exceed the value offered by competitors. This means getting the most out of distribution networks, reducing stockholding, quickening turnover of stock and optimising use of warehousing facilities.

The added problem for retailers operating across Europe is that they face a likely upheaval due to the introduction of European Monetary Union (EMU), which is set to force both legal and business change on the retail industry. Compliance with EMU is no longer optional, though the UK is unlikely to go into the first round of the process. Retailers and distributors trading with customers or suppliers across Europe may be paying, being paid and reporting in a number of different currencies during the handover. They will certainly have to operate twin base ledgers in Euros and local currencies for several years.

Apart from settlement issues, there will be an impact on supply chains where any part of them (customer or supplier) is in Europe. Whether the UK is inside the Union or not, EMU will affect retail businesses in lots of ways. EMU presents a unique set of business, IT and organisational challenges for retailers and distributors; the question is whether they see those challenges as a threat or an opportunity. Bearing in mind the fact that change almost always involves cost, the most positive way to view this is to make a choice between doing the minimum and simply complying with EMU, or turning it into an investment to be taken advantage of. Looking at the advantages of EMU, perhaps the biggest is that it will introduce currency transparency, which will mean that there is less risk involved in moving stock around Europe. At the moment, it is difficult to predict costs in a supply chain that moves through a number of different countries, because exchange rates do change daily. With a single currency, distributors and retailers can say with some certainty what it will cost to store and move products, and what profit margins will be. Retail organisations will benefit from this not only because the cost of hedging against currency changes will be eliminated but also because it will be easier to plan the future more effectively alongside partners.

Translation costs will also be reduced considerably. However, this is small change compared with the changes in the market and some of the changes in the macro-economically driven retail marketing environment. Discount rates, for example, are likely to change significantly, changing the way that capital is raised. From a supply chain perspective, this foreign exchange risk *per se* is

▶

147

perhaps not as important as the changes that will occur in the market as a result of pricing transparency. The ability of retailers to compare prices without the volatility of exchange rates complicating the picture means that consumers will buy more widely and the competitive landscape will widen considerably. This is likely to have a massive impact in the supply chain and represents both an opportunity and a threat to retail organisations throughout Europe. Importantly, this issue does not change whether the UK goes into the EMU in the first wave or not. The competitive environment on the Continent will change anyway, and UK suppliers and customers need to get themselves into a better position to take advantage of it or protect themselves, as the case may be.

The trend towards outsourcing in the supply chain – where specialists in different processes (such as distribution) provide services – means that there are closer working relationships than ever before between suppliers, customers and contractors. Another trend is the changing role of suppliers in the supply chain process. Manufacturers, for example, expect component suppliers to deliver their products in the right numbers, in a convenient format, direct to the shop floor. Retailers are beginning to push responsibility for category management and replenishment up the supply chain to manufacturers. One effect of this is that most retailers are rationalising their supplier network, which simplifies and reduces costs in the supply chain. The changing role of suppliers moves the boundaries, making relationships simpler and easier to manage, and allowing people to focus on relationships instead of mechanics.

There is now a real need for tighter integration between retailers' supply chains, if retailers are to react swiftly and accurately to customer demand. It means that retailers, distributors and manufacturers increasingly need access to information held in partners' IT systems. The tool that enables this approach is called 'electronic commerce': a collection of technologies and processes that allows closer links, better information to customers, and relationship management. Using a web-style interface, a retailer can browse through partners' systems to check availability, make orders or even schedule deliveries.

The key benefit of this activity is to be able to align activity in the supply chain with customer orders and enquiries on a global or pan-European basis. Rather than just finding out whether suppliers can provide components, manufacturers can choose to buy components from the most cost-effective source – comparing the cost of raw materials, say, between sources in different countries. Of course, none of this can happen without the right IT foundations in place.

Questions for discussion

1 What do you consider to be the advantages of European Monetary Union (EMU) to UK retailers in terms of retail marketing operations in other European countries?

2 Discuss the implications of EMU for a UK-based retailer in terms of supply chain management.

REFERENCES

Bucklin, L.P.A. (1966) Theory of Distribution Channel Structure. Institute of Business and Economic Research, University of California, Berkeley.

Cooper, J., Brown, M. and Peters, M. (1993) *European Logistics: Markets, Management, and Strategy*. 2nd edn. Oxford: Blackwell.

Ellram, L.M. (1991) 'Supply chain management: the industrial organisation perspective', *International Journal of Physical Distribution and Logistics Management*, 21(1): 13–22.

Ellram, L.M. and Cooper, Martha C. (1990) 'Supply chain management, partnerships, and the shipper-third party relationship', *The International Journal of Logistics Management*, 1(2): 1–10.

Horscroft, Peter and Braithwaite, Alan (1990) 'Enhancing supply chain efficiency: the strategic lead time approach'. *The International Journal of Logistics Management*, 1(2): 47–52.

Kotler, P. (1991) *Marketing Management*. 7th edn. Hemel Hempsted: Prentice-Hall.

Lambert, D.M. and Stock, J.R. (1993) *Strategic Logistics Management*. 3rd edn. Boston: Irwin Homewood.

Larson, P.D. and Sijbrands, M.J. (1991) 'Quick response retailing in Canada and The Netherlands', *International Journal of Retail and Distribution Management*, 19(7): 10.

McGoldrick, P. (1990) *Retail Marketing*. London: McGraw-Hill.

Mercer, D. (1996) *Marketing*. 2nd edn. Oxford: Blackwell. pp. 289–302.

Moore, E.J. (1991) 'Grocery distribution in the UK', *International Journal of Retail and Distribution Management*, 19(7): 18.

Stern, Louis W. and El-Ansary, Adel (1982) *Marketing Channels*. 2nd edn. Englewood Cliffs, NJ: Prentice-Hall.

Sussams, J.E. (1991) 'The impact of logistics on retailing and physical distribution', *International Journal of Retail and Distribution Management*, 19(7): 4.

Whitley, R. and Cox, B. (1989) 'Logistics in Retailing', *Management Services*, (April): 6.

7

Store location and assessment of market potential

LEARNING OBJECTIVES

After reading this chapter you should be able to:

- understand how and on what basis the store location policy is developed;
- understand the importance of the location decision to the retailer's marketing strategy;
- analyse the spatial characteristics of sites within different locations;
- identify trade areas for an existing store and for a new store;
- explain the method of site selection and assessing market potential for retailers.

The importance of location in the retailer's overall marketing plan can hardly be overstated (Gist, 1968). Whether selling goods or services, perhaps the most important decision a retailer must take is to choose an outlet location. A number of considerations make this decision so critical. To a large extent, the location determines the type and number of people the store will attract. Good locations provide ready access to large numbers of target consumers and increase potential sales. In a highly competitive retail environment, even a slight difference in location can have a significant impact on market share and profitability. A poor location is a liability that is not easy to overcome. In the development of competitive strategies, retailers can match prices, extend and improve services, double sales, and imitate promotion, but an effective location strategy is difficult to assail or neutralise (Ghosh, 1994).

The decision to locate a store may arise in a large variety of situations. The retail organisation makes this decision every time a new lease is signed, and because it is locating the store with that signature, though the store may have been in the same place for many years. The firm which owns its own building locates the business every morning when the front door of the store is unlocked. Thus, the decision to select a location is made with great frequency, though it may be an unconscious decision, manifested merely by an unwillingness to move. The firm would normally analyse the location periodically with the same care as if it were locating a new store. Many grocery or variety chains monitor their location strategy every year to find potential gaps in the market saturation pattern, to change some units to better locations, or to eliminate poor locations. Some chains do this work themselves; others use consultants (Omar, 1992). The principles followed in reaching a decision to remain in a location are the same as those for selecting a new one, and they should be reapplied continually.

This chapter presents a careful analysis of the **store location** process, discussing the various aspects of the retailer's location decision and the types of analyses that must be performed in order to develop a coherent location strategy. The chapter also provides a systematic framework to follow in selecting specific sites in which to locate new outlets. Each step in the location decision-making process is discussed, with particular emphasis being placed on the types of information needed and their sources.

Location policy principles

The location policy is the outline for achieving the retailer's marketing objectives and expansion plans. It translates the retailer's marketing strategy into a concrete policy that is sensitive to the spatial pattern of demand and the availability of desirable sites, and targets the retailer's investments toward specific locations and market areas. The process of store location starts with the analysis of the retailer's marketing strategy and an understanding of the target market. The location decision, like other retail marketing mix decisions, must be consistent with the firm's overall strategy. Next, the firm must analyse the spatial aspects of different geographical market areas. The spatial analysis process starts with regional analysis, which is the identification of regional markets such as cities, towns and metropolitan areas in which to locate new stores (Berman and Evans, 1995). The retailer is concerned here with regional variations in demand for goods and services and with variations in the level of retail competition. The retailer compares regional demand and supply and then ranks regional areas according to their potential for supporting new outlets.

Both the population characteristics and the level of retail activity may vary considerably between areas within a city or town; area analysis focuses, therefore, on the immediate area surrounding potential sites. The demographic and socio-economic characteristics of the population surrounding each site must be carefully evaluated, since they will ultimately determine the sales potential of the site. The final step in this process is site evaluation, which focuses on the characteristics of the sites at which a new store may be located. The characteristics of each site are analysed with respect to traffic flow, accessibility and **compatibility.** A retailer who aims to be successful needs to formulate a strategy for store location. The steps leading to the development of site selection and store location policy are discussed in this chapter.

The store location decisions

Opening a new store is inherently risky, entailing significant monetary costs, including the rising costs of land and building construction. Since location decisions cannot be changed easily, the greatest risk in opening a new outlet is the possibility that it will never achieve its sales potential. The failure of a store at a new location can have a significant negative impact on the store's image. A retail chain that operates many outlets in the same area may feel the effects of the failure of any one store throughout the entire chain. Even for a firm that operates only a single store in an area, store closure or relocation can be quite damaging. A relocated store may lose many of its loyal customers to whom the new site is inconvenient, requiring the firm to rebuild its customer base at the new site (Simkin *et al.*, 1986). The long-term nature of the store location decision and the substantial financial investments it puts at risk compel the retailer to take great care in making the decision.

The location problem can be subdivided into two distinct tasks. The first task involves a general evaluation of the potential available in a competitive market. The question that must be asked is: 'Does the market contain enough potential profitably to support an addition to currently existing stores?'. The second task involves the specific delineation of the potential market in terms of the exact location for retailers. The question may be asked as: 'Given sufficient potential, where is the best location to serve the available potential?'. An additional problem is faced by retailers with several stores in the same general market area. A multiple store retailer must evaluate a specific site, based on both the site's potential volume and its place in a multiple store network (Markin, 1971). The development of a retail chain for the multiple store operation then involves the question of individual site profitability and optimum network expansion. Several methodological approaches, including marketing strategy and regional and area analytical approaches, could be employed and these are discussed in the following sections.

Marketing strategy approach

Since each type of store has a unique target market, each has its own location requirements. Home improvement centres, for example, rely on home owners for a major portion of their sales. Therefore, in selecting a location for this type of store, the managers must pay special attention to the number of home owners who will be attracted to the site. A supermarket, on the other hand, is more concerned with the general level of population in the area than with home owners in particular. Similarly, in selecting a site for a children's clothing store, the number of families with children requires careful attention, whereas multimedia speciality store must look at the number of teenagers and young families in the area, since these population groups patronise multimedia stores most frequently.

Stores selling similar types of merchandise may even have different location requirements, because their positions on the shopping opportunity line may differ. As discussed in other chapters, stores with different positions on the shopping opportunity line attract different types of customer. Thus, although both discount stores and speciality boutiques sell clothing, they attract very different consumer groups. This variation in target markets gives them differing location requirements; fashion-oriented clothing stores tend to locate in central business districts or regional shopping centres, whereas discount stores are often located in districts or regional shopping centres, or as free-standing units.

The location policies of service retailers also differ because of differences in their marketing strategies (Gist, 1968). The impact of marketing strategy on location policy can be seen especially clearly in the case of restaurants. High priced, up-market restaurants usually locate in high-income neighbourhoods. Family-oriented restaurants, on the other hand, tend to locate in middle-income suburbs where large numbers of families with children live. Even the ideal locations for fast-food restaurants vary: some that cater to lunchtime crowds seek locations near busy commercial areas. Other fast-food outlets serve travellers and locate near roads, airports, and tourist spots. Finally, yet another group of fast-food restaurants locates in communities where many families with children live. The specific population segment served by each type of fast-food restaurant dictates, to a large extent, its location policies. Since a firm's location policy must be consistent with its policies on price, promotion and merchandise, a change in the marketing strategy often necessitates a similar change in location policy too.

The location policy of a retail organisation is an integral part of its overall marketing strategy, and it must be consistent with the other elements of the retailer's marketing mix. The marketing strategy dictates the criteria by which the firm evaluates different market areas and selects the sites at which to locate new outlets.

Regional and area analysis

The retail potential or attractiveness of a region depends on the interplay between the demand for and supply of retail goods and services. To support a new outlet, an area must have adequate population and income to create sufficient demand (Davies, 1973). Moreover, the demographic and socio-economic characteristics of the population must be consistent with the firm's target market. However, higher levels of supply (that is, more existing stores) make regions less attractive for new stores. Many commercial firms also compile demographic and socio-economic information for different geographical markets from a variety of sources and make it available to retailers.

Measuring demand

Retail demand in an area can be measured in a number of ways. The number of people living in the region for example, provides a quick but approximate estimate of demand. More specifically, however, one should look at the total retail purchasing power in the region. This information is available from secondary sources. The

Office for National Statistics (ONS) compiles information on population size and composition for all geographical regions in the UK. Information on per capita expenditure is usually available from the published statistics.

The buying power of population

Total retail sales in an area are closely correlated with the **buying power** of the nearby population. The number of people employed, the number of households with use of a car, the total payrolls of retailers located in the community and the average wage, the regularity and frequency of payment of wages and salaries, social security payments to the elderly, and the amount of, and trend in, bank deposits are among the significant sources and indicators of consumer purchasing power. In fact, skilled retailers can frequently use these factors as the basis for a reasonably accurate estimate of the community's potential expenditures. The **buying power index** (BPI) measures the overall retail demand in an area expressed as a percentage of total demand in the UK. In essence, the BPI measures the market's ability to buy (Huff, 1983). The index is a weighted average of the area's population size, income, and total retail sales in the preceding year, computed as follows:

BPI = 0.5 × (percentage of total effective buying income)
+ 0.3 × (percentage of total retail sales)
+ 0.2 × (percentage of total population)

Note: **income is weighted 5; retail sales 3; and population 2**

Of the three factors, most importance is given to effective buying income (that is, an individual's income after taxes). The index gives least weight to population size, and the preceding year's retail sales have an intermediate weight. The weights are based on the perceived importance of each factor in predicting the total retail demand in an area.

Index of retail saturation

In the retail segment it is possible to calculate the amount of retail sales available in any geographical area with reasonable accuracy. It is also possible to quantify certain characteristics of retail facilities in any geographical area. These two factors can be combined to form an index of retail saturation (Rudelius *et al.*, 1972). This index could be defined as 'an index number providing a relative measure of retail store's saturation in any given trading area'. It may also be expressed as a functional relationship:

$$\text{IRS}_1 = \frac{C_1 \times \text{RE}_1}{\text{RF}_1}$$

Where: IRS_1 = Index of retail saturation for Area 1
C_1 = Number of consumers in Area 1
RE_1 = Retail expenditures per consumer in Area 1
RF_1 = Retail facilities in Area 1 (selling space)

Using the IRS to measure saturation in a groceries market

Consider the following case in analysing a supermarket's potential in Market A where there are 100 000 consumers who each spend an average of £5.50 per week on groceries in food stores. If there are 15 supermarkets serving Market A, with a total of 144 000 square feet of selling space, the IRS for Market A could be calculated as:

$$IRS_A = \frac{100\ 000 \times 5.50}{144\ 000} = \frac{550\ 000}{144\ 000} = £3.82$$

The £3.82 per square foot of selling space measured against the monetary value per square foot necessary to break even would provide the measure of saturation in Market A. The £3.82 figure would also be useful in evaluating relative opportunity in different market areas. The sales-per-square-foot calculation is a common measurement tool in supermarkets. However, the inputs into the system and the measurement of saturation would vary with the segment of the retail structure being analysed. In the case of hotels, in the service segment, for example, retail facility (RF) might be calculated by the number of available rooms during a given time period.

There are several problems of methodology that are immediately evident. The major factors among these problems are the operational definition of terms, and the delineation of the market area. Careful development of methodology should either eliminate or minimise the above problem areas. It should also be recognised that the index of retail saturation is a static type of analysis and its calculations have value for only one point in time (Omar, 1992).

The development of an index of retail saturation could have both practical and theoretical significance. The practical significance of the index stems from its usefulness as a decision-making guide for the location analyst. From a theoretical point of view, the index could be used to study the relationship between retail saturation and characteristics of retail operation and competition. The index of retail saturation provides valuable insights for retailers into the evaluation of available potential in any market. It provides a superior measurement to the simple analysis of **market potential**, since it would take into account both the demand side (potential) and the supply side (retail facilities) in evaluating a market.

After the construction of an index, retailers may still face the problem of specific site selection. Borrowing from the methodology developed by the clinical approach, distinctive store location types can be developed. A store location type can be defined as a distinctive classification of stores possessing certain measurable location characteristics. Such an approach and its complete methodology is beyond the scope of this book.

Market expansion potential (MEP)

The index of retail saturation gives an indication of demand and supply in an area, as determined by existing buying patterns and expenditures. The attractiveness of different market areas also depends on the scope for expanding the market the existing potential is a reflection on the marketing skills of retailers already located in the area. A low per-capita retail expenditure in the area may reflect the inability of existing retailers to satisfy consumers needs completely. Shoppers are likely to go elsewhere for their shopping if not satisfied. Retailers must consider an area's potential for creating new demand, its market potential, along with its index of retail saturation, to assess its attractiveness for locating new outlets.

Market classification schemes

Evaluation of the desirability of opening new stores requires consideration of both the index of retail saturation (IRS) and the market expansion potential (MEP) for an area (*see* Figure 7.1). IRS indicates existing conditions while MEP is more future oriented (Ingene and Lush, 1980). The most attractive markets (those with high ratings on both IRS and MEP), appear in the upper left-hand quadrant (1). The high IRS values indicate low saturation in the markets, so competition is not too intense. In addition, these markets have high expansion potentials; that is, their total demand can be increased. The markets in the lower right-hand quadrant (4), on the other hand, are low on both IRS and MEP, indicating highly competitive markets with little scope for expansion – which would discourage new stores from locating here. The attractiveness of markets in the other two quadrants depends on the entering firm's competitive strength. Markets in quadrant 2 have low levels of existing competition (high IRS), but lack growth potential (low MEP). The lack of growth potential reduces the attractiveness of these markets, despite the relatively mild competition. Markets in quadrant 3 have high growth potentials, but they also have high levels of existing competition (low IRS). This implies that the new entrant can gain sales only by aggressively taking them away from existing stores.

Fig.7.1 MARKET CLASSIFICATION SCHEME

	Market expansion potential (MEP)	
	High	Low
High Index of retail saturation (IRS)	1 Current competition is low High expansion potential	2 Current competition is low Low expansion potential
Low	3 Current competition is high High expansion potential	4 Current competition is high Low expansion potential

Site selection and evaluation

Site evaluation systematically examines the characteristics of each site to determine their feasibility as locations for new stores (*see* Figure 7.2). (On a practical note, to keep track of the large number and wide variety of factors that affect site evaluation, retailers generally develop a checklist such as that in Figure 7.2 to aid the evaluation process.) The essence of site evaluation is to find a 100 per cent location, that is, one with all the desirable characteristics of a good site. Unfortunately, finding a 100 per cent location may not be an easy task. The retailer must first determine what characteristics to look for, since desirable characteristics vary from one type of store to another: the 100 per cent location for a specialist clothing store may not be appropriate for a food store. It is necessary first to look at the procedures for selecting a site, then to evaluate the site.

Fig. 7.2 SITE EVALUATION CRITERIA CHECKLIST

Traffic flow and accessibility

- number and types of vehicles
- number and types of pedestrians
- access to major roads
- availability of mass transit
- quality of streets within the area

Retail structure

- number of competitors in area
- similarity of other stores
- proximity to business area
- collaborative retail promotion

Site characteristics

- available number of car parking spaces
- distance of store to car park
- visibility of site
- ease of entrance and exit
- public image of the area

Legal and cost factors

- type of zoning
- length of leasing
- local authority responsibility

Site selection procedure

Any firm that operates retail outlets must implement a well-thought-out location policy that is consistent with its overall marketing strategy. In addition to traditional retail firms such as department stores, discount outlets, speciality stores and supermarkets, location planning is important for such diverse organisations as banks, hospitals and medical clinics, restaurants and fast-food outlets, chemists, convenience outlets, cinemas and concert halls, and so on.

A much higher percentage of new locations are being given thorough analysis in the 1990s than ever before. There are two types of site selection procedures (Simkin *et al.*, 1986):

1 The retail organisation undertakes a scientific analysis of the market served and desired to be served, laying out a pattern of areas in which a store should be located or relocated by cataloguing all possible sites and preparing volume estimates for each to determine the best option.

2 The firm makes its interest in the new location known among estate agents and studies the proposals that are submitted in response. Volume estimate potentials are prepared on those locations which appear most desirable, for the purpose of selecting the best of those proposed.

The first technique is preferred from the standpoint of achieving maximum business volume and market saturation. The second has the advantage of leaving the retailer in a better negotiating or bargaining position, as the initiative then rests with the building owner or developer. The most successful of the chains use a combination of these procedures, in order to maximise volume and retain bargaining power at the same time. The need for relocation may come about for a variety of reasons: a store requires additional space which cannot be obtained at its current site, experience has proved that the existing location is inadequate, the rent is too high, the landlord will not renew the lease, the building is destroyed by fire – the list goes on (Simkin *et al.*, 1986). All of these come under the heading of changing location. New locations, on the other hand, involve retailers who are establishing a business for the first time or already own a store or chain of stores but wish to have an additional outlet.

Exhibit 7.1 | **New locations may be difficult to secure**

Finding a new site to locate in may be more difficult in practice than in theory. When Tesco tried to open a new 34 000 square foot store at Gerrards Cross in Buckinghamshire, local residents objected and it was never built. Tesco submitted its plan for the store to be built on a raft over the railway tracks at the station in the centre of the town. The residents' objections were that the store was too big, would generate unmanageable traffic in an already traffic-congested town, and it would ruin local businesses – and the planners upheld their views.

It is not only the retailer who locates; building owners are is also responsible for locating a store when they rent store space or sell a building. Much the same sort of site selection technique applies in selecting the kind of occupant who will be the best tenant and, at the same time, benefit other tenant stores. The landlord follows the same procedure when he or she renews the lease of an existing tenant. Developers, in choosing a site and then either selling buildings or selecting tenants, also use these techniques in order to maximise their own profit.

Accessibility of site to trading area

One of the main reasons for choosing a particular site is to secure maximum accessibility to a **trading area** and to have available as much of the business potential as possible. The choice may be positive, being an attempt to put a store in the way of as many people as possible; however, it may be negative, merely involving the choosing of a site which is not inaccessible. Accessibility must be measured in terms of the source of various types of business. First the potential from various sources must be isolated and then the possible capture estimated for each source.

Generative business is produced by the store itself through heavy advertising, and by a reputation for unique merchandise or merchandising style; it must be calculated for each segment of the trading area. Public knowledge that a large variety of merchandise is available in one spot is of itself generative. This is a basic factor in the generative power of a department store, which is really a bazaar of departments carrying clothing, jewellery, furniture, appliances and other goods. A store that generates all its own business will want to be in the most accessible location commensurate with cost. The dealer's showroom or discount house which generates 95 per cent of its business through advertising expenditure might find the most accessible location at the junction of two major streets or close to a motorway junction. A corner at such an intersection, however, is likely to be priced at several times that of an equivalent 'non-corner' piece of land nearby. The slight decline in accessibility of the off-corner location may be more than compensated for by lower costs. Business share is also secured by a store as a result of the generative power of its neighbours. This business is represented by customers who, although making purchases at the store, have as their main purpose a visit to a neighbouring store. A large part of Boots's business in London's Oxford Street, for instance, comes from this source.

Compatibility

In site selection, the principle of compatibility requires that there be no interruption in shopper traffic and that customer interchange be at a maximum. The rules of compatibility indicate that maximum business potential is available in a location where the compatibility principle operates. Some businesses are compatible, others are not. The measure of compatibility is the degree to which the two businesses interchange customers. The measure of their compatibility, therefore, lies in the answers to the questions: 'Does business A next door help business B, or does it harm business B, or does it apparently have no effect on business B?'. Sometimes the answer may be the single most important location factor in the success of a retail business. The experienced shopping centre developer takes compatibility carefully into account in planning the placement of stores, and the individual retailer should give it equal attention in selecting a location (Ghosh, 1994).

A high degree of compatibility exists between two businesses which, because of their proximity achieve more sales together than they would if separated. This high compatibility may come about because these businesses are complementary in nature or because, though competitive, they carry goods of different styles, lines and prices, thereby increasing total patronage through **cumulative attraction** in locations that have a trade area adequate to support two stores. It can be seen that high compatibility may have a significant and positive effect on overall **shopper attraction**.

Competition and site economics factors

The site selection and business volume projections should take into account the location, character, size and type of existing competitive units so that possible business losses due to these competitors are considered. There may also be vacant stores or sites which could be occupied in the future by competitors. The principle of minimising competitive threat should lead the retailer to select locations where there are few competitors.

The application of the principles of site economics involves analysis of the site in terms of the relationship between its cost and its productivity. The efficiency of the site, its size, shape, topography, and load-bearing qualities, adjacent amenities like street lighting, availability of utilities, condition of kerb and street, and other immediate off-site factors which affect its cost or desirability, must all be examined in detail. Also under this heading come the effectiveness and cost of any existing building which might be rented or purchased by the retailer. The retailer must study the size and efficiency of the building, the load-bearing quality of its floors, its modernity, the character of its store front, heating and air-conditioning facilities, attractiveness, cost of maintenance, and all other factors affecting building valuation. Also to be considered are such items as availability of labour and adequate advertising media.

Site evaluation

Although the specific factors firms look for in individual sites vary from one situation to another, there are some factors that must always be considered in site evaluation including: type of location and physical characteristics of site.

Type of location

It is possible to distinguish among four types of sites: sites located in the central **business districts** of urban areas; sites within planned shopping centres; free-standing sites located near one another along major traffic arteries; and free-standing sites located in relatively isolated places that are not a part of any store cluster. Business districts are usually unplanned store clusters found mainly in urban areas. Shopping centres, on the other hand, are a carefully planned, well-balanced mix of stores within a single complex; they are typically located in suburban areas.

Physical site characteristics

The physical characteristics of a site determine the type of structure that can be built there, the visibility for potential customers (*see* Figure 7.2), and the ease with which they can enter and exit. A vacant piece of flat land with good visibility and access is ideal. However, a vacant piece of land can be costly to develop. Alternatively, if an available site has an existing structure, a retailer must decide whether the existing structure can be modified or whether the entire structure or any part of it needs to be reconstructed. Whether a potential site is a vacant piece of land or a vacant store, its visibility is important. A store that has a small frontage at the end of a shopping centre or in a small side street is not as visible as one located on a major street or near the main entrance of a mall. Similarly, a site in a strip development that is set far back from the major road may not be easily seen by potential customers driving along the road. Although this can sometimes be remedied by constructing large, clearly visible signs, the danger of losing a significant amount of business remains.

Along with visibility, the position of the site is another important consideration. This is especially true for sites in strip developments. Generally a corner site at the intersection of two roads is better than one in the middle of a row of other shops. Many stores will pay higher rents to gain the easier access of corner sites. Corner sites also provide greater opportunity for window displays and separation of exits and entrances to the car park.

Another important physical characteristic of a site is the availability of car parking space. Most out-of-town shopping centres provide adequate free parking facilities. In central business districts (CBD), however, car parking can be a major problem. Although in many CBDs parking is provided by the local authority or through cooperative arrangements among retailers, it often falls short of need – often desperately so. In some cases, even when parking space is available, it tends to be costly. In order to make it easier to shop in the CBD, some stores (The Co-op, Somerfield and Kwik Save, for example) have arranged for free parking with proof of purchase. Despite these efforts, the lack of car parking can be a major deterrent to shopping in central business districts.

Trade area delineation

A method for estimating the geographical market for a city or a major regional shopping centre is a technique called retail trade area analysis. The term refers to studies that assess the relative drawing power of alternative retail locations. This task can be accomplished in a variety of ways. Shoppers may be polled and asked for their residence locations, driving times, frequency of shopping trips, and so on. Similarly, the addresses of credit customers with active accounts at an existing store may be plotted on a map to indicate the service area of a shopping centre or a proposed site for a similar type of retailer. Some of these techniques, which are frequently used by retailers, are discussed in this section. Since the size and the nature of a trade area determines a store's potential to generate revenues, delineating trade areas is an important part of location analysis. To define the geographical area from which the customers of the outlet come, researchers employ a technique known as customer spotting.

Customer spotting

The customer spotting method is used by retailers to help determine the spatial extent of a store's trade area. In using this method, a sample of the store's customers are interviewed to determine their geographical origin (street address), demographic characteristics and shopping habits. While customer spotting is simple, it must be done with considerable care if it is to provide accurate results. One important consideration is to ensure that a representative sample of shoppers is interviewed; that is, to ensure that all types of customers and not a particular group of shoppers are contacted (Ghosh, 1994). A number of important steps are necessary to ensure a representative sample. First, it is very important that the survey is spread over different days of the week and different times of the day. A survey that interviewed shoppers on weekdays only, for example, may miss important customer groups who shop at weekends; similarly, interviews should be conducted throughout the day.

It is better that an independent group rather than the store's regular employees conduct the interviews. Experience has shown that when asked to conduct such surveys in addition to their normal work, store employees have a tendency to neglect or ignore the survey when the shop is busy. This, however, may be the prime time for conducting interviews. Shopper interviews by store employees are typically conducted at the point-of-sale, when the customer is paying. An important drawback of this practice is that it slows down the checkout process and has the potential to alienate customers. The only way to overcome these problems is to employ trained, independent interviewers, although the cost of conducting the interviews may be high.

Survey of customer records

Although the most accurate customer spotting techniques are based on customer interviews, the customer origin map may be drawn based on addresses from customer cheques or in-store credit cards. Cheque and credit card information reduces the cost and time requirements of data collection, but such information should be used with some caution because the customer origin map may not accurately reflect the store's trade area if it totally ignores cash customers. This is especially true when an analyst draws customer origin maps based solely on the addresses of credit card customers who may be unrepresentative of the store's customer base as a whole. It is advisable, therefore, to sample credit card, check, and cash customers to assure adequate representation of all customer groups. The latest development has come about through the introduction of 'data mining software', which enables retailers to manipulate their customer databases through the use of loyalty cards.

Customer origin maps

Customer origin maps provide important information for retailers. They contribute in a number of ways to the development of various retail policies. Identification of useful trading areas for instance may lead to effective feasibility analyses and capital need determination. Such identification tasks include the following (Gist, 1968):

1 Determination of the critical mass of population likely to be customers of the proposed retail store.

2 The proportion of these people who are located in the area must be determined. If, for instance, 55 to 70 per cent of the store's customers live in that area, it is called a **primary trading area**. If 15 to 25 per cent of the customers are located in that area, it is called **secondary trading area**; and finally, the remaining proportion of the customers are located at the **fringe trading area**.

3 Determination of what proportion of the purchases of these people will take place in the store. This implies determining the effectiveness of competing stores in the trading area.

4 Determination of the demographic and socio-economic characteristics of the store's customers.

5 The key aspects of advertising activity must be decided upon.

6 Key location sites for a new store, a new branch, or an existing store that may be considering relocation must be examined.

7 An estimation of future growth or decline, and the number of stores the area can reasonably handle must be made.

Law of retail gravitation

Another technique used to assess where customers come from is the law of **retail gravitation**, sometimes called Reilly's law after its originator, William J. Reilly (1929). The law of retail gravitation, originally formulated in the 1920s, delineates the retail trade area of a potential site on the basis of mileage between alternative locations and relative populations (Rudelins *et al.*, 1972). The formula is as follows:

$$\text{Breaking point in miles from B} = \frac{\text{Miles between A and B}}{1 + \sqrt{\dfrac{\text{Population of A}}{\text{Population of B}}}}$$

Assume a retailer is considering locating a new outlet in either Town A or Town B, which are located 60 miles from each other. The population of Town A is 80 000; the population of Town B is 20 000. One of the questions that concerns the retailer is where the people who live in a small rural community located between the two towns, 25 miles from B, are likely to shop.

According to the law of retail gravitation, these rural shoppers would more likely shop in Town A, although it is 10 miles farther away than Town B. The retail trade area of A extends 40 miles toward B, and the target rural community is located only 35 miles away. The complete trade area for A or B could be calculated by similar calculations with other communities.

$$\text{Breaking point in miles from B} = \frac{60}{1 + \sqrt{\dfrac{80\,000}{20\,000}}}$$

$$= \frac{60}{1 + \sqrt{4}}$$

$$= \frac{60}{3}$$

$$= 20 \text{ miles}$$

The application of this technique is limited in an era of urban sprawl, regional shopping centres, and consumers who measure distances in terms of driving time. As a result, a more contemporary version of retail trade area analysis has been offered by David Huff (1983). Huff's work is an inter-urban model that assesses the likelihood that a consumer will patronise a specific shopping centre. The Huff model takes account of modern trends like shopping centres and the emphasis on travel time. The main outcome is that trading areas are expressed in terms of a series of probable relationships. The probability that a consumer will patronise a specific shopping centre is related to the size of the centre, travel time, and the type of merchandise the shopper is looking for.

With the trade area delineated, the retailer can analyse the demographic and socio-economic characteristics of its potential customers. Such analysis provides valuable guidelines for streamlining the store's merchandising and pricing policies and for responding more directly to customer needs. A supermarket chain with a number of outlets in an urban area, for example, may use trade area analysis to determine the ethnic composition of each store's customer base. It may then care-fully select the merchandise offered at individual outlets to meet the needs of their local customers, since differing ethnic groups may vary in their preferences for par-ticular grocery items. The next section discusses how retailers may measure their sales value and the buying power of their potential customers.

Market assessment and sales forecasting

The final decision whether or not to open a new outlet depends, to a large extent, on market assessment results and the level of sales that the store can expect to generate at a site. Similarly, when faced with a choice among a number of alternative sites for opening a new store, a retailer will choose the site with the highest market and sales potential. These criteria make accurate market assessment and sales forecasts essential for the efficient and successful selection of new sites. This section examines market potential in terms of market opportunity for a new outlet, and the quality of competing stores already in a location. It then reviews briefly the key sales forecasting methods.

Market opportunities for new outlets

Determining the adequate number of retail organisations in a given area can effectively indicate whether or not there is room for the proposed retail organisation. The commercial structure model for an area is determined by a series of three equations. In the first equation, the total expenditure for current consumption by residents of the area is determined:

$$T = (d)(E)(e)(f)$$

where T = expenditures in retail and service stores in the market area
       d = percentage allocation of expenditures for current consumption (E) by type of store
       e = shopping pattern ratio
       f = trade flow ratio

The second equation allocates the total expenditures for current consumption on the basis of the data on shopping behaviour (Markin, 1971). It therefore, facilitates the calculation of estimated annual expenditures in retail and service facilities in the market area.

$$S = \frac{T}{gh}$$

where S = recommended number of establishments for each line of retail and service trade
       g = pound or (dollar) sales per square foot for each line of trade
       h = recommended average establishment size in square feet for each line of trade

The recommended number of stores for each line of product and service trade is then determined by the following equation:

$$E = (C)(I)(a)(b)$$

where E = expenditures for current consumption
       C = consumption units (families and unrelated individuals)
       I = median family income (before taxes)
       a = tax ratio
       b = expenditures ratio

These three equations combine to provide information about existing opportunities – or lack of them in any given area.

Quality of the competition

The quality of the competition must be delineated so that the proposed retail organisation can determine its opportunities fully (Omar, 1992). The evaluation process can be achieved through consumer surveys and observation of existing stores. Consumer surveys indicate where people shop and intend to shop. If consumers appear to be very loyal to existing competing stores and if the competition appears to be strong, then the proposed store may not find the existing opportunities very enticing. The same observations are true for an existing store.

Systematic observation of established stores can reveal valuable information about the existing competition. In this context, observation may be divided into internal and external observation. Internal observation may include noting factors such as size of the store, internal layout, merchandise depth and breadth, prices, quality, customer in-store movements, and many other important bits of information that can add up into a rounded picture of a stores activity.

Sales forecasting for new outlets

Although market potential analyses approximate the possible sales volume of a retail organisation, they do not give specific sales volume estimates. Thus, the final step in market potential and feasibility analysis is the estimate of sales potential. Two common methods for forecasting sales of retail outlets are the analogue method and the regression analysis. These two methods are briefly discussed here.

Each method estimates a trade area and the sales it will generate, using a different technique. The discussion of these methods simply highlights when their application is appropriate.

Analogue method

Popularised in 1966 by William Applebaum, the analogue method was one of the first systematic procedures put forward to forecast retail sales. To forecast sales for a new store, the analogue method studies a similar store that is already in operation as an 'analogue'. The analyst determines the analogue store's trade area and market penetration by customer spotting. The sales pattern of the analogue store then serves as the basis for forecasting the sales of a new outlet.

The most important step in implementing the analogue procedure is to identify an analogue store that closely resembles the proposed new store. The analogue store should be similar in terms of size, store services, pricing and merchandising policies, the level of competition, and site characteristics. The ideal analogue is an existing outlet operated by the same chain. After identifying the analogue store, customer spotting reveals the geographical pattern of its customer base. Next, concentric circles of different radii drawn on the customer origin map determine the analogue store's trade area. Based on the information from customer spotting analysis, the firm calculates the drawing power of the analogue store and its per capita sales from each distance zone.

The pattern of per-capita sales achieved by the analogue store is the key to forecasting the sales for the new store. This forecast assumes that the new store will

MINI-CASE

Ogenmar's store

Consider the case of Ogenmar's store, a single, independent store located in a residential area of a major city. Three concentric areas – A, B and C – indicate walking distances of 1 minute, 1.5 to 3 minutes, and 3 to 4.5 minutes respectively from the shop. Area A represents 2 per cent of our census area, whereas B and C each represent 4 per cent. Assume that a survey was conducted to determine to what extent the residents bought groceries at Ogenmar's store and the results were as shown in Table A. It becomes clear that Ogenmar's store is dealing with a £382 955 market potential. A fraction of the population was purchasing all of their groceries at Ogenmar's store (*see* Table B).

Table A
INFORMATION ABOUT AREAS A, B, AND Cª

Areas	Estimated no. of families	Average income (£)	Proportion spent of food (%)	Total purchases (£)
A	50	£25 000	23.0	287 500
B	40	20 000	27.0	216 000
C	110	15 000	30.0	495 000

ª Hypothetical data. Similar data could be abstracted from *Census Tract* data and *Labour Statistics* of consumer spending data.

Table B
PROPORTION OF GROCERIES BOUGHT AT OGENMAR'S STORE

Proportional groceries purchased	Area A (%)	Area B (%)	Area C (%)
All (100%)	20	13	00
Part (50%)	55	40	40
A fraction (25%)	27	20	40
None (0%)	00	27	20
Total	100	100	100

If Ogenmar's store was to go on sale, major food chains would not consider it because of its potential. However, a 7–Eleven type of convenience grocery store might find it very attractive.

If a prospective grocery store was to consider locating near Ogenmar's store, there would be £615 545 worth of market potential not tapped by Ogenmar. If the new proposed store could capture a large proportion of this part of the market, it would then be quite attractive for a competing convenience grocery chain. However, there would still be insufficient reason for a major supermarket to consider buying Ogenmar's store.

have a sales pattern similar to that of the analogue store. This crucial assumption requires that the analogue store closely resembles the store that is to be opened. Unless the stores are very similar it would not be reasonable to assume that the patterns of their trade areas would be similar.

The analogue procedure has a major advantage in that it is easy to implement and reflects actual shopping patterns. It depends partly 'on quantified experience and partly on subjective judgement'. Considerable judgement is required in selecting the analogue store, and even then the forecast may need adjustment to take account of differences between the analogue store and the new outlet. The new store may, for example, have more aggressive competitors and so may not achieve the same market penetration as the analogue store.

The analyst can overcome this drawback by using more than one analogue store. Instead of relying on only one store as the analogue, the analyst may obtain patronage patterns from a number of similar stores. After making an initial series of forecasts based on the data for each analogue store, these separate forecasts are then averaged to estimate the sales at the new site. Although averaging figures for a number of analogue stores increases the cost of implementing the procedure, it reduces the possibility of error in the sales forecast due to the idiosyncrasies of a single store.

Regression analysis

Retail chains that operate many stores can apply the sales experience of all the existing outlets, instead of a single analogue store, to forecast sales at a new location through regression analysis. Regression analysis allows the retailer systematically to incorporate information from a number of existing stores in sales forecasts for new sites. Regression methods quantify the relationship between sales at different stores and the trade area, and store and site characteristics of the respective outlets. From this relationship, the retailer can calculate the expected sales at a new site. Since regression forecasting models require information from a large number of existing stores (at least thirty to forty stores), they are mainly used by retail chains that operate many outlets. Regression forecasting systems are based on two major assumptions: they assume that the sales a store generates depend on the characteristics of the store, its site, and its trade area; and the relative impact of each of these factors on sales can be measured by a statistical procedure called regression analysis.

The regression model

To implement a regression procedure, one must first select a list of store, site, and trade area characteristics that may affect store sales. Since these characteristics explain the variation in sales among different stores, they are called explanatory variables. Store performance, on the other hand, is a dependent variable since its value depends on those of the explanatory variables. In general, regression sales forecasting models have the following form:

$$Sales = b_0 + b_1 + b_2X_2 + ... + b_nX_n$$

where: b_0 = the intercept term
$X_1, X_2 ... X_n$ = explanatory variables
$b_1, b_2 ... b_n$ = regression coefficients that measure the impact of each of the explanatory variables on sales

The **regression model** develops a quantitative relationship between the explanatory variables, and the dependent variables: sales. The impact of each explanatory variable (the Xs) on sales is measured by the regression coefficient (the b value) associated with that variable. Larger numerical values of the coefficients indicate stronger impact on sales. The sign of the coefficient is important, too. A negative sign implies that a variable is inversely related to sales: as the value of the explanatory variable increases, sales drop. A positive coefficient, on the other hand, implies that sales increase as the value of the coefficient gets larger. The explanatory variables included in a particular model depend on the type of retail store, but they must always include the store, site, and trade area characteristics discussed earlier in this chapter.

Finally, market potential assessment and sales forecasting are important steps in developing store location strategy and selecting sites for new outlets. The trade area is the geographical area from which the store draws its customers. The nature and size of the trade area determine, to a large extent, the size and composition of the store's customer base. Since the sales of a store depend to a large extent on its location, the firm must compare expected sales at a number of alternative sites prior to making a final site selection decision.

SUMMARY

The location policy is one of the key elements for achieving the firm's marketing objectives and expression plans. It has to be sensitive to the spatial pattern of demand and the availability of desirable sites, and target the firm's investment towards specific locations and market areas. Developing a location policy involves analysis of retail marketing strategy, regional and area analysis, and site evaluation. Like all retail marketing policies, the location decision must be consistent with the firm's overall corporate goals and marketing strategy. The firm's marketing strategy and the target market it intends to serve strongly influence its location policy. Since each store has a unique target market, each has its own location requirements. It must be emphasised that even stores selling similar types of merchandise may have different location requirements, because their positions in the shopping opportunity lines may differ. A firm's location policy must also be consistent with its policies on price, promotion and merchandise. A change in the overall marketing strategy, therefore, often requires a change in location policy.

Regional analysis involves the selection of geographical market at the level of county, city, town or metropolitan area in which to locate the store. The key to regional analysis is to assess the retail potential in the region by comparing supply and demand. A number of sources provide data to measure demand and supply, and, based on these data, the retailer can calculate the index of retail saturation and the market expansion potential of an area. These indices together indicate the attractiveness of locating a new store in a particular area.

Site selection involves evaluating the traffic history, and parking facility aspects of the site. Assessing market potentials begins with studying the levels of business activity. Next, the commercial structure is analysed. Identification and evaluation of the quality of competition are the next steps. Customer analysis is performed to determine market potentials. A sales potential estimate is the last step in the overall market potential and feasibility analyses. It is necessary to reduce the analysis to the point where the retailer's sales volume can be estimated. This chapter presents a specific model to accomplish this task. Different techniques are available to determine the expected sales volume of the proposed store. Perhaps it is necessary to use more than one technique and to establish a range rather than a single figure upon which a decision will rest.

KEY TERMS

business district	fringe trading area	secondary trading area
buying power	generative business	shopper attraction
buying power index	market potential	store location
compatibility	primary trading area	trading area
consumption unit	regression model	
cumulative attraction	retail gravitation	

ASSIGNMENT

Spanish fashion designer Adolf Dominguez is to open two new stores in London, and he is looking at various sites in London and surrounding areas. Although Señor Dominguez has owned a store in London's South Molton Street for nearly ten years, he is still confused about which areas in London to consider as possible new sites and the criteria to use in making selection decisions.

Task

You are required to advise Adolf Dominguez with respect to site selection procedures, giving reasons for your suggestions.

REVISION QUESTIONS

1 Why is the location decision so critical for retailers and on what basis is a location decision made?

2 Using examples of some local retailers, explain how a firm's overall retail marketing strategy affects its location decisions.

3 Explain how retailers can measure retail demand in a given local area. What other factors besides demand must be considered in assessing and measuring the desirability of an area for the opening of a new store?

4 Explain, with examples, the term 'store compatibility'.

5 Explain how the market expansion potential and the index of retail saturation help to develop a market classification scheme for evaluating areas for expansion.

6   The law of retail gravitation, sometimes called Reilly's law, delineates the trade area potential site on the basis of mileage between alternative locations and relative population groups. Explain, with examples, the usefulness of this law to retailers seeking to locate a new store.

7   Briefly discuss two methods for delineating a store's trade area.

8   What steps are involved in using analogue methods for forecasting sales for a new store?

9   What steps are involved in using the regression model to forecast sales of a new store outlet?

10 Once a site is selected, it is still necessary to identify the prospective store's market and determine its potential. Why?

CASE STUDY

Store location problem for Tesco at Clapham Common, South London

Supermarket giants are desperate to build stores in the south-east of England, especially in London. In many cases, however, they are locked in battle with residents who claim superstores are unwanted because they kill off local trade and create pollution. This case study reports on the clash between the residents of Clapham Common, South London, and Tesco, who wanted to locate a supermarket in their local area. Clapham Common, according to a detailed survey by upmarket agents Savills, is emerging as a 'prime' London location for superstores – even ahead of Islington. However, residents fear that their peaceful neighbourhood will be destroyed by a Tesco supermarket which is proposed for the site of the former South London Hospital for Women.

A spokesperson for the residents says that she was told by a senior planning officer that Tesco offered the council £2 million worth of 'sweeteners' in the form of housing units, a library and a tree replacement scheme. It was alleged that, in return, the local planners are prepared to side with the supermarket against the residents. The outrage is fuelled by the fact that in the Local Plan – approved by Lambeth Council, the local authority within which Clapham Common falls – the site is designated for: 'mixed needs; health and social facilities; housing, including special needs; some frontage shopping' etc. The Plan also states that the council wants to see supermarkets located 'within or adjacent to established shopping centres'. The proposed site is in a Conservation Area, surrounded by terraced houses in Englewood Road, Hazelbourne Road and Anchor Mews. It is opposite Clapham Common, across the A24, which is a red route trunk road.

The old hospital was built in 1916 and closed in 1984. In 1986 planning permission was granted for housing, but it was never taken up. In 1992, the Minnie Kidd Nursing Home was built. The council's own planning brief for the site describes it as being within a 'predominantly residential area'. The brief is mostly about housing and the encouragement of 'health and social uses'. As for shopping, it could not be clearer; the site is not considered suitable for a large retail development. In view of all these firm statements to the contrary, the residents'

▶

disapproval when they discovered that local planning officers were recommending approval for a Tesco supermarket with 157 parking spaces, in addition to 112 flats in a nine-storey tower and a library, is unsurprising. Tesco tried to minimise local worries by describing the new supermarket as a 'Metro', one of the compact, upmarket stores they had pioneered in inner city locations. But the residents do not seem to be taken in. Tesco has commissioned reports showing the new store would have little impact in terms of traffic, noise and pollution. On the basis of experience at other stores, the residents simply did not believe them. Some homes in Anchor Mews are only a wooden fence away from the proposed development site.

Tesco is desperate for the site, having lost another Clapham Common site to Sainsbury, which had also recently enlarged its Balham store. Faced with an officers' recommendation to approve the Tesco plan, it was up to the eight-strong planning committee to decide. The three Labour members voted against it, as did one of the three Liberal Democrats. One of the two Conservatives the committee chairman, voted in favour. But to the delight and relief of the residents, his colleague abstained; he later explained that he will not be told how to vote by Conservative Central Office. The plan was defeated but Tesco are to appeal. Those who support the plan said the scheme would be of benefit to local residents – produce jobs, especially part-time jobs for women, and reduce traffic not increase it. They said they feared the council would lose the appeal and be made to pay heavy costs. Tesco says the scheme is an opportunity to replace a derelict site with a flagship development. They say the nine-storey tower was put in because Lambeth requested a landmark feature. Although Tesco has appealed against the decision, it has also put in a second application for a slightly smaller store but one which is still totally unacceptable to locals.

Source: Evening Standard – Home & Property, 8 October 1997

Questions for discussion

1 Discuss why, in your opinion, the residents are opposed to the Tesco plan despite Tesco's aim of developing an area it claims to be a derelict site.

2 What would you consider to be the major attraction of this location to Tesco?

REFERENCES

Berman, B. and Evans, J.B. (1995) *Retail Management.* New York: Macmillan.

Davies, R.L. (1973) 'Evaluation of retail store attributes and sales performances', *European Journal of Marketing,* 7(2): 89–102.

Ghosh, A. (1994) *Retail Management.* New York: The Dryden Press.

Gist, R. (1968) *Retailing Concepts and Decisions.* New York: John Wiley.

Huff, D.L. (1983) 'A probabilistic analysis of shopping trade areas, *Land Economics,* 39: 81–90.

Ingene, C.A., and Lusch, R.F. (1980) 'Market selection decisions for department stores', *Journal of Retailing,* (Autumn): 23–30.

Markin, R.J. (1971) *Retailing Management.* 2nd edn. New York: Macmillan.

Omar, O.E. (1992) 'Grocery shopping behaviour and retailers' own-label food brands', PhD. thesis, The Manchester Metropolitan University, UK.

Reilly, W.J. (1929) *The Law of Retail Gravitation.* New York: Pilsbury.

Rudelius, W., Hoel, R.F. and Kerin, R. (1972) 'Assessing retail opportunities in low-income areas', *Journal of Retailing,* (Autumn) 99–108.

Simkin, L.P., Doyle, P. and Saunders, J. (1986) 'Store Location Assessment', *Property Management,* 4(4): 333–43.

8

Product selection, buying and merchandising management

LEARNING OBJECTIVES

After reading this chapter you should be able to:

■ understand how a retailer's merchandise decisions are related to its retail marketing and financial objectives;

■ describe the criteria for selection and explain how merchandise suppliers are selected;

■ understand the buying functions and the buyer-related aspects of merchandise acquisition;

■ recognise how retailers use merchandise lists to plan assortments (merchandise mix planning);

■ understand the importance of inventory level planning and the stock control process.

The essence of retailing is **merchandising**; although this statement may over-simplify the challenges of retail marketing, it does point to the central role of merchandising in retail stores. The merchandise (the mix of products a store offers for sale) is at the heart of the retail operation. Central to the store's success is the merchandise selection that matches the tastes, preferences and expectations of its target customers (Ghosh, 1994).

Merchandise decisions affect all aspects of retail operations. They affect the amount of funds the firm will have to invest to maintain merchandise inventory, along with the amount of space, labour and equipment it will require for stock and display. The sales and profits generated by a store also depend on the merchandise. The merchandise selection determines the types of customers the store is able to attract. Of all the factors that influence a customer's decision to shop at a particular store, none is individually more important than the selection of merchandise offered. The quality, price and selectivity of merchandise strongly influences customers' perceptions of a store's image (McGoldrick, 1990). The firm must fully integrate merchandising decisions with its overall marketing strategy and with the elements of the retail marketing mix, as stated in Chapter 1.

This chapter discusses merchandise selection, **supplier selection**, and the **buying function** as they relate to merchandise mix management. The discussion is wide ranging, covering planning for buying as well as overall **merchandise planning** for depth, width, breadth and **merchandise consistency** in the overall stocks of the retail establishment. The control function which, as discussed here and elsewhere in this book, implies feedback and corrective action regarding the **merchandise mix** is also examined.

Merchandise selection

The objective of **merchandising strategy** is to select the right mix of products or services to sell at the store. To develop the merchandise selection, the retailer must meet the four merchandise objectives identified in Figure 8.1. As indicated in the Figure, to be 'right' the merchandise selection must be consistent with the firm's retail marketing strategy and its financial objectives.

Merchandise consistency with retail marketing strategy

The store's merchandise is its primary means of satisfying customer needs. A key element of a successful retail marketing is, therefore, a merchandise mix that satisfies the tastes and preferences of the target market while being consistent with the store's position in the market. A merchandise selection that ideally suits one retailer will not necessarily be appropriate for another retailer that follows a different retail marketing strategy (Samli, 1989).

A retailer's product and supplier selection must reflect its retail marketing strategy. This is well illustrated by examining the merchandise selection of razors for women in New Zealand.

Fig. 8.1 MERCHANDISE PLANNING FRAMEWORK

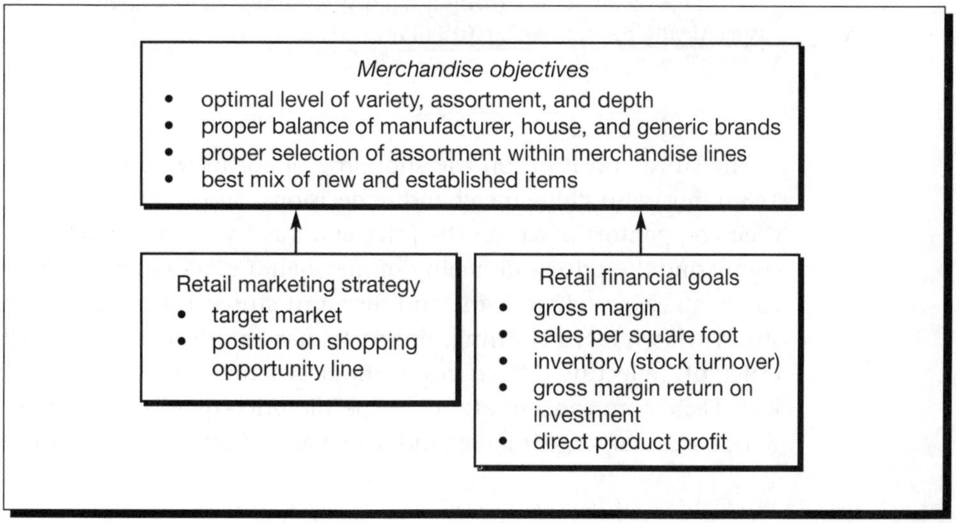

Merchandise objectives
- optimal level of variety, assortment, and depth
- proper balance of manufacturer, house, and generic brands
- proper selection of assortment within merchandise lines
- best mix of new and established items

Retail marketing strategy
- target market
- position on shopping opportunity line

Retail financial goals
- gross margin
- sales per square foot
- inventory (stock turnover)
- gross margin return on investment
- direct product profit

Exhibit 8.1

In order to appeal to their target markets, American-based stores such as Magnin, Neiman-Marcus, and Brooks Brothers, carry 'fashion-forward merchandise' that reflect the latest styles and trends within their market segments. In contrast, stores such as Sears and K mart tend to follow the market trends in fashion rather than lead. Cut-price clothing stores, on the other hand, often rely on bankrupt stock, and late-season merchandise to maintain their low prices.

MINI-CASE ## Women's razors in New Zealand

For many years the New Zealand's 1.6 million female population have shaved their underarms and legs, but the subject was considered a private and delicate matter. Until 1989 none of the retailers and shaving supplies companies actively promoted shaving equipment (razors) for use by women. It was simply assumed that women used their husbands' razors. A private survey surprised Wilkinson Sword by revealing that over 60 per cent of New Zealand's women bought blades for themselves rather than using those of their husband. The survey also disclosed that 80 per cent of those women who shaved used the wet shaving method; 13 per cent used creams and depilatory techniques; and the remaining 7 per cent used electric shavers.

Based on these results, Wilkinson Sword decided to market a ladies razor – the only company to consider it worthwhile. The marketing required a change of colour and packaging so that the product was more attractive to females, and active promotion aimed at women using television and in-store displays. A special Mother's Day promotion and sponsorship of women's sporting events also took place. As women's use of razors is different from that of men (women use razors in the bath or shower, and their hair is longer and finer), new features designed to cater for these differences were incorporated. Since then many retailers have stocked razors for women and many suppliers have entered this market. The overall image of razors for women is an up-market, more expensive product designed specifically for women's particular needs.

The store's position on the shopping opportunity line (Ettenson and Wagner, 1986) must also guide merchandise decisions. Stores differentiate themselves from their competitors based on the price and quality of the merchandise they carry, as comparing the price and quality of merchandise offered by traditional department stores, mass merchandisers, and discount stores makes clear. While all of these stores sell women's clothing, the particular brands and styles each sells are quite different, reflecting differences in the needs and expectations of their target markets. Each store concentrates on a specific price–quality range that suits the needs of its particular target market and which also differentiates it from others.

| Exhibit 8.2 | **The impact of marketing strategy on merchandise selection** |

Department stores, discount stores, chemists and supermarkets all sell after-shave lotions and colognes. Each type of store, however, typically sells quite different brands. Supermarkets usually sell a limited number of low-priced brands such as Brut 33, Mennen, and Old Spice. Chemists, discount stores, and mass merchandise outlets also sell Old Spice. These stores also carry British Sterling, English Leather, Aqua Velva, and Brut (higher-priced than Brut 33) – all of which cost more than the supermarket brands. Department stores carry a more exclusive array of brands, many of them associated with well-known designer names such as Ralph Lauren, Pierre Cardin, Armani and so on. These products cost significantly more than the brands sold by the other types of store.

A store's merchandise reflects its retail marketing strategy and the merchandise selection has a profound influence on how consumers perceive the store's image. As is shown in Exhibit 8.2, certain types of retail outlet carry particular categories of a specific type of merchanidise – such as aftershave – and customers will look for the items they want in the appropriate stores, that is in the shops in which they expect to find them. The retailer must, therefore, take great care in its **product selection** to meet the expectations of its target market and to create the image for which it aims.

Merchandise consistency with financial objectives

A store must also keep its merchandising decisions consistent with its financial objectives; after all, it is the sale of merchandise that creates the potential for profit. Merchandise decisions affect many aspects of the store's financial performance, including its sales and margins. The size of the merchandise selection determines the amount of funds the firm will have to invest in maintaining inventory and the amount of space, labour and equipment it will need for stock and display. The store's profitability depends, to a large extent, on its merchandising policies.

Retailers use a number of different measures to monitor merchandise performance, three of the most common are shown in Figure 8.1. The first, **gross margin,** shows the difference between the retail value of the merchandise and the cost of goods. Higher margins mean that more money is available to cover expenses and generate profits. Maintaining a healthy gross profit is a prime objective of merchandise managers. The second common measure for judging merchandise performance is sales per square foot. Few retailers have enough space to stock all the items they would like to (*see* Berman and Evans, 1995) so they must use the available space productively. Sales per square foot indicate the relationship of sales to the amount of space used to stock and display the merchandise. The higher the sales per square foot figure, the more productive use of available space is.

The third measure, inventory or **stock turnover,** measures how quickly the merchandise sells. Turnover shows the relationship between the amount of merchandise the store sells (net sales) and the amount it keeps in inventory (retail value of average inventory). Higher turnover indicates a higher level of sales compared to the amount of money invested in inventory. The following expression is one way to measure merchandise turnover:

$$\text{Turnover} = \frac{\text{Net sales}}{\text{Retail value of average inventory}}$$

Retailers must continuously monitor merchandise sales and inventory in order to improve their financial performance. To do this, they should calculate two figures based on sales, margin, turnover, and cost information, called **gross margin return on investment (GMROI)** and the direct product profit (DPP), for each item in the merchandise mix. GMROI measures the gross margins each item produces by dividing the gross margin by the **cost of average inventory:**

$$\text{GMROI} = \frac{\text{Gross margin}}{\text{Cost of average inventory}}$$

A retailer may set GMROI targets for the entire store and for different merchandise classifications. From these guidelines, they formulate merchandise plans and evaluate the performance of merchandise items. The DPP measures the net income an item generates after accounting for all direct costs. The retailer should evaluate the profit on each item separately based on these criteria in order to identify products that are performing badly, to eliminate them from the merchandise mix, and to exploit opportunities for improving the profit of remaining items to the fullest.

Product selection

A retailer cannot operate without having at least some idea of what will be needed to serve customer demand during the forthcoming period (Nilsson and Host, 1987). Retailers normally prepare their merchandise plan based on the past experience and current market information regarding the items customers want and what products suppliers will have available. However, customer preferences change and new products appear on the market at various times, stimulating **merchandise purchase** in response to demand. All buying plans must, therefore, be considered as tentative and subject to constant review. **Product selection** is not an exact science; however, care and continuous attention to up-to-date retail information reduce its risks.

Breadth of selection

The store must decide not only on how many and what classifications of goods will be carried, but also on how wide a selection will be carried within each classification, that is, the **breadth of selection** (*see* Exhibit 8.3).

Exhibit 8.3

Breadth of merchandise selection

A recorded music store, for instance, must decide whether to sell compact discs (CD), tapes and/or sell records or whether to concentrate on popular and country titles, or also to have operatic and classical albums and sets. The shop may also have to decide on how extensive a range of titles, artists and price lines it should offer within each category. A wide selection permits a closer match with the individual preferences of a greater number of potential customers. It has been noted that many customers seem to like to shop in stores such as EMI, HMV and Virgin which offer great width and depth of choice.

Nevertheless offering additional titles, as is suggested in Exhibit 8.3 involves disadvantages and costs that must be balanced against the attractiveness of carrying a large selection. Each new item that is added requires some additional display and storage space. Since the available space is usually limited, and additional space even if obtainable is usually costly, the extra items will reduce the space that can be devoted to the basic items in the assortment. Every additional item will also use funds that could be invested in a deeper stock of the core products. Adding too many marginal items is likely to lead to the retailer carrying an inadequate supply of the basic, most-desired products, due to pressure on space for stock or, more importantly, pressure on financial resources. This increases the danger of being out-of-stock when customers want to purchase those products. Furthermore, the marginal items normally sell more slowly than the basic ones, yet still require a substantial inventory. Consequently, a wide selection usually results in a slower stock turnover rate than an **assortment** that is concentrated on the most popular items. That is why many discount store operators try to plan assortments that are 'strong on the best [sellers] and forget the rest' (Nilsson and Host, 1987). Of course, each **buyer** must make decisions in terms of the particular items involved (for example, most customers do not particularly desire a choice of brands when buying shoelaces, although they may feel very differently about toothpaste or hairspray), store policies, price levels, competition (a store selling at relatively high prices in a market with many competitors will generally have to provide wider selections than a store with low prices or a monopoly location), and most important of all, customer desires.

Balanced assortment

The buyer will often want to include items in the assortment to serve a variety of merchandising objectives. Some very new styles or innovative items and some luxurious or prestigious merchandise may be added to improve the department's image. The store may expect to sell only very limited amounts of these items and will not invest in a large supply. But such merchandise will help give the whole department a reputation for leadership in introducing the best products. It may be obvious that 'high style products' may make up only a small percentage of a retailer's sales, but shrewd management knows these products are very important because they bring customers into the store. Similarly, decisions will have to be made about the ratio of own-label brand to national brands (*see* Chapter 9), and the extent to which the buyer wants to emphasise the most profitable lines.

Supplier selection

Success in merchandising depends on the buyer's ability to identify potential sources of supply, evaluate alternative suppliers, and negotiate purchase agreements with them (Shipley, 1985). This section of the chapter discusses supplier selection, with the following section looking at and the process of negotiation between buyers and suppliers.

Evaluating sources of supply

There are many potential sources of supply for most retailers. Some manufacture the products themselves, and others are wholesalers and distributors which represent producers. Many retailers concentrate supply policy, buying specific core products from a few, established suppliers, although some buy from many suppliers based on the best opportunity at any given time (Shipley, 1985).

Concentration of purchases with a few suppliers has a number of advantages; it fosters a long term cooperative relationship between a retailer and its suppliers. Such cooperation can lead to a more active retailer–supplier interaction in the design of new products and improve retail marketing activity. Furthermore, suppliers are likely to favour their established customers in distributing a limited supply of popular items. Concentration of suppliers can also lead to cost savings due to **quantity discounts** and better inventory management. Whether a firm decides to deal with a few or many suppliers, it must carefully research the strengths and weakness of all prospective suppliers before selection takes place. The selection of suppliers by the retailer must, therefore, take several important factors into consideration as indicated in Table 8.1.

Table 8.1
SUPPLIER SELECTION FACTORS

Factor	Relevance
Reputation of supplier	Department stores and mass merchandisers consider a supplier's reputation to be the most important criterion in supplier selection.
Brand names	The suitability of a supply source depends on whether its merchandise is appropriate for the store's target customers.
Brand images	The image of the brand must be consistent with the store's merchandise strategy.
Price and payment terms	Wholesale prices can vary, even for similar products. Price list, quantity discount schedules, and payment terms of different suppliers must be carefully compared.
Supplier reliability	Buyers attach crucial importance to a supplier's service standards. Suppliers must deliver at the right time and in the agreed quantity.
Support provision	Retailers prefer suppliers that provide promotional assistance, such as cooperative advertising, point-of-purchase displays and product demonstrations.

Matrix approach to supplier selection

Although buyers typically select suppliers by subjectively evaluating alternative sources of supply based on the criteria listed in Table 8.1, they can employ a more systematic procedure for supplier selection called the decision matrix approach (*see* Table 8.2).

Table 8.2
DECISION MATRIX FOR SUPPLIER SELECTION

| Basis for evaluation | Weight | Supplier | | | |
		A	B	C	D
Reputation	4	7	5	6	3
Cooperation	3	5	5	6	9
Brand image	3	9	6	7	5
Price	4	7	6	5	8
Reliability	5	6	6	7	7
Promotion	3	5	7	7	6
Support	5	6	7	6	8
Weighted score		173	163	169	179
Rank		2	4	3	1

Note: Figures are arbitrarily derived for the purpose of explanation.

The decision matrix approach (Table 8.2) involves the following steps (*see* Lucas *et al.*, 1994):

1 List the factors to be considered in evaluating suppliers. This list of factors will resemble the one that appears in Table 8.2, but may change from one situation to another depending on the type of merchandise being considered.

2 Assess the importance of each of the factors identified in Step 1 and assign to each factor an importance weight measured on a five-point scale, with larger numbers denoting greater importance. The importance weights will change for each application because of the differing needs relating to different types of merchandise. For a staple product, for example, supplier reliability is likely to be much more important than promotional support; for a new item, on the other hand, promotional support may be the most important criterion.

3 Assign a score to each potential supplier on each criterion listed in Step 1, based on an evaluation of the supplier's programme. As with importance weights, retailers typically use a five- or ten-point scale for this purpose.

4 Compute a weighted score for each supplier by multiplying each criterion score by the importance weight for that criterion and summing.

5 Rank suppliers according to their scores – the higher the weighted score, the higher the supplier's rank.

The decision matrix approach has the advantage that it bases the decision on quantitative assessments of the relative abilities of individual suppliers to meet explicitly defined criteria. As shown in Table 8.2, this yields a summary measure of the relative strengths and weaknesses of each potential supplier. The quantitative approach eliminates reliance on *ad hoc*, subjective judgements and forces decision makers to gather complete information prior to making final supplier selections.

Negotiating with suppliers

One of the important yardsticks by which firms evaluate the performance of retail buyers is the amount of profit the store earns from selling the merchandise they buy. Buyers must, therefore, negotiate the best deal they can with each supplier to improve their profits. Three factors are particularly important in supplier **negotiations**: discounts, **shipping charges**, and **promotional allowances.** Each of these factors has an effect on the final cost of goods to the retailer.

Discounts

Suppliers should normally charge the same price to all retailers for goods of like grade and quality. Suppliers therefore maintain list prices that, on the face of it, apply uniformly to all retailers. The list price, however, is far from firm since the supplier can offer various types of discounts. The types and amounts of retailers' discounts depend on the terms and conditions under which they actually purchase the goods. A price discount is legal as long as the purchase quantity, buying method (payment timing, for example), or timing of the purchase reduces the supplier's cost of doing business. Moreover, the supplier must offer the discounts to all retailers who meet the same terms and conditions.

Quantity discounts

Most suppliers do offer quantity discounts to retailers who buy in bulk. Since large orders reduce the supplier's handling, billing, transportation, and inventory costs, it can legally pass these cost savings on to retailers in the form of discounts from list prices. Quantity discounts reduce the cost of goods to retailers and allow them to lower price without sacrificing profitability.

Seasonal discounts

Manufacturers of seasonal products usually offer discounts to increase sales during off seasons and, thereby, even out production schedules. Since fashions change from season to season, suppliers often find themselves burdened with excess supply at the end of a selling season. Retailers willing to purchase end-of-season merchandise can often negotiate substantial discounts. Suppliers also give discounts to those willing to buy lines that are to be discontinued. Buyers from cut-price clothing stores take advantage of such discounts to reduce the costs of goods inward and so allow their resale at much lower prices.

Cash discounts

Suppliers offer **cash discounts** to encourage prompt payment by retailers. Suppliers often permit retailers to deduct a certain percentage from the net invoice amount – that is, the net amount of the order less all quantity and seasonal discounts – if they pay within a specified time period. Early payment by retailers benefits suppliers since it maintans their cash flow and reduces their potential borrowing requirements.

Anticipation

Cash discounts encourage retailers to pay within a specified time period to reduce the cost of the invoice. But what happens when a retailer pays before the expiration of the cash discount period? Should they receive a further discount? For example, suppose a retailer which has negotiated a 2 per cent discount for paying within 10 days actually pays in 2 days. In many cases such early payment can entitle retailers to additional discounts over and above negotiated cash discounts. This form of discounting, known as anticipation, would allow the retailer in the above example to deduct 8 days of anticipation at an agreed upon daily discount rate.

Multiple retailers, such as Tesco, Sainsbury (food retailers), PC World (in computing) and especially those with surplus cash, generally negotiate favourable anticipation terms to further reduce their cost of goods. A store cannot automatically claim an anticipation discount when it pays its bill early; anticipation is a matter of negotiation between the retailer and the supplier.

Shipping charges

A retailer which pays the cost of shipping merchandise from the supplier to their retail outlet must add that cost to the cost of the goods. Thus, retail buyers must always negotiate to reduce shipping charges. The factors which are important in negotiating shipping terms may include: responsibility for the cost of transportation; the bearer of shipping charges; and when title to the goods change hands (Lucas *et al.*, 1994). In some instances, someone other than the party which pays directly for transportation may ultimately bear the cost. The supplier, for example, may pay for transportation, but add the cost to the retailer's invoice.

The question of when legal title to the goods passes from the supplier to the retailer is also important in negotiating shipping terms. When title for the goods passes to the retailer, the retail business becomes responsible for any loss or damage to the merchandise. This means that if the retailer assumes title before the supplier ships the merchandise, the retailer is responsible for any damage or loss occurring during shipment and, therefore, has to pay for insurance during transit.

Promotional allowances

Most manufacturers offer various promotional allowances to encourage retailers to stock their products. Retail buyers must actively negotiate for these allowances since they, too, reduce the retailer's cost. One common type of promotional allowance – cooperative advertising – offers the retailer an allowance to underwrite all or a part of the cost of retailer advertising featuring the manufacturer's product, generally within certain prescribed limits. Cooperative advertising benefits both the retailer and the manufacturer – stretching the retailer's advertising budget, and promoting the manufacturer's product and increasing its sales (*see* Chapter 11).

Some suppliers also offer promotional allowances to retailers who put on in-store demonstrations of their products or give them prominent shelf space in the store.

The management of the merchandise mix

A retail firm would cease to exist without appropriate goods and services to sell. In order to be effective in buying, the critical characteristics of buying must be explored – and the skills of buyers in these areas must be excellent. There are several objectives in managing a merchandise mix effectively including (see Cook and Walters, 1991):

- providing a highly desirable merchandise mix;
- adjusting the mix to suit changing consumer needs;
- pre-purchase planning;
- maintaining an internal consistency;
- taking into consideration the external variables.

These factors are briefly discussed here in terms of a firm's ability to select and buy a blend of merchandise suited to the needs of the consumers within the retail outlet's market segments.

Buying a desirable merchandise mix

The objective of providing a desirable merchandise mix is the main focus of merchandise management. The reason for a retail organisation to provide a highly desirable merchandise mix is obviously related to its survival and profitability objectives. A high degree of desirability implies a number of features: first, it must be different from those of the competitors, otherwise, the retail firm cannot establish a differential advantage. Second, a particular mix must be appropriate for the market segment at which the retailer is aiming. In fact, this appropriateness is one of the most important of the factors that combine to produce differentiation between the customer's self-image and the store image held by the same customer. This self-identification will lead to customer satisfaction and, subsequently, to customer loyalty. The merchandise mix should not only be different and appropriate, but it must also have appropriate features in terms of depth, width, breadth, consistency, and flexibility (Samli, 1989).

1 **Depth** – the number of brands and styles within a particular generic class of product.

2 **Width** – the number of different generic classes of products which a store may carry. For example, a store selling only boots has a 'narrow' line in comparison with a store carrying boots, hunting equipment, golfing equipment, sporting footwear, and so on.

3 Breadth – the number of units in each brand and style within given generic classes of products. The store that carries ten each of the different types of chocolate bars has more breadth than the one with only six of each.

4 Consistency – the degree to which the different types of products that comprise the merchandise assortment are related. Merchandise assortments are highly consistent when all the brands are closely related in use, value, appeal, and perceived brand images.

5 Flexibility – Some retailers are able to buy at favourable price no matter the type of merchandise.

These five merchandise mix features are not prescriptive in the sense that they imply that there is only one way of managing merchandise. Different options are available to a retailer, and specific options may be appropriate for particular types of retail establishments. For example, the retail businesses position on consistency–inconsistency continuum does not imply a value judgement – that it has a good or bad merchandising policy – rather it is a means of identifying the retailer's choice of options. Within the given overall retail marketing strategy, any two of these continuums may account for a merchandise mix policy. Table 8.3 lists at least six such policies.

The retail marketing strategies discussed earlier in this book are partially implemented by these merchandise mix policies. This implementation process takes very specific forms so that the policies can go some way to fulfilling a company's goals, via its properly implemented retailing strategies. For example, Marks & Spencer would not aim to carry a shallow and narrow assortment when it is trying to differentiate itself as the ideal store for the upper-middle-class shopper; whereas Tiffany's must have a deep and narrow assortment reflecting the characteristics of its speciality stores and its effective philosophy of segmentation.

Adjusting the mix to suit changing consumer needs

This objective seeks to develop the ability to reflect changes taking place in the market. To be effective, this response should be sensitive and quick, occurring at an early stage in the process. Retailers must understand the specific product needs of consumers and adjust their buying strategy accordingly. Retailers that fail to pay attention to changing trends or cannot understand them are likely to go out of

Table 8.3
MERCHANDISE MIX POLICIES

Policy statement	Application
Deep and narrow assortments	They reflect speciality store philosophy. A speciality store must have numerous brands and styles of the speciality area it represents.
Deep and wide assortments	They suggest the general store merchandising philosophy which features good selections of diverse product lines.
Shallow and narrow assortments	They follow the concept of the convenience stores, such as Tie Rack or 7-Eleven which sell only frequently needed lines with little selection or depth in any given line.
Shallow and wide assortments	They reflect the 'five-and-dime' type of store philosophy. Discount stores typically carry a few brands and styles of a wide variety of generic product classes. Warehouse clubs follow this pattern of retailing.
Consistent and compatible assortments	They imply that within a department or among departments as well as within the store as a whole, quality, class, and selection of merchandise are consistent. There are no extremely good and extremely bad product lines and/or departments. In other words they are all compatible.
Flexible and localised assortments	They typify any type of bargain basement or bargain type of store such as charity stores. Furthermore, they typify decentralised buying such as is displayed by the Co-op stores. These stores have very good produce departments that buy the best a community offers.

business. In an era of increasing leisure and informality, for example, a traditional, casual wear store will have to assess whether the market remains large enough for it to survive; if in doubt, it must take drastic measures – perhaps totally changing its product lines and becoming a sportswear store.

Retailers need to be sure that they are able to detect the trends and strive to keep abreast of changes in the market, by adjusting the merchandise mix to the changing retail marketing needs. This objective can be fulfilled through effective feedback and retail marketing control functions, which are discussed in Chapter 14 in this book. However, a brief discussion is presented here to reinforce the necessity of keeping up to date with the market in terms to the merchandise plan. Maintaining up-to-date knowledge of the market is accomplished by merchandise mix pre-planning analyses, as seen in Figure 8.2.

Pre-purchase planning

In developing an appropriate merchandise plan, changes in the market must be assessed and fed forward: this is called pre-planning for the merchandise mix. As demonstrated in the pre-planning analysis in Figure 8.2, before the next year's merchandise mix is planned, two items of information are needed: an assessment of the past year's merchandise mixes; and an evaluation of the forces affecting the market.

Fig. 8.2 MERCHANDISE PRE-PLANNING ANALYSIS

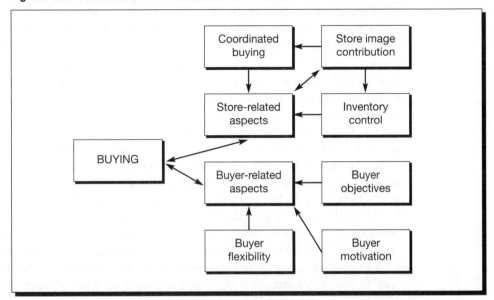

Merchandise mixes of past years show some subtle and obvious changes. It is necessary to examine the fast moving, slow moving, more popular and less popular items, and to ascertain the strengths and weaknesses of recent merchandise in stock within the store (McGoldrick, 1990). Similarly, the retailer must know which are the growth components and which the declining components of the merchandise mix. If, for instance, a bookseller's most noticeable growth in sales has been in the area of fiction and the greatest decline in cookery, the retailer may well decide to allocate more space and resources to carry a wider and deeper fiction selection; the necessary resources may be reallocated from the cookbooks section to this new growth area.

Exhibit 8.4 **Redirecting resources – the control provided by IT**

In fashion retailing, large retailers such as the Burton Group, Sears, The British Shoe Corporation reallocated funds from the declining sectors of their businesses into information technology (IT) in the 1970s and 1980s and gained market domination in their respective sectors partly through the control this gave them. Towards the end of the 1990s many fashion retailers in the USA and Australia invested heavily in IT and performed very well, despite an uncertain economic climate. In the UK, companies such as Marks & Spencer, Next and River Island all increased their market share due to the redirection of funds from declining sectors of their businesses to the growth sectors. The success of these companies in the redirection of funds from slow growth to fast growing sectors, has motivated other companies, such as Oasis and New Look, to invest heavily in retail information technology which gives the necessary information and control to identify which are the declining and which the deemed as fast growing sectors.

Retailers must take into consideration competitive factors within the context of the market. Any change in competition, and the changing competitive position of other retailers, implies some changes in the store's merchandise are necessary. If, for instance, a new competitor appears to be capturing the women's clothes market because the women of the area are predominantly professionals and this new store has the most complete line of professional women's outfits, existing stores must make adjustments in their merchandise mixes. These adjustments may be positive or negative: the decision may be to compete in terms of improved choice, making the merchandise stocked as good as or better than that offered by the new comer to the market. Alternatively, they may abandon this line completely, focusing attention and resources elsewhere. By establishing the directions in which the merchandise mix is to be adjusted on the basis of deviations from the past, changing trends and changing competition, merchandise planning is effectively facilitated. As pre-planning for the coming year's merchandise mix is considered, the actual image and expected image changes of the store need to be considered so that the merchandise mix can be adjusted accordingly. If a fashion retailer considers changing their image from an emphasis on 'formal and expensive' to one on 'casual, attractive and good value for money', then the retailer must plan the inventory mix changes with extreme care.

Maintaining consistency

In achieving and maintaining image differentiation, the retailer must pay particular attention to the merchandise mix. The merchandise mix is one of the retailer's most significant extrinsic cues for developing an image which, in turn, will be instrumental in achieving the desired differential congruence. It must be reiterated that the effectiveness of these external cues is subject primarily to the intrinsic consistency that the retail store achieves between its merchandise mix and other variables. If, for instance, the store is handling the most up-to-date fashion lines but its salespeople are all middle aged and not very well dressed, the store's interior is extremely conservative, and customer services such as credit, stock taking or liberal returns policy are not appropriately administered, then the store does not have the internal consistency essential to achieving the desired differential advantage – the store is sending conflicting cues to the market. Similar and perhaps more alarming situations can occur if a store's departments lack internal consistency. While one department may be known for its good value, high quality and fashionable merchandise, another may develop a reputation for poor quality and cheap merchandise. Again, the store is sending conflicting cues to the market and damaging its chances of developing the synergistic effect that is achieved through the creation of a uniform image.

Consideration of external variables

The retailer must understand external trends and changing retail marketing needs. Furthermore, the firm must assess each of the trends and needs as they influence the store's well-being. In addition to changing consumer needs (discussed above), the retailer must be aware of at least four external variables: increasing competition; worsening economic conditions; increasing international competition; and major population movements. Swift reaction to changes in any of these variables is vital; ignoring them is especially detrimental to small retailers, who are always trading at the margins (Samli, 1989). These variables as well as possible merchandise mix adjustment policies are depicted in Table 8.4.

Table 8.4
A PARTIAL LIST OF EXTERNAL VARIABLES

Factor	Merchansise mix adjustment
Increasing competition	Place more emphasis on product differentiation leading to specialisation.
Worsening economic conditions	Streamline the merchandise mix and change merchandise composition in terms of having more economical and lower priced products.
Changing import restrictions	Reassess the imported and importable components of the overall merchandise mix.
Major population movements in or out of the trading area	Readjust the merchandise mix. Provide more attractive quality and variety. Differentiate to make the store more attractive. Consider relocation.

Buying the merchandise

Once the features of an attractive and adequate merchandise mix are determined, they must be explored from the perspective of differential advantage, objectives and implementation. As indicated in Figure 8.3, two groups of considerations are particularly important: the store-related aspects of buying; and the buyer-related aspects of buying. In buying, perhaps the most important consideration is either the continuity of the store image, if that is what is needed, or revision of this image according to information recieved through the feedback and control functions. Although the buying function in retailing is a personal creative expression, this display of creativity cannot be an independant activity; buyers must not pull in opposing directions or risk frustrating efforts to build up the desired differential advantage.

Store-related aspects of buying

There are three critical store-related aspects of buying: the store image; **inventory control**; and coordinated buying (*see* Figure 8.3).

Fig. 8.3 MERCHANDISE MIX BUYING FACTORS

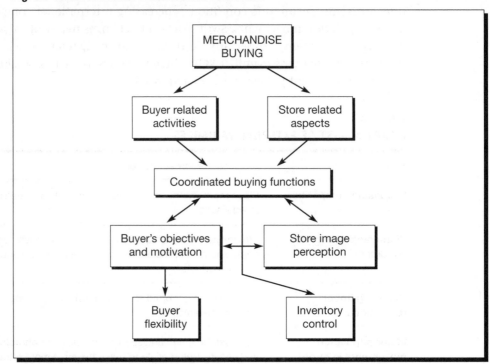

Store image contribution and continuation

The merchandise mix is an important contributor to the store image. Thus, the store image must be evaluated regularly and the actual contribution to the overall image must be assessed periodically.

Inventory control

Inventory must be controlled within a given business context dictated by factors such as cost constraints, time limits and – above all – store image goals. Inventory feedback is extremely important in fulfilling the buying function; as in many areas of retail marketing management, the judicious and prompt use of this information may deliver long-term benefits.

Coordinated buying

Assume, for instance, that TopMan in Exhibit 8.5 has three people buying for the firm and that these buyers have a completely different perception of TopMan's image. While one of them is buying bargain merchandise, the second one is buying only the most expensive formal wear and the third buyer feels that TopMan's lines should be competing with Marks & Spencer lines. Unless the buying function is coordinated among the three people buying for the firm, and they understand the store's present image and its image goals, TopMan cannot expect to be able to establish a differential and competitive advantage.

| Exhibit 8.5 | **Keeping buying within budgetary and image constraints** |

Consider the following hypothetical situation. 'TopMan' is a very elegant and rather expensive men's clothing store. Its inventory controls indicate a shortage in its lower priced men's suits, just before the beginning of preparations for the Christmas season. The buyer has found a job lot of suits in a local store which is going out of business. Although this bargain stock does not fit TopMan's image precisely and is larger than the store needs, the buyer purchases the lot.

As a result, the company's open-to-buy budget (*see* section on planning purchases below) has been spent and the newly acquired stock is taking up too much space in the store. The company will lose large sums of money because it is not ready for the Christmas season, and the newly acquired merchandise has altered the store's image.

This imaginary scenario may all too easily become a reality; it demonstrates that the buying function must be within both the budgetary and the image constraints.

The buyer-related aspects of buying

Buyer-related aspects of merchandise acquisition are based on buyer flexibility, motivation and objectives.

Buyer flexibility

All buyers must be flexible as to the sources, quality and styles of merchandise. The buyer is the person who pursues that mixture of art and science that is the activity of buying the merchandise which will fulfil the store's retail marketing objectives. It is termed the 'art' of buying because good merchandise has many aesthetic features such as colour, style and fashion. However, not only must buyers have good taste but their judgement must also reflect the taste of a store's customers. Furthermore, if a store employs multiple buyers, their tastes or sense of style must not be too different from each other – otherwise, it will be almost impossible for a store to maintain a consistent image.

The scientific aspect of buying is reflected in the knowledge and use of certain merchandise planning tools such as stock lists, mark-ups, mark downs, expense control factors, contribution returns, stock turnover analyses, return on merchandise investment and capital turnover, weighting technique, open-to-buyer computations, and so on.

Buyer motivation

Buyer motivation is extremely important in acquiring the most desirable merchandise mix. (Table 8.5 provides a summary of some factors influencing buyer motivation.) The important point is that if the buyer is not sufficiently motivated, the resultant deficient performance will be reflected in all phases of the retail marketing function. If, for instance, the image of the firm is questionable and the buyer is aware of this flaw, it may be difficult for the buyer to be motivated.

Table 8.5
SOME KEY BUYER MOTIVATION FACTORS

Factor	Brief description
High morale	Favourable balance of work life and private life. Positive work conditions and market conditions, e.g. good company name, good merchandise to work with, good suppliers to deal with.
Reasonable remuneration	A reasonable income with some bonus and other incentives or benefits. Knowing that the company takes care of the individual.
Interaction with management	Good working relationships with immediate supervisor and with other buyers. Good communication with department managers.
Seeing the results of efforts	Being able to work with department managers in terms of providing inputs as to the department's overall merchandise mix. Knowing the results of selling efforts.
Positive feedback	Managers, other buyers and salespeople have a sensitive approach to making suggestions for changes (if necessary) or to offering praise (if and when possible).
Adequate training	The buyers should undergo training in terms of acquiring necessary skills such as communication skills and the ability to negotiate.
Proper information for buyers	Information must be available for buyers as to how the market is doing, how the most recent merchandise lot purchased by the buyer has performed and existing options regarding sources of merchandise.

Similarly, if the buyer is not paid adequately, this may well have a demotivating effect on self-esteem; in addition more effort may be devoted to managing personal finances than to turning in a good professional performance.

Buyers must be well trained and their training updated periodically. They also need to possess certain critical skills such as the ability to communicate with the key persons in the industry and with departmental managers as well as sales staff. Similarly, the ability to negotiate and to establish strong relationships with people is extremely important for the success of buyers and hence the need for their motivation. It is generally time to say that a well-informed buyer is a highly motivated buyer. Specific information imparted by the firm will motivate the buyer. Among other information requirements, the condition of the market, the behaviour of competitors, and new and changing sources of merchandise are all essential ingredients in the buyer's satisfactory performance.

Buyer objectives

A close relationship exists between buyer motivation and buyer objectives. As individual professionals, buyers will have some clear-cut objectives. They must understand that these personal objectives have a significant impact on the well-being of the retail organisation. The match between the buyer's self-image and the store image has an interesting twist in this context. Buyers reflect their art and science through their performance. This performance is consistent with the buyer's objectives. If the buyer has clear-cut professional objectives, such as seeing that their firm obtains a greater return on investment, then the buyer is more likely to be successful; in this case, success implies well-being for both the buyer and the store. Thus, in one sense, the retailer's well-being is a direct function of the buyer's degree of professionalism.

It is generally anticipated that the buyer will be a mature professional, properly motivated and with mature personal objectives of advancement and success. Since buyer motivation and objectives are so important to the well-being of the retail store, and both motivation and objectives are – in part at least – a function of the buyer's degree of professionalism, the retail organisation must make a special effort to play an important role in the buyer's professional maturation process.

Merchandise purchase planning and control

The development of a successful merchandise plan is related to effective buying and control. Following the discussion of effective buying above, this section deals with merchandise mix planning – an internal process that deals with the quantities and mixture of the total merchandise within a given period of time for a given sum of money. Effective merchandise planning tools and the rigorous use of them are extremely important if the firm is to fulfil its goals. Three special merchandise lists are used in planning the merchandise mix: basic stock lists, model stock lists and never-out lists.

The basic stock lists include the items that have a stable sales pattern. Since these patterns are often predictable, these lists are very specific and detailed. Model stock lists are constructed primarily for certain shopping goods and fashion merchandise. Since their sales are not as predictable as the stable products, model stock lists are not nearly as detailed as basic stock lists. They are merely skeletons indicating the size, price, quality and colour groups rather than the specific products.

'Never-out' lists deal with products that the store must keep on hand at all times. These products are either the core of the store's product line or contribute significantly to the image of the retail organisation. Customers may equate the retailer with these products and, if the store sells out of these products, a credibility gap may be created.

On the basis of these lists and a great deal of additional information, a general merchandise plan can be prepared. This additional information is in the form of sales, end of the month inventory, reductions, beginning of the month inventory, and **open-to-buy.** Typically, the average merchandise plan covers a six-month period. By constructing such a plan, a retailer can physically see relationships and associations among various product categories and other variables. Merchandise plans are formulated by using six steps including the selection of control units; forecasting sales; inventory level planning; reduction planning; purchases planning; and planning profit margins.

Selection of control units

Control units can be selected by using department-wide classifications such as jewellery and sports goods in a department store (Ghosh, 1994). In addition, within-department classifications may also be used. The jewellery department may feature fashion jewellery, gold jewellery, diamonds and other valuable stones, watches, and the like. As opposed to departments in smaller stores, standard merchandise classifications may be used as control units. Every firm has its own merchandise classification, however, for typical stores some commonly accepted merchandise classifications may be considered standard. At no time should a retailer rely solely on its own internal classifications. Small firms should seek information from outside: for example, other data classifications and trade association data.

Sales forecasts

These are necessary for preparing a general merchandise plan. There are many different forecasting techniques. It is beyond the scope of this book to enter into a detailed technical discussion here; without getting into a discussion of various techniques, the retailer has to look at three separate groups of indicators: external, internal and seasonal factors. External factors, such as changing personal income in the trading area, or changing population of the trading area, may be used; internal factors such, as changing total sales in pounds sterling or units should be considered, as should seasonality factors. Seasonality is more important for some retailers than for others. The following formula is used to calculate sales volume for a store:

$$S = f(X, Y, Z)$$

where: S = sales volume
X = external factors
Y = internal factors
Z = seasonal variations

This formula implies that the store's sales volume is a function of external factors, internal factors, and seasonal variations. Individual retailers have their own sales volumes which interact differently with these variables. It is of the utmost importance that they identify these relationships and use them for predicting the future.

Similarly, the retailer can estimate future sales by analysing past trends and future growth. However, such forecasts must be revised and further adjusted on the basis of subjective evaluations and expected changes; indeed, the retail organisation may have experienced a situation similar to that displayed in Table 8.6 (note that the detail in Table 8.6 includes only a few critical product lines). Forecasts in the tabular example are based on an expected eight per cent growth in the economy combined with the average growth each product has experienced; however,

Table 8.6
A CLOTHING STORE EXAMPLE

Key product lines	Five years average sales	Average increase	Expected growth	Additional adjustments
Top coats	30 000	2.0	32 400	30 000
Men's suits	50 000	3.0	55 500	53 000
Ladies' suits	35 000	5.0	45 000	48 000
Slacks	25 000	7.0	28 750	30 000
Jumpers	10 000	0.0	10 800	10 000

Note: Based on an anticipated 8 per cent growth in the economy adjusted to past experiences.

they are further adjusted on the basis of subjective criteria. Since sales of overcoats have been shrinking, plans were made to maintain the inventory at the same level. Stocks of men's suits are scaled down because of increased local competition whereas ladies' suits and slacks have shown particularly noticeable increases – the forecasts, therefore, are adjusted upward. Jumpers and sweaters are expected only to maintain their sales level in this store.

Inventory level planning

This is an essential component of merchandise plans. If a retail store does not have adequate stocks, it loses; however, if it is overstocked, it also loses. Hence, any retailer who can develop a system to plan purchases on time and in adequate quantities is likely to be ahead of the competition and to be more profitable than the average.

In planning the inventory, three concepts are important: average monthly stock, which implies that portion of the total inventory plan expected to be on hand; average monthly sales, based on actual sales data; and calculated on the basis of planned monthly sales. These latter are derived from forecasts. Planned inventory is calculated on the basis of planned monthly and basic stock. The concept can be illustrated as follows:

$$PI = PMS + BS; \text{ and } BS = AMS - ASM$$

Therefore,

$$PI = PMS + (AMS - ASM)$$

where: PI = Planned inventories
PMS = Planned monthly sales
BS = Basic stock
AMS = Average monthly stock
ASM = Average monthly sales

Clearly, a good deal of sophistication is required to develop effective inventory plans. Inventory planners must have carefully developed analyses of the average monthly stock and average monthly sales to hand. Furthermore, they must have developed reasonable forecasts from which planned monthly sales can be derived. Despite the availability of a massive literature relating to these issues, small retail firms are likely to approach them in a relatively pragmatic manner. Further research is needed to develop these concepts for the particular use of small retail firms or for formulation of similar concepts for easy planning.

Reduction planning

Some reduction in retailing is always necessary. Every retailer must use variable markdowns for effective marketing and particularly for effective promotion. Thus, most retailers not only use reductions but also plan them.

Another type of reduction is planned reduction in the planned inventories. If the firm can develop a level of logistics sophistication which will help to reduce inventories without losing sales, then the retailer plans such reductions not for promotional purposes but for financial efficiency. A third type of reduction is one that is imposed on the retailer. This form of reduction is referred to as shoplifting, though many UK retail organisations now prefer to use the term 'theft'. It has been estimated that shoplifting accounts for more than 20 per cent of stock shortages in the UK. Discussing this aspect of 'merchandise reduction' is not within the scope of this book; students are referred to standard retailing textbooks.

Planning purchases

Planned purchases can be illustrated as follows:

$$PP = AMS + PMS + PMR$$

Where: PP   = Planned purchases
AMS = Average monthly stock
PMR = Planned monthly reductions
PMS = Planned monthly sales

It is probable that one of the most important concepts related to purchase plans is open-to-buy (OTB). This concept depicts the difference between **planned purchases** and actual purchase commitments made by a buyer during the month. It is important that buyers have some degree of flexibility; each buyer should be allowed a budget with a reasonable sum of OTB (Cook and Walters, 1991). This will mean that a buyer not only has the flexibility to take advantage of special offers and opportunities, but also will feel more involved in the well-being of the store – and therefore, be more highly motivated.

Planning profit margins

In many retail situations, profitability and sales are regarded by many retailers to be the ultimate criteria within buying decisions, all other factors acting as indicators of how well these criteria are likely to be met. Thus, increasing the number of brands stocked within a product group will not normally increase total sales volume. It may reduce individual sales volumes, increase pressure upon distribution and shelf-space and result in poor buying terms. An addition is therefore usually accompanied by a deletion, so a potential supplier will have to show that his product offers advantages, in terms of profit margins, over one which is currently stocked.

The decision on merchandise selection is closely intertwined with consideration of the costs and revenue that the store will experience from its purchases. Moreover, most large and many small retailers place great emphasis upon the percentage gross margin rate (usually expressed as a percent of retail sales). This figure recieves so much attention since gross margin must cover the store's expenses and any remainder will constitute the net profit before tax. Consequently, many retail organisations include gross margin and profit planning in their merchandise budgeting process.

Economic constraints

As plans for purchase are developed, some criteria must be established for reordering the merchandise that has been sold and certain economic constraints must be considered in this process. Retailers like to order in large quantities because it enables them to reduce the cost of reordering and capitalise on quantity discounts. On the other hand, ordering in small quantities will reduce the excessive costs of carrying large inventories. These are two key constraints which are recognised and utilised by the concept of economic order quantity (EOQ) which can be calculated using the following formula:

$$EOQ = \frac{2DS}{PC}$$

where: EOQ = Economic order quantity in units
D = Annual demand in units
S = Costs of placing an order
P = Percentage of annual carrying cost to unit cost
C = Unit cost of an item

Such a formula may facilitate attempts to optimise buying efforts by minimising overstocking and understocking episodes. As estimated demand and costs change, EOQ is revised periodically (Berman and Evans, 1995).

Merchandise controls

Most aspects of planning explored in this chapter also provide criteria for controls. Each time a financial criterion (such as planned monthly sales) or a quantitative criterion (such as a model stock plan) is discussed for planning purposes, control criteria are also established. This is due to the fact that planning criteria set forth certain limits, and the control comes from comparing the difference between the planned and the actual. Thus, whereas model stock lists, basic stock lists, and never-out lists provide unit control criteria, the six-step merchandise planning process discussed in this chapter provides financial control criteria.

Figure 8.4 illustrates the merchandise control process. If, for instance, the firm has been cultivating the image of an elegant but medium-priced apparel speciality shop, and research shows that the market views the present merchandise as too high class and extremely expensive, the store may be forced to provide a larger space in the model stock plan for lower priced products. The purchase plan will be adjusted accordingly and more purchases reductions will be planned for these products. In order to obtain these products, the buyers may not only have to change suppliers but may also have to change their behaviour in that the new group of suppliers may respond to different interaction patterns. The suppliers of very expensive merchandise, for example, may exhibit snobbish behaviour, with buyers not being expected to treat them as peers, whereas the suppliers of more modest merchandise lines may expect to be treated as peers.

Fig. 8.4 MERCHANDISE CONTROL PROCESS

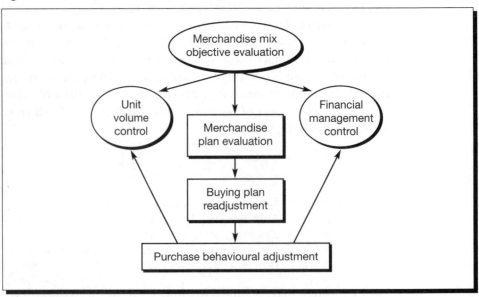

SUMMARY

This chapter posits that effective merchandise mix management means effective buying through planning and careful control. It is further emphasised that buying is part of the lifeblood of retailing. The four objectives of merchandise mix management are identified as: providing a highly desirable merchandise mix; adjusting the mix to changing needs; maintaining an internal consistency; and considering external variables. Five specific merchandise policies were discussed: deep and narrow assortment; deep and wide assortment; shallow and narrow assortment; shallow and wide assortment; consistent assortment; and flexible assortment (*see* Table 8.3). Merchandise mix is first pre-planned on the basis of external variables such as changes in competition, consumer trends and past performances. On the basis of the pre-planned merchandise mix, the chapter singled out certain buying factors such as: high morale; reasonable remuneration; interaction with management; recognition of the results of efforts; positive feedback; adequate training; and planning purchases.

Merchandise management controls are classified as financial and unit controls. It is emphasised that the control function has a hierarchical effect, and, therefore, that the whole merchandise mix system must be controlled rather than simply constitute one or two steps in the total hierarchy. In the merchandise mix management and control areas, the role of brands must be considered carefully. The retailer can use product or brand image as a force to establish a competitive edge or may use the store's own image. Variations of these two strategic tools provide numerous alternatives for the retailer (*see* Chapter 9).

KEY TERMS		
assortment	inventory control	product selection
breath of selection	merchandise consistency	promotion allowances
buyer	merchandise mix	quantity discount
buying function	merchandise planning	shipping charges
cash discount	merchandise purchase	stock turnover
cost of average inventory	merchandise strategy	supplier selection
depth	merchandising	width
gross margin	negotiation	
gross margin return on investment (GMROI)	open-to-buy	
	planned purchase	

ASSIGNMENT

Mr Lou Wang came to Britain from Taiwan just over four years ago. One year after he arrived in Britain, he bought a progressive fashion store in the centre of Manchester city. The store was selling mainly women's outerwear, targeting the age group ranging from 24 to 45 years. It was doing well but the former owner had sold it because he was moving to another business in Japan.

The location of the store was very attractive to Mr Wang, who is aware that traffic is the lifeblood of a store like his. Two years later things began to go wrong and sales dropped dramatically – to a disturbing level.

Soon after he took over, Mr Wang changed the merchandise mix composition and began to stock a high percentage of Chinese-related fashion items in an area with less than 4000 Chinese residents.

Task

You are required to advise Mr Wang with respect to his merchandise mix strategy and suggest possible ways of improvement (1800 words).

REVISION QUESTIONS

1 One of the key elements of successful retail marketing is a merchandise mix that satisfies the taste and preferences of the target customer while being consistent with the store's position in the market. Agree or disagree with this statement.

2 Discuss how the retailer's product and supplier selection must reflect the store's retail marketing strategy.

3 How can a store keep its merchandise decisions consistent with its financial objectives?

4 Not only should the merchandise mix of a store be different from competitors and appropriate for consumers, it must also have features observed in terms of depth, width, breadth, consistency and flexibility. Explain.

5 One of the yardsticks by which retailers evaluate the performance of buyers is the amount of profit the store earns from selling the goods they buy. What role does the buyer's ability to negotiate with suppliers play in their buying performance?

6 Why is pre-purchase planning necessary in the management of store merchandise?

7 The buying function in retailing is a personal creative expression. Discuss.

8 Discuss the view that a match between the buyer's self-image and store image must always exist for successful buying objectives to be achieved.

9 The rigorous use of effective merchandise planning tools is extremely important if the store is to fulfil its goals. Briefly explain this statement in the light of merchandise purchase planning and control.

10 The importance of inventory level planning is due to the notion that if a store does not have adequate stock it will lose customers and money, but if it carries too much stock it will also lose money. How may retailers plan their inventory to avoid losses either way?

CASE STUDY

Commercialising Christian related merchandise

'What Would Jesus Do?' (WWJD) is the latest craze to grip America's increasingly influential Christian consumers. Bracelets inscribed with 'WWJD?' are all the rage, as are VeggieTales, videos starring vegetables that deliver cheery Christian messages. *Where's God When I'm S-scared?* – a Veggie/Tales featuring a cucumber and a tomato – has just been launched in stores such as Wal-Mart, Target, and K mart, and it is already America's second most popular non-movie children's video after Sesame Street's *'Elmo Palooza'*.

Religion has always sold well, for example, Chaucer's Pardoner made a career out of hawking fake holy relics. More recently, Christian products have been supplied largely by family-run stores which were in business more for love than profit. But the segment is being 'born again'. Secular companies have seen potential in the Christian market and retailers have responded by becoming better organised and creating shelf space for merchandise suited to Christian consumers. The Christian Booksellers Association (CBA), representing 70 per cent of

America's 3500 Christian retailers, estimates that Christian merchandise worth $3 billion is sold in America each year. The number of Christian stores with a turnover of at least $1m has nearly quadrupled since 1989. In 1997, Christian fiction was the fastest-growing genre in America; modern Christian music is bigger than jazz and classical. Market evidence from CBA indicates that sales of Christian merchandise assortments will double in the next five years. This growth is being driven partly by church-members' increased spending power. The average Christian shopper in America is a well-educated Caucasian, aged between 30 and 49 years, with a net income of more than $40 000. In addition, spirituality and the search for 'meaning' are in vogue. The managing director of Family Christian Stores, the largest Christian retailer with 270 shops in 35 states, was quoted as saying, 'the approaching millennium is prompting people to reassess their beliefs, and hence their Christian-product requirements'.

Similarly, the Chief Executive Officer (CEO) of Big Idea, which makes VeggieTales, was also reported as saying that ageing babyboomers are 'hungry for ways to teach values to their kids that are fun, not sappy'. In *Dave and the Giant Pickle,* a modern version of David and Goliath, peas hurl abuse at the Israelites, whose ranks include a host of gourds. The Grapes of Wrath teach Asparagus how to 'rub along' with fruit. Secular companies have spotted the potential. Wal-Mart is devoting more shelf space to religious products. Seven out of ten religious books are sold by chains such as Barnes & Noble. Christian music labels are being bought by media giants. Gaylord Entertainment, Zomba Music and EMI have, between them, bought seven Christian labels since 1994. As a result, a handful of such artists are finding mainstream success. Bob Carlisle's album *Butterfly Kisses* was the first by a modern Christian artist to reach *Billboard's* Top 200.

Now Christian retailers are responding. Many independents have joined buying groups, such as the Parable Group and Munce Marketing, to give their marketing and purchasing more weight. Consolidation is also under way; America's biggest chain, Family Christian Bookstores, bought the second biggest, Joshua's Christian Stores in May 1998. Mr Dietzman, Family Christian Bookstore's CEO, is a former Wal-Mart executive and says that since more independents are run as ministries with little retail experience, there is scope for the big firms to get bigger. Taking his cue from the likes of Barnes & Noble, Mr Dietzman has introduced coffee shops, book signings and listening areas for music into the FCB stores.

Shops are also becoming larger in America, for example, FCB in Dallas is some forty thousand square feet compared with the usual two thousand square feet. FCB, which has grown from sales of $79 million in 1992 to $168 million in 1997, plans a stock market flotation in the next few years – underlining the industry's capitalist leanings. Mr Dietzman is not shy about commercialism, recalling that 'Jesus criticised the man who buried his talents so he would not lose them'.

Christian retailers are moving on to the Internet. St Jude (www.st-jude.com), based in Philadelphia, offers a range of merchandise on-line including 'wash and wear clergy shirts designed to be comfortable yet dignified'. With more clergy hooked up to computers, demand is growing for specialist software, often sold on-line. The best-seller at Britain's Churchill Systems is parish management software, which organises church services.

Source: The Economist (1998) 'Christian retailing', May 23: 93.

Questions for discussion

1 Religion has always sold well in America. Discuss why you think the market for Christian related merchandise is growing at a rapid pace.

2 Merchandising for profit (commercialism) is generally regarded as being inappropriate and against most religious faiths. Basing your argument on the evidence of this case, do you consider Mr Dietzman's defence of religious commercialism justified?

REFERENCES

Berman, B. and Evans, J. (1995) *Retail Management*. New York: Macmillan.

Cook, D. and Walters, D. (1991) *Retail Marketing: Theory and Practice*. London: Prentice Hall.

Ettenson, R. and Wagner, J. (1986) 'Retail buyers' saleability judgements: a comparison of information use across three levels of experience', *Journal of Retailing*, 62(1): 41–6.

Ghosh, A. (1994) *Retail Management*. 2nd edn. New York: The Dryden Press.

Lucas, G.H., Bush, R.P. and Gresham, L.G. (1994) *Retailing*. Boston, USA: Houghton Mifflin.

McGoldrick, P. (1990), *Retail Marketing*. London: McGraw-Hill.

Nilsson, J. and Host, V. (1987) *Reseller Assortment Decision Criteria*. Aarhus: Aarhus University Press.

Samli, A.C. (1989) *Retail Marketing Strategy: Planning, Implementation and Control*. New York: Quorum Books.

Shipley, D.D. (1985) 'Resellers' supplier selection criteria for different consumer products', *European Journal of Marketing*, 19(7): 26–36.

9

The retailers' own-brand marketing management

LEARNING OBJECTIVES

After reading this chapter, you should be able to:

- understand and differentiate between the manufacturer's and retailer's own brands;
- determine the strategies for own-label branding;
- understand the advantages of own-label brands to the retailer;
- determine the likely strategy for manufacturers in fighting off the own-label threats;
- understand the implications of manufacturers supplying own-label to retailers.

Products sold under a retail organisation's **house brand** name are sold exclusively through that retail organisation's outlets. There are, however, many different approaches to ownbranding, some of which push against the boundaries of this definition.

Exhibit 9.1	Six main 'species' of private branding

- the own brand using the retailer's own name, such as Bhs and Sainsbury;
- the own brand using a different name, which may become as well known as that of the retailer itself – such as St Michael products at Marks & Spencer;
- 'super' own brands, such as the Sainsbury Supreme range;
- generics, a plain-label variant upon the own-brand concept, such as the Tesco Economy brand;
- the 'exclusive', introduced usually as a temporary promotion but not using the retailer's usual own brand name. For example, 'House of Fraser Exclusives', which do not use the company's usual own-brand name, Allander;
- surrogate brands – not truly a retailer brand but a manufacturer brand that is exclusive to a chain of stores; for example, Cover Plus is manufactured by MacPhersons for the Woolworth group.

Customer loyalty and shopping habits are the major factors in the battle between the retailers' own labels and the manufacturers' **national brands.** The differences in consumer shopping behaviour among British shoppers tend to be reflected in their selection of retail outlets and their responsiveness to specific marketing policies (Omar and Kent, 1995). Thus the power of brand loyalty is the main factor underlying consumer shopping and **brand usage** habits (the habit of using a particular brand). Similarly, research evidence indicates that there are differences in the demographic characteristics of those who are likely to buy **own labels** and those who are likely to buy national brands. Those who shop for national brands are likely to be motivated by several factors, including brand image, store image, brand perceived quality, shopping experience, and convenience. On the other hand, those who shop for own labels may be motivated by **low price**, value for money and store loyalty.

A major cornerstone of retail marketing in recent years has been the development of the retailer's name as a brand, rather than simply a name over the shop. A situation has developed where the names of major retailers are better known to consumers than any but the biggest manufacturers' brand names. An important part of this change has been the evolution and growth of retailers' own-brand products, to the point where they represent a high proportion of retail turnover in the UK and elsewhere in Europe. It is also noticeable that some of the most successful retail companies have a very strong commitment to own brands. Marks & Spencer has 100 per cent commitment in its **own label**, selling only St Michael's in all its stores worldwide. This represents just one reason why the topic of own brands merits individual consideration, rather than treating it as a special issue within retail pricing and merchandising.

This chapter first examines the development of **own brands** within different retail sectors and specific companies. Attention is then turned to the various strategies of own branding, the opportunities and threats to retailers, approaches and problems in recruiting suppliers, and the task of positioning the range(s). The final section considers responses to own brands, their purchase patterns, and their perceptions of price and quality.

Developments in own-label brands

In one sense, the history of own brands is as long as that of retailing itself, with individual tailors, shoemakers, bakers, etc., making and selling their own products – and building up a clientele for them. In another sense, own brands are a relatively recent phenomenon, representing an integral component of retailers' increasing power and marketing sophistication. Own brands started to be widely noted as a threat to **manufacturers' brands** in the late 1960s, especially in packaged grocery markets. Surprisingly little attention was given to their growth in other markets. It tended to be taken for granted that many clothes were sold as own brands and that all of Marks & Spencer's sales were in own brands. This situation changed rapidly in the late 1970s, when it was acknowledged that few product markets had escaped significant inroads from retailers' own brands.

The percentage or units accounted for by **private labels** varies widely by category. To some degree, the variation is a function of time – private-label canned foods, for example, have been on the market longer and in broader distribution than private-label disposable nappies. Several factors may be identified which favour own-brand penetration and these are summarised in Table 9.1.

There are various explanations for the obvious stagnation of own brands in the late 1970s. McGoldrick (1990) pointed to the anxiety among some multiples that consumer choice was being limited, especially by 'me too' own brands offering few innovative features. The own-label versus national-brand price differentials had declined rapidly – in some cases they had been halved in two years. Successful discount stores, such as Kwik Save and Asda, had previously concentrated mainly or even entirely upon manufacturers' brands but, by the late 1990s, all of these stores had begun to sell own-label brands. Some retailers, such as Sainsbury, had started to use **fighting brands** as their lowest price offering, to avoid devaluing the image of their own brand. Temporary shortages in the early 1970s had adversely affected some own-brand supplies. These are examples of the hazards of own-brand development, some of which could affect other sectors in the future.

The 1990s, however, saw renewed confidence in own brands and a recognition by retailers that the most successful own brands tend to offer more than just a price reduction. This renewed vigour also reflects the growth of major multiples with a strong commitment to own brands. Own-label penetration began stabilising in the early 1990s when the emergence of the discount retailers brought an upsurge in the availability of **'value brands'** at prices significantly below those of own brands, which in turn were cheaper than national brands. Market leaders in the grocery sector (Tesco and Sainsbury), which had vigorously protected their own-label quality and image, were forced to stock value or **economy brands** to ensure they did not alienate customers for whom price was paramount. This could be regarded as attitude of mind because some of Tesco's brands are more expensive than national brands.

A strong link inevitably exists between retail concentration and the share of trade taken by **retailer brands.** This point was demonstrated in an international comparison by Akehurst and Alexander (1995), who illustrated high levels of retailer concentration and branding in the UK and USA, and low levels of both in Italy and Belgium. European comparisons of retailer branding within grocery product classes have been presented by A.C. Nielsen (the high-profile consumer survey company). Table 9.2 shows that grocery own brands increased their share in most European countries between 1989 and 1996, especially in Austria, The Netherlands and Germany. However, these data are based on volume trends and on selected product classes. Turning to comparisons between product sectors, Table 9.2 also shows the estimated share of own-brand sales through each category of outlet.

Table 9.1
MARKET DEVELOPMENT FACTORS

Market factors	*Market penetration determinants*
Product category characteristics	■ The product is an inexpensive, easy, low-risk purchase for the consumer. ■ It is easy to make from commodity ingredients. ■ The product is perishable and therefore local suppliers are advantaged. ■ Product category sales are large and growing, so private labels can more easily garner sufficient volume to be profitable. ■ The category is dominated by a few national-brand manufacturers, so retailers promote private labels to reduce dependency on them.
New-product activity	■ National brands are offered in few varieties, enabling a private label with a narrow line to represent a clear alternative to the consumer. ■ National-brand, new-product introductions are infrequent or easy to copy. ■ Consumers can easily make side-by-side comparisons of national brands and private labels.
Private-label characteristics	■ Private-label goods have been available to consumers for many years. ■ Distribution is well-developed. ■ Variability in quality is low. ■ Quality in comparison with national brands is high and improving. ■ Consumers have confidence in their ability to make comparisons about quality.
Price and promotion factors	■ Retail gross margins in the product category are relatively high. ■ Price gaps between national brands and private labels are wide. ■ National-brand expenditures on price promotions as a percentage of sales are high, increasing price sensitivity and encouraging consumers to switch brands. ■ The credibility of national-brand prices is low because of frequent and deep price promotions. ■ National-brand expenditures on advertising as a percentage of sales are low.
Retailer characteristics	■ The retailer is part of a stable oligopoly and, therefore, sells national brands at relatively high prices. ■ The retailer has the size and resources to invest in high-quality private-label development.

Table 9.2
OWN-BRAND GROCERY VOLUME SHARES – EUROPEAN COMPARISONS

Country	No. of product classes measured	1989 (%)	1996 (%)
Great Britain	12	17.5	22.1
Sweden	22	20.0	18.4
France	09	17.8	18.4
Austria	06	12.5	18.1
The Netherlands	12	13.7	18.0
Belgium	14	15.5	16.6
Norway	19	n/a	10.7
Switzerland	09	10.7	10.1
Germany	15	03.8	09.7
Italy	11	04.3	05.3
Mean	12	12.9	15.3

Source: Based on Nielsen data (1997).

A consistent pattern has emerged, in the research data: own-brand shares have increased in every major category. In the clothing sector, own brands have traditionally been stronger in menswear than in womenswear, although the growth of the multiples is helping to increase their penetration in both these categories (Omar and Kent, 1995). In footwear, the high level of vertical integration, including the extensive retail interests of the British Shoe Corporation, has ensured a strong presence of own brands. Growth has been slower in the durable goods categories, where the perceived risks of purchase are higher. Progress has, however, been made in DIY with the rapid spread of multiples such as B&Q. This also applies to some self-assembly furniture categories of products, such as those available from retailers like MFI and IKEA, for example.

In that own-brand growth is strongly related to the growth of the multiples, this process of own-brand share increase is likely to continue, but probably at a slower rate. Average of Great Britain (AGB) forecast that the pace of growth would slacken in the late 1990s, partly because multiples will be cautious of accusations that they are reducing consumers' real choice. In some sectors, concentration has also come close to the level at which government intervention may well occur. There is, however, a growing tendency towards more innovative retailer brands, which should ensure continued growth.

Retailers' brand developments

The biggest own brand in the UK is Marks & Spencer's 'St Michael'. Although sold only through the company's outlets, this represents a major brand in its own right. The own-brand percentage share at Sainsbury has varied somewhat over the years.

To an extent, this fluctuation reflected the opening of many larger stores by that company, prompting the need and providing the opportunity to diversify into new products more quickly. The company also cultivated manufacturer-named fighting brands in the late 1970s, largely in response to the competition from other retailers' generic ranges. In spite of the high turnover share of the Sainsbury brand, however, it comprises only about a third of the product range sold by the company. This is indicative of an emphasis on the higher-volume items, plus a strong marketing effort behind the own brand. The own-brand range does, however, extend into some speciality areas.

The Co-op represents a major own-brand retailer across a wide spectrum of commodity groups. Traditionally, this reflected the large manufacturing and farming capacity of the Co-operative movement. Its manufacturing and wholesaling division has increasingly been obliged to compete with outside suppliers and also to become suppliers to other organisations. The Co-op biscuit factories, for example, have produced own-brand products for other retailers such as Asda, Kwik Save, Waitrose, etc. Possibly the best known of the Co-op branded items is their '99 tea', which holds 14 per cent of the packet tea market.

In the pharmacy sector the dominant company is Boots. Like the Co-op, its high level of own-brand participation has its roots in a large manufacturing division; the manufacturing arm is also a major supplier to the chemists' trade in general. Boots manufactures many products that do not carry the company brand name: for example, Optrex eye care products, Virol baby foods, and Strepsils throat lozenges. As the Boots stores have diversified into many new fields, such as photographic goods and speciality foods, the powerful Boots brand name has been increasingly used on products brought from outside suppliers. W.H. Smith is another company that has used own labels as a strategy for diversification from its original product base. That company also introduced special own-brand names with just a low-key mention of the W.H. Smith name, such as 'Messenger' prestige products and 'Expressions' gift stationery.

It would be incorrect to assume that own brands are restricted to large stores operated by the multiples. Symbol groups, such as Spar in the grocery sector and Numark in the chemists' sector, have also been active in own-brand development. The UK's biggest group of convenience stores, Spar, also developed a number of own-brand ranges. There may seem little scope for own brands to be sold in completely independent outlets, but those of cash-and-carry groups are normally sold via independent stores. The wholesaler's name probably means little to the independent store's customers, but some advantages of own brands can still be achieved through this type of operation. In the case of symbol groups, own brands offer an additional method of cohesion for stores that are typically more diverse than is ideal. For cash-and-carry wholesalers, own brands attempt also to increase the loyalty of independent retailers, as the own brands become established within their stores.

Brand competitive dimensions (brand wars)

Taken together, the trends in the growth of market share of own brands may seem daunting to manufacturers of national brand-name products. But they tell only half the story. The increased strength of private labels does not mean that the death of national brands should be heralded. Competition between categories of brands continues – sometimes referred to as the **brand wars**.

National brands

With the increase in penetration by own brands, national brands require a more dedicated marketing management to compete. Several factors may help to illustrate this point:

- the **shopping process**;
- **brand preference** and choice;
- the value factor.

The shopping process

The purchase process in many sectors are known to favours brand-name products. Brand names exist because consumers still require an assurance of quality when they do not have the time, opportunity, or ability to inspect alternatives at the point of sale. In any cluttered **product category**, brand names simplify the selection process; in the time-pressured, dual income households of the 1990s, national brands are needed more than ever. Exhibit 9.2 backs up this claim.

Exhibit 9.2	The strength of national brands

A 1994 DDB Needham survey indicated that 60 per cent of consumers still agree that they prefer the comfort, security and value of a national brand over a private label. Although this percentage is lower than the 75 per cent figure common in the 1970s, it has remained fairly constant since the late 1980s. Brand-name goods have a solid foundation on which to build current advantage. Put simply, brands have a running start. The strongest national brands have built their consumer equities over decades of advertising and through delivery of consistent quality. From year to year, there is little change in consumers' rankings of the strongest national brands. In contrast, retailer brand names are not prominent.

Brand preference and choice

National-brand strength is known to parallel the strength of the economic situation, with many consumers preferring national brands on most shopping occasions. As the UK emerged from recession in the 1990s, manufacturers of national brands increased advertising and won back some consumers who had turned to private labels. Sales of premium-quality, premium-priced brands were on the rise by the mid-1990s.

The value factor

National brands have a value for retailers which they cannot afford to ignore; retailers cannot afford to cast off national brands that consumers expect to find widely distributed. When a store does not carry a popular brand, consumers are put off and may switch to another store (Omar, 1996). Retailers must not only stock but also promote, often at a loss, those popular national brands – such as Kit-Kat, Heinz tomato ketchup and Campbell's soup – that consumers use to gauge overall store prices. Even if, in theory, retailers can make more profit per unit on private-label products, those products (with rare exceptions such as the St Michael brand) do not have the traffic-building power of national-brand goods.

Own brands

Several factors suggest that the private-label threat is serious and may remain so, regardless of economic conditions. These factors may be listed as:

- the improved quality of own-label products;
- the development of premium own-label brands;
- European supermarkets' success with own-label products;
- the emergence of new retail marketing channels;
- the creation of new categories.

Table 9.3 lists these factors and summarises the corresponding marketing actions.

Generic products

A **generic product** is a distributor's label that does not have a traditional brand name on its label. Distributive colours, designs or other brand marks may be used, but generic products are distinguished by the absence of a traditional brand name. A generic product is a plainly packaged, less expensive version of a product, such as paper towels, canned fruit, potato chips and coffee filters.

Generics were originated in France, in 1976, by Carrefour whose strategy was simply to position generic products at the same quality levels as national brands, but make them more competitive in price. When they were introduced into the US in 1977, a different strategy was adopted. Generics were positioned as a lower-quality line with a substantially lower price. This was done so that generics would not be in conflict with sales of own-label products. The reasons for the growth of generics are both economic and strategic. As one would expect, by eliminating advertising and promotional costs, using simple, economy packaging and – in many cases – lower quality ingredients, retailers were able to offer such products to the consumer at substantially lower prices.

Table 9.3
MARKETING FACTORS FOR OWN BRAND GROWTH

Factors	Market action
Improved quality	Private-label quality levels are much higher than ever before. They are more consistent, especially in categories historically characterised by little product innovation. Retailers that contract for private-label production have improved their procurement processes and are more careful about monitoring quality.
Premium brands	Innovative retailers in the UK have shown the rest of the world how to develop a private-label line that delivers quality superior to that of national brands. Consider, for example, St Michael's numerous fashion and food brands, which includes the leading brands sold in the UK. As a result of careful, worldwide procurement, Marks & Spencer can squeeze national brands between its top-of-the-range (St Michael label) and the regular private-label line. This is despite the St Michael label not being sold outside Marks & Spencer's own stores.
Supermarkets' success	In European supermarkets, higher private-label sales result in higher average pre-tax profits. But the reasons for the strengths of private labels in Europe are partly structural due to regulated television markets, which means that cumulative retail advertising for name brands is low.
New channels	Mass merchandisers, warehouse clubs, and other channels account for a growing percentage of sales of dry groceries, household cleaning products, and health and beauty aids. Some national-brand manufacturers have encouraged the growth of new retail marketing channels, but they may come to regret this later. Unlike supermarkets, mass merchandisers and warehouse clubs are national chains; they have the incentive to develop their own national brands through private-label lines, and they have the procurement 'clout' to ensure consistent quality at low cost.
New categories	Private labels are continually expanding into new and diverse categories. Their growth follows some general trends. In supermarkets, for example, private labels have developed well beyond the traditional staples such as milk and tinned peas to include health and beauty aids, paper products such as disposable nappies and soft drinks. Private-label sales have also increased in categories such as clothing and beer. With such expansion comes increased acceptance by consumers. The more quality private-label products on the market, the more readily will consumers choose a private label over a higher-priced national-brand. The stigma that was attached to buying private labels is being eroded due to improved product quality.

Competitive considerations have also fostered the growth of generics. Retailers have introduced generics as either an offensive or defensive strategy. The addition of a range of generic items allows retailers to expand by broadening the range of customers who may be attracted to their stores. This is a particularly important factor for the large superstores, with their one-stop shopping orientation. These large stores require a huge variety to appeal to a broader base of customers and to generate the high volume of sales needed to be profitable. A defensive strategy has typically involved establishing a 'store-within-a-store' approach, in which operators of ordinary supermarkets have set up special sections and end-of-aisle displays for generics.

The introduction of generics has intensified the battle for shelf space in the supermarket and has often meant a reduction in facings and in the range of sizes or packs carried for advertised brands – in some categories, this has even led to the elimination of national brands with minor market shares. One response to this shift of power to retailers has been the dramatic increase in the money being spent by manufacturers on trade deals and allowances. Manufacturers have considered this to be necessary as a means of providing retailers with increased gross margins on their advertised brands – as protection against the retailers' lower-priced generics. Other strategies implemented by national-brand producers involve:

- reducing and, in some cases, eliminating national advertising in order to lower the price on product;
- major national advertising campaigns promoting the perception of quality of a brand-name product;
- producing products at various quality levels with comparable prices in order to attract buyers of generics and private labels;
- promoting taste tests in an effort to discourage consumers from purchasing generic products.

Regardless of the above strategies many experts believe that generic products have entered the maturity stage of the product life cycle and their sales are slowing down as part of the natural progression. However, generic products have conspicuous strengths, some of which are listed below.

1 Generic products have been accepted by retailers as an option for the consumer, and have enabled retailers to secure a significant increase in the share of the market held by private labels. Therefore, they are being given their own sections, or more and better shelf space.

2 The fact that generic products continued to grow through two recessions may indicate that consumers accept generics as a value purchase.

3 Generic products have successfully expanded product lines, thus providing the consumer with a wide array of choices in terms of price and quality.

4 With tight inventory controls, annual inventory turns for generic items can be 50 per cent higher than those of non-generic products.

The weaknesses of generic products include the following.

1 The market for generics has matured. Therefore, retailers who have been followers have been unable to match the sales levels of those who were first in their market to introduce generics.

2 Overall, generics have not contributed to category growth. While generics may attract a few new shoppers, generic sales have basically been at the expense of national brands and private labels. This change in sales mix can have, and in many cases has had, an adverse affect on the retailer's gross profit.

3 Without tight inventory controls, generics can have an adverse impact on the retailer with regard to inventory carrying costs. Introducing generics into a category may reduce inventory turnover for the category as a whole, thus increasing a retailer's carrying costs.

4 The adverse effect on inventory turnover is most obvious when a retailer introduces generics into product categories which traditionally have had higher than average turns because of being delivered directly to stores by suppliers (for example, beer, soft drinks and biscuits). A major reason for higher turns in these categories is the store delivery and service by vendors.

Since generics are not advertised, they need to be placed in a prominent location by the retailer to attract customers' attention. This is an opportunity cost to the retailer if a product yielding a higher profit could have been placed in that space. Although many retailers have used generics to support and stimulate own-label sales, they have traditionally taken business away from the retailer's own-label items. This reduction in own-label sales is pure cannibalisation, with the same profit implications as those discussed earlier.

Table 9.4 offers a useful summarising comparison of the three types of brands discussed in these central sections of this chapter: national, own label and generic.

Strategies for own branding

From the brief account of own-brand developments given, it will be apparent that very different levels of success have been achieved by different retailers. At Marks & Spencer, for example, own-brand development has been the sole brand at the heart of the company's growth. The route to a successful own-branding strategy is to determine the precise objectives to be fulfilled by the introduction of the range(s); and appropriate sources of supply must be found that can deliver the required price–quality mix. Through their launch and development, own brand(s) must be clearly differentiated, both within the store's own assortment and within the retail sector as a whole. The overall objective of own branding is to achieve

Table 9.4

CHARACTERISTIC COMPARISON OF NATIONAL, OWN-LABEL, AND GENERIC BRANDS

Characteristic	National brand	Own-label brand	Generic Product
Target market	Risk avoider, quality conscious, brand loyal, status conscious, quick shopper	Price conscious, comparison shopper, quality conscious, moderate risk taker, store loyal	Price conscious, careful shopper, willing to accept lower quality, large family
Product	Well-known, trusted, best quality control, clearly identifiable, deep product line	Same overall quality as national, less emphasis on packaging, less assortment, not known to non-store shoppers	Usually less overall quality than national, little emphasis on packaging, very limited assortment, not well known
Distribution	Usually sold at many competing stores	Only available in the outlets of a single retailer	Varies and depends on the owner
Promotion	Manufacturer-sponsored advertisements, cooperative advertisements	Retailer-sponsored advertisements promoting the retailer's name	Few advertisements, secondary shelf space
Price	Highest, usually controlled by manufacturer	Moderate, usually controlled by retailer	Lowest, usually controlled by retailer
Marketing focus	To generate brand loyalty and manufacturer control	To generate store loyalty and control	To offer a low-priced, lesser-quality item to those desiring one

competitive advantage, although there may be many forms that this may take. The potential advantages to the retailer can be broadly classified as   relating to:

■ store image and/or customer loyalty;

■ **competitive edge** and/or extra turnover;

■ higher profits and/or better margins.

These potential advantages are detailed in Table 9.5 under the headings:

■ store image/customer loyalty;

■ competitive edge/extra turnover;

■ higher profit/better margins.

Table 9.5
ADVANTAGES OF OWN BRAND FOR RETAILERS

Store image/customer loyalty	Competitive edge/extra turnover	Higher profit/better margins
■ Good value enhances store image	■ Advantage over competitors with no own brand	■ Margins tend to be 5–10% better
■ Good value builds loyalty to the store and own brand	■ Offer benefits distinct from competitors	■ Manufacturers' promotional expenses are avoided
■ Own brand may be perceived as equal to or better than manufacturers' brand	■ More control of product specification and quality	■ Display space can be manipulated for better returns
■ It is widely assumed that own brands are made by leading manufacturers	■ Allows more retailer-led product innovation	■ Sales can be promoted by placing own brands next to major brands
■ Own brands can give a distinctive corporate image	■ More control over composition of product range	■ Tighter control is usually possible
■ Own brands carry the retailer's name into the consumer's home	■ Own-brand products cannot be obtained elsewhere	■ There is more control over pricing
■ Retailer advertising can benefit both the stores and the own brand	■ Own-brand products can be sold at lower prices	■ Favourable buying terms occur where excess supply capacity exists
■ Better design coordination can be achieved between the stores and the products	■ Offer more price variety to the consumer	■ Bargaining power increases as it becomes easier to switch suppliers
	■ Inducement to use the store, leading to other purchases	■ They can help to break down manufacturers' hold over certain markets

A successful own-brand range is likely to yield benefits under each of these three headings, although it is most unlikely that all the cited advantages will apply. The objective of building customer loyalty and store image must be a major long-term consideration. Some of the most respected and sought after own brands are also those that have been longest established, such as the Sainsbury and St Michael brands.

The objective of achieving a competitive edge through own branding can be pursued in various ways. The most common approach has tended to be to present the own brands as a lower-priced alternative. Unfortunately, this ceases to provide a competitive edge if most competitors are doing the same, and if leading brands are also being heavily discounted. As a result, more retailers have sought to follow alternative methods of differentiation through quality, innovation and/or design.

Any initiative involving own branding is likely to see profit improvement as a major objective, although there are different routes to achieving this. In some cases an objective is to break down a monopoly and/or oligopoly position when strong manufacturers dominate specific markets. At the very least, the existence of the **private brand** is likely to increase bargaining power, both with suppliers of the own brand and with those competing for the remaining shelf space. Own-brand programmes may be one means by which retailers secure greater control within the marketing channel; other advantages of own brands for retailers are summarised in Table 9.5.

Unlike the manufacturer, a retailer is able directly to control the selling environment of its brands so as to enhance their turnover and, hopefully, profitability. It is quite usual for leading brands to be displayed alongside the own-brand alternatives, to provide an attraction to the section and to emphasise own-brand advantages. Manufacturers of national brands often claim that retailers give a disproportionate amount of display space to their own brands; at least in the packaged grocery sector this tends to be true. Some retailers can defend this in terms of the superior sales volume of their own brands, although excessive bias in space allocation can damage the retailer's image in terms of product choice. Retailers must carefully balance the objectives to be achieved through own branding.

Manufacturers' competitive strategy options

Strategies to fight private labels

Manufacturers of national brands could take several actions to prevent private-label products from achieving any further share gains. Such strategic actions may include:

- investing in brand equities;
- innovating wisely;
- using fighting brands sparingly;
- building trade relationships;
- managing the **price spread**;
- exploiting sales-promotion tactics;
- managing each product category;
- using category profit pools as a performance measure;
- taking private labels seriously.

Invest in brand equity

A brand could be described as the capital value of the trust between a company and its customer. **Brand equity** – the added value that a brand name gives to the underlying product – must be carefully nurtured by each successive brand manager. Managers must continually monitor how consumers perceive the brand. Consistent, clear positioning – supported by periodic product improvements that keep the brand contemporary without distorting its fundamental meaning – is essential.

Exhibit 9.3	**Keeping ahead of the competition – and keeping the faith**

Proctor & Gamble has made 70 separate improvements to Persil laundry detergent since its launch in 1956, but the brand's core promise that it will get clothes cleaner than any other product has never been compromised. Consistent investment in product improvements enhances a brand's perceived superiority, provides the basis for informative and provocative advertising, increases the brand's sustainable price premium over the competition, and raises the costs to own-label imitators who are constantly forced to play catch-up.

Wise innovation and use of fighting brands

Desperate to increase sales and presence on the shelves and to earn quick promotions, too many national-brand managers launch line extensions. Most are of marginal value to customers, dilute rather than enhance the core-brand franchise, add complexity and administrative costs, impair the accuracy of demand forecasts, and are unprofitable on a full-cost basis. Too many line extensions confuse consumers, the trade, and the salesforce, and reduce the manufacturer's credibility with the trade as an expert on the category. Brand additions should represent substantial new innovation and should be introduced wisely.

Fighting brands should be treated with similar caution and handled wisely. Their use should be limited though they may have a role – strictly controlled – in defending an existing national brand which is under attack from a private-label competitor. It must be remembered that there are always casualties, and a fighting brand is highly unlikely to make a profit.

Exhibit 9.4	Managers should be wary of launching fighting brands; these are products which are price positioned between private labels and the national brands they aim to defend. The purpose of a fighting brand is to avoid the huge contribution loss that would occur if a leading national brand tried to stem share losses to private labels by dropping its price; the fighting brand gives the price-sensitive consumer a low-cost branded alternative.

Philip Morris has effectively used fighting brands L & M, Basic, and Chesterfield around the world to flank Marlboro. Likewise, Heinz has used fighting brands well in pet foods. However, the fighting brand can end up competing with the national brand for consumers who would not have switched to private-label products anyway. For this reason, Procter & Gamble recently phased out White Cloud toilet tissue and Oxydol laundry detergent.

Rarely do fighting brands make money. The management time that these products absorb would often be better invested in building the equity of the national brand.

Learning Resources
Centre

Build trade relationships

Manufacturers must leverage their knowledge to create a win–win proposition for their trade accounts. Retailers and national-brand producers can both maximise their profits, without excessive emphasis on private labels. This is possible if manufacturers:

- collaborate with retailers in both marketing and distribution steps;
- offer to examine retailers' purchase scanner data. Invariably, the shopper who buys a national-brand item rather than a private-label one in the same category spends more per supermarket visit and delivers a higher absolute and percentage margin to the retailer;
- subsidise in-store experiments. Retailers' views of how many consumers are attracted to their stores by private labels are often inflated. Manufacturers can suggest, and pay for, tests that compare the sales and profitability of a control store's current shelf-space allocation plan with the sales and profitability of a shelf-space plan offering fewer or no private-label goods.

By responding to customers and managing categories more efficiently, leading manufacturers have found new ways of favouring trade accounts that support their brands over private labels; they have also found ways of not being quite so helpful to those that do not.

Price spread management and the use of sales promotion tactics

During the 1980s, manufacturers increased prices ahead of inflation (the easiest way to add bottom-line profit in the short term) and then offered periodic reductions on their artificially inflated list prices to distributors and consumers who demanded them. As long as some customers paid full price, this price discrimination was thought to be profitable. Over time, however, such a high proportion of the typical brand's volume was being sold at a deep discount that the list prices no longer had credibility. Further, the added manufacturing and logistics costs of the promotions and the increased price sensitivity they stimulated played into the hands of private labels. When Marlboro cut its list prices, it correspondingly reduced the level and frequency of its promotions; the list price was restored to a more credible level while the hidden costs from the brand's use of promotions were reduced.

Manufacturers must monitor the price gap both to the distributor and to the end consumer between each national brand and the other brands, including private labels, in every market. They must also understand what the price elasticity of demand is for each national brand – that is, the manufacturer must be aware of what effect a change in price would have on consumers in terms of each branded product line.

Brand category management and taking private labels seriously

Brand **category management** is not a straightforward process; what works for detergents may not necessarily work for soft drinks. Categories differ widely in terms of private-label penetration, the price–quality gap between private labels and

| Exhibit 9.5 | **The effects of price changes on national and private-label brands** |

In a price experiment conducted for Asda superstores, it was found that a 5 per cent increase over the private-label price in the price premium of a sample national brand resulted in a 2 per cent loss of share. But an increase of 10 per cent resulted in an additional 3 per cent loss. With an increase between 10 and 15 per cent, only 2 per cent more was lost because the remaining national-brand customers were the less-price-sensitive and loyal customers (Omar, 1992). Knowing the shape of the brand's price elasticity curve is essential to adequate pricing and to maximising the brand's profitability. A price reduction on a popular national brand may result in a lower profit contribution, but studies show that private-label sales are twice as sensitive as national brands are to changes in the price gap. In other words, a decrease in the price gap would swing twice as many sales from private labels to national brands as a corresponding increase would swing sales to private labels from national brands.

national brands, and the relative profitability and potential cannibalisation cost of any private-label brand. Thus, in categories with:

- low private-label penetration such as breakfast cereals and baby food, managers must understand and sustain the barriers to entry – with frequent technological improvements within the category;

- emerging private-label penetration, it is useful to consider value-added packaging changes and line extensions – strategies which may make the product stand out on the shelf, since it is important that consumers' attention remains focused on the national brands;

- well-established private-label penetration, the goal is containment. The emphasis must be on lowering the costs in the supply chain – through minimum order size, truckload and direct shipment discounts, more efficient trade deals, and the elimination of slow-moving stock-keeping units – to save money for reinvestment in the brand.

| Exhibit 9.6 | **Fighting the own-label challenge** |

Consider the results of the Coca-Cola Company's response to Cott in Canada, where the market for private-label soft drink sales was strong. After Coca-Cola retaliated aggressively against Cott in 1994, the latter's profits as a percentage of sales plummeted along with its stock price; the company then moderated its ambitions to extend its private-label success formula to other product categories. Cott executives stated that the company's growth would thereafter come as a result of overall market expansion and at the expense of competitors smaller than Coca-Cola. By taking firm, considered action, national-brand manufacturers can successfully fight the own-label challenge.

Manufacturers can use some or all of the strategies outlined above to wage the battle against private-label producers. Whatever strategy is used, however, the basic lesson that must be learned is that private labels should be treated with respect.

Own-label sourcing

As retailers became more demanding in their product specifications and the sheer volume of own brands increases, the choice of suppliers with the required capability becomes more limited. Also, the identification of suitable sources for new own-brand products may require extensive information and more management and/or buyer time than some retailers are able to devote to the task.

It could be argued that organisations with their own manufacturing capacity, such as the Co-op, Boots and the British Shoe Corporation (with retail outlets such as Dolcis), encounter fewer supply problems. In none of these cases, however, is the manufacturing division the sole source of supply; vertical integration may also be regarded, at least by the retail divisions, as an obstacle to aggressive buying. Britain's largest own-brand retailer, Marks & Spencer, has no manufacturing capacity under its direct control. Due to its close involvement in the design and production of own brands, Marks & Spencer has been described as a 'manufacturer without factories' (Tse, 1985). The company has set new standards in specification buying, which attempts to leave no aspect of the product to chance or to arbitrary decisions by suppliers.

There are about seven hundred suppliers producing St Michael goods, ranging from major brand manufacturers such as United Biscuits and Lotus Shoes, to small manufacturers in North Africa and India. The major supplier of St Michael foods is Northern Foods. This company operates what is sometimes termed a 'mixed brand' policy, producing own labels and a number of well-known brands, such as Fox's Biscuits and Bowyers. A very close involvement is maintained between Northern Foods and Marks & Spencer, from senior management to shop-floor levels. Generally, there is a surprisingly high level of manufacturers' involvement with own-brand production. Only a small number of manufacturers refuse to supply own brands (Kellogg's is a well-known example), and there is no guarantee that these will not supply them in the future. Among those companies that currently supply own-brand products, a small number at least formulate some of the own brands specifically for the particular retailer(s). For manufacturers, there are both advantages and disadvantages inherent in the supplying of own brands (de Chernatony and McDonald, 1992).

Advantages:

- excess production capacity can be utilised;
- there is a more efficient utilisation of manufacturing and distribution facilities, exploiting economies of scale;
- own brands help absorb fixed costs;

- supplying own brands may prevent the retail buyer from transferring their business to competitors who will supply them;
- own brands may provide a base for expansion;
- small manufacturers can enter/stay in the market without incurring costs associated with branding;
- some warranty liabilities may transfer to the retailers;
- large manufacturers using a mixed-brand policy may retain more control and discriminate between product images, specifications and prices;
- brand leaders may benefit as own brands have tended to compete more with minor brands;
- retailers may refuse to stock a manufacturer's brand unless it agrees also to produce own brands;
- own-brand supply fosters a closer relationship between manufacturer and retailer;
- the retailer has an equal interest in selling the goods.

Disadvantages:

- advantages may be short-lived;
- it may be difficult to re-establish the position of a manufacturer's brand once promotion and advertising have been phased down;
- own brands may undermine sales of a manufacturer's brands in the same store;
- retailers may restrict display and promotion of manufacturer brands to emphasise own brands;
- own brands can lead to excessive reliance on a few trade customers (at worst, just one large customer);
- negotiating power is reduced – even lost – since the retailer usually has the ability to switch to alternative channels of supply;
- using own brands to recover overheads may simply be treating the symptoms not the disease and postpone solving the real problem of excessive overheads;
- investment in technical development and competitive advantage is given away 'free' to own brands;
- expertise developed at great expense and effort may, in effect, be handed over to rival domestic or foreign manufacturers if a retailer decides to switch suppliers;
- margins may be much lower – around 20 per cent less – and own-brand supply tends to achieve lower profitability.

A variety of reasons have been cited by manufacturers for becoming involved in or staying out of the supply of own brands. The arguments most frequently given in favour of supplying own brands relate to the economic factors. When excess capacity exists, the production of own labels at least helps to absorb fixed costs. Greater economies of scale can also be achieved, an argument that may also be applied to distribution facilities. In this case, however, the strategy may backfire; for example, a frozen food manufacturer with a mixed-brand policy found that its expensive ware-housing and transport system was increasingly difficult to sustain, as their own brands were increasingly distributed by the retailers or their agency distributors.

Own-brand differentiation and positioning

The majority of retailers have used price as a major method of achieving competitive advantage for their own brands. As manufacturers have responded to the challenge, by paring down their own costs and margins, it has become increasingly difficult to achieve successful differentiation through price alone. Where private label and man-ufacturer's brands compete directly, however, there are still a few examples of own brands being sold at the same or higher prices, though it is normally assumed that the equivalent own brand will be noticeably cheaper than the national brand.

A variety of positioning strategies may be employed in developing own brands. Three types of role could be fulfilled by own brands; in terms of consumers' moti-vations, these may be defined as:

- the cheapest will do – motivated by economy or lack of pressure to select any-thing else. Shopping in this mood clearly favours own brands, including generics;

- rational choice – a conscious judgement of quality versus value strongly associ-ated with the store itself. This could favour own brands or **premium brands**, depending on the shopper's feelings about the store;

- worth paying for quality – where there is some rejection of economy or even rationality, or when the shopper is under pressure to make an impression on others. This kind of motivation favours premium brands or the own brands of up-market stores, for example, Harrods.

It is clearly important for the retailer to identify the particular position within the relevant market(s) to be filled by the own brands. The tendency to introduce 'me too' own-brand ranges – mainly because everyone else seems to have them – will not lead to clear positioning, and indeterminacy in positioning is unlikely to result in success in own branding. Furthermore, the positioning does not have to be based mainly on price. The most successful own brands have been those with clearly differentiated 'product pluses' in comparison to existing branded products. These 'pluses' may relate to several factors including quality, convenience, innova-tion, assortment and price.

As noted earlier, two of the most successful own-brand retailers, J. Sainsbury and Marks & Spencer, have made massive investments in the specification of quality products and the development of unusual additions to their assortments. Innovative forms of convenience packaging have also contributed to the success of St Michael foods. IKEA and MFI have achieved considerable success with their self-assembly furniture, which can usually be paid for, collected and transported immediately by the customers. This innovation incorporated the major 'pluses' of convenience and price, relative to standard furniture retailing. There are also many other examples of differentiation through product design, such as new safety features on Mothercare's products and the natural preparations developed by The Body Shop and within an ethical business framework.

In view of the success of these approaches, it seems inevitable that retailers will take an increasingly strong role in product development and innovation. Without this, they would have to be content with competing from a primarily price-based platform, which is a difficult position from which to maintain competitive advantage in the long term. It is often pointed out that the retailer is far closer to the customer than the manufacturer, although the identification of needs and the interpretation of these into successful product concepts is unlikely to happen through proximity alone. In the future, it is likely that more retailers will adopt the type of role that is already ascribed to Marks & Spencer, that of a 'manufacturer without factories'.

Consumer response to own brands

In common with any marketing strategy, own branding requires close monitoring of consumers' reactions, in terms of both perceptions and actual purchase patterns. It tends to be assumed, for example, that own brands increase loyalty – which may or may not be true in relation to a particular retailer's brand. It may also be assumed that consumers perceive a particular range to represent high value, but these perceptions should be regularly checked. This section looks briefly at some of the studies undertaken to assess consumer reactions to own-brand ranges. From the earlier discussion, however, it will be recognised that own brands come in many different forms; the results of any one specific study, therefore, should not be assumed to apply to own brands in general.

Own-brand purchasers

There has been considerable research interest in identifying the types of consumer most likely to purchase own brands. Early studies in the UK generally confirmed a slightly higher propensity to purchase own brands among upmarket and young consumers (Uncles and Ellis, 1989). This has been attributed to the higher perceived risk involved in buying own brands, and the greater security of these upmarket consumers and reduced risk aversion displayed among the young. This, obviously, cannot be generalised across all own brands. St Michael and Sainsbury brand products, for example, are regarded as extremely 'safe' purchases. Clearly, the extent of the perceived risk depends upon the length of time that the own brand has been established, the marketing support invested by the retailer, and consumers' perceptions of the retailer's overall reputation.

Many upmarket shoppers patronise Sainsbury and Tesco, and therefore have extensive opportunities to buy own labels. Research has sworn that consumers who preferred own brands tended to transfer that preference, even when they switched to another store. The concept of own-brands appealing to the more discerning consumers has been effectively harnessed by a number of retailers. Tesco, for example, pursued a strong programme of nutritional labelling in product categories where this had not generally been provided (Omar, 1994).

It will become increasingly difficult to find meaningful differences between generics users and non-users as the purchase of generics becomes more widely diffused throughout the population. It may well be that marketing scholars have overemphasised the analysis of consumer descriptors while neglecting the study of the determinants of quality perceptions and their role in the consumer decision-making process for generics.

Price and quality perception

Objective quality data, such as the Consumers' Association test reports (published in *Which?* magazine), are available on a limited scale but are not used by the majority of consumers. Perceptions of quality are, therefore, a key determinant of the positioning achieved by own brands. Over a period of many years, the St Michael own brand has achieved an enviable reputation for quality and value. Within the UK, a high proportion of shoppers would single out Marks & Spencer as a shop with particularly good-value own-brand products. This type of reputation cannot, however, be achieved overnight; the process of establishing a new own-brand range inevitably takes time and/or a good deal of marketing support. In the vigorous early growth period for many own brands in the 1970s, there was some concern about quality perceptions. The available evidence, however, suggested that the standing of own brands started to converge with that of manufacturers' brands in the 1980s; by the late 1990s most shoppers considered own-brand products to be of the same quality as well-known national brands.

Exhibit 9.7	**Matching a retailer's reputation to own branding**

There is inevitably a dilemma facing a retailer launching an own brand based primarily upon a low-price proposition. Consumers have a propensity to impute quality on the basis of price, particularly when there are no other strong quality cues available (Rothe and Lamount, 1973). One such cue, of course, is the reputation of the retailer itself. It is significant that Asda postponed the main development of its own brands until the mid-1980s, by which time it had established its own 'name'. In the early 1970s, the company was still trading largely from converted old mills and was unknown in most parts of the country. After years of new store development, geographical expansion and heavy media advertising, Asda achieved a solid, national reputation. The time had, therefore, arrived to start expanding by retailing an own-brand range – when the quality of the own-brand range would be backed by Asda's reputation for good quality, low-priced retailing.

Depicting own brands in terms of price and quality perceptions illustrates that there is a limited amount of space within which successfully to position an own-brand range. Considerable buying power and operating efficiency is required to achieve the reasonable price/good quality position attained by Marks & Spencer and J. Sainsbury. Some of the lower perceived quality positions, while possibly commanding a viable share of turnover, may be in conflict with the retailer's over-all need to develop a quality image. As discussed in the previous section, it is increasingly necessary to look at dimensions beyond those of price and quality if a retailer is to achieve successful own-brand differentiation.

SUMMARY

Many alternative terms are used to describe own brands, including 'private labels', 'own labels', 'house brands' and 'retailer brands'. These are all descriptions of prod-uct ranges that are sold only within the stores of a particular retail organisation. The range may carry the name of the retailer or a brand name specific to that retailer. There are also variants upon the own-brand concept, including generics, retailer 'exclusives' and 'me-too' brands.

Own branding is particularly strong in footwear, menswear, chemists, grocery and large 'mixed' retail businesses. The proportion of own branding in the UK is higher than in other European countries, reflecting the particular strength of the UK multiples, although most countries have seen increases during the 1990s Many own-brand ranges rank alongside major manufacturer brands in scale; Marks & Spencer, Sainsbury, the Co-op and Tesco have successful own brands, each with a high annual turnover. Own brands have grown with the major multiples, although not all multiples have been committed to their development. Neither are own brands to be found solely in the multiples and co-operatives. In the symbol sector (e.g. Spar) own brands have been developed partly to maintain group cohesion, and in the cash-and-carry sector they have helped to increase the loyalty of inde-pendent retailers.

Generic ranges, otherwise known as 'brand-free' and 'no-names', have been introduced by some retailers, especially in the grocery sector (e.g. Tesco's Value range). These products use very basic labelling and sell at prices well below those of leading brands. Their growth has been limited in the UK, partly because of diffi-culties in positioning them alongside existing own brands. Generics have achieved rather more impact in other countries, such as France, Germany and the USA. Some own brands have been introduced as defensive, 'me-too' ranges; others have demonstrated more positive approaches to gaining competitive advantage.

KEY TERMS		
brand equity	generic product	price spread
brand preference	house brand	private brand
brand usage	low price	private label
brand wars	manufacturer's brand	product category
category management	'me-too' brand	retailers' brand
competitive edge	national brands	shopping process
customer loyalty	own brand	value brand
economy brand	own label	
fighting brand	premium brand	

ASSIGNMENT

Average of Great Britain (AGB) Superpanel data suggest private labels in the packaged grocery market have risen from under 37 per cent at the beginning of 1994 to over 43 per cent by mid-1998, with the increase concentrated in Tesco, Sainsbury, Asda, Safeway and Somerfield. It all adds to the pressure on manufacturers, but those that will benefit are the manufacturers which invest in 'unique brands whose genuine points of difference' cannot easily be copied by own-label producers.

Task

You recently graduated with a degree in Retail Management and working for a reputable national-brand manufacturer which also supplies own-label products to several retailers. Discuss the implications of the AGB Superpanel data suggestions for your organisation. What strategic option would you recommend to your employer? Your essay must not exceed 1500 words.

REVISION QUESTIONS

1 What do you consider to be the key factors that have influenced the pattern of growth in own branding in the UK? Do you expect this growth to continue?

2 Explain why own brands have achieved far more impact in some product sectors than in others.

3 To what extent have retailers' marketing activities influenced the development and growth of own brands within the supermarket sector?

4 Briefly describe the importance of stocking generic products for grocery retailers.

5 From the viewpoint of a major grocery retailer, how would you appraise the opportunities and the threats of introducing a range of generics?

6 What would you consider to be the principal objectives for food retailers in developing own-brand products?

7 What factors could motivate a manufacturer of branded goods also to supply own brands? What risks are involved in this strategy?

8 'The most successful own brands have been those with clearly differentiated "product pluses" in comparison with existing branded products'. Discuss.

9 Why do some own-brand positioning strategies fail to achieve high consumer loyalty to the range?

10 What strategic marketing actions would you suggest to national-brand manufacturers who are fighting against retailers' own-label products?

CASE STUDY

Nisa-Today's own-brand marketing

Own-brand products first appeared in the UK during the latter part of the nineteenth century, with the Co-operative Society unveiling its range of private label biscuits. In the 1970s, retailers found they needed new business strategies in order to grapple with the recession in consumer spending. Food retailers began to concentrate on volume sales of staple items, often using own-label products as 'loss leaders' to tempt shoppers into their stores and to increase sales.

A major change in private-label retailing occurred during the 1980s, when some of the best-known retailers extended the reach of own-brand goods by launching their own high-profile product ranges. It was about this time that Nisa entered the fray. The first products launched under the Nisa label were high volume, commodity lines such as canned vegetables, baked beans and soft drinks. Consumer interest in the first own-label venture of Nisa-Today's was very encouraging. The growth in the UK's own-label sector has accelerated rapidly since then, mirroring the surge in interest for private-label products across the country. By the 1990s, the UK had become the country with the highest own-brand penetration in Europe; furthermore, many of these products had become market leaders in their respective fields.

The underlying reason for the growth in own-label brand sales is the fierce competition that has developed between grocery multiples in an attempt to build brand allegiance. Own-brand share of overall retail sales in the UK has grown steadily, reflecting the UK's position as Europe's leading own-brand market. This unexpected prosperity of the private-label sector also resulted in a more than favourable outcome for Today's range.

According to the marketing director of Nisa-Today's, 'our experience in own-label quickly benefited our Today's wholesale members, when we launched the successful Today's brand some fifteen years ago'. The Today's private labels are performing above market expectations, and forecasts from within the organisation estimated a volume growth in excess of 40 per cent per annum. All areas of private-label business are reported to be performing extremely well, but the most impressive include: paperware (up 20.2 per cent); soft drinks (up 30.1 per cent); hot beverages (up 12.9 per cent); household items (up 17.1 per cent); and biscuits (up 13.4 per cent).

Formed in 1977 to protect the interests of the UK independent retail community, Nisa-Today's is now the largest self-governing buying organisation in the UK, boasting national membership and a turnover of over £10.5 billion. Initially, Nisa-Today's concentrated on offering the best stock deals possible to independent retailers on well-known brand names, enjoying a considerable level of brand loyalty. This gave smaller independent outlets the chance to compete with the multiples.

Nisa-Today's in the late 1990s offers comprehensive, high quality private-label ranges – including Today's which takes in over 300 lines – spanning all the major

▶

product categories. This provides small independent retailers, using cash and carry and wholesaler deliveries of stock, with an opportunity to achieve the same sort of on-shelf impact enjoyed by the major supermarket groups. Own-label represents an important factor in the success of every progressive independent. From the consumer's point of view, it provides an alternative to the leading brands. Developed to meet the needs of every type of outlet, the Today's private-label portfolio provides a comprehensive arsenal for an independent retailer – from price-fighting products to upmarket lines – in packaging that reflects the quality of this competitively-priced range.

All the products in the Today's range have one fundamental thing in common – the highest possible quality. This is ensured by the Quality Assurance Team (QAT) which tests each product to monitor standards to be sure that the quality, on which the group prides itself, is maintained. Nisa-Today's product quality compares favourably with all competition in the independent sector, most favourably so with those of the major supermarket chains.

Like the multiples, Nisa-Today's also have export customers. To achieve this status, they were audited by a third party body and came out with a higher score than any major brand on the high street. Nisa-Today's has a very experienced QAT but third party laboratories are used for micro and analytical testing, along with consumer test panels where appropriate. All factories manufacturing private-label lines are visited by Nisa-Today's representatives at least once a year. The QA department works on all brands controlled at the centre; the strict procedures they practice protect the brand and the buyer, but, most importantly, they safeguard members' interests, by making sure their customers receive the best own-label products available on the UK market.

The British have become seasoned purchasers of own-brand goods, accepting them as a regular and essential part of their shopping. Moreover, the recent bout of price competition between major multiples has intensified own-brand sales. Consumers are confident of own-brand goods, perceiving them as being innovative, inexpensive, competitive and good quality. They now compare own-brands and this has led to retailers paying increased attention to both the quality and price-positioning of their own-brand selection.

In 1997, Nisa-Today's carried out a market research programme into price-marking own-brand products. It discovered that price-marking led to an increase in consumer confidence at the point of purchase. This ushered in the update and re-launch of Today's as a price-marked range that sits comfortably with the quality and value image that features on every pack.

The competition created by the growing number of private label products arriving on the UK market has led to a situation whereby few branded manufacturers feel able to remain outside this increasingly lucrative area. HJ Heinz's decision in 1996 to enter the fray of private-label manufacturing, for the first time, set a historic precedent – one for others to follow into the twenty-first century.

Questions for discussions

1 Why are branded manufacturers no longer able to stay out of own-label production and marketing? Discuss this question, giving your own views.

2 What reasons could you suggest as factors for Nisa-Today's success with own-label marketing; and why are own-label products more popular in Britain than other European countries?

REFERENCES

Akehurst, G. and Alexander, N. (1995) *The Internationalisation of Retailing*. London: Frank Cass.

de Chernatony, L. and McDonald, M.H.B. (1992) *Creating Powerful Brands*. London: Butterworth/Heinmann.

McGoldrick, P. (1990) *Retail Marketing*. Maidenhead: McGraw-Hill.

Omar, O.E. (1992) 'Grocery shopping behaviour and retailers' own-label food brands'. PhD thesis. Department of Retailing and Marketing, The Manchester Metropolitan University, Manchester, UK.

Omar, O.E. (1994) 'Comparative product testing for own-label marketing', *International Journal of Retail and Distribution Management*, 22(2): 12–17.

Omar, O.E. (1996) 'Grocery purchase behaviour for national and own-label brands', *The Services Industry Journal*, 16(1): 58–66.

Omar, O.E. and Kent, A. (1995) 'Manufacturers' food brands: assessment of marketing opportunities in the UK supermarkets', *The Journal of Brand Management*, 3(5): 327–36.

Rothe, J.T. and Lamount, L.M. (1973) 'Purchase behaviour and brand choice determinants for national and private brand major appliances', *Journal of Retailing*, 49(3): 19–33.

Tse, K.K. (1985) *Marks & Spencer: Anatomy of Britain's Most Efficiently Managed Company*. Oxford: Pergamon.

Uncles, M.D. and Ellis, K. (1989) 'The buying of own-labels', *European Journal of Marketing*, 23(3): 57.

10

Pricing in retail marketing management

LEARNING OBJECTIVES

After reading this chapter you should:

■ understand what is meant by retail pricing;

■ understand how demand and supply affect pricing policy and price elasticity;

■ understand the various roles played by price in retailing;

■ be able to evaluate various pricing strategies adopted by retailers based on their competitive strategies;

■ know how manufacturers give discounts to retailers and other sales agents.

As we saw in Chapter 1, retail marketing involves the two-way exchange of something of value. Value is used here to mean a measure of the power one product or service has to attract another product or service in exchange. But while it may be possible to value every product in terms of every other product, such a system would be extremely complicated. It is far easier to express these many values in terms of the single variable of money. Price is a statement of value, because it is the amount of money or other consideration given in exchange for a product or service. In the UK, it is most commonly expressed in pounds and pence.

Price has many names, and these names vary according to tradition or the interests of the seller. For instance, we may refer to price as rent, fee, donation, toll, bonus, etc. in specific exchange situations. Some sellers avoid the use of the word price to make what is offered for sale appear to be of a quality that price cannot fully describe. Thus, the student pays tuition fees – for education is beyond price; the London underground commuter pays a fare; a suspension bridge user pays a toll; and a private medical doctor charges a fee for a professional consultation. In general, however, governments, universities, teachers and doctors all sell their services for a price, irrespective of what this price is called. As far as the exchange of things of value is concerned, the name commonly used to describe this value is 'price'.

Retailers' use of price

Price is probably the most responsive and potent weapon in the retail marketing mix. Yet the markets in which **price wars** are fought are littered with corporate casualties and pyrrhic victories. Exhibit 10.1 gives some background to the use of price in food and household goods retailing in its present form.

Exhibit 10.1	**Price discounting to achieve high volume sales**

The retail sector provides obvious evidence of the most blatant use of price to attract shoppers into the stores. High volumes and low price are the key features of retail strategy, and this has led to greater concentration among the major multiples and the demise of the corner shop. In food and household goods, price competition is particularly fierce – usually in the form of discounting of selected lines, combined with promotion of own-label and/or generic or no frills products. This trend probably assumed its modern character in 1977 with Tesco's 'Operation Check-out', followed by Sainsbury's 'Discount 78'; and several of other catchy campaign slogans such as Asda's 'Pocket the Difference', Woolworth's 'Crackdown' and the Co-op's 'Price Right'. These campaigns generally boosted market shares – some more successfully than others.

The meaning of price

Bearing in mind the above explanation of what price is, we may all mean different things when we talk about 'price'. Specifically the buyer and the seller may have different views, and such differences may create problems between them and delay or prevent the basic agreement necessary for a sale to take place. Examples of the ways sellers and buyers may look upon price are given in Table 10.1.

Although price is important in itself, its role in the overall retail marketing strategy is diverse and of particular note. Exhibit 10.2 shows how price is used by Uno, one of Britain's large upholstery superstores, to present their products strongly and with an accompanying quality/price assurance.

Often, pricing is not used as part of the overall marketing strategy; rather, it is maintained in a situation of neutrality, with the prices determined on a cost-plus basis or by using the manufacturers' suggested prices. In either case, pricing plays an active role in the retailer's overall marketing strategy.

The right price

Now that you have some idea of what price is, the next question is: 'What is the right price for retailers to set for the items they sell in their stores'? In answering this question, most people may say 'what the market will bear' or, simply, 'what

Table 10.1
MEANING OF PRICE TO THE SELLER AND THE BUYER

Price to the seller	*Price to the buyer*
1 An element in the retail marketing mix, or the store promotional mix, which can be manipulated within a defined range to achieve corporate objectives, e.g. to promote sales, to create an image, to forestall competition.	1 A measure of the value of the total bundle of satisfaction they are offered, with the corollary that the significance of price may vary within the decision-making process.
2 Part of the relationship which, when taken in conjunction with the sales volume, yields a revenue fund from which costs can be met and a profit obtained.	2 A cost, particularly where the purchase is for industrial or commercial purposes. It is also a measure of quality. That means 'you only get what you pay for', etc.
3 A measure of the risks to the seller involved in the sale, and/or an insurance premium against the maturing of these risks.	3 A measure of the alternatives foregone: either directly, i.e. directly competitive products or substitutes, or indirectly, i.e. alternative uses for the money to be spent.
4 Part of an overall bundle of factors, including discounts, settlement terms, credit terms which can be used to affect both the 'willingness' and the 'ability' of the customer to purchase.	4 Part of a conglomerate of things which the buyer often takes into account under the heading of price – discounts, settlement terms, credit-terms, part-exchange or trade-in-terms, guarantees which may affect his/her 'willingness' or 'ability' to purchase.

Exhibit 10.2 | **Price and quality assurance as part of the overall strategy**

Uno's price promotional campaign and price guarantee reads: 'if you imagine buying a beautiful, new 3-piece suite, knowing it's at Britain's lowest price – guaranteed; imagine choosing from Britain's biggest display of 3 seaters, 2 seaters, sofa beds, chairs and recliners, plus a superb range of leathers; imagine being given £3000 instantly on Uno's easy payment plan and your payments not starting until September 1998; imagine every suite being covered by an exclusive 5 year quality guarantee. Imagine no more. Uno turns your dreams into reality'.

In terms of price guarantee, Uno's promise is that if you 'buy your suite from Uno and if within one year of purchase you see that our price (including services) is not at least 10 per cent cheaper than that for the identical perfect product (including services) on show anywhere else in Britain, you are entitled to claim a refund of the difference between the total price you paid Uno and the total competitor's price less a further 10 per cent. This is in addition to your statutory rights'.

consumers are willing to pay'. But what does that mean? Does it mean the price at which the retailer can sell most of their product, or perhaps the highest or lowest price at which any item is sold? The correct definition of the right price is 'the price which will bring the largest contribution to overheads and profit'.

Exhibit 10.3

Setting price to maximise profit

Take a simple example of a St Michael range of women's dresses costing £60 per unit to make for Marks & Spencer (see Table 10.2 for details).

Table 10.2

Forecast sales (units)	Unit price (£)	Unit contribution (£)	Total sales (£000)	Total contribution (£000)
60	120	60	7.2	3.6
90	110	50	9.9	4.5
100	100	40	10.0	4.0
120	90	30	10.8	3.6

In price-sensitive retail sector, the higher you set your price, the fewer units you will sell, but – up to a point – the higher will be your unit contribution to profit and overheads. The trick is to find the price at which the largest contribution to overheads and profit will be made. In this simple Marks & Spencer case, increasing the unit price from £100 to £110 results in 10 per cent fewer units being sold and a 1 per cent reduction in total sales value, but increases the total contribution by 12.5 per cent. A further increase in price reduces both total sales and total contribution. The maximum contribution comes from the price increase which reduces total sales slightly.

This example shows that retailers, both large and small, should beware of chasing turnover at all costs because the price that brings the maximum profit may not necessarily be the one which brings maximum sales.

External influences on price

This section concerns itself with external factors affecting pricing in retail organisations. Since the retailing process takes place in the market, certain factors prevailing in the market directly influence retail price policy and management, including demand, price elasticity and competition, and price-perceived quality.

Demand and price relationship

Demand is reflected in the ability and willingness of customers to buy the products the retailer is selling. If no potential can be realised in terms of sales, the store does not have a chance of succeeding. However, if there is potential, its success in terms of being converted into sales is substantial, depending on the store's pricing strategy. All other factors being equal, if the store charges the 'right' price, then it will sell more. The concept of right price, however, is subject to careful scrutiny.

Consumers have a mental picture of the value of a product. This mental picture includes a range as well as a psychological dimension. These price ranges are likely to vary on the basis of how much importance is attached to the product and each consumer's socio-economic background. Thus, instead of the demand curve customarily illustrated in economics texts, the demand curve for the retailer is likely to be a disjointed rather than a continuous demand function. Figure 10.1 shows that if a retailer were to raise prices from L to N in the conventional demand curve, a volume loss equivalent to B A would be the result (that is, the demand curve would move to the left). On the other hand, if the price range theory were accepted, the retailer could raise the price from L to N without losing any volume. Hence, the total revenue for the retailer would be substantially greater than the conventional demand function would indicate.

The range concept of price is related to an individual's psyche. To the extent that an individual would like to buy a certain brand or to patronise a store, he or she will not have one specific price in mind. Within reason, this individual will not insist on a particular price but will be willing to pay a little more or less to buy that specific product or to buy in the chosen store. The individual's brand loyalty or store loyalty is part of his or her psyche. Another pricing concept that involves consideration of the individual's psyche is known as **psychological pricing**. It has been suggested that odd prices are psychologically more attractive to customers. Thus, consumers typically opt for a product priced at £5.99 as opposed to the even price of £6.00 (Berman and Evans, 1995). This psychological point is important only if demand for the product or the store exists.

Fig. 10.1 PRICE RANGE INCLUDED DEMAND FUNCTION VERSUS CONVENTIONAL DEMAND FUNCTION

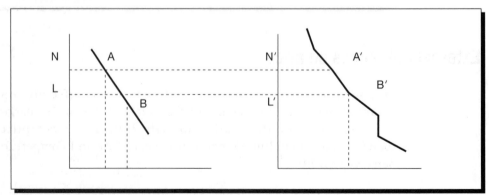

Price elasticity and competition

Price elasticity, though discussed in marketing literature, is rarely practised by the practitioner and rarely advocated by marketing academics as an important pricing tool because it is too difficult to compute. However, both retailers and manufacturers need to understand price elasticity because it guides management pricing actions as suggested in Exhibit 10.4. As a concept, **price elasticity of demand** implies the consumer's reaction to price changes. It may be defined as the change in quantity demanded which is attributable to a 1 per cent change in price. If the quantity demanded exceeds 1 per cent, demand is considered to be price elastic, but if it is smaller than 1 per cent demand is considered to be price inelastic. It is calculated using the following formula:

$$\frac{\% \, \Delta \, Q}{\% \, \Delta \, P}$$

where % Δ Q = per cent change in quantity demanded
% Δ P = per cent change in price

Any standard economics text will offer a reasonable explanation and discussion of this concept. From a retail marketing perspective, elasticity is important as an indicator of the store's competitive advantage or monopolistic power. If the demand that a store commands is such that price increases yield a less than proportionate

---

| **Exhibit 10.4** | **Why marketers need to understand price elasticity** |

With retailers making big inroads into market shares and competition increasingly focusing on price, it is vital that manufacturers have a full understanding of price elasticity. This is necessary because leading brands' price promotions may have only a small impact on sales, and marketers will need other ways of building volume. In this scenario, marketing mix decisions need to take account of the sensitivity of sales to changes in price. Price elasticity, the ratio of sales change to price change, captures price sensitivity as a promotional effect. Price elasticity assumptions guide management actions. Thus, when a brand shows high elasticity, managers may favour price promotions; if elasticity is low, more emphasis may well be placed on other components of marketing.

Practically, if the price elasticity for Fairy washing-up liquid is –1.58, this could be interpreted to mean a 15 per cent increase in sales for every 10 per cent cut in price. Three techniques can be used to measure price elasticity including: analysis of store-level data, field experiments, and regression analysis. Analysis of price elasticity is vital in markets where price is under pressure, as in retailing. It makes more sense to advertise brand leaders rather than to promote them. Price premium is a way to increase revenues on existing volume. There are five traditional ways to build brand share: through increased advertising, increased promotion, multibuy, price premium, or distribution. For many manufacturers, building new channels will be key, and it may be necessary to innovate and communicate with the customers.

decline in quantities, then it is implied that the demand is inelastic and that the store has a substantial degree of **monopoly** power. In such cases, the store does not have to engage in price competition; rather, it may more readily engage in non-price competition, emphasising other variables of the retail marketing mix.

It is dangerous for any firm to experiment with this kind of retail marketing behaviour without measuring the demand elasticity. Perhaps a better approach would be to approximate the demand elasticity (Samli, 1989) by using a series of factors, including the following:

1 Competition implies the availability of close substitutes. If the store's product line has close substitutes or, in general, the store has some very close competitors that are quite similar to itself, then it may be deduced that customers of the store could easily go to the competitors' stores. The demand is, therefore, elastic.

2 Importance of products – if the store's products are important to customers or if the store, in general, is very important to customers, then in the minds of consumers neither the store nor its products can have substitutes. The demand is, therefore, inelastic.

3 Urgency of need. Even though the products of the store – for example medicine or spare parts for an imported sports car – may not be very important in absolute terms, because of the urgency of need the demand for the store could be inelastic. The whole range of small convenience shops; open from '8 until late', is enjoying such demand based on urgency – despite relatively higher prices.

4 Ease of want satisfaction. If the store's products are dealing with consumer wants that are readily satisfied, the demand cannot be expanded by lower prices and, thus, demand is inelastic.

5 Impact of total price. If the prices of the store as a whole or the prices of some products in the store become too high, the customer may be forced to find substitutes. Hence, at a certain price level, demand may become elastic.

6 Economic conditions. In times of recession, demand may be somewhat price elastic in terms of price increases and price inelastic in terms of reductions. In other words, consumers may cut down their purchases but are not likely to increase their purchases.

Generally, when demand is relatively inelastic, price reduction may not increase the purchase volume more than proportionately. On the other hand if, in times of recession, retailers were to increase their prices, they would experience a more than proportionate decrease in sales volumes. It appears that while demand is elastic when prices are raised, it is inelastic when prices are reduced. It may be concluded that within certain price ranges during recessions demand is inelastic.

Table 10.3 illustrates these conditions as they affect retail price-level strategies.

Table 10.3
CONDITIONS DICTATING PRICE-LEVEL STRATEGIES

	Price strategy		
	Below market	Market	Above market
Low competition	−	+	+
High-level product importance	−	+	+
Urgent needs	−	+	+
Easy to satisfy wants	−	+	−
Total prices are reasonable	−	+	−
Economy is experiencing a recession	−	+	−
High competition	+	+	−
Low level product importance	+	+	−
Needs are not urgent	+	+	−
Wants are not easy to satisfy	+	−	−
Total prices are too high	+	−	−
Economy is experiencing a boom	+	−	−

Price-perceived quality

A number of pricing studies indicate that price perception does not always mean cost or sacrifice to the customer (Hoch *et al.*, 1994). In fact, these studies have shown that a perceived quality is implied by price and, in some cases, buyers may tend to prefer higher priced products. The second tendency is particularly valid when consumers do not have any other information in addition to the price. The key question is whether or not the same situation can be applied to retail marketing. The answer to this question lies in the concept of 'price thresholds'. As discussed earlier, consumers may have individual 'limits' for prices and, accordingly, exhibit varying degrees of responsiveness to price changes. The Weber-Fechner law posits that 'if some lower price thresholds are established below the actual low prices, consumers will think that perhaps the product is undesirable for purchase. Hence, consumers will opt for higher prices if these products are sold in certain stores' (Mulhern and Leone, 1991).

If a certain convenience product, such as tinned peas, is sold in a convenience shop or supermarket, the consumer will not attach much special value to them – one tin of peas is rather like another. However, another convenience product, such as men's underwear, privately branded and sold at Marks & Spencer may have a special value that is reflected in a higher price. Thus, price-perceived quality reinforced by the store's reputation or image is a plausible proposition in retailing. Price-perceived quality relationships have been used by several car manufacturers to build image and maintain reputation, a classic example being Rolls-Royce.

Exhibit 10.5 The supply of Rolls-Royce cars is constrained (quite tightly) by a highly skilled, non-automated production line. Skilled image-building has ensured that Rolls-Royce has a superb reputation and that the cars are, therefore, highly desirable. The shortage of production allied to this reputation, enables Rolls-Royce to sell its cars at very high prices through a very limited dealer network. Despite their exceptionally solid reputation, Roll-Royce also offer a quick and effective after-sales service should things go wrong.

Certain speciality products, namely expensive appliances or jewellery, may gain price-perceived value as their prices are raised within a certain range (Bang and Olifson hi-fi's, Tiffany's jewellery). The price-perceived value is related to price-perceived quality. In other words, as price goes up, the perceived quality of the product increases proportionately. Increased perceived quality further accelerates the perceived value.

Internal influences on price

Three groups of factors that influence the retail prices internally are: price objectives, strategic alternatives, and goal-related strategies.

Price objectives

At least four price objectives can be cited: achieving a certain sales volume, a certain amount of profit in money terms, certain expected returns on investment, and early recovery of cash for improving cash flow.

Achieving a certain sales volume has been, and remains, a strong objective for many retailers. For many years Tesco aimed for and achieved the number one position in the UK grocery market by achieving the largest sales volume – the 'pile it high; sell it cheap' principle originally. Many retailers use pricing in order to attain a certain profit level in money terms. For example, if a company is determined to make £1 000 000 in profits in a year, such an expected return on investment can be achieved by pricing. Thus, the company may manipulate its prices to reach the desired return on investment (ROI). For many retailers, particularly during recessions, cash flows are critical for survival. Retailers can supplement their cash flow position by using special prices. By providing **cash discounts** and lowering prices, the retailer can facilitate cash flow and eliminate the cash flow problems that are common – and may even be fatal – during recessions.

Strategic alternatives

Retail pricing is an important tool to fulfil the retailer's particular strategic alternative, irrespective of what that strategy may be. If, for example, the store is exercising a segmentation strategy, its prices must reflect this strategic preference;

Littlewoods and British Home Stores (Bhs) cater for the lower middle class and the middle class for whom price-perceived quality is not that relevant, whereas Harrods positions itself within a given segment (primarily upper class) where price-perceived quality is very pertinent. Similarly, store strategies related to life cycle can also be implemented with significant help from pricing. Asda, particularly during its growth era, promoted its pricing as the most reasonable for the product value received.

Goal-related strategies

In order to fulfil corporate objectives, goals are established which, in turn, are interpreted as pricing strategies. At least two types of pricing strategies can be identified in this context: price strategy related to market level, and price strategy related to leadership. Pricing strategy related to market level implies being above, at, or below the market level. A **price above the market** policy means that the retailer sets many prices above their competitors' level. This strategy is appropriate if the retailer deals with market segments where price-perceived quality is important. Once again, profit maximisation is achieved by establishing a strong price-perceived quality relationship for the particular store.

Most big name stores in retailing such as Marks & Spencer, Miss Selfridge, Dixons, W.H. Smith, Tesco, Sainsbury, and so on practice an above the market price policy to some extent. The store's image is so highly regarded and accepted that customers feel they are receiving something more than just the merchandise; they are not buying just a tie but the retailer's name and image (Omar, 1997). In common economic parlance, the situation implies that the store's demand curve is relatively inelastic, and customers display a strong degree of store loyalty. The middle-class general merchandise department and discount department stores opt for meeting the competition type of pricing policy – pricing at the market level. Debenham's, and TopMan, both belong to this category. The general orientation is primarily toward a low profile on price and heavy emphasis on non-price competition. Position is often exercised by pointing out that the retailer offers strong price to value relationships as opposed to some exclusive and expensive brands and prices (e.g. John Lewis). Both Miss Selfridge and Sears are middle-of-the-road retailers. As they position themselves against each other, they position themselves primarily below very high and prestigious name brands such as Harvey Nichols and Harrods (Collins, 1992).

Finally, a **price below the market** policy is emphasised by those discount stores and discount chains that cater to lower middle-class market segments. For Littlewoods, Argos, and others in this category, the emphasis is on price competition, with few or no frills regarding customer services and sales promotion. They do not promote labels or brands. Instead, they emphasise basic practicalities: cash only, limited returns and exchanges policy, and few or no delivery services – on the whole, low-cost practices. A comparative analysis of pricing strategy related to market level is presented in Table 10.4. The 11 **retail mix variables** used by Berman and Evans (1995) in the analyses are identified and grouped into merchandise-related, service-related, store atmospherics-related, and general strategy-related factors (*see* Table 10.4).

Table 10.4
MARKET-LEVEL-RELATED PRICING STRATEGY

Retail mix variable	Pricing below the market	Pricing at the market	Pricing above the market
Merchandise related			
Product assortment	Concentration on best sellers	Medium assortment	Broad and deep assortment
Merchandise lines carried	Private labels, name-brand out-of-stock, small manufacturers' products	Name brands	Exclusive brands
Merchandise differentiation	Undifferentiated merchandise, emphasis on price competition	Differentiated merchandise	Highly differentiated merchandise based on exclusivity
Role of fashion assortment	Fashion follower, conservative	Concentration on accepted best sellers	Fashion leader
Service related			
Personal service	Self-service, little product knowledge on part of salespeople, no displays	Moderate assistance by sales personnel	High levels of personal selling, delivery, liberal exchanges, alterations, adjustments, etc.
Special services	Cash and carry	Not available or extra charge to customers	Included in price
Store atmospherics related			
Location	Poor, inconvenient site	Close to competitors	Absence of strong competitors, convenient to consumers
Atmosphere	Inexpensive fixtures, little or no carpeting, no basic decoration, racks for merchandise	Moderate atmosphere, neutral and somewhat attractive	Very attractive, pleasant decor with many creative displays
Image	Store known for its bargains and low prices	Store known for price–quality combination, considered a middle-class place	Store known for exclusivity, it appeals to upper economic class
External appearance	Modest and unassuming	Reasonably nice but very flashy	Extremely flashy
General strategy related			
Key strategy emphasis	Mass merchandiser with limited differentiation and segmentation	Mass merchandiser with heavy emphasis on differentiation	Heavy segmenter and positioner

Source: Adapted and expanded from Berman and Evans, 1995.

Whether or not the retailer has some degree of leadership in the marketplace may imply that the store has options to use variable mark-ups. **Mark-up pricing** policies are also used to fulfil specific goals. If the store pursues a general merchandiser strategy, it tries to appeal to all segments, which implies a rather flexible pricing policy. Price flexibility means flexible and variable mark-up practices. Flexible mark-up suggests that either the store has numerous special sales where mark-ups are all adjusted or that the store is somewhat amenable to haggling – adjusting price downwards to match a competitor or 'throwing in' additional services.

Haggling is much more common in Third World countries than in the UK. However, haggling is very common in open market operations in Europe. Variable mark-up, on the other hand, means using different mark-ups for different products or product lines. The basic principle is low mark-ups for fast-moving merchandise; high mark-ups for slow-moving merchandise, though these high mark-ups may be changed periodically for some big sales. A variable mark-up policy offers a better opportunity to appeal to different markets more effectively and establish some degree of market leadership position.

Many retailers segment the market strategically. One very successful chain has segmented the market on the basis of one specific benefit–convenience. The 7–Eleven stores use a single mark-up approach across the board for all of their products. Such stores have performed particularly well in the marketplace, with their number increasing continually. Thus, it may be reiterated, many consumers prefer convenience over price when buying small items.

General price policies

The general price policies that retailers adopt will be influenced by the customers (the market) to whom they hope to appeal, the character of the stores they plan to operate (which also should be related to the market), and competition. Moreover, making the right decisions involves as much judgement and artistry as science, but the aim should always be to further the long-term objectives of the business. These elements of pricing are examined in this section.

The market

Some consumers are much more price conscious than others. One might expect low-income consumers to be more sensitive to price than high-income ones, but this is not always the case. Sometimes lower-income buyers may, of necessity, be more interested in the availability of credit or other services than price. Customer awareness of, and interest in, price may also vary with education, occupation, age, type of goods involved and other factors. Retailers, therefore, should watch how potential and/or present customers seem to respond to various pricing and service practices in their stores and in competitive outlets (Bolton, 1989).

Retail marketing mix consistency

Price policies should be consistent with the other parts of the store's marketing mix – its merchandise, display, advertising and services. For example, shoppers may be doubtful that a supermarket is following a low-price policy – even though it actually charges less than the competition – if it also offers above average levels of service and has more modern fixtures than is the norm. A retailer who plans to charge relatively high prices will have to offer the atmosphere, merchandise, convenience and/or services that will make those prices acceptable to potential customers. One important decision in this context relates to which services will be subject to extra charge and which will be included in the price of the merchandise.

Strategic view

The retailer should also always maintain a strategic view of pricing. Upon opening a business, a retailer may plan to sell at very low prices for the first few months in order to build up trade. Short-term earnings may suffer as a result of this policy, but it may attract enough customers and build sufficient repeat business to maximise profits in the long term. In the long term, the retailer may want to keep prices at a fairly low level; selling at high prices does not necessarily produce maximum profits. Profits result from the relationships among sales, prices, costs of merchandise, and expenses of operation. Sometimes these factors will indicate that raising prices will improve profits, but other times they will show that lowering prices will improve earnings.

One price policy

The retailer following a **one price policy** charges the same price to everyone who buys the same item in comparable quantities under similar conditions. If the price for a Cannon's 'Camberley' double oven gas cooker is £859.89 at British Gas Energy Centre, every purchaser – regardless of who that may be – will be charged £859.89 for that brand of gas cooker. Of course, a one price policy does not prevent a store from having clearance sales or special promotions. It simply means that if the store reduces its price for any item, the lower price becomes available to all customers.

This policy builds up customer confidence since no one has to worry about being charged more than someone else. It also saves a great deal of time and skill that might otherwise have to be spent in bargaining with customers. Although one price policies are the general rule in the UK today, store employees are often allowed discounts on the merchandise they buy. Occasionally, a retailer may set up a special discount arrangement for a particular group, such as the members of a sports club or the workers in a nearby factory, in the hope of obtaining a large share of their purchases. Airport retailers generally give discounts to airport employees who prefer to shop at airport stores. Such systematic discounts affect only a very small percentage of all retail sales. The risks of becoming known as a retailer who is willing to bargain argue against the use of such practices. A one-price policy builds confidence and successful retailing is built on confidence.

Range of prices

Another policy decision, closely related to merchandising decisions, concerns whether there will be goods at a range of prices available in the store. Provision of 'something for everyone', ranging from relatively inexpensive merchandise to elegant high-priced goods, is known as **range pricing**. A very large store can do this relatively easily, to some extent and in some merchandise lines, by grouping different price levels in different departments. It may sell budget dresses in one department, medium-priced and better models in another, and expensive designer clothes in a third section. Most merchandise categories do not generate sufficient sales volume to warrant creating several price-based departments, and even large stores find that an attempt to cover too extensive a range may result in customers perceiving a confused store image (Grewal *et al.*, 1996). Consequently, most retailers will tend to concentrate on a limited price and quality range.

Price lines

Price lining consists of selecting certain prices and carrying assortments of merchandise only at those prices, except when markdowns apply. Customers desire a wide assortment when buying shopping goods (to which price lining is especially applicable) but become confused by small price differences among the various items. Confining the assortments to a few specific price points reduces the confusion.

Having only a few price points helps salespeople become well acquainted with their prices and reduces mistakes (Collins, 1992). This facilitates selling and improves customer goodwill. Price lining may reduce the size of the store's inventory, increase turnover, decrease markdowns, simplify stock control, and reduce interest and storage costs. It also enables the store buyer to concentrate on items that can be sold profitably at the pre-set price levels. Price lines are usually established through a careful analysis of past sales, picking out those prices at which the bulk of the sales were made. In some cases, however, past sales are disregarded; the retailer simply selects new price lines which the salespeople are then expected to 'push'. Although the number of price lines needed will vary in different situations, a retailer will usually want at least one below and one above the basic medium-price line.

Some of the advantages of price lining are lost if the price lines are not far enough apart to indicate definite differences in quality; the customer will still be confused, with several goods selling at fairly comparable prices. The retailer should have full assortments at each price line to serve the customers attracted by that line. Retailers may check competitors' price lines frequently to make sure that they have not found ones with greater customer appeal.

Effects of general price level changes

Retailers face difficult problems in maintaining traditional price lines when prices in general are changing rapidly. These problems become especially troublesome in combined inflation and recession periods. Normally prices rise during periods of prosperity, with most customers being willing to accept new and higher price lines if the retailer cannot secure satisfactory merchandise to sell at the old price levels. During depressed periods, when customers want to 'trade down' to lower price points, most suppliers usually recognise the necessity of reducing their wholesale charges to obtain business (Mulhern and Leone, 1991). In either case, some retailers will be tempted to lower the quality of each regular price line. For example, when wholesale costs rise they will want to substitute inferior merchandise to avoid changing a traditional price point; during depressed business they will reduce quality so as to lower the retail price even more than the wholesale cost has fallen. But this is generally unwise. If possible, it is better to maintain the character of the goods in a price line to preserve customer confidence in the store's offerings. This may require some upward or downward adjustment in the prices of the lines during severe inflation or deflation; it may also be advisable to add extra higher or lower priced lines, as appropriate, to meet changed demand.

The drawbacks of price lining

Price lining reduces the buyer's range of alternatives in selecting goods for the store. The buyer must secure merchandise that will provide a profit when sold at the store's established price lines. This requirement can increase the difficulty of obtaining adequate assortments and more than offset whatever advantages result from having to consider only those items that fit the store's price lines. Its main disadvantages may include (*see* Samli, 1989):

- limitations on the store's ability to meet competitive prices;
- a danger that the price lines selected will not be suited to the preferences of customers and prospective customers;
- difficulties in maintaining uniform quality during periods of changes in price levels;
- the likelihood that price lines will multiply over a period of time;
- a tendency to focus attention on price rather than on the merchandise.

Nevertheless, price lining's advantages have resulted in widespread use of the practice in selling clothing and other shopping goods. It is not as useful, however, in selling staples such as foods and toiletries, where customers generally do not want to compare an assortment of styles, colours, or sizes at one price (Raju *et al.*, 1990).

Competitive posture

The most basic pricing decisions retailers make concern the relationship between their prices and those of competitors. As one might expect, most retailers tend to set their prices close to those of their major competitors (Samli, 1989). But this statement needs clarification:

1 Most retailers tend to think of other retailers of the same type as their major competitors. Thus a small independent grocer will usually consider other nearby independent grocers, rather than large supermarket chains, as the competitors whose prices must be met.

2 Retailers, such as supermarket operators, who sell wide assortments of convenience and non-shopping goods, will generally not try to match their competitors' prices item for item. They expect to be higher on some items and lower on others, and are more concerned with the general price image or impression their store reflects.

Many shopping goods retailers, on the other hand, pay strict attention to item-by-item price comparisons. Practically every department store and most large speciality stores employ comparison shopping staff that check their store's prices, merchandise and service against its competitors. Some department stores may decide to run specific departments (for example toiletries or small electric appliances) at a loss, if need be, in order to compete with discount stores. For example, Comet, the electrical stores, even offer to give a refund to any customer who finds the same item at a lower price in any other store in town.

Pricing below competitors' level

Some retailers go one step beyond simply meeting competition and actually try to undersell their competitors. Many chain store, mail order, supermarket, and discount houses among others, believe in seeking their profits through the use of relatively low prices to attract a large volume of sales. The net result, of course, has been a rise in their customers' standard of living, as well as an advance in the retailers' profits.

These retailers are 'hard' buyers, since they must acquire their merchandise at low cost to permit the profitable use of low prices (Berman and Evans, 1995). They often operate with relatively low-cost physical facilities and may dispense with many services that other stores offer. They frequently limit their stocks to the fast-moving items. These retailers are often strong advocates of own-label brands, the prices of which cannot be precisely compared with competitors' offerings; and these stores generally devote their advertising to announcing price 'specials' (Rosenbloom, 1981).

Retailers who adopt a low-price policy must use consistent policies in the other aspects of their business, such as merchandise mix, services offered and advertising. Those who do not will soon find themselves threatened by the rapidly changing retail environment.

Discount pricing

Discount stores exhibit many of the low-price retailing characteristics discussed above. Having set the overall price, the supplier then has the option of offering different prices (usually on the basis of a discount) to cover different circumstances. The types of discount most often offered and the conditions under which they are offered are shown in Table 10.5. Though included in the list of discounts, one of them – **optional features** – is not a discount. This works, rather, by offering a basic product but with extra features, for the same price.

Table 10.5
RANGE OF DISCOUNT PRICES

Type of discount	Offer conditions
Trade discounts	To wholesalers, retailers and middlemen for services provided on behalf of the manufacturer
Quantity discount	To those who buy a large quantity of particular product
Cash discount	Offered as an incentive for prompt cash payment
Allowances	Used by manufacturers to persuade consumers to buy a new product, e.g. trade-in their old product,
Seasonal discounts	Used in service offerings such as the holiday market
Promotional pricing	Suppliers may use price discount as promotional device
Individual pricing	Used mainly in business-to-business buying negotiations – a form of haggling
Optional features	Instead of a discount, customers are offered a basic product to which they can add features
Product bundling	Customers are offered a bundle of related products for much less than they would cost if bought separately
Psychological pricing	Some suppliers deliberately set high recommended prices in order to offer seemingly very high discount.

Price wars

A price war develops when a number of competitors try to undersell each other. The warring retailers keep reducing their prices, in tit-for-tat fashion, in an effort to attract each others' customers. The war will often be confined to a few fast-moving items, such as milk, cigarettes, petrol or bread, but those items may be reduced to one-half or one-third of their normal price before the battle is over. Price wars are particularly destructive because at one end of the chain it destroys the profit of the

MINI-CASE ## Discounting – who pays the price?

One of the major questions to answer in terms of price discounting is 'who pays the price?' – that is, who bears the cost of the discount? It is interesting that drug companies were unable to answer this question and were very angry over Asda's cut-price vitamins, even when Asda admitted it was swallowing the costs of the discount itself. By all accounts this is what usually happens with discounting – the retailer bears the cost. In some instances, if retailers have a very strong relationship with the manufacturer, it may be agreed that the manufacturer will take a reduced margin; but usually it is the retailer that bears the costs. That is not to say the retailer loses on the transaction. The trade-off is that by cutting prices the retailer pulls in more customers. The retailer is going for volume and could end up by making rather than losing a lot of money.

Asda is thought to have spent tens of thousands of pounds on its campaign against value added tax (VAT) on sanitary protection products, by slashing 17.5 per cent off national brands and own-label prices. The campaign probably has a lot of support from customers, and other retailers, and presumably sales have risen accordingly. In the case of vitamins and minerals, supermarkets can discount their own-label products in any way they want. Supermarket own-label vitamins are, on average, 20 per cent cheaper than national brands; Sainsbury's claims that its own-label medicines are up to 40 per cent cheaper (*Supermarketing*, 1997). After Asda, Sainsbury's cut prices on selected vitamin and mineral brands, most of them Seven Seas and Roche. Similarly, Tesco has been known to have secretly bought Sony electrical products and to have sold them at heavy discount prices in 150 stores. It has previously discounted Levi 501 jeans; Adidas sportswear, fashion clothing and trainers; and Calvin Klein underwear and jeans. Under the slogan 'Just do it for less', Tesco usually buys these products by turning to the so-called 'grey market' – an increasingly popular route for retailers which circumvents normal supply channels.

But why should the manufacturers be worried if the retailer is bearing the cost, and if more of their products are shifting off the shelves? When the brand owners Seven Seas and Roche went to the High Court over Asda's cuts in their products in 1995, they were not litigating for the fun of it – and it is a very expensive option. As Seven Seas explained, they would not take out an injunction on any of their major customers without considerable thought, but that they have to protect their brands' reputation. The suppliers are demanding for the rules surrounding resale price maintenance (rpm) to be clarified. They think it is unfair for their products to be discounted in supermarkets and not with their other customers such as the small chemists. Brand manufacturers are clearly concerned that they could eventually have to pay some of the cost of discounting.

suppliers (and with it the capacity to invest in the future of the market) and at the other because it often destroys the belief of the consumer in the quality of what is being offered (and, thus, in their expectations of development of the market). Some of the reasons for indulging in the very risky pursuit of price competition include: volume sales, price reduction stimuli (*see* Figure 10.2), and minor brands.

Fig.10.2 PRICE REDUCTION STIMULI

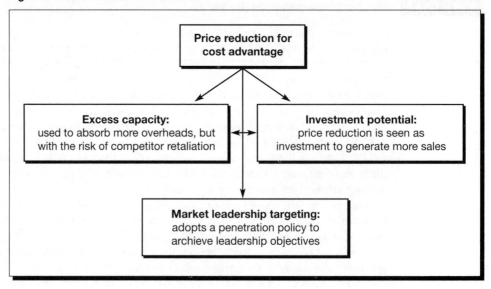

Volume sales

Not all price reductions are destructive. Some result in such increases in the volume of purchases that absolute profit is increased, despite the relative reductions in price (and economies of scale may mean that even the relative profit per unit increases), and the whole market expands rapidly. The key to making a success of price competition is in ensuring that it reflects a genuine cost advantage. Economies of scale, and hence the justification of lower prices to increase volumes, are one aspect. Another is that the own cost structure of the business planning to cut prices must offer advantages over those of their competitors. When these factors apply in the price reducer's favour, then price competition can be very advantageous – in exactly the same way that any other 'product' advantage would be (Corstjens and Corstjens, 1995).

Unfortunately, most price competition occurs between companies with very similar cost structures, frequently leading to debilitating price wars. In general, the dangers of initiating a price war may include:

- low-quality image – a low price may be equated with low quality (and may actually represent just that, as the opponents shave quality in order to fund the cost cutting);

- temporary advantage – a price advantage is often only held in the short term and consumers will be rapidly attracted to the even lower one, which will surely appear eventually);

- investment potential – above all, price reductions should be seen as an investment to generate greater sales; (if they do not, they result only in reduced profits). It is wise, in these circumstances, to work out which company has the

---

MINI-CASE **Grocery stores spreading out**

The market share of chemists is gradually being eroded by the grocery sector according to Mintel's report on personal healthcare. It tells us that supermarkets have made particular healthy strides in vitamins, mineral supplements, and cough and cold remedies. The story is the same in many non-food sectors. Verdict Research, on the other hand, noted that grocers are taking an increasing share of the market in music and videos, newspapers and magazines, books, toiletries, cosmetics and petrol. Although their market share in areas like books remained small (about 1.5 per cent in 1996), they had captured 12.9 per cent of the newspapers and magazines market and an estimated one-fifth of petrol sales. Market analysts predict that their shares of all these markets will continue to grow.

By early 1997, grocers accounted for 23.9 per cent of consumer spending on healthcare products, compared to just 19.3 per cent five years earlier. By contrast, chemists accounted for only 68.4 per cent of consumer spending in 1997 compared to 75 per cent in 1992. Mintel's figures on toiletries and cosmetics draw similar conclusions. In 1990, chemists took 48.8 per cent of spending on these products, and in 1996 that had dropped to 42.3 per cent. Department stores and variety stores have also lost out to grocers, which in 1997 took 40.2 per cent of spending compared to 36.2 in 1992.

deepest pockets and can afford to invest in such a war of attrition. The firm with most resources will hold out the longest. History tends to show that it is often the initiator of the war who is the first casualty (*see* Exhibit 10.6).

These price wars end in various ways. All of the competitors may simply withdraw from the struggle when they find that their rivals quickly match their price reductions. In other cases, the retailers or their suppliers may have to take some

---

Exhibit 10.6 **The first casualty in the airfare price wars**

During the early 1980s, airlines vying for business on international routes – the North Atlantic, London to New York route in particular, led to unprecedented cuts in air fares. At the centre of the debate was Sir Freddie Laker, hailed by some as the 'entrepreneur of our time' and accused by his competitors of 'reckless pricing' and 'providing a catalyst for the industry's problems'. According to the International Air Transport Association (IATA), a cartel of which Laker was not a member, international airlines were expected to record operating losses of the order US $1.9 billion on scheduled services in 1982.

Before the collapse of Laker Airlines, Laker boasted that he could offer lower fares than his much larger competitors because he had lower costs. Unfortunately he was caught out by his inability to service debts. The root of Laker's problem was that his small company could not withstand the hostile environment over time in the way that the then state-owned British Airways and other loss-making foreign airlines which similarly symbolised national pride could.

form of joint action before prices move upward. Sometimes the retailers hold a meeting and, in effect, agree upon a truce. In other cases, suppliers have used various methods to call a halt to the retail price cutting. For example, major oil companies have terminated some local petrol price wars by supplying their petrol to the service stations on consignment and thus retaining the right to fix final selling prices.

Pricing above competitors' level

Other retailers regularly sell some or all of their merchandise at prices above those of their competitors. Retailers who follow this policy recognise that many non-price considerations, such as those outlined below, may attract customers to their stores. These retailers often can operate their businesses successfully, in spite of charging higher prices, if they offer some of the following features.

1 Satisfactory services – many customers will pay somewhat higher prices in order to receive the desired services. They will patronise the store that provides more helpful personal attention or that has more generous delivery, credit and goods return policies, even if its prices are slightly above those of its competitors.

2 Prestige – a store that has historically set the standard for quality in its community, as for example Marks & Spencer, may have acquired considerable prestige in the eyes of its customers. This prestige helps to remove the store from direct price competition with other retailers and sometimes enables it to charge a higher price than other stores.

3 Convenient location – some people will pay a premium for the convenience of being able to shop at a handy location. Corner shops, grocery and DIY stores, for example, tend to have higher prices but some customers will pay a little extra rather than travel to the lower-priced outlets. Airport terminal stores, a hamburger stand in a football stadium, or a village shop in an isolated community may have virtually captive markets because of their locations and thus be able to command unusually high prices.

4 Extended opening hours – a store that is open when the other shops are closed may be able to charge more than its early-closing competitors. Many small shops do a large share of their business in the evening and on Sundays. Chains of convenience stores, which sell a limited assortment of the most popular items and stay open very long hours, have become an important part of grocery retailing. The price advantage that comes from long hours tends to disappear, however, as more and more supermarkets, discount houses and shopping centres stay open evenings and on Sundays.

5 Exclusive merchandise – an assortment of items or brands that are not available in competitive stores will also give a retailer some freedom from direct price competition. Sometimes a retailer will obtain an exclusive agency for a certain manufacturer's products so as to make certain that no immediate competitors can get the same goods.

Escaping price competition

Manufacturers and retailers generally tend to prefer non-price competition to price competition because they believe that customers who are attracted by non-price factors will be more loyal than those who shop around for low prices; and competitors will have more difficulty in matching non-price factors than in meeting price changes. However, a retailer can seldom completely escape price competition in spite of a preference for non-price rivalry. A store may be able to charge somewhat higher prices for reasons already suggested, but too broad a difference will drive customers away. In fact, any price difference causes a store to lose some customers, since there are some who have little regard for a store's services or prestige. The wider the price differences become, the more customers leave and go over to the lower-priced store. Of course, customers sometimes become suspicious that the quality of merchandise is dubious if prices seem too low. This is one reason why pricing calls for skill and judgement.

Moreover, it is particularly difficult to escape price competition on staple clothing, household and recreational items, and well-known brand merchandise. The thriftier buyers of these items can go from store to store and learn the prices that various retailers are asking for comparable goods. Retailers who sell style items are somewhat less likely to be affected by competitive prices since customers cannot always make direct price comparisons on these items. Paradoxically retailers, such as supermarket firms, that sell very wide assortments of low-priced staples will also escape direct price competition on many items, since most consumers seem to select only certain key products for price shopping.

Most stores find that they have some competitors who have equal prestige and offer as many services as they do. Even a relatively minor price differential between such stores may cause a fairly rapid shift of business to the lower-priced retailer. A retailer must keep such comparable stores in mind when setting prices; there may be no opportunity to charge more than others do.

Own-label brands

Some retailers gain a certain amount of freedom from direct competition by offering some own-label brands instead of manufacturers' national brand items. A consumer cannot compare the values of two different own-label brands sold by two different retailers with anywhere near the precision that is possible in comparing the same two retailers' prices for a specific national brand product. Some prestige stores are able to command fairly high prices for own-label brands that have won consumer acceptance.

Retailers can legally discriminate in pricing products by selling national brands and own-labels at whatever prices they wish. Of course, as noted earlier, a competitor's pricing strategy can influence a store's pricing differentials. There is no general rule about own-label pricing. Each store has its own philosophy on how to structure mark-up or markdowns. But there are certain options open to the retailer. Own-labels can be priced:

- as a regular price – traditional mark-up without a measure against the national brand;

- at a premium price – higher than the national brand, because the private label is of superior quality;

- at a competitive price – the same as the national brand pricing;

- as a price differential – below the national brand pricing;

- as a **loss leader** – sold at or below cost, or given away in a coupon offer;

- discount price – buy one and get another free or promoted at a much reduced price.

The most effective pricing strategy for own-label brands involves a balancing of these different strategies. Woolworth's does this very effectively, using different departments to draw in customers. Some products are featured with a mark-up of less than 20 per cent, while other items carry a 40 per cent mark-up. The first reaction to a price reduction should always be to consider the situation carefully before taking any form of action.

Successful retail price setting is an art as well as a science. Formulas and general price policies provide a basis for price making, but any experienced retailer will then use judgement, intuition, and trial and error to adjust the resultant prices. Even so, one cannot be absolutely certain as to how customers will react to any specific price. Sometimes raising the price will make the item more appealing to customers; in other instances a reduction may be needed to move the goods. But, over time, successful retailers develop a feel or sense for the prices that are appropriate to their costs, market and competitive situations. In the pages that follow, we will look first at **mark-up pricing**, and **markdowns** which express the relationship between merchandise cost to the store and retail price.

Other aspects of pricing strategies

In the long-term, whether prices are raised or lowered is the most important point to be emphasised. Here, we carefully examine mark-ups, which are perhaps more market and **demand oriented**, and markdowns which are more internal or **cost oriented**. The reason for this distinction is that price level faces more consumer and competitor retaliation. Markdowns are considered to be tactical and are used primarily to move merchandise that has not been moving satisfactorily (Samli, 1989). Other parts of this section look specifically at aspects of pricing in market stagflation, **everyday low prices**, **high–low price**, and the use of coupons.

Mark-ups

This is a form of cost-based pricing in which prices are set by calculating per-unit merchandise costs and then determining the mark-up percentages that are needed to cover selling costs and profit. The margin between the cost and the retail price is extremely important because, in terms of overall volume of the store, it is success of effective mark-up which will provide the effective price. As opposed to an internal markdown orientation which, unfortunately, is quite widespread among retailers, mark-up must be based primarily on external factors. Both the total market potential, the demand elasticity; and competitors' expected reaction are of specific interest. What will be the market's long-range reaction? Is the demand inelastic enough to raise the price and increase the mark-up? And will competitors retaliate by not raising their prices or even by lowering their prices? Without appropriate answers to these questions, it will not pay to raise the price through an increased mark-up.

Markdowns

This is a reduction from the original retail price of an item to meet lower prices of competitors, to counteract overstocking of merchandise, to clear out an assortment of odds and ends, or to increase customer traffic. Unlike mark-ups, markdowns are likely to be internally oriented. They are generally used to take care of internal merchandising problems. However, their excessive use or abuse has significant implications for external pricing strategy. Markdowns are widespread in retailing. Some merchandise will not sell at the original price and sooner or later will have to be marked down. Many retailers use markdowns to:

■ remedy buying errors;

■ compensate for changes in customer needs;

■ retaliate against competitors' actions;

■ provide a principal feature of a promotional event.

Both manufacturers and retailers have regular promotional events such as stock-taking sales, end of season clearance sales or pre-season sales, during which time markdowns become the focal point of the overall activity. In such cases, markdowns help to:

■ sell merchandise that is not moving fast enough;

■ attract customers who are drawn to special sales;

■ build customer loyalty among these groups of customers;

■ sell other merchandise not marked down;

■ stimulate excitement about the store.

Using markdowns in such cases is an ongoing activity. Figure 10.3 illustrates this process. One important aspect of the figure is that it demonstrates the continuity of the process, emphasising that after the specified time period of the markdown the whole situation is reviewed and a decision on further markdowns is made. Thus, the most important activity relating to markdown decisions is the continuous scrutiny of the merchandise to distinguish the unsold items from those that are selling well and then to determine why these items or lines are not selling.

Fig. 10.3 MARKDOWN DECISION FLOW

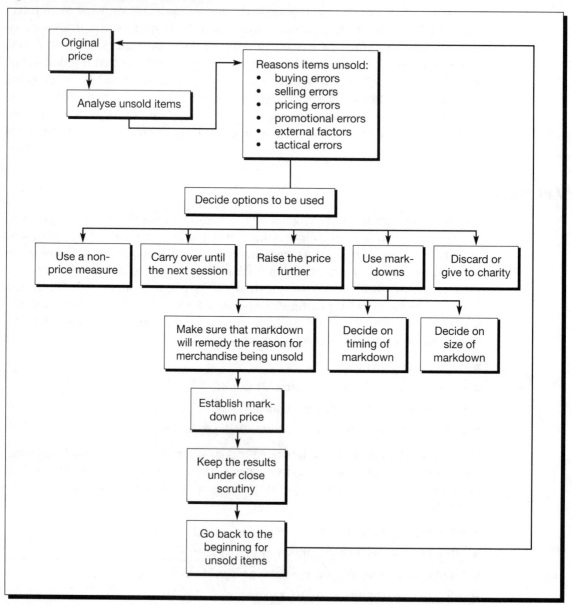

Source: Adapted from Samli (1989).

Pricing in market stagflation

During the late 1970s and early 1980s, the British economy was very sluggish and was experiencing a great many difficulties, as were others in the international community. One of the specific problems manifested in this situation was simultaneous inflation and recession; this is termed stagflation. When stagflation prevails, conditions for retailers in particular deteriorate. During the prolonged British stagflation, many small retailers went bankrupt. In order to avoid such a dramatic end retailers must understand the nature of stagflation – even try to benefit from it.

During stagflation, prices tend to go up while the total business volume shrinks. As a result of stagflation, retailers may find themselves facing both declining sales *and* worsening profit margins. For those who do not connect internal conditions with the adversities of the environment, the quickest solution may appear to be along the lines of: 'since I cannot increase the sales volume in the midst of this stagflation, I may be able to recoup my losses by cutting down my expenses as much as I can and by raising my prices as well'. The outcome of such an orientation may be twofold:

1 Retailers may try to cut down their expenses by reducing promotional activities, streamlining stocks and inventories, and decreasing the sales effort.

2 Retailers may raise their prices on a cost basis or at times simply indiscriminately. Sometimes prices are raised on the basis of types of 'independent' criteria such as the national consumer price index.

Reduced volume and increasingly unused capacities in retailing become devastatingly dangerous for retailers in an era of stagflation. Business failures in times of stagflation increase dramatically. The strategic options available to cope with stagflation are the proper use of promotional activity, pricing, and product–service adjustments.

Selective pricing

Some stores apply different prices for the same product or service in specified ways, as shown in Table 10.6. Customer group pricing, peak pricing and service level pricing are particularly prevalent in the service industries, where the supplier is in direct contact with the customer and often bypasses the retailer (Rosenbloom, 1981). Above all, the main temptation to avoid is the assumption that price is the most important variable in the retail marketing mix.

Table 10.6
SELECTIVE PRICING

Pricing strategy	Application
Category pricing	Covers the range of price categories from cheap to expensive price with a range of brands of the same product
Customer group pricing	Ability of various groups to pay the prices may be met, e.g. gate fees paid by football fans.
Peak pricing	High price for 'peak times' and lower price for 'off-peak period' e.g. railway travel companies, package holidays, etc.
Service level pricing	Level of services provided determines the price, e.g. health care provision

Everyday low prices (EDLP)

Recently it is the 'everyday low price' (EDLP) format that has experienced rapid growth and media popularity. The EDLP retailer charges a constant, lower everyday price with no temporary price discounts. These constant everyday prices at the EDLP outlet eliminate week-to-week price uncertainty and represent a contrast to the high–low (Hi–Lo) pricing of promotion-oriented competitors.

Discount stores like Kwik-Save have led the EDLP wave and successfully made in-roads into the traditional markets of supermarkets, department and chemist's stores by advertising that their everyday prices are always the lowest to be found. Similarly, warehouse club operators like Costco and others have grown rapidly by pursuing limited assortment and limited service EDLP price strategies, while also using well-known brand names as a draw. Non-retail organisations have adopted versions of EDLP, notably many airlines and some car manufacturers (Hoch *et al.*, 1994).

Various rationales for adopting EDLP have been advanced. First, heavy price promotion tends to erode consumer confidence in the credibility of everyday shelf price (Ortmeyer *et al.*, 1991). With an EDLP approach, it may be possible to restore price credibility. Since EDLP is simple and consistent, it may be easier to communicate to consumers and, therefore, to increase the chances of establishing a low price image through advertising. It also reduces managerial costs because it is easy to implement by simply matching or beating the most aggressive local competition. This assumes, of course, that the retailer has an appropriate cost structure in place. Second, EDLP often is assumed to involve lower operating costs. These lower costs can be achieved through: reduced service and assortment, reduced stocks and warehousing handling costs, and lower in-store labour costs. Warehouse operators gain additional cost savings due to their less expensive locations.

High–low pricing (Hi–Lo)

The Hi–Lo retailer charges higher prices on an everyday basis but then runs frequent promotions in which prices are temporarily lowered below the EDLP level. Many retailers may not use Hi–Lo pricing because they can price discriminate between consumers that vary in price sensitivity. When heavy users of a product have higher inventory holding costs, retailers can use temporary price cuts to effectively charge them higher average prices. With a Hi–Lo policy, retailers can attract price-sensitive switchers with promotions to build store traffic while store-loyalty consumers buy merchandise both on discount and higher everyday prices. Temporary price discounts also can lead to higher product sales in ready to use brands. Many Hi–Lo retailers also believe that aggressive temporary price reductions help to sustain a low-price value image (Berman and Evans, 1995).

The use of coupons

Couponing can be defined as a printed price offer made to a target group of customers, using a variety of media including direct mail leaflets, printed advertisements, in and on packs and so on. It usually requires that potential customers take the printed offer to a retailer of their own choice for a redemption against the named product. Thus the price reduction is associated with the manufacturer rather than the retailer. This is an important feature since the abolition of retail price maintenance (rpm) removed, to a large extent, discretion on pricing from the hands of the producer. The increasing use of coupons is probably due to competition for the limited available shelf space as supermarkets have rationalised the number of items and national brands stocked. Also, the late 1980s and 1990s have seen the concentration of buying power in the hands of a few supermarket groups – such as Tesco, Sainsbury, Asda and Safeways. These massive supermarket groups are now more powerful than many of the manufacturers whose brands they sell. This has made it difficult for manufacturers to control their sales purely through consumer advertising, using a 'pull strategy'. As a result of these factors, 'below-the-line' activities designed specifically to influence the trade have become increasingly important. Couponing is one way that manufacturers persuade retailers to stock or display the product, as it can stimulate substantial short-term sales increases for the brand being promoted.

SUMMARY

Successful retail price setting is an art as well as a science. Formulas and general price policies provide a basis for price making, but any experienced retailer will then use judgement, intuition, and trial and error to adjust the resultant prices. Even so, no one can predict with absolute certainty how customers will react to any specific price. Sometimes raising the price will make the item more appealing to shoppers; in other instances a reduction may be needed to move the goods. Successful retailers develop a sense for the prices that are appropriate to their costs, market and competitive situations.

KEY TERMS		
cash discount	mark-up pricing	price lining
cost oriented	monopoly	price wars
demand oriented	one price policy	psychological pricing
everyday low prices	optional features	range pricing
high–low prices	price above the market	retail mix variables
loss leader	price below the market	
markdown	price elasticity of demand	

ASSIGNMENT

One basic pricing decision involves whether or not a retailer should use everyday low pricing (EDLP). With EDLP, retailers charge relatively low prices for all of their goods and services throughout the year. An opposite approach to EDLP is known as 'high–low' pricing (Hi–Lo), in which retailers regularly offer specials on a few items, but charge higher prices on their other products. Retailers with an EDLP philosophy feel that EDLP builds brand and store loyalty, reduces their advertising costs, lessens staffing needs, and reduces inventory costs. To stablise prices, EDLP retailers often pay the same amount for specific items on an annual basis. They also do not get promotional allowances from suppliers for putting items on sale.

In contrast, retailers favouring Hi–Lo believe that special promotions add excitement and provide a stimulus for consumers to shop during limited sale periods. Hi–Lo retailers have a steady stream of in-store promotions and sales designed to keep customers coming back. The amount paid by these retailers for the same items varies. Often, these retail firms stock up when they are offered special deals. Research on the effectiveness of EDLP and Hi–Lo has yielded mixed results, and no absolute preference was suggested.

Task

On the basis of such divided opinion, write an essay (no longer than 1500 words) advising your retail marketing manager which of these pricing strategies to adopt. You must give reasons for your favoured option.

REVISION QUESTIONS

1 Price has many names and these names vary according to the interests of the seller. What do you understand by the term price?

2 We may all mean different things when we talk about price. Describe the meaning of price to both the retailer and the shopper.

3 The right price is the one which will bring the largest contribution to overheads and profits. Discuss this statement.

4 One of the pricing concepts that enters the individual's psyche is labelled psychological pricing. What is psychological pricing, and how is it used by retailers to set a price?

5 Price elasticity, though discussed in marketing literature, is rarely practised. Why do marketers need to understand the concept of price elasticity?

6 Price is one of the most responsive and potent weapons in the retail marketing mix, yet the markets in which price wars are fought are littered with corporate casualties and pyrrhic victories. Explain, with the aid of examples, why this is so.

7 What internal factors influence retail pricing? Briefly discuss these factors.

8 Distinguish between mark-up and markdown pricing strategy. Explain the application of each of the two strategic pricing tools.

9 Both the everyday low price (EDLP) and Hi–Lo price strategies have their advantages and drawbacks. Discuss.

10 As a result of stagflation, retailers normally find themselves facing at least two adverse conditions: declining sales and worsening profit margins. What suitable action could retailers take to correct the situation?

CASE STUDY

The right price is the one that favours consumers

Supermarket prices may be 'right' but, as prices on non-food come down, so too do retailers' shares. This case study shows how the multiples are bidding to draw attention to themselves, and improve books and magazine sales volumes. Life in the supermarket in the past decade has been more intriguing than any retail analyst could have predicted. Generally, retail prices have gone up for almost everything from turkeys to unleaded petrol. During 1997, there have been headaches and wrangles over the prospect of cheap non-prescription medicines, and a war of words has been waged in the late 1990s over how magazines and newspapers are sold in the supermarkets.

Asda, the fourth largest UK supermarket, has more or less taken the credit for abolishing the Net Book Agreement, and looks set to do the same thing for non-prescription medicines. The Office of Fair Trading (OFT) was, in fact, already looking into both of these areas – it has been looking at medicine pricing since as far back as 1994 – but Asda's action undoubtedly hurried things along. Days after Asda's announcement that it was cutting prices on around eighty vitamins and minerals, the OFT announced an official inquiry into the rules governing the pricing of certain over-the-counter medicines, creams and health food products.

One thing the OFT will have to prove is that there has been a market change, and what Asda did should be considered as a market change. It is irrelevant that Asda was forced by some of the big drug companies to back down and return the prices to what they had been – its action set the ball rolling. Immediately following the OFT's announcement that it would investigate, Sainsbury's joined the fray with its own discounts, but has since raised prices on these seventy or so vitamin and mineral products. The investigation, which could take up to six months, is expected to come out in favour of abolishing the resale price maintenance rules on medicine, books and magazines, newspapers, vitamins, and health-food products.

Tesco has been similarly shrewd in its handling of magazine and newspaper distribution. Chairman Sir Ian MacLaurin chose a meeting of the British Society of Magazine Editors to criticise the way retailers are supplied with fixed allocations of magazines, on a sale-or-return basis. Tesco's frustration was expressed in the following terms:

> we're talking about a system that was designed years ago for a very different market. The magazines are lumped together at the start of the month and you get an allocation and that's your lot for the month. We run out of some issues and we're unable to order more.

More crucially, it means that Tesco cannot run the promotions on magazines it would like to, despite the fact that more magazines would mean more multi-save and link-save promotions. These are techniques which work well in other areas and which Tesco and other supermarkets could use on magazines to help increase sales. Thus, if Tesco got its way, magazines could be one of the next targets for price promotions.

HOW THE PRICES COMPARED ONE DAY (OCTOBER 1997)

	Safeway	Tesco	Asda	Sainsbury
Produce				
Bananas per lb	0.19	0.19	0.19	0.19
Frozen turkey per lb	0.35	0.54	0.45	–
Frozen turkey per kilo	0.77	–	–	0.99
Fuel				
1 litre of unleaded fuel	0.49.2	0.49.9	0.49.9	0.49.9
Books				
The Rainmaker by John Grisham	9.99	–	–	–
Tinker's Girl by Catherine Cookson	–	3.99	–	–
The Chamber by John Grisham	–	–	3.99	–
Sheba by Jack Higgins	–	–	–	3.99
Albums				
(What's the Story?) Morning Glory by Oasis	11.99	11.99	11.99	12.99
Videos				
The Lion King	13.99	13.99	13.99	13.99

Note: Food retailers' percentage shares of sales are music and video 4.9; newspapers and magazines 12.8; books 1.2; and health and beauty, toiletries, cosmetics, medicines 21.3.

With promotions on everything from bananas to best-selling books (see 'How the prices compared' table), it doesn't look like there are many areas left for discounting apart from the toiletries market. The whole area of toiletries is ripe for price cutting. Toiletries are high-margin products and there is no reason why they should be. The whole health and beauty area is one of the few sectors where retail analysts expect to see sustainable real growth into the first few years of the twenty-first century. It is an area in which food retailers will want to increase their shares and whether they want to do that now or later, they have started to use price already. It seems obvious that more price activity on toiletries is inevitable. In both short and long term, more competition between Boots and Superdrug is anticipated. Superdrug, in particular, is responsible for much of the retail pricing activity in this area, using price as a competitive marketing weapon.

Superdrug already beats the supermarkets hands down on own-label health supplements; it has 70 own-label vitamins and minerals compared to Asda's five, and it could afford 20 per cent cuts on a selection of its own brands without prejudicing its annual development plans. Another area where we can expect to see more low pricing is fine fragrances; Superdrug led a campaign two years ago to try and open up supply of fine fragrances to retailers other than Boots and the big department stores. Despite an official government ruling which basically endorsed the status quo, Superdrug is quietly persuading some of the big perfume houses to supply their stores directly. Without direct supplies Superdrug and the supermarkets have to rely on the so-called 'grey market', which is too erratic and unreliable.

Although price is not exclusively important and it is not the only marketing weapon, when consumer spending looks shaky, price remains important. However, discounting can be taken too far and toiletries may be a sensitive area. In general, if a product is discounted too heavily it loses credibility. With toiletries, part of the value is in the pricing. People believe that products are not delivering that special element of luxury if they go too low in price and there is a risk that discounting is also undermining the brand. A better and safer way is to offer added-value products like extra-volume packs and two for the price of one, as Boots does. Retailers should leave heavy discounting to commodity items without any individual brand values – vitamins, CDs and videos are good examples. If any price-fixing problems need to be addressed and solved, it seems the supermarkets will be the ones to do it; and as we have seen with books and drugs, they are willing to stick their necks out in the drive to cut prices.

Finally, the current rules on magazine and newspaper distribution were largely endorsed by the Monopolies and Mergers Commission in 1998. But if things change, the wholesalers are not likely to take it lying down. In the meantime, the supermarkets continue to be the young upstarts, ready to flout the law if necessary to prove a point, while their market share is high. Meanwhile, though the price may not be right for lots of supermarket suppliers out there, for the customers in the shops it certainly is.

Questions for discussion

1 Discuss the key issues involved in this case.

2 Do you think there is probably a hidden agenda in retailers' actions; that is, what are their motives?

3 How could the situations discussed in the case be corrected?

REFERENCES

Berman, B. and Evans, J. (1995) *Retail Management: A Strategic Approach*. 6th edn. Englewood Cliffs, NJ: Prentice-Hall.

Bolton, R.W. (1989) 'Relationship between market characteristics and promotional price elasticity', *Marketing Science*, 8 (Spring): 153–69.

Collins, A. (1992) *Competitive Retail Marketing: Dynamic Strategies for Winning and Keeping Customers*. London: McGraw-Hill.

Corstjens, J. and Corstjens, M. (1995) *Store Wars: The Battle for Mindspace and Shelf-space*. Chichester: John Wiley.

Grewal, D., Marmorstein, H. and Sharma A. (1996) 'Communicating price information through semantic cues: the moderating effects of situation and discount size', *Journal of Consumer Research*, 23 (September): 148–53.

Hoch, S.J., Dreze, X. and Purk, M.E. (1994) 'EDLP, Hi–Lo, and margin arithmetic', *Journal of Marketing*, 58 (October): 16–27.

Mulhern, F.J. and Leone, R.P. (1991) 'Implicit price bundling of retail products: a multiple product approach to maximising store profitability,' *Journal of Marketing*, 55(4): 63–76.

Omar, O.E. (1997) 'Target pricing: a marketing management tool for pricing new cars', *Pricing Strategy & Practice*, 5(2): 61–9.

Ortmeyer, G., Quelch, J.A. and Salmon, W. (1991) 'Restoring credibility to retail pricing', *Sloan Management Review*, Fall: 55–66.

Raju, J., Srinivasan, V. and Lal, R. (1990) 'The effect of brand loyalty on competitive price promotional strategies', *Management Science*, 36 (March): 276–304.

Rosenbloom, B. (1981) *Retail Marketing*. New York: Random House.

Samli, A.C. (1989) *Retail Marketing Strategy: Planning, Implementation and Control*. New York: Quorum Books.

11

Retail promotion and advertising management

LEARNING OBJECTIVES

After reading this chapter, you should:

- understand the meaning and functions of sales promotion within the retail communication mix;

- understand the role of advertising as the most visible manifestation of retail marketing;

- be able to evaluate the role of public relations within the retail organisation and its influence in achieving corporate objectives;

- understand the use of display as a visual merchandising tool within the retail organisation;

- be aware of the benefits of special sales events that promote the retailer and/or merchandise without mass media.

In many retailing situations, **sales promotion** and **advertising** are the most active elements in the marketing mix. Basically, retailing is a business of buying for resale. The first task of any retailer before the doors open for business is, therefore, to buy a stock of merchandise that may be sold at a profitable price. In understanding the needs and wants of the shoppers that the retailer wishes to serve, products must be stocked in the order that the shoppers may wish to buy, at the prices that they are able and willing to pay, at the time when they are ready to do their shopping, and in the quantities that they require. Unless the retailer provides a stock that measures up to all these requirements, success will be unlikely.

Once the necessary merchandise has been acquired, the retailer must then set out to accomplish the ultimate corporate objective by selling at a profit the products and services that have been bought for resale. In effect, shoppers must be found who need and want to buy the products. To achieve this goal, retailers must use every appropriate means of informing potential shoppers about their businesses and of attracting them to their stores.

This chapter is viewed from two broad perspectives:

- retail promotion;
- retail advertising and display.

It explores the relative role of promotion, in general, and its role in different retail marketing strategies in particular. There is a well-developed range of theories which addresses how both sales promotion and advertising communicate, and the various elements of these factors are examined. The chapter also observes that the traditional theories of promotion are being challenged by the use of 'conviction marketing': conviction marketing is based on both personal vision and research. The chapter first reviews the application of retail sales promotion techniques and then explores the use of retail advertising and display as means of creating store awareness among the shopping public.

Retail promotion

Retail promotion involves informing, persuading and/or reminding customers through advertising, **publicity,** personal selling and sales promotion. Among the various facets of the marketing mix, the promotional aspects are most likely to arouse controversy both within and outside the organisation. Internally, promotion can arouse controversy because problems are created by the inability to measure the results of expenditure on promotion. Externally, the controversy stems from the belief of many that promotion, and the money spent on it, operate against the best social and economic interests of the customer. Promotion can be taken to cover three separate activities (Table 11.1) including, sales promotion, advertising and publicity.

Table 11.1
COMPOSITION OF RETAIL PROMOTION ACTIVITIES

Retail sales promotion	Retail advertising	Public relations
Leaflets	National press	Publications
Catalogues	Local press	Events
Direct mail	Magazines	Press
Showcards	Books	In-house journals
Signs	Outdoor	Advertising
Exhibitions	Cinema	Non-media
Packaging	Television	Sponsorships
In-store selling	Radio	Store cards
Display		Donations
Gifts		

Since developing a retail marketing strategy is almost synonymous with image manipulation, the role of retail promotion becomes obvious. The manipulation of retail image can be achieved through communication (Samli, 1989). As image basically means the sum total of impressions that different shoppers perceive about a retail organisation, by definition retail promotion communicates the image. The creation and portrayal of an appropriate image by the retailer requires a calculated and tightly controlled communication activity, regardless of the size and nature of the retail organisation. Taking a very broad view, retail promotion embraces all activities and devices that are designed to sell merchandise, either directly or indirectly. Accordingly, there is a sales promotion aspect to practically every phase of retail marketing, from buying, through pricing, to store layout. A more commonly accepted view, however, is that sales promotion concerns only those activities and devices whose primary function is to invite, persuade, and otherwise encourage and stimulate shopping. Included in this are the major forces of advertising, **display**, personal selling, and other associated activities such as special sales shows, discounts, and loyalty storecards.

The relative importance and effectiveness of the different types of promotional effort vary considerably from store to store and from time to time. Success with these sales-building tools depends upon ability to organise and coordinate them into a unified programme, tailored to the specific needs of a particular store and its merchandising situation.

The retail promotion programme of a retailer is likely to be much more nebulous, consisting of many strands that are difficult to separate from one another and from other aspects of store operation. The grocery and pharmaceutical trade press are probably the best reference points for confirmation of what is happening in terms of retail promotions. But a visit to a supermarket is as good a way as any of seeing retail sales promotion working down at the store level. Since retail sales promotion is essentially a practical, down-to-earth activity, it is without doubt at the actual point of sale that it really counts and where it can best be seen.

Planning for retail sales promotion

A retail organisation, like any other social or economic institution, communicates with its actual and potential publics regularly, both directly and indirectly. Planning this communication entails developing a promotional programmes. This section discusses promotional objectives and the promotional mix; the other four areas are outlined in the major sections that follows.

Promotional objectives

The retail store's **promotional objectives** must be consistent with the image development and image manipulation process. If the store wants to project an image as the fashion leader in the area and it promotes only its prices and its conservative orientation to fashion merchandising, it cannot fulfil its promotional objectives. Table 11.2 illustrates the points of emphasis in different retail marketing strategic options. These points of emphasis either explicitly or implicitly identify promotional objectives. In the case of **general merchandiser** for instance, mass information about all of the store's merchandise as well as the store itself needs to be promoted. This has to be done in a form that involves least cost for the widest amount of information dissemination (Samli, 1989)

It is not necessary for retailers to pursue a single strategy only. In most cases a combination of strategic options is necessary. Consider, for example, a retailer that is a **differentiator** and is at the stage of being a fast grower. In such a case the retail store will be researching not only its differences and strengths but will also enhance these special characteristics. As a result, that store will gain further acceptance in the market segment at which it has been aiming its attention. Thus, the two strategic objectives are likely to reinforce each other for more effective performance.

Table 11.2

STRATEGIC ALTERNATIVES AND PROMOTIONAL OBJECTIVES EMPHASIS

Strategic options	*Promotional emphasis*
General merchandiser	Mass information about all of the merchandise and the store
Differentiator	Emphasis on showing differences and strengths of the store
Segmenter	Emphasising the key characteristics of the store which will satisfy the obvious needs of an identified segment
Positioner	Comparative advertising to reassure and capture the position that is aimed for
Store versus merchandise congruence	Emphasising the store characteristics and matching product groups to the store image
Beginner	High level of information dissemination to promote the store (information)
Fast grower	Enhancing the store characteristics to gain stronger acceptance in view of increasing competition (persuasion)
Mature	Maintaining successful image and position in a changing market (reminding)
Declining store: ■ scaling down ■ revitalisation ■ redirection	Overall decline in promotional efforts. All-out emphasis on one new feature. Renewed emphasis on features that have been somewhat neglected up to that time
Speciality store: ■ speciality goods ■ shopping goods ■ convenience goods	Maintaining differential advantages of the store and its image by the uniqueness of its selection service and advertising
Discount store: ■ speciality goods ■ shopping goods ■ convenience goods	Advertising extensively the prices for even the best brands

Promotional mix

All promotion must be seen in the context of the whole marketing mix, of which promotion is just one of the four elements. Price and place may be just as important in terms of the mix as a whole, and they also have an impact on any promotion. For example, a high-priced product sold through specialist outlets will demand a very different form of promotion to that of a cut-price brand sold through supermarkets. Fourth, the most important element of the marketing mix must almost always be the product or service itself. Despite widely held misconceptions, it is a hard fact of the brand promotional life that consumers will not buy (at least not more than once) a product or service which does not meet their needs – no matter how persuasive the promotion (Duncan and Hollander, 1977). At the same time, the form of the promotion itself, the message and even the medium, may be largely determined by the specification of that product or service. Thus, by defining the product, the whole marketing mix is largely defined; and all the elements of the marketing mix contribute to the overall promotion of a product, service or company.

Although, retail and marketing promotional mix components are basically the same, the relative points of emphasis in the retailing promotional mix differ substantially from those of the marketing promotional mix. In retailing, for instance, the local nature of the business and the immediacy of promotion message imply much heavier emphasis on local radio and local newspapers. The delay in promotional scheduling makes media less appealing. The development of the retail **promotional mix** depends on at least seven factors (Samli, 1989):

- strategic objectives
- the audience to be reached
- the size of the market
- the message or product that is going to be promoted
- the relative cost of available media
- the amount of lead time required before an advertisement is run
- general retail marketing practices.

In pursuit of strategic objectives the general merchandiser, the differentiator, the **segmenter,** or the **positioner** (*see* Table 11.2), has to use selective media such as television and selective magazines. If the merchandise in question is related to fashion, it becomes important to use effective visual promotion, such as television and some special fashion-related national or local magazines. The role of the visual is, clearly, important.

Simple recognition can affect perceptions because people tend to like known brands, even if they have never used them. Brand visibility can signal leadership, success, quality, substance and excitement, even before the product is used. Exhibit 11.1 illustrates this, recounting how Hugo Boss used brand visibility to create and sustain an exclusive image that was translated into sales.

Exhibit 11.1   **High visibility and a high media profile lead to international sales**

Hugo Boss, a fine clothier, created its image of exclusivity and high quality through the effective use of sponsorships. In the early 1970s, Hugo Boss sponsored Porsche in Formula One races to capitalise on Porsche's strong exclusive image and international presence. Over the years that followed, the company also took on the sponsorship of international tennis, golf, and ski competitions; It funded exhibitions and artists; and it sponsored television drama such as *Miami Vice* and *LA Law* – both of which featured Hugo Boss's garments. The visibility gained through Hugo Boss's sponsorships quickly paid off with high volume sales and international recognition. Hugo Boss's garments are sold in 57 countries and more than half its sales come from outside Germany, its country of origin.

A speciality store that sells primarily speciality goods will use television or magazines to promote the store itself and newspaper or radio for the speciality goods it is promoting. In contrast, a convenience store promoting convenience products is not likely to use major **mass media** such as television or magazines; it will rely heavily on its appearance and location, and will use more specialised promotional devices.

Exhibit 11.2   Grand Met launched Häagen-Dazs (a brand of luxury ice-cream) in Europe in 1989, despite an economic recession and high competition. Häagen-Dazs used both location and traditional values to promote its image. It pursued additional strategies to fuel word-of-mouth communication: branded freezers in food retail stores; sponsorship of cultural events; and a relatively low-budget, steamy, print-media campaign with the theme 'the ultimate experience in personal pleasure'. Linking the brand to arts sponsorship was a particularly smart move. At one arts event, the Opera Factory's production of *Don Giovanni* in London, the ice cream was even incorporated into the show. When the Don called for sorbet, he received a container of Häagen-Dazs. The result was a good free publicity spread among target consumers.

The company's coordinated brand-building efforts were overwhelmingly successful. Häagen-Dazs' brand awareness in the UK reached more than 50 per cent within a few months.

In general, Samli (1989) noted that there are some notable patterns to the ways in which different groups with varying strategic objectives direct their promotional activity. These can be grouped under three headings for ease of discussion:

- strategy types
- life cycle stages
- store types

Strategy types

1 Discount stores which are general merchandisers (grocers or chemists) generally use newspapers and, in the main, disseminate information about their merchandise in a most cost-effective manner.

2 Differentiators proceed more readily with long-lasting print media (magazines) and pay attention to store appearance. They emphasise the differentiating characteristics of their store.

3 Segmenters behave basically like differentiators; however, they emphasise the differentiating characteristics of their store that are geared specially to the segment to which the store is aiming. They use primarily long-lasting print media (magazines), some television, and the store appearance.

4 Positioners are usually engaged in comparative advertising. As such, they rely on visual media (magazines, television, and newspapers).

5 Store-merchandise congruence emphasisers rely heavily on the store's appearance and on disseminating information about both the store and the merchandise. They are likely to use local print media or radio.

Life cycle stages

1 New entrants (retail stores which are opening up, in this context) try to disseminate as much information about themselves and their activities as possible. In addition to trying to obtain public information coverage – such as news items in the local newspaper – they use heavy radio and newspaper advertising. General store site promotion, along with direct mail, is a further option

2 **Fast growers** try to persuade by more long-lasting messages in local magazines, newspapers, store displays and the store's appearance.

3 The matured firm continues using the promotional activity that has enabled the store to achieve its current position. Unlike the fast grower, it needs more immediate impact; hence, it may emphasise newspaper and radio advertising.

4 The declining store has three alternatives:
   - if it is scaling down its activities, the major emphasis is likely to be on low-cost immediate promotion using radio, newspapers, and point of purchase displays;
   - if the store is attempting to revitalise, it is almost in the same position as the new entrant and must behave similarly;
   - if it is trying to redirect its efforts, the store may be likened to the fast grower and should behave in a similar way.

Store types

1 The speciality store, regardless of the products it carries, must project the image of a speciality store. Maintaining the differential advantages of a speciality store requires at least three special arrangements:
   - advertising in particular media, prestigious magazines, specific newspaper advertising on special occasions, and paying particular attention to the store's appearance;

    – if the company operates on a national basis, national network television and major magazine advertising;

    – if the company is very local, the emphasis should be on its image, merchandise, and service.

2 The shopping store, regardless of its merchandise emphases, must communicate the idea that there are gains to be made and economies to be enjoyed in this store. It has to emphasise local promotional efforts by using local newspapers and radio stations on a regular basis.

3 Unless it is very large, a convenience store relies on the shopper traffic drawn by the stores around it. A convenience store typically does not have the means to advertise unless it can get into a **co-operative advertising** effort with a manufacturer who is advertising a product that the store is carrying. The promotional tools a convenience shop may use include direct mail, the store atmosphere, its merchandise and service.

Media mix and selection process

Assuming that strategic promotion management decisions have been made, that the market segments and customer profiles are known, and that promotional objectives have been decided on, it may be concluded that reaching the audience implies the development of an effective media mix – that is, **media planning.**

The retailer can choose from among newspapers, telephone directories (*Yellow Pages, Thomson Local*), direct mail, television, magazines, outdoor billboards, and transit media (found in or on buses or taxis). Each one of these media reaches a special audience. Duncan and Hollander (1997) present a detailed account of the strengths and weaknesses of each medium. Suffice it to say here that the retailer must have a clear idea about the store's market segment so that the appropriate media mix may be put together to reach it. It is quite well known that individual local radio stations have distinctive characters, which result in them each developing a following – their own market segment. This does not apply only to local radio; the same is true of other media. For example, teenagers and senior citizens listen to different radio stations; they also watch different television channels and, with some notable exceptions like *Coronation Street* and *EastEnders*, different television programmes. Thus, the retailer must know not only the specific target markets they are aiming for, but also the relevant audiences of the various media. Different retailers have different media mixes that are appropriate for their purposes. In order to develop an effective media mix, an intermedia selection process must take place so that different media classes are compared and analysed, enabling the most appropriate media mix to be developed. Here at least six critical factors (Kotler, 1997) come into play:

1 **Quintile analysis** is a special market research technique which indicates different socio-economic market segments in quintiles and their media exposure.

2 **Media objectives** – this factor deals with broadness of coverage in terms of reach or depth of the media in terms of frequency. For instance, if the retail

organisation wants to expand its market, it may emphasise reach, whereas the organisation that may be trying to penetrate a certain specified segment will emphasise frequency.

3 **Audience selectivity** – the audience the retailer wants to reach is a significant factor in choosing one media class over another. Obviously, radio listeners and *Reader's Digest* or *Cosmopolitan* readers constitute very different groups of people. The media classes as well as the specific medium within the media class will be selected depending on the target audience to be reached.

4 **Message tone** – this factor refers to the nature of the message that is going to be communicated. The message may or may not be matched with the medium or media. To the extent that the retail organisation is trying to project its forward-looking aspects, it should not use media which consumers may identify as being traditional or conservative. In particular, the message tone may not be consistent with the rationale of the message magazine or newspaper. Similarly, the emotionality or rationale of the message calls for the promotional team to analyse the media message tone carefully.

5 **Media sense modality** – this factor is related to the media's impact on consumer perception. The medium may have movement, visual or audio effect, or be a combination of all three. The retail organisation that finds motion desirable will, of course, choose television as their medium of preference – all other things being equal.

6 **Geographical dispersion** – each medium has a different reach, which can be measured in terms of socio-economic as well as geographic dimensions. When the retail organisation has a good idea about its target markets and trading areas, it becomes necessary to match this information against the geographical reach of the media. The best matches are the most desirable objective that leads to better media group selection.

The most important point here is that the components of the media mix are decided on by the promotional objectives. Without clear promotional objectives, it becomes impossible to put together an effective promotional mix. The second most important point to remember is that every retailer has a distinctive promotional mix. This implies the presence of multiple media. Retailers use a combination of mutually reinforcing promotional forms (Davies and Brooks, 1989). A combination of media may be better than single medium advertising but, in general, the following factors may be considered:

■ size of the trading area
■ the message and the product
■ relative cost
■ amount of lead time
■ general trade practices.

Size of the trading area

The size of the trading area has a strong and definite impact on the promotional mix. All other considerations aside, the retail organisation will need the most appropriate coverage for its trading area. The greater the extent of the trading area, the more viable radio and television become since newspapers may not cover large geographical areas. Furthermore, in such situations, where the trading area is wide-spread outdoor advertising – namely, on billboards – can become important. The smaller the trading area, the greater the dependence on store appearance, direct mail, and outside promotional activity. The smallness of the trading area is usually related to the size of the retail organisation. Small retailers are unlikely to be able to afford advertising in expensive media such as television or magazines.

The message and the product

There is need for basic congruence between the message and the media. As an example, take the retail firm that is attempting to establish its reputation and is positioning itself. If the medium (or media) it uses does not possess the kind of credibility the message is trying to get across, it should not be used – indeed it may even be counter-productive. Similarly, the retail store that is trying to establish a liberal, forward looking, vibrant image would be well advised not to advertise on television before or after a political party broadcast. If the message needs visual effect, certain types of media (for example, radio) are unsuitable; if colour is important for the message, monochrome media such as black and white newspapers are not ideal.

In addition to congruence between message and media, congruence between product and media is also important. Certain products such as fashion goods need visual impact, therefore, only newspapers, television or other print media can be used; some well-known brand appliances do not rely on visual effect, hence, a special sale of these products can easily be advertised on the radio. Although each case is unique and must be considered on its own merits, generalisations such as those presented here are useful to increase the retailer's awareness of the factors relating to the promotional mix. Each retail store must find the most suitable promotional mix for itself.

Relative cost

Cost is always one of the most important factors in making media decisions. Most advertising books deal with the measures of relative cost (the cost of one medium against the others). The two measures are **milline rate** (measures used in calculating promotional costs) and cost per thousand. All things being equal, the choice is always to use the lowest relative costs.

Amount of lead time

For many retail advertisements timing is very important, and usually there is little lead time to prepare the advertisements. The supermarket advertisements, for instance, appear in local newspapers one day and are expected to create traffic the next day; moreover, the sales of that week are different from those of the previous week. Thus, most grocery retailers and others who promote special sales need to use local media that do not need much lead time to prepare advertisements. For image-building or for media with long-lasting impact, as well as for those types of retailers who need **illustrations** and colour, a long lead time is required. Argos's catalogue, advertisements in major magazines or television commercials, for example, all involve extensive periods for preparation – that is, they have long lead times.

General trade practices

Trade practices inevitably influence retailers' promotional mixes. In most cases, retailers feel obligated to match or excel their competitors. If their competitors are advertising heavily in the local print media, other retailers in the same market will often do the same. For example, when McDonald's is engaged in massive television advertising, Burger King follows suit. These factors are instrumental in determining the promotional mix for the retail organisation.

Special sales events

An important part of the retailers' promotion programme is the planning and execution of **special sales events** – that is, the heavy promotion of merchandise at reduced prices for a limited period of time. Most retailers believe these events contribute significantly to sales and profits, and that they maintain the customers' interest in the store. Three kinds of special sales events may be identified as:

- **distress sales** (auctions) – those designed to raise money quickly regardless of their effect on future business;
- turnover sales – those conducted to sell slow-moving merchandise or to sell out a line or brand;
- Promotion sales – those used to attract new customers, introduce new goods, or secure favourable publicity.

These events may include a clearance sale, anniversary sale, white goods sale, new year sale, back-to-school sale, Mother's Day sale and Christmas sale. In addition to special sales events which feature reduced prices, many large retailers conduct special events which may attract considerable publicity and arouse customer interest. Small retailers are, in most cases, unable to afford these special sales events. The types of special sales events used by a retailer (Duncan and Hollander, 1977) and their frequency will depend upon many factors, including:

- past experience;
- the competitive situation;
- group efforts undertaken with other retailers;

- assistance received from manufacturers;
- the accumulation of slow-moving merchandise.

Many large stores use special sales extensively to obtain a satisfactory sales volume; however, when used too frequently, they may undermine customer confidence in 'regular' prices. In addition, customers become indifferent to such events, employees lose their enthusiasm, accounting and control problems are complicated, and merchandise returns are increased. Special sales events often require extra sales personnel and great diligence in controlling shoplifting while satisfactorily handling large numbers of customers.

Collaborative promotions

Special sales events are often organised by groups of retailers. The growth of shopping centres (McGoldrick, 1990) and retailer/manufacturer collaboration have brought group promotional activities to a new peak. Retailers in these centres have long engaged in joint promotions, often organised around the visit of a celebrity, an art exhibition or a concert. As shopping centres grew in size and number, and as they became competitive with one another, special sales events became even more desirable as a means of drawing customers to a particular centre.

Planning special sales events

Special sales events must be planned with care so that all activities are effectively coordinated. Store-wide sales, for instance, are often planned three to six months in advance, with store buyers approaching sources in ample time to obtain the best price concessions – frequently made available by negotiation during off-peak production periods. When these arrangements are completed, time is required for production, delivery to the store, receiving, and marking. Time is needed also for preparation and for securing additional selling and non-selling employees to handle the customer traffic. Otherwise, the value of promotion in bringing customers into the store will be reduced because customers are likely to become disgruntled due to the resultant poor service.

Retail advertising management

Retail promotion efforts are of two major types:

- those of a non-personal nature, such as advertising, **window display** and mail order;
- those of a personal nature, involving personal selling abilities and requiring an individual conversation between a customer and a store employee.

Once a store has been properly equipped and well-balanced assortments of merchandise have been assembled to meet the needs of prospective customers, measures must be adopted to attract those customers into the store and to induce them to make purchases. When such measures are effective, they build goodwill for the store and ensure continuous patronage from satisfied customers. It is retail advertising which generally performs such tasks (Ogilvy, 1983).

Functions and goals of retail advertising

Advertising is 'any paid form of nonpersonal presentation and promotion of ideas, goods, or services by an identified sponsor' (Ogilvy, 1983). Retailers may use it to tell people what goods and services they have available, to stimulate desire for those items, to keep people interested in their stores between visits, and to develop goodwill. In other words, its main function from the retailer's standpoint is to create a desirable image of their business in the customer's mind.

Advertising has become a very important part of many retail businesses. In 1997, for example, 50 large UK retailing companies spent a total of around £2.6 billion on advertising – not including the costs of window or interior displays. Total retail advertising expenditures were, of course, substantially greater than those figures. One of the top UK food retailers, Sainsbury, alone invested about £4.0 million in newspaper, radio, television and magazine advertising – quite a change for a company that until 1978 relied almost entirely on window displays and location in the mainstream of pedestrian traffic to attract trade (McGoldrick, 1990). But retailers know that customers shop differently in the 1990s from the way they did in the 1950s – or even in the 1970s. Consumers now have a choice of several shopping centres rather than automatically drifting to one location; they often travel by car rather than walk; and they may be unwilling or unable to visit all possible stores in the time available for shopping. Consequently, retailers frequently need advertising to attract potential consumers and to 'pre-sell' to them.

Advertising will not accomplish its goals unless it is carefully planned, prepared, tested, placed in appropriate media at the right times, and reviewed frequently (Abraham and Lodish, 1990). Moreover, it must be coordinated with other activities of the store to obtain maximum benefits. Advertising is not a panacea for all the retailer's management problems. Some small retailers may avoid advertising (other than window displays) because they are aware of the difficulty of making a strong impression with a limited budget. However, those retailers, whatever their size, who recognise the limitations of advertising programmes and plan their programmes accordingly, will derive the greatest benefit from such efforts. They should keep in mind that advertising cannot:

■ sell merchandise that people do not want to buy;

■ sell merchandise in profitable quantities without the backing of every other division of the store;

■ succeed to the fullest extent unless it is used continuously (Mercer, 1996).

This clear warning emphasises that if advertising is to be effective in the long term it must be believable, truthful and provide the customer with helpful information. There are two main types of retail advertising: direct-action advertising and indirect-action advertising. Most advertisements represent a blending of both types.

Direct-action advertising

The main purpose of this type of advertising is to bring customers into the store to purchase specific items of merchandise. Advertising with this emphasis constitutes the greater proportion of total retail advertising. It may take the form of:

- regular-price advertising, where the appeal is based on the desirability of the goods;
- 'bargain' advertising, which features price appeal in relation to value;
- clearance-sale advertising, the main purpose of which is to sell off slow-moving items and sell remnants at reduced prices.

Indirect-action advertising

Institutional or indirect action seeks to develop goodwill for the store, to create confidence in its merchandise and services, with the aim of building permanent patronage. The forms used to achieve this include prestige advertising and service advertising. Prestige advertising emphasises the store's or the department's character and leadership in style, merchandise quality or positive social responsibility. Often these characteristics are suggested by the use of appropriate typefaces and illustrations rather than by flat statements in the advertisement. Service advertising seeks to attract patronage by stressing the various services and facilities offered by the store which make it such a desirable place in which to shop.

Institutional advertising

Every retail advertisement helps create some impression in the reader's or viewer's mind about the store or to add to or detract from an already existing general impression. So all retail advertising has some institutional effect, although the resultant image may be accurate or inaccurate, consistent or confusing, and helpful or harmful to the store. A retailer must recognise the institutional impact of every contribution to their promotional advertising, and select both items and messages that will contribute to the production or enhancement of a favourable image. Among three leading London speciality shops, for example, one stresses elegance in its copy and illustrations, another focuses on avant-garde or very original fashions, while a third emphasises their appeal to a broad spectrum of fashion conscious customers. Other retailers go beyond this and skillfully blend institutional themes and item information in the advertisement.

Food store advertising, often cited (incorrectly) as promotional in nature, illustrates well a combination of the two main types of retail advertising. A study of the advertisements of four competing food chains in Manchester in 1992 concluded that the adverts were used to create a favourable image to attract customers – not necessarily to buy the specific items mentioned, but to highlight the store's general assortments (Davies and Brooks, 1989). The typical advertisement was one of three categories, with the first two classes greatly predominating:

- adverts focusing on items which differentiate the advertiser from competitors, that is items not stocked or not featured by other chains;

- adverts serving as a sort of shopping reminder list – to inform customers of the retailer's name and of the breadth of stock;

- adverts, run by a limited number of retailers, to neutralise the previous advertisements of competitors based on price, that is items on which competitors' advertised prices were met.

Public relations

Institutional advertising (which promotes a company, not the product) and **public relations** are used to create an image, correct an image, and communicate a corporate philosophy.

Exhibit 11.3 | **Mobil's public relations – using advertising to establish credibility**

After the 1973 oil embargo, Mobil Oil Corporation corrected the erroneous impression that it was part of a conspiracy to raise oil prices. It used two distinctly different media: 'masterpiece theatre' on public television and editorial-type advertisements in the national newspapers. The public broadcasting was claimed to be a goodwill umbrella, while the newspaper advertisements stressed the need for a national policy on energy.

Mobil established credibility in its domestic market; established a constituency of people who recognised that it was 'different', established a leadership position in oil industry communications, and established a policy of speaking out on relevant issues necessary for its strategic development planning. Other major oil corporations including Shell and BP, adopted similar strategies for their national and international campaigns.

Trademarks

There is always the danger that an advertising and promotional campaign will become so successful that the trademark becomes the generic name for the product – aspirin, nylon, sellotape, cellophane, Hoover, and cola were all proprietary trademarks at one time. The trademarks of Kodak, Kleenex, Xerox and Frigidaire have become generic names in the minds of some consumers, despite the companies' strong promotional efforts to stop this happening.

After losing cellophane as a trademark in 1936, duPont learned its lesson. Since then the company has been careful to protect its legal rights in Teflon and its annual investment of £4.8 million in advertising. It won a case against a Japanese firm for using the trademark 'Eflon'. DuPont won the case in what became a battle of opposing research. The duPont survey established that 68 per cent of the respondents identified 'Teflon' as a brand name and that only 31 per cent thought it was a generic term. DuPont has a trademark-protection programme that involves its legal department, its advertising department, and its advertising agency.

Co-operative advertising

The retailer generally assumes complete responsibility for the preparation and cost of the store's advertising. At times, however, retailers may be able to engage in co-operative advertising, in which they share responsibility and cost with manufacturers or wholesalers. To illustrate how this works, the product is advertised with the retailer's name with the resource (the manufacturer or wholesaler) paying part – perhaps 50 per cent – of the media cost up to a maximum amount, for example, 5 per cent of the retailer's purchases. Perhaps as much as £2 billion is spent each year by manufacturers on co-operative advertising (Carter, 1994). The resource gains from the added interest shown by the retailer in its product, from the retailer's prestige, from the extra space or time purchased by the retailer's contribution to the media cost, and from the fact that retailers usually buy newspaper space at lower 'local' rates than national advertisers are charged. Despite these advantages, many manufacturers dislike co-operative advertising. They are not satisfied with the return they obtain from the advertising allowance, and often prefer to deal directly with the media. Consequently, the trade press sometimes publishes stories of manufacturer dissatisfaction with the arrangement.

To the retailer, co-operative advertising yields benefits such as assistance in preparing advertisements, the tie-in posters and displays supplied for use in the store, and in the increase in the total advertising space that can be afforded. The retailer should, however, be fully aware of the obligations involved and should be sure that the product has a suitable reputation. Moreover, retailers may be held responsible for the truthfulness of the claims made in co-operative advertisements that the manufacturers or wholesalers have prepared. On balance, the retailer should probably engage in some co-operative advertising, but be careful to select the best deals available.

Advertising strategy formulation

Having no distinct and unconfused understanding of the advertising process, a substantial amount of advertising is conducted without a clear idea of the future benefits. But it is impossible to develop and implement a successful advertising strategy for a product unless the objectives are clearly specified. One factor which inhibits this is a general resistance to control and a feeling that creative activity cannot be measured; another is the difficulty of differentiating between marketing and advertising objectives. An increase in market share is a valid marketing objective. But what is the advertising objective, one that advertising alone can achieve, which is consonant with the increase in share? It is common practice to distinguish sales from non-sales objectives for advertising, such as awareness, trial, attitudes, and so on. Any quantitative treatment of advertising must relate these non-sales measures to their sales effectiveness. An advertising campaign which increased awareness but left sales unaltered should not have been run – and certainly must not be repeated. Specification of the advertising strategy for a product requires that decisions be made in each of the following areas (Duncan and Hollander, 1977):

1 Who is the firm trying to reach? What segment of consumers and users is the advertising to be directed towards?

2 What is the objective of the advertising and what should it say? What is its theme?

3 How much should be spent on the campaign?

4 How should this budget be allocated in terms of media, geographical areas, products and over time?

5 What procedures are required in terms of pre-testing and monitoring the results of the campaign?

Developing such an advertising strategy is itself a multi-stage process. The first step in this process is market analysis – an integrated series of measures to describe the current competitive status of the product in terms of sales, market share and awareness, trial and penetration rates, an analysis of the buyers, the extent of brand loyalty, and so on. Included in this analysis is a definition of the product class – how the product is to be positioned. It has been suggested that research be directed toward establishing whether the conventional product class can be expanded or whether additional segmentation is possible. On the basis of such an analysis, the target market for the product can be defined using attitudinal measures. Attitudinal research is used to aid the creative step of generating the potential concepts and themes to be used. These concepts are then tested against a sample, drawn from the target audience, and reaction to the concepts in terms of importance, interest and believability are ascertained. Specific advertisements may then be generated and pre-tested. Such an intensive procedure is likely to be followed only for a major campaign.

Budget strategies

The subjectivity and creativity of advertising help to explain why it is so difficult to determine the level of an **advertising budget** (Farris and Buzzel, 1979). Central to this budgeting decision is the difficulty of relating advertising expenditures to profits; advertising is only one element in the retail marketing mix which created a sale. Furthermore, the time lag between retail advertising and sales varies across products and market segments, which makes it difficult to link a specific retail advertising effort to a particular profit period. There are two basic budget strategies:

■ the breakdown method

■ the build-up method.

The breakdown method determines the size of the budget and then breaks it down into the copy and media strategies. The breakdown methods include percentage of sales, a fixed amount per unit, competitive parity, return on investment, and the marginal approach. A brief description of each of these would be helpful here.

The *percentage of sales* approach seems like one of the easiest methods to implement until the question is asked, 'Which sales figure do we use?'. If historical sales are used, then it is a simple method. To use historical sales, however, makes advertising dependent on sales – the opposite of the intended relationship of the advertising determining sales. Using forecasted sales makes it more difficult and introduces a further uncertainty, that of forecasting. The most logical sales figure to use is potential sales, because this relates the advertising budget to market opportunity. But estimating sales potential is difficult and requires research.

A *fixed amount per unit* is used in those industries in which the advertiser has considerable experience and, therefore, may be able to estimate how much advertising will be required to sell a unit of the product. Packaged grocery and car manufacturers use this method when giving trade allowances for co-operative advertising. Using units sold rather than money-amount sold makes the advertising effort independent of changes in price. Otherwise, a decision to change the price would automatically change the advertising budget in the same direction, which may be unrelated to the advertising task at hand.

Return on investment approaches view advertising strategies as investment portfolios (Farris and Buzzel, 1979). The strategy is sound, but the implementation is difficult except when advertising is the sole determinant of sales and when sales can be linked directly to advertising effort. Direct mail marketing is one of the few situations that meet these two conditions, where sales can be linked to a specific promotional piece or catalogue.

The *marginal* approach is based on the sound economic theory that advertising effort should be added in small increments until the cost of the additional unit of advertising and the profit generated by this unit are equal. This economic concept states that profit will be maximised when the marginal cost equals the marginal revenue. The theory cannot be questioned, but the implementation is possible only in the case of a single-product firm that uses easily measured units of advertising effort Few businesses or advertising budgets in the real world meet these criteria.

The build-up method estimates the costs to execute all of the advertising strategies. These costs are added to build up to a total budget. It is also known as the objective-and-task method because it begins with a statement of the advertising objective and estimates the costs of the tasks to meet the objective. The most common objectives are communication ones – changes in brand recall, benefit awareness, attitudes, etc. Direct-action advertising, such as direct mail advertising, may define the objective in terms of sales. Trade advertising may define the objective in terms of percentage of distribution or the number of point-of-purchase displays used. The build-up method seems more logical than the breakdown methods, but it suffers from the cost and delay in establishing the costs to perform the tasks. Unless adequate research has been performed, the costs estimates may be reduced to subjective guesstimates.

Effective advertising

Once objectives are established (Samli, 1989), conducting effective advertising involves:

- determining the advertising appropriation;
- planning the advertising;
- selecting appropriate media;
- preparing the actual advertisements;
- testing the advertisements.

These steps should be coordinated into a complete advertising programme, perhaps with the aid of an advertising agency. Some retail trade associations, such as the National Retail Furniture Association, and the National Retail Hardware Association, also prepare helpful materials for their members and some assistance (although not always unbiased) is often offered by suppliers and media representatives.

The advertising appropriation

The amount a store needs to spend on advertising will depend primarily upon its objectives. Does it want to dominate the media and have the most prominent advertising in its community, increase sales by a certain percentage, build up certain departments or lines of merchandise, attract a certain number of new customers – perhaps from a particular age or income segment of the market – or does it simply want to remind old customers of its existence? The expense of achieving one of these objectives will be influenced by such factors as the store's age, policies, size, location, competition, trading area, and the image it has already created. Other influential factors include media costs and circulation, business conditions, and competitors' marketing strategies.

What a retailer really needs to spend to achieve a stated objective may be beyond the business's resources. Perhaps some of the objectives will be impossible to attain or will cost more than will be recouped in view of the store's present market position. In such cases, the retailer must reconsider goals and settle for ones that are more practical, more achievable or more profitable. The retailer must also remember that advertising results will depend not only on how much is spent and how much time and space is bought, but also on the planning and timing of the programme, and the wise selection of items and prices to be featured. Nevertheless, one should not expect miracles from small advertising expenditures. Store policies will also have a strong impact on results since advertising can only build potential goodwill; this may be easily lost if the store does not live up to the customer expectations raised by the advertising.

Advertising process and planning

In general, there are three main groups of activities which retail advertising wishes to achieve (Mercer, 1996):

1 Building awareness (informing). The first task of any advertising is to make the audience appreciate that the product or service exists, and to explain exactly what it is.

2 Creating favourable attitudes (persuasion). The second stage, and the one that preoccupies most advertisers, is to create the favourable attitudes to the brand which will eventually lead consumers to switch their purchasing patterns.

3 Maintenance of loyalty (reinforcement). One of the tasks which is often forgotten is that of maintaining the loyalty of existing customers, who will almost always represent the main source of future sales.

These objectives are likely to be achieved by creating a suitable and effective message. To achieve this result, it will need to communicate a clear message which may include: awareness, interest, attitudes and buying decision.

Communicating a clear message

Awareness

The first task must be to achieve awareness, to gain the **attention** of the target audience. All of the different models are, predictably, in agreement on this first step. According to Ogilvy (1983) unless the headline sells the product, advertising has wasted 90 per cent of the money. Achieving awareness means, therefore, that the messages must first of all be seen and 'read'. They must grab the audience's attention. Advertising agencies have spent decades tracking down the techniques involved: from challenging headlines (like the famous Avis 'We try harder') in the press to memorable images on television (such as the Coca-Cola 'We'd like to teach the world to sing' advertisement of the 1970s). There is often a tendency by advertising agencies to concentrate almost exclusively on this element of awareness, however, though it impresses the copywriter's peers in other agencies, it does not necessarily achieve the end result of making the sale.

'Attention getting' is in part a function of 'size'. A full page advertisement is more likely to command attention than a quarter page one; a two-minute commercial will command more attention than a 15-second one. In part, having some feature which breaks through the apathy of the reader or viewer – using a 'visual' or a headline which is out of the ordinary and demands attention – is useful. It must be remembered that this has to be achieved in an environment in which every other advertiser is attempting the same trick. This may be so successful, indeed, that the advertising becomes almost 'generic' – for example, that for Guinness. Arguably, then creativity is the key to this first stage.

Interest

It is not sufficient to grab the reader's attention for a second or so, until it wanders again. In that brief time the message must take hold of the reader's interest and persuade him or her to 'read' on. The content of the message(s) must be meaningful and relevant to the target audience's needs. This is where marketing research can come into its own as the basis for effective advertising. In the first instance, the 'advertiser' needs to know exactly who the target audience is. Then the advertiser has to understand the audience's interests and needs, which must be addressed, and what are the exact benefits which the product or service will provide. In short, the message must be in the language of the consumer and must make an offer which is of real interest to the specific audience. This may mean that the message is boring to all other audiences (including those who are commissioning and creating the advertisement), but that is not the point; it has to be of interest only to the specific target audience. The messages which are of interest to teenage CD buyers may well be very different to those aimed at middle-aged buyers of Volvo cars; and if middle-aged people are commissioning advertising campaigns aimed at teenage music fans, they had better appreciate the differences. This second stage, therefore, largely depends upon a full appreciation of the results of market research.

Attitudes

The message must persuade the audience to adopt a positive attitude towards the product or service so that individuals will purchase it, albeit on a trial basis. There is no adequate way of describing how this may be achieved. It is down to the creative magic of the copywriter's art, based on the strength of the product or service itself.

Buying decision

All of the above stages may happen in a few minutes while the reader is considering the advertisement. On the other hand, the final decision to buy may take place some time later when the prospective buyer is actually in a shop which stocks the product. This means that the basic message will probably need to be reinforced, by repeats, until the potential buyer is finally in the position to buy. Above all, it also means that the product or service must be distributed widely enough for the prospective buyer to be able to find it.

These stages are most evident in the Attention, Interest, Desire, Action (AIDA) model, which is frequently advocated as the structure for the selling process. Similar stages are also described in the Hierarchy of Effects model (where interest and understanding are paralleled by knowledge, liking and preference). After AIDA, the most often quoted model within the advertising industry is Defining Advertising Goals for Measuring Advertising Results (DAGMAR), which breaks the process down to the four steps of Awareness, Comprehension, Conviction and Action. There are a number of other models in the literature, but they all tend to describe the same processes from differing points of view.

Effective planning

The care with which advertising plans are made will determine the results they produce (Carter, 1994). Careful planning has many benefits:

1 It provides a definite concrete plan based on facts rather than indefinite, last-minute decisions based on opinions and guesswork.

2 It forces a review of past experience, thus focusing attention on past mistakes and successes.

3 It requires looking ahead – adopting a long-range perspective.

4 It considers and ensures attention is given to all phases of the advertising programme, including seasonal promotions, the need for clearance sales, etc.

5 It provides balanced attention to the needs of each department and each branch in departmentalised and chain stores.

6 It schedules appropriate promotional activity to accompany planned developments such as the addition of a major new merchandise line or a change in store and service policy.

7 It considers probable changes in competitors' policies and programmes.

8 It facilitates coordination between various types of advertising and between advertising merchandising, store management, and control activities.

Advertising should be planned in stores of all sizes, even in the small shop where the proprietor exercises direct supervision over all promotion. As in the merchandise plan or budget, the advertising plan should cover a period of several months and be subdivided into months, weeks or short special promotions. It should set forth programmes for various types of promotions, including selection of merchandise to be advertised and choice of advertising media. It should also provide for the coordination of advertising and special forms of sales promotions, as well as for adjustments to meet unforeseen conditions.

Proper timing

Proper timing is vital in the planning of advertising efforts. Food retailers in London for example, concentrate their advertising in Wednesday afternoon and Thursday morning newspapers since Thursday, Friday and Saturday are the days when the majority of customers usually make large purchases of groceries. Department and speciality stores often advertise heavily on Sundays on the assumption that Sunday newspapers are read more thoroughly than those published on weekdays (McGoldrick, 1990). For retailers of high-fashion goods, timing in terms of weather is particularly important. A large amount spent on advertising autumn fashions during a warm spell may produce few sales; likewise the promotion of lightweight summer dresses during a summer cold spell may result in a large outlay with little customer response. Some retailers study the monthly weather forecasts of the UK Meteorological Office and adjust their promotions accordingly.

Suitable merchandise

Perhaps the greatest waste of retail advertising money is promoting the wrong merchandise. The best advertisements cannot sell goods the customer does not want. In contrast, relatively poor advertising is often effective in moving merchandise that customers want. In selecting goods to advertise, the retailer should be guided by past experience regarding proven best-sellers; by the merchandise that is selling well in other stores; by pre-testing goods to determine their probable rate of sale; by the desire to promote private brands; by the advice of salespeople (and by department heads in large stores); and by considerations of timeliness, buying habits of the community, variety, frequency of purchase, and contribution to store image. New fashion items and prestige brands are often used to enhance store image. Retail advertising should feature items and values that are attractive to many customers, that are purchased frequently, and that will not absorb the customer's total purchasing power.

Too often retailers advertise specific items without first making certain that adequate quantities are on hand to meet reasonable sales expectations (Davies and Brooks, 1989). When stocks are exhausted, customers unable to buy the goods advertised are annoyed and encouraged to make their purchases elsewhere. Many shrewd retailers specify limited quantities or broken sizes and colours in their **advertising copy** if their stocks may be inadequate to meet customer demands.

Preparing advertisements

Television commercials are almost always prepared by specialists: by outside advertising agencies, by a merchandise supplier under a co-operative programme, or, in some large retail firms, by the company's own television expert. The most important rules a retailer should remember in working with the television specialist, in providing merchandise and in approving commercials apply to all advertising include:

- each advertisement should contain a 'unique selling proposition' – it should show why an item, an idea or a store image ought to appeal to the customer;
- the more specific the advertisement the better;
- only a limited amount of information can be transmitted in any one advertisement.

Print advertising is more likely to be prepared in the store and involves three steps:

- writing copy;
- selecting illustrations;
- designing the layout.

The term 'copy' refers to the reading matter of an advertisement, including both the text and the headline. Copy may be said to be the heart of a retail advertisement, although colour, illustrations and typography must be coordinated with it to obtain the desired results.

Retailers frequently use illustrations to attract attention, to show the merchandise and/or its use, to lend 'atmosphere', and to confine the reader's attention within the advertisement. Small retailers find the advice and assistance of the local printer and the manufacturers whose products they handle invaluable in choosing illustrations. Large retailers have their own specialists who, singly or in co-operation with advertising agencies or newspaper artists, devise appropriate illustrations to create the desired effect. The illustration should be simple, clear and appropriate; focus attention on the points desired; help sell the product or the ideas being advertised; and 'face' into the advertisement and toward the copy if possible, to draw the reader into the heart of the message. Otherwise the reader's eyes may be directed toward a competing advertisement in the next column.

The layout is a sketch showing the location of the text, headline and illustration in the advertisement. It enables the advertiser to visualise the complete advertisement and to provide instructions to the printer for setting up the advertisement.

Display management

The growth of self-service has brought increased emphasis on display in both small and large stores. In the past, window display was neglected by retail outlets, especially the multiples, but this situation changed rapidly. Most retailers are now aware that window displays which occupy the most valuable footage along the front and sides of a building can be used effectively to stop passers-by from passing by. Similarly, windows that face pedestrian concourse in a shopping centre may be a major factor inducing customers to enter the store. Good interior display (according to Duncan and Hollander, 1977):

- contributes to the atmosphere of the store;
- breaks up the monotony of a rectangular layout;
- enhances the featured merchandise;
- stimulates impulse buying.

It is important that retailers are aware that display warrants very close attention.

Window displays

Stores normally use their window display to feature merchandise items, although some may occasionally be used to display fascinating scenes for children at Christmas. The careful selection of merchandise for the display – items which are distinctive, timely, stylish, or particularly good value – contributes to the successful sale of those items. At the same time, the use of appropriate merchandise, careful choice of the right fixtures and mannequins, and taste and imagination in designing and executing the displays contributes greatly to the overall store image.

In department stores, window display experts are usually part of the regular staff, sometimes supplemented with outside professionals who provide ideas and materials for special occasions such as the Christmas season or a store anniversary. These large stores usually:

- plan their window displays several weeks in advance;
- carefully select the merchandise to be displayed;
- arrange definite time schedules for each window;
- assign display space to various departments upon the basis of need, etc.

Unfortunately, many small retailers neglect to plan their window displays properly, to dress them effectively, or to change them frequently. Independent retailers often consider window dressing as a waste of money, delegate the responsibility to employees uninterested in such work, and refuse to spend money on fixtures and supplies necessary to do the job properly. The inevitable result is that sales are lost because the store appears unprogressive or just plain tatty.

Actually a small retailer does not have to spend a fortune on display equipment to create effective window displays. Generally, the emphasis should be on the merchandise rather than on background or fixtures. The window and the display area should be kept scrupulously clean and well dusted. Any discoloured items should be removed from the display and the window should be checked frequently so that any items that have fallen out of place may be quickly restored to position. Manufacturer-supplied display materials can be very helpful in trimming windows in the small store, but they should be reviewed carefully to ensure that they fit in with the store's own selling requirements. A creative window display can usually convey effectively a positive image message.

The value of window displays is, to some extent, increased by the frequency with which they are changed. The management should also make sure that the sales-people are thoroughly familiar and keep up to date with the merchandise in the windows so they can properly respond to customer enquiries about it.

Interior displays

Interior displays constitutes practically the only method of inside sales promotion other than window displays in some stores particularly supermarkets, variety stores, and many small grocery, drug, and hardware stores. Other retailers coordinate such internal displays with newspaper advertising featuring the same kinds of merchandise. Most of the purchases made in some types of store are probably the result of decisions made by the customer after entering the store – so called impulse buying. As impulse buying is so prevalent in many stores, the correct use of interior displays requires continuous attention. Among food chains, the number and use of special displays continues to increase. Duncan and Hollander (1977) suggested that a combination of media advertising and point-of-purchase displays to promote identical items may prove especially effective.

Types of interior display

Interior displays may be conveniently classified into three groups: merchandise displays, point-of-sale displays, and store signs and decorations. These classifications are rather arbitrary and some overlapping among them is inevitable. *Merchandise displays* constitute the main type of interior displays and may include open, closed and architectural displays:

1 Open displays are those that make merchandise accessible to customers for examination without the aid of a salesperson. Open displays permit customers to handle merchandise, are readily adjustable to meet variations in customers' demands, are simple and inexpensive to set up, and use space that otherwise might be wasted.

2 Closed displays consist of merchandise shown inside a showcase and are inaccessible to the customer without the aid of a salesperson. Their chief advantages are protection against theft and maintenance of merchandise in a saleable condition. For example, jewellery, fur coats, silverware, porcelain and expensive perfumes are so valuable and/or susceptible to becoming damaged or shop-soiled that close control must be exercised.

3 Architectural displays provide an appropriate setting showing various articles of merchandise in use, such as model homes and complete kitchens or bathrooms. Their main advantage is that they dramatise the merchandise by showing it in a realistic setting.

Point-of-sale displays consist of signs, banners, display racks, and other selling aids provided by the manufacturer, including those used in windows. Some manufacturers supply audio-visual units that show taped commercials for their products. Point-of-sale displays encourage sales in two ways: by reminding salespeople of the product and its merits, thus encouraging suggestion selling; and, more significantly, by informing the shopper of a product at the very moment he or she is in a buying mood. From the manufacturer's point of view, such displays present the advantages of the product pictorially. This presentation is made to the very people most interested in the product since they are in a store where such products are sold.

The term *store signs* includes counter signs, price cards, window signs, hanging signs, posters, flags, banners and similar devices. These selling aids are used to some degree by all retailers but mostly by stores making frequent use of special promotions and sales events. They are helpful in directing customers to items being featured and in calling attention to particular merchandise values. *Decorations* refer to distinctive displays and other related preparations for such occasions as Christmas and New Year sales.

Other special events that offer customer entertainment or information, rather than price bargains, also draw people to the store, contribute to the store atmosphere and add excitement to the shopping experience in the store as a whole. Merchandise stunts, such as inviting a star football player to a department store to meet customers and assist them in their purchases or to autograph goods purchased, often stimulate sales. Similarly, the authors of best-sellers may be invited to a bookshop to autograph their books. Fashion shows, in which the newest designs in women's ready-to-wear are showcased by live models, are widely used by department stores, and by some speciality and limited line stores. Bridal fairs, which may be sponsored by an individual store or a group of retailers, provide an opportunity to display wedding fashions for both bride and groom, bridal bouquets, wedding invitations, jewellery, furniture, and honeymoon travel. Flower shows, such as the famous Chelsea Flower Show, attract numerous observers and undoubtedly many buyers. Contests of various sorts – related to cooking, photography and craftsmanship, for example – are sometimes used by retailers.

In many communities, retailers cooperate in the planning of an annual crafts fair to attract customers to the shopping district and thus to increase sales. Some US stores sponsor parades to advertise the store and promote business. The variety of such events that a store may conduct is limited only by the imagination and energy of its personnel, and by its promotion budget. As suggested by the preceding comments, manufacturers and other suppliers will sometimes cooperate and absorb much of the cost if their items are featured. As a practical matter, large stores are more likely to receive such assistance than small stores. Even the large stores must scrutinise offers of cooperation carefully and make certain that the items and promotional techniques involved meet store standards and are acceptable to their customers.

SUMMARY

A six-step promotional model is presented in this chapter. These steps are: determine promotional objectives; establish the components of the mix; develop an overall promotional budget; review, revise and finalise; develop a programme of implementation; and control. Advertising budget is advocated to be a task-objective type. Hence, it has to follow the promotional objectives and the promotional mix of the retail organisation.

The reviewing, revising and finalising process follows the budgeting activity. It is the completion of the total communication activity of the retailer with its prospective (and/or actual) market(s). Since the completeness or comprehensiveness of the total programme does not mean much without implementation, an implementation plan is based on time, effort and money. Hence, scheduling, programming and budgeting are all tools of implementation.

Finally, control is related to information in-flow on effectiveness. Such feedback can be used before, during or after the advertising activity in order to redirect it and hence to improve its effectiveness. The consistency theory purports that the informal and non-commercial communication of retail establishments must be consistent with their formal and commercial communication efforts.

KEY TERMS

advertising	general merchandiser	promotional mix
advertising budget	geographic dispersion	promotional objective
advertising copy	illustration	publicity
attention	mass media	public relation
audience selectivity	media objectives	quintile analysis
cooperative advertising	media planning	sales promotion
differentiator	media sense modality	segmenter
display	message tone	special sales event
distress sales	milline rate	window display
fast grower	positioner	

ASSIGNMENT

A 'Television Shows Store' which sells merchandise related to television programmes, both current and archive, shown on independent television (ITV) channels or the British Broadcasting Corporation (BBC) has recently opened in London's West End. The store is proposing to investigate suitable promotion objectives and a media mix for its new concept.

Task

You are required to write an essay (1500 words maximum), describing suitable promotion objectives for such merchandise in London's West End, and suggesting a possible media mix for the store.

REVISION QUESTIONS

1 Explain the reasons for the growing importance of advertising in stores' sales promotion.

2 Retail promotion can be taken to cover three key activities; discuss briefly each of these activities.

3 Promotional objectives may vary depending on the store type, life cycle stage, and the type of strategy the store is pursuing. Explain this statement using specific examples from the UK retail sector.

4 What do you consider to be the main elements of promotional mix?

5 Some companies prefer brand promotion without mass media. Suggest reason why this has worked well for Hugo Boss and Häagen-Dazs in the European market.

6 What are the main functions of advertising? What does the advertising message need to do to perform these functions efficiently?

7 The communication mix (sales promotion, advertising and display) of the store must be consistent within itself. Discuss.

8 What schedule of special sales events would you recommend for a store that sells expensive and rather conservatively styled men's clothing?

9 Suggest special sales events that may be appropriate for a toy store that wants to increase its business during the winter, spring and summer seasons.

10 An association of small retailers who do not have display directors have asked you to talk to them on the subject of: 'Planning, timing and preparing good window displays'. Write your speech (1000 words).

CASE STUDY

Building brands without mass media – The Body Shop approach

It is obvious that retailers and manufacturers must build strong brands to be competitive. But the question is how? Traditionally, mass-media advertising has long been the cornerstone of most brand-building efforts. But this norm is threatened with obsolescence. Fragmentation and rising costs are already inhibiting marketing through traditional mass media like radio and television. New communication channels which allow individuals to bypass advertising as they peruse entertainment, obtain information or shop are already in use.

Media options for branded manufacturers in Europe historically have been limited and relatively ineffective compared to those available in the United States. European retailers have had access to fewer commercial television stations, many of which bundle advertisements to avoid programme interruptions. It is still rare to see media spanning several countries, despite the hype. Due to the limitation of media availability, costs have been high. Even as new cable and satellite television channels were gradually added in European countries, costs did not decline because of retailers' own brands being added to the demand. Leading retailers in many countries usurp much of the available media capacity to engage in corporate advertising and to strengthen own-label branding efforts. Retailers in Europe have found that communication through traditional mass media has been ineffective, inefficient and costly. They are, therefore, relying on alternative communication channels to create product awareness, convey brand associations, and develop loyal customer bases. They are building brands without the use of mass media, as The Body Shop approach demonstrates.

The brand concept (identity) from the brand owner's perspective is the foundation of any good brand-building programme. Whether pursuing alternative brand-building approaches, accessing multiple media, or both, the retailer must have a clear brand identity with depth and texture so that those designing and implementing the communications programmes do not inadvertently send conflicting or confusing messages to customers. A clear and effective brand identity, one for which there is understanding and buy-in throughout the organisation, should be linked to the business's vision, and its organisational culture and values. It should provide guidance as to which programmes and communications will support and reinforce the brand. The Body Shop's approach illustrates the concept of a strong clear brand identity particularly well.

The Body Shop's core brand identity is, in essence, its profits-with-a-principle philosophy. The soul of the brand, the philosophy sends a clear message to employees and customers alike. Consider how the company – in spite of the criticisms of its detractors – 'walks the walk' in terms of developing programmes reflecting the core identity. The company opposes testing on animals, helps Third World economies through its 'Trade, Not Aid' mission, contributes to rainforest preservation efforts, is active in women's issues, and sets an example for

▶

recycling. It participates in 'Save the Whales' rallies, advocates for other endangered species (a line of its children's bath products, for example, comes with informative storybooks about various endangered animals), and supports the development of alternative energy sources. One summer, employees and supporters sent 500 000 signatures to the president of Brazil to urge the Brazilian government to stop the burning of trees there.

These efforts are not ancillary to The Body Shop brand; they *are* the brand. The vision carries right through the customers' in-store experience. Enter a branch of The Body Shop, and you are greeted by a salesperson who not only wears a The Body Shop T-shirt bearing a social message but also believes in the company's causes, values and products. Displayed among the store's goods and tester samples are posters and colourful handouts (printed on recycled paper) that provide information about the products, about social causes the company supporters, and about how customers can get involved in rallies, social-cause advocacy groups, and the like.

Compare The Body Shop's brand identity with those of its competitors. Most skin care and cosmetic lines are indistinguishable, focusing on similar product attributes and 'health-and beauty' promises. Their customers are not involved with even their favourite brands – except to make a transaction or to receive a broadcast-style advertising message. Clearly, The Body Shop has transformed the skin care and cosmetics experience into something more than it has ever been.

It is probable that The Body Shop did not deliberately seek to pursue alternative brand-building methods rather than mass media advertising. Instead, they were blessed with liabilities (lack of funds) that encouraged them to be creative. Although not every retailer is blessed with such liabilities, the lessons The Body Shop learned are valuable and transferable. Similarly, developing a set of alternative approaches to brand building is not easy, especially for retailers who have relied on media promotion as the cornerstone of their brand-building efforts. But with dedication and commitment from senior managers, building brands without resorting to using the mass media could be a worthwhile investment.

Questions for discussion

1 What do you consider to be the key factors in The Body Shop's approach to brand building without using the mass media?

2 Discuss the possibility of this approach – brand building without the mass media – for any other European retailer of your choice.

REFERENCES

Abraham, M.M. and Lodish, L.M. (1990) 'Getting the most out of advertising and promotion', *Harvard Business Review,* May/June.

Carter, M. (1994) 'Direct response ads gain respect', *Marketing Week,* 5 July.

Davies, G. and Brooks, M.J. (1989) *Positioning Strategy in Retailing.* London: Paul Chapman.

Duncan, D.J. and Hollander, S.C. (1977) *Modern Retailing Management: Basic Concepts and Practices.* 9th edn. Homewood, IL: Richard Irwin.

Farris, P.W. and Buzzell, R.D. (1979) 'Why advertising and promotional costs vary: some cross-sectional analysis', *Journal of Marketing,* Fall.

Kotler, P. (1997) 'Reconceptualising marketing: an interview with Philip Kotler', *European Management Journal,* 12(4).

McGoldrick, P. (1990) *Retail Marketing.* London: McGraw-Hill.

Mercer, D. (1996) *Marketing.* 2nd edn. Oxford: Blackwell.

Ogilvy, D. (1983) *Ogilvy on Advertising.* London: Pan Books.

Samli, A.C. (1989) *Retail Marketing Strategy: Planning, Implementation, and Control.* New York: Quorum.

12

Retail service provision and management

LEARNING OBJECTIVES

After reading this chapter you should be able to:

- explain the role and requirements for self-service in retailing;
- describe the role and steps in the personal selling process;
- explain the characteristics and the nature of financial services in retailing;
- evaluate the role of service mix and innovation in improving transaction efficiency;
- explain the different ways in which retailers provide customer support services to their customers within their market segments.

One of the major problems associated with store arrangement concerns the retailer's decision regarding the extent to which access to merchandise will be allowed. Should customers be permitted to serve themselves, with aid being provided by sales personnel if needed. This decision obviously influences the entire layout of the store as well as the kind and amount of store equipment and fixtures purchased.

This decision also has an impact on the type and level of sales personnel required in the store. In general, many shoppers tend to regard salespeople and other personal service employees as inadequately trained; and many salespeople do not appear motivated enough to help customers adequately. Many retail managers also tend to agree that improving the level of **personal service** at a store continues to be one of the greatest challenges they face (Duncan and Hollander, 1977).

Personal service is especially important for retailers who sell services instead of tangible products (Ghosh, 1994). Hotels, estate agents, banks, dry cleaners, insurance brokers and beauty salons, for example, are all engaged in retailing since they serve the needs of individual customers. The service sector has grown phenomenally since the 1950s, and firms such as McDonald's, Pizza Hut, Holiday Inn, the Automobile Association (AA), and many others, now form an integral part of the retail industry. The service product provided by the retailer must be consistent with the overall strategy and with the image the retailer seeks to portray – a quality product, whether it be goods or service, requires **quality service.**

The efficiency, appearance, attitude, availability and product knowledge of store personnel are important issues for many shoppers (Ogwo, 1981). Financial services have grown, and continue to grow, as an influential force in retailing – both as a contributory factor in increased transaction efficiency and as a branch of the services industry in their own right.

Exhibit 12.1	**The growth of the financial services in retailing**

Among the financial services, the emergence of the store card and many other forms of credit have contributed both to transaction efficiency and to marketing effectiveness. Creative thinking, for instance, can be rewarded with a tremendous growth in business volume. Thus some financial institutions, including Barclays Bank and NatWest Bank, are expanding their provision by offering one-stop services, including estate development, investment management, credit card services, leasing services, safety deposit facilities, insurance coverage, savings facilities, travel scheduling, accounting services, and other money related activities.

Times of opening have also become an important form of differentiation between stores, as retailers increasingly cater for those unable or unwilling to shop at 'normal' times. Further services are aimed at reducing the perceived risks of product purchases, such as changing rooms, favourable returns policies and extended warranty offers; yet others are aimed at enhancing convenience, such as free carrier bags and carry-out services. It is, therefore, essential that a retailer should develop an integrated service policy, based upon a clear understanding of the needs and preferences of the target segments to which they cater.

This chapter adopts a more specific connotation of service, focusing upon **self-service**, personal service, financial services and other elements designed to reduce risks and make shopping easier, more efficient and hopefully more pleasant. These services as provided by the retailer are discussed in relation to the retailer's marketing strategy. **Service provision** has become a strong differentiator, with profits being linked in some areas of retailing with **perceived quality of service** among target customers.

Self-service in retailing

The management of most stores continue to face unremitting pressures to adopt increasing degrees of self-service or impersonal selling. When a store is operated on a self-service basis, merchandise is displayed and arranged to enable the customer to make a selection without the aid of a salesperson. Typically, open display shelves are used, frequently supplemented by racks, stands and free-standing islands. Once the selection is made, the merchandise is usually taken to a checkout point where payment is made and the purchase is wrapped and put in 'carrier-bags' for the customer. Most major stores provide free carrier-bags with the store's name on them; and intended for customers to carry out the purchased items. Credit, delivery, and other special customer services commonly found in personal service stores, may not be offered by the self-service store, since a low operating cost is one of its major objectives (Duncan and Hollander, 1977). Although the term 'self-service store' refers – strictly speaking – to a store with all of its sales on this basis, many stores described as self-service handle a substantial amount of business on a personal service basis. Many discount stores regarded as self-service stores, for example, provide personal service for merchandise such as jewellery, cameras, major appliances, bakery products, meat, delicatessen, fruit and vegetables in their supermarkets.

Requirements for self-service

In general, shelf arrangement for self-service operation is motivated by the layout of the store and is determined by: the store's attractiveness and convenience from the customer point of view, exposure of merchandise for sale, satisfactory sales volume, and economical operation from the point of view of the retailer. The attainment of these goals is not an easy matter and, whether a new store is being opened or the conversion of a service store into one providing less service is being analysed and planned, the favourable and unfavourable elements of the self-service plans should be studied carefully. According to Duncan and Hollander (1977), both retailers' and customers' experiences reveal that among the factors essential to success are the following:

1 Stores arranged on the self-service plan have wider aisles with fewer obstructions, thus encouraging circulation of customers and minimising congestion in customer traffic.

2 Many customers prefer self-service because it enables them to examine merchandise at their leisure, make selections based upon their own judgement, and overcome their dependency on salespeople who may lack the courtesy and helpfulness expected.

3 Fewer salespeople and other personnel are required, thus reducing bad selling experience and personnel problems.

4 Economies in operation make it possible to sell at lower prices than other stores and to appeal to customers on this basis.

5 Self-service arrangements permit larger and better displays of merchandise which, in turn, contribute to greater sales.

6 Customers of self-service stores purchase more at one time, both in amount and in variety, than patrons of other stores. This occurs because customers shop in a more leisurely manner and examine more merchandise. Self-service also encourages impulse purchasing.

On the other hand, the publicity given to successful stores using the self-service plan frequently has resulted in failure to consider the shortcomings of this type of operation. Since a self-service arrangement requires more floor space for a given sales volume than the counter-service plan, the physical makeup of the store (its size, shape and location) may not be adaptable to self-service (Ghosh, 1994). Many customers may prefer to be served by salespeople; they dislike having to locate the merchandise they want and take it to the **checkout point.** The large sales volume of some stores also creates congestion at checkout points, especially during peak times. The result is likely to be inconvenience for the customer and more errors by the checkout operators. Shoplifting and theft are generally easier and more prevalent in self-service stores; consequently, losses are greater. Certain types of high-priced products such as electronic and technical goods usually require the advice and service of salespeople, and so self-service may not be suitable for these types of products.

Despite these drawbacks, evidence of increased acceptance of self-service is not hard to find. Under a host of modified titles – self-selection, selective open selling, simplified selling, open selling, display merchandising – self-service or impersonal selling is being applied to ever more heterogeneous assortments. Increasing degrees of self-service are employed in many departments such as stationery, household-wares, CDs and tapes, chemist, cosmetics, toys and so on.

Exhibit 12.2	**The successful expansion of self-service**

Some department stores such as Bhs, Miss Selfridge, John Lewis, and so on have successfully tried the supermarket versions of self-service in such departments as toys, greeting cards, haberdashery, and books. The increased encouragement that customers receive to use automatic vending machines, mail-order catalogues, coupons, and telephone ordering facilities is presumably based on the belief that more customers may favour this self-service type of marketing ideology.

It is also possible that there is a shift among customers towards self-servicing selling as a reaction against what is perceived as inadequate **personal selling.** It may well be the case that modern face-to-face **personal selling** in the stores lacks some of the warmth or genuine concern that it possessed in the past.

Personal selling in retailing

In a highly competitive environment, the quality of personal selling and customer service is an important way in which retailers differentiate themselves. Two often-cited examples of good practice are Marks & Spencer and Tesco. Shoppers at Marks & Spencer, for example, receive a high level of personal attention from Marks & Spencer's well-trained salespeople should they require it. The salespeople actively help customers find the merchandise they want and complete the retail transaction smoothly. In this way, they augment the 'value' customers receive at the store. Due to the self-selection environment at Tesco customers there require less individual attention, yet the level of service at the store is excellent. Each customer is greeted at the store and shop-floor employees are always willing to help locate merchandise and provide other relevant information to customers.

All retail employees who come in contact with customers are a vital part of the retailer's marketing strategy. They are the most direct means by which retailers communicate with their customers. Thus, they facilitate the exchange process by providing information to shoppers and matching the retailer's offering to consumers' needs (McGoldrick, 1990). The quality, ability and co-operation of shop-floor employees have a major influence on how customers perceive the store. By providing adequate services through well-trained employees, retailers may encourage positive consumer attitudes toward their stores (Lucas *et al.*, 1994). Their employees may also increase sales by turning browsers into buyers and by building long-term relationships with customers. Sales staff may have direct responsibility for managing the shop floor: speeding up transactions, handling customer complaints, accepting returns, and even watching for shoplifters. However, the importance attached to the role of salespeople may vary considerably among stores, as is shown in Exhibit 12.3.

Exhibit 12.3	**The varying role of the salesperson**

Supermarkets and discount stores stress self-service and self-selection by customers, so their shop-floor employees mainly manage retail transactions and direct customers to merchandise sections, answer queries about stock, etc. Speciality stores, department stores, and jewellery stores, on the other hand, employ salespeople who actively interact with customers to communicate merchandise information and persuade them to buy at the store. This does not imply, however, that personal service is any less important in stores that encourage self-service.

Even in a self-service environment, customers must have adequate information and the retail transaction process must proceed smoothly. An efficient transaction process is a basic service required of all stores, irrespective of the merchandise they sell and the customers they attract.

Personal selling involves the two-way flow of communication between retail employees and their customers. The basic role of retail selling is to facilitate customer decision making by providing relevant information about products and store policies and to make shopping a pleasant experience. The ultimate aim is to build a strong relationship with customers. To fulfil their role, sales personnel must perform several tasks: providing information that helps customers better to define their shopping needs; explaining the various features of different products; providing information about new merchandise, fashion trends and innovations; helping customers to compare the relative merits of merchandise items and demonstrate the products; assisting customers in finding merchandise that best fits their needs; drawing attention to support services (such as delivery, gift wrapping, and repair services) which may influence the customer's decision to purchase; and speeding up the retail transaction process.

The personal selling process

Selling is a complex task. In order to help understand the different actions and tasks involved, the selling process is best viewed as comprising a sequence of steps as shown in Figure 12.1. Figure 12.1 presents the five steps in the retail selling process as: approaching the customer; determining customer needs; presenting merchandise; closing the sale; and follow-up.

Fig. 12.1 THE RETAIL SELLING PROCESS AND STEPS

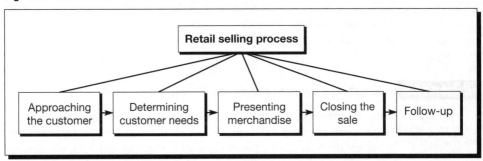

Approaching the customer

One major difference between retail selling and other forms of selling is that retail salespeople do not have to search for their customers. They usually rely on the other elements of the retailer's marketing strategy to bring prospective customers into the store. However, the selling process will be greatly influenced by the attitude of retail salespeople present to these customers. If, for example, a courteous greeting makes the customer feel welcome, the selling process gets off to a good start, whereas neglecting customers may lose sales. The salesperson's opening remark when approaching the customer often critically affects the development of the interaction between the customer and the salesperson. Too often salespeople approach customers with such phrases as 'May I help you, Madam?' or 'Do you need help Sir?'. These opening approaches usually elicit responses along the lines of 'No, thank you' or 'Just looking'. The salesperson cannot then continue the approach without appearing aggressive and pushy. The ideal approach allows the salesperson to initiate a conversation with the customer and discover his or her needs (Ghosh, 1994).

Determining customers' needs

To sell effectively, a salesperson must understand the customer's need and find the merchandise that best satisfies that need. Thus, the salesperson must learn as much as possible about the customer's requirements, from the purpose for which

---

Exhibit 12.4 | **Approaching potential customers**

The salesperson in a clothing store may approach a browsing customer by asking: 'What size were you looking for?', 'Have you seen these new styles?' or 'Did you have something special in mind?'. All these phrases offer assistance to the customer without the customer asking for it and without inviting an immediate 'brush off' response from the customer. At the same time, the answers given may help the salesperson to get a better idea of the customer's needs and shopping expectations. The manner in which the salesperson approaches the customer is as important as the particular approach he or she uses.

---

the product will be used the budget for the purchase, and so on. Only then can the salesperson complete the exchange process by finding the merchandise that best matches what the customer wants. Since a wide variety of people shop at retail stores, determining an individual customer's needs can be one of the most difficult steps in retail selling.

Exhibit 12.5 | **Assisting a customer to define their product needs**

Some customers may walk into a store with a clear idea of what product they need and even the brand they want to buy; some may know what product they want to buy, but not the brand. Yet others may want something, but not know precisely what – a person shopping for a gift for a friend's birthday or for a Christmas gift, for example, may walk into a store without any clear idea of what to buy. The salesperson must first determine, broadly, the customer's need and decide what information will be relevant in helping the customer define that need more precisely.

Selling is an act of communication (Duncan and Hollander, 1977). It is not always an easy matter to judge what a customer wants or needs from a product by mere observation. For this reason, good salespeople must be expert listeners rather than just talkers. The basis for effective selling is listening to customers to ascertain their needs and identify the criteria by which they will select merchandise. Only then can the salesperson find a product that will satisfy customer.

Presenting the merchandise

With knowledge of the customer's needs, the salesperson can begin to present the merchandise to the customer. The salesperson should present merchandise that reflects what he or she believes will best suit the customer. Presentation involves more than just physical demonstration of products. It includes three distinct tasks: providing customers with information about the merchandise; refining the salesperson's understanding of the customer's need; and handling customer objections (McGoldrick, 1990).

1 Providing merchandise information – the salesperson must show the customer merchandise items and explain how they fit his or her needs.

2 Refining their understanding of customer needs – while presenting merchandise, the salesperson must pay close attention to how the customer responds to each item so that appropriate action may be taken to assist the customer.

3 Handling customer objections – to make a sale, the salesperson must overcome any customer objections to the merchandise being presented.

Closing the sale

The sale is the ultimate objective of selling. Once all customer objections have been handled, the salesperson must attempt to close the sale by asking for an order. According to a number of studies, sales personnel are often reluctant to ask for an order and close the sale. Retail salespeople commonly try to close sales with statements such as: 'Shall I wrap this up for you?' 'Will this be cash or account?', 'Would you like it delivered?', and so on. The question prompts the customer to a number of common closing techniques. The most important decision in closing is timing. The salesperson can lose the sale by attempting the close either too quickly or too slowly. Attempting to close too early may make the customer resentful of being pushed by the salesperson. On the other hand, stores often lose sales when the close is delayed too long and the customer postpones the decision to buy.

In deciding when to close, the salesperson must consider each shopper individually. No single rule can cover all of them; Table 12.1 offers various approaches and the procedures that accompany them. As mentioned earlier, some customers walk into the store with a relatively clear idea of their needs and they may well be ready

Table 12.1
APPROACHES TO CLOSING THE SALE

Approach	Procedures
The summary close	The salesperson summarises all the benefits of the product.
The balance sheet close	The salesperson writes down the reasons for buying the product on a sheet of paper.
The continuous yes close	The salesperson asks a series of questions, each worded in such a way that the customer will answer 'yes' to them all. The final question requests the customer to buy.
The assumptive close	The salesperson acts as if the customer has already agreed to buy. For instance, the salesperson can close by saying, 'I will write the order for you'.
The standing-room-only close	The salesperson tries to get the customer to buy immediately instead of postponing, saying, for instance, 'The sales ends today; you will have to pay more if you wait until tomorrow'.

to close early. Some, on the other hand, may require more time to make their decision and would not like to be rushed to a close. The salesperson must judge a customer's position for themselves; each potential customer will provide verbal and non-verbal cues suggesting the best time for the salesperson to initiate a close.

Follow-up

The selling process does not stop with the closing of the sale. Good salespeople follow up on their sales to make sure that customers are completely satisfied. Some follow-up is necessary before the customer leaves the store. Successful selling is dependent upon building a long-term relationship with the customer and the **follow-up** is essential to build these long-term relationships – because it increases customer loyalty and provides an opportunity for new sales.

Suggestion selling and trading up

The total sales that the store achieves at the end of any day depends on the average amount of money taken for each sales transaction and the number of transactions completed during the day. The total amount of sales may be calculated using the following formula:

Total sales = average revenue per transaction × number of transaction

In order to increase sales, therefore, the store must either increase the number of transactions by attracting more customers or increase the amount customers spend at the store per transaction. **Suggestion selling** and **trading up** are two ways in which salespeople try to increase average transaction size.

Suggestion selling

Suggestion selling increases transaction size by **cross selling** related items to the same customer. In the time between **closing the sale** and ringing it up, a salesperson has the opportunity to suggest merchandise that is related to the article the customer has just bought. A salesperson may, for example, suggest a tie to go with a new suit or a Kodak film for a new Kodak camera. Unfortunately, many salespeople lose the opportunity for suggestion selling because they neglect to ask or fail to make the suggestion in an appropriate way.

Trading up

Trading up is another technique for increasing the size of transactions. In this process, the salesperson tries to sell a better quality and higher-priced product than the one the customer originally intended to buy. After first showing items within the price range requested by the customer, a good salesperson will also show higher-priced alternatives, explaining their relative advantages over the lower-priced brands. The customer then has the opportunity to consider the cost and benefits of all the alternatives and reassess his or her need. Often customers choose an item that costs more than they had originally contemplated spending once they become aware of the additional benefits offered. Trading up is a time-honoured sales technique for increasing transaction size. It should, however, result from a genuine re-evaluation of needs and expectations by the customer and not from aggressive or deceptive selling on the part of the salesperson.

In spite of all these efforts, buying decisions are normally made depending on the ability of the shopper to pay for the chosen item, and the retailer's provision of credit facilities for the shopper. Such financial aspects are the subject of the next section.

Financial services in retailing

The ease with which customers can pay, both in terms of efficiency and available credit, has become an important influence upon store choice and transaction size. Retailers have a long history of providing credit for regular customers, a practice that first became formalised into customer accounts and has evolved into the present generation of store cards. For many years, credit tended to be associated with more expensive purchases; the spread of credit cards and the tendency towards fewer, larger shopping trips has brought credit usage into nearly all sectors of retailing. The development of 'own-brand' credit cards has also opened up many new marketing opportunities for retailers (Conneran and Lawlor, 1997).

This section first examines the growth of credit cards and some characteristics of their usage in the stores. The strategy of retail store cards is then considered, specifically the advantages, techniques and possible problems of operating a card system. The progression by some retailers from store cards into other forms of financial services is also briefly reviewed.

The growth of credit cards

Credit cards have experienced a considerable rate of growth since the launch of the first bank credit card by Barclays in 1966. The holding of credit cards has proved particularly attractive in the UK. No other European country has a comparable number of cards on issue, and there is a greater reluctance to use credit to pay for minor purchases in some countries (Uncles, 1994). In the UK there remains scope for development, since over half of men and about two-thirds of women still do not hold a credit card. This could be compared with the USA where, on average, there are 7.2 cards per person – over half of which are retail credit cards (McGoldrick, 1990).

In the 1980s the combined number of Access and Visa accounts was reported to be growing at the rate of 64 per cent annually, and the usage of the accounts – in terms of transactions, turnover and credit outstanding, – was also growing considerably. By comparison, retailer's 'own-brand' credit cards had achieved more limited penetration but were growing very rapidly (Ogwo, 1981). The number of retail outlets accepting Access and Visa cards has grown progressively as retailers have realised they are able to increase sales revenue through this mode of payment (Omar, 1995).

Exhibit 12.6 **Debenhams's credit facilities**

Well before the recent boom in store cards, many retailers including Debenhams gained experience in offering various types of credit facilities. The forms of credit offered by Debenhams, for instance, included:

- option charge accounts – like bank credit cards, these provide the option of being used as a charge account, attracting no interest if the monthly account is paid within the specified period after the statement date;
- budget accounts – the customer establishes a monthly banker's order and is allowed credit of up to 24 times the basic monthly payment;
- credit terms – these are long-term facilities, available over periods of up to three years, to assist major purchases. Such arrangements may include the incentive of zero interest if the account is settled within the first few months.

The credit formats of the new generation of store cards have become relatively standardised, although different names are used by the various retailers. Next, for example, refers to its card as 'Option Account'; Marks & Spencer calls its card 'Chargecard'; the Sears card is known simply as 'Sears Card'; and Tesco's is called 'Club card'. In each case, the card may be used as a charge card, interest-free, or payments may be spread over a longer period and interest incurred. The term 'credit card' tends to be avoided because of negative connotations and the more upmarket/exclusive images of the well established charge cards, such as American Express and Diners Club (Hirschman and Goldstucker, 1978).

One element that is certainly not standardised between the store cards is the rate of interest charged if the credit option is used. In general, the annual percentage rate (APR) of store cards tends to be higher than those of the main bank-issued cards (Ogwo, 1981).

In that some retailers' APRs are more than double the level of others, it is clear that most consumers are insensitive to interest rates. The Save and Prosper financial services company had a disappointing response to its Visa card – even with the lowest available APR at 17.4 per cent – when it was first introduced. The conventional wisdom in the financial services business seems to be that people are simply interest rate insensitive (Hawkes, 1996). In part, this insensitivity may reflect an optimism that the account can be settled in full each month, thereby making the APR irrelevant. Over half of credit card holders in the UK use their cards in this way. There is, however, also widespread ignorance as to the way in which interest is calculated.

The store card strategy

An own-label store card can offer numerous advantages and opportunities for a retailer, if operated, promoted and used effectively. It is possible that a store card could become a powerful marketing tool. The main benefits of running a store card system are as follows (Uncles, 1994):

1 Customer transaction sizes tend to be larger, with more unplanned purchasing.

2 Loyalty to the store increases and can be nurtured by improved communication and the feeling of exclusiveness.

3 Detailed information is gained about customer characteristics and spending patterns.

4 Direct mail can be targeted to appeal to specific customer types.

5 The effects of promotions can be more precisely monitored.

6 Other financial services can be developed and promoted.

7 Costs may be lower than those incurred by accepting bank-issued credit cards.

To an extent, customers who are able and inclined to obtain a retail card are also likely to have a higher spending propensity (Conneran and Lawlor, 1997). The retail card can, however, reinforce this and help to ensure that a higher proportion of that spending is obtained by the specific retailer. Whereas bank-issued credit cards have been promoted primarily as a convenient form of payment, store cards also attempt to convey the 'club concept'. They enable a special relationship to be developed between retailers and their best customers, encouraging further involvement and loyalty (Uncles, 1994). Common 'privileges' for card holders usually include exclusive offers, special shopping evenings and previews of sale events.

Exhibit 12.7
Marks & Spencer occasionally run Charge Card evenings outside normal opening hours, sometimes offering free wine and live music as additional attractions. Store cards enable retailers to get to know a great deal about their customers, offering the high-technology equivalent of the small retailer–loyal customer relationship (see Omar, 1995).

Although the bank-issued credit card companies have much customer information on file, they are unable to disclose this to retailers. Store cards, therefore, provide an unprecedented insight into the cardholder's personal details, habits, tastes and spending patterns (McGoldrick, 1990). The personal details disclosed on card application forms are used initially for credit-scoring, then for segmentation and target marketing. Such application forms are likely to obtain some or all of the following details: full name and address; property ownership; type of residence; length of residence; age; number of children and their age(s); marital status; occupation and employer; length of service; salary; previous occupation; occupation/salary of spouse; bank account(s) held; and other credit or charge cards used.

Armed with such a formidable array of data, there are numerous opportunities for precisely targeted direct mail advertising, possibly also including the most appropriate financial inducements (Hirschman and Goldstucker, 1978). The data continue to accumulate as reactions of specific customers to specific types of offer can be monitored. In that monthly statements are sent to card holders, selected advertising enclosures, or 'free-riders', are usually enclosed at little extra cost. With detailed information on card-based transactions, personalised letters may also be produced to suggest appropriate supplementary purchases; however, care must be taken not to appear too intrusive or to be invading customers' privacy.

The evaluation of store card strategy

In evaluating the store card strategy, a retailer must also consider the costs and potential dangers. In theory, a well managed card provision can represent a cost saving, particularly when compared with the percentage of sales charged to the retailer by bank-issued credit cards. The store card can also lead to more highly automated transactions, reducing clutter and congestion at the checkouts. However, not all the store cards have broken-even and some of the major banks believe the provision of 'own-label' cards by retailers to be unprofitable. From the retailer's viewpoint, the overall evaluation of profitability must consider not only the 'hard' costs and savings but also the many other benefits in terms of improved marketing opportunities. The skill and commitment of store card management will inevitably influence the cost-effectiveness of the strategy. It is obvious that:

- many of the defensive, 'me-too' card schemes are not harnessing the full potential marketing benefits;
- the administration is complex and expensive if not done properly;
- credit scoring is a sensitive job which cannot be done without upsetting some customers;
- the credit balances need to be financed and accounted carefully;
- it is easy to underestimate the care and work necessary to make the cards a fully integrated part of the retail operation.

The inadequate assessment techniques of some retailers brought store credit cards in general a bad name and left many retailers with bad debts. The adverse publicity concerning interest rates and credit scoring contributed to the initial decision of some major retailers to withdraw their store cards from the market. Since then, both Tesco, Sainsbury and Safeway now offer their own credit cards.

Diversification into other financial services

The experience gained in operating store cards and credit systems could lead to more diversification into other financial services. One approach is to enter the general credit card business, with a card acceptable in a wide range of outlets (Exhibit 12.8).

The range of financial services that retailers may provide, either by direct marketing or within their branches, are very wide and may include in-store banking, charge cards, credit facilities, credit protection plans, extended product warranties, mortgages, estate agencies, property insurance, life assurance, and pensions. Retailers have a number of advantages in diversifying into these areas because they

Exhibit 12.8	In the USA, Sears Roebuck has achieved excellent penetration with its 'Discover' card. In the UK, Marks & Spencer have a sufficient customer base and marketing advantage to take a similar step – though they have not yet taken this step. In Scotland, the 'Style' card, initially limited to the Goldberg chain was subsequently accepted by many other companies; it became the largest credit card operation in Scotland. Control of this card has been acquired now by the Royal Bank of Scotland, so the range of financial services offered to cardholders have increased further.

tend to enjoy a friendly and more approachable image than most of the major financial institutions. Retailers also tend to have more experience in fiercely competitive environments. The upmarket profile and the high rate of home ownership among store card holders provides a very sound basis for the selling of many financial services.

There are, of course, dangers in treating financial services as just another product category. Retailers tend to feel that they have superior marketing skills to those of bankers, but financial services do represent a very fundamental diversification. Another major issue is the role of the retail outlets; their quality and location must be appropriate to the financial services envisaged, and some services may be sold equally effectively by direct marketing. It seems likely that more retailers will acquire, or form partnerships with, financial institutions in order to develop the required expertise. Other retailers may choose to take the pure retailing role and will become aggressive retailers of financial services bought from a wide range of institutions.

Customer loyalty schemes

The recent focus on customer loyalty schemes stems from an increasing recognition of the benefits loyalty has to offer, including the knowledge that loyal customers buy more, pay premium prices, and bring in new customers through referrals. Loyalty schemes are appropriate in mature, concentrated industries (food, fashion, etc.) where differentiation is difficult to achieve and switching costs are low. As price is no longer the major source of competitive advantage in these matured industries, retailers are forced to find other areas in which to differentiate themselves. In the UK some retailers, such as Tesco, Sainsbury, etc., launched their card-based loyalty schemes as a thank you to loyal customers – and an attempt to induce loyalty in their less loyal patrons.

Upon membership the customer receives a card with a bar code. The customer's name appears when the card is swiped through the electronic slot thereby facilitating customer relations. Customers receive club points for every pound spent in the store. The main potential of the scheme, from the participating outlet's point of view, is the resulting database which facilitates direct marketing. This allows participating retailers to carry out promotions via direct mail without the knowledge of competitors. In a competitive industry such as the grocery industry where differentiation is difficult to achieve, this advantage may prove to be critical to their success. Success of the scheme is based on each participant benefiting from the scheme. The customers benefit from 'getting something for nothing' (as most people would see it); the retailer's benefit comes from increased customer traffic, better sales, and individualised customer communications; and merchandise suppliers benefit through the increase in sales and profits achieved by offering bonus points on their products.

Loyalty schemes contrast with the traditional view of sales promotion. They are more sophisticated, longer term in focus, and have a strategic orientation. Customer loyalty schemes, if carefully implemented and integrated with other marketing communication tools, may prove to be suitable as brand-building tools (Hirschman and Goldstucker, 1978). These schemes are delayed gratification schemes, the advantage being that they create greater excitement and consumer involvement, also offering the opportunity to build lasting relationships. However, their success is determined by participation rather than what they do for the brand or how they effect attitudes. In order to achieve maximum results from the scheme, it must be integrated into the retailer's marketing strategy. The loyalty scheme needs the initial financial investment but also investment in staff training. While management commitment to the loyalty scheme is a prerequisite for its success, shop-floor staff must be involved in the day-to-day running of the scheme to ensure a successful outcome.

Extended opening hours and Sunday trading

The days and hours of the week stores are open to serve their customers is an increasingly important problem. Although customer preferences are probably the key determinant, competitors' policies, employee attitudes, and government regulations are also basic considerations. Retailers' desires to serve their customers have led to long hours of business for retail stores in comparison to other firms. The present trend towards all-day and Sunday openings has extended current store hours substantially. Major changes in consumer lifestyles – such as the growth of two-career households and the demand for other leisure activities at weekends – have forced many retailers to extend their opening hours and to open every day of the week, including Sundays.

Although scant attention has been given to opening hours as a possible determinant of retail patronage in the past, it is nevertheless an important factor. Extended hours can greatly increase the true accessibility of a store, possibly influencing the size and shape of its trading area and the profile of shoppers attracted to it. A retailer considering a major extension of hours must ensure that sufficient staffing and logistical support is available, plus the financial resources to back the increase in staff costs until the new hours start to 'pay for themselves'.

Sunday trading

The Sunday Trading Act 1994 came into force on Friday, 26 August 1994. It clarifies the right of shops and other retailers to open on Sundays, but at the same time gives most shop staff the right to refuse to work on the Sabbath. The Act applies in England and Wales, but not Scotland or Northern Ireland.

Sunday opening hours

There are now no special Sunday restrictions on the opening hours of any shop, the sale and display area of which does not exceed 280 square metres (although the special provisions regulating the hours during which intoxicating liquor may be sold will remain). Larger shops may open for six hours only, between the hours of 10 am and 6 pm. Half an hour's 'shopping-up' time is allowed: that is to say, if the permitted opening hours are 10 am to 4 pm, customers may not be admitted after 4 pm but they may be given until 4.30 pm to complete their purchases.

A 'shop' is defined as 'any premises where there is carried on a trade or business consisting wholly or mainly of the sale of goods' (Sunday Trading Act 1994, HMSO). Fourteen days' notice must be given to the relevant local authority before Sunday opening begins and the permitted Sunday trading hours must be 'displayed in a conspicuous position inside and outside the shop'. The local Magistrates' Court may punish unauthorised Sunday trading with a fine of up to £50 000. By way of exception to the general rule, some large shops may open for whatever hours they choose. These shops include:

■ farm shops;
■ shops selling motor and cycle supplies and accessories;
■ pharmacies (if open only for the sale of medicines and surgical appliances);
■ shops 'where the trade or business carried on consists wholly or mainly of the sales of intoxicating liquor' (but these will remain subject to the existing law limiting the hours during which alcohol may be sold);
■ shops at petrol filling stations and motorway service stations;
■ shops at airports and railway stations; and
■ shops serving the needs of boats arriving at, or departing from, port.

Finally, no shop over 280 square metres may open on Easter Sunday or Christmas Day, if that falls on a Sunday.

Shops closing on Saturday

If the owner of a large shop is of a religion or denomination which observes the Sabbath on Saturday, he/she may (by notifying the local authority) elect to close the shop on Saturday and open it on Sunday. He/she may not, however, open for six hours on Saturday and then all day on Sunday!

The Act also deals with two consequential matters. First, local authorities are given the power to make bye-laws prohibiting the loading and unloading of lorries at large shops before 9 am on Sunday morning. Second, a provision in a lease, entered into before 26 August 1994, that a shop shall be kept open during normal trading hours, shall not be read as requiring the shop to open on Sundays. However, a specific provision requiring Sunday opening remains valid.

Employment rights for shop staff

New employment protection rights have been given to all 'shop workers' except those employed to work only on Sundays. These rights may therefore be claimed by those who work for corner shops as well as those who work in out-of-town superstores. A 'shop worker' is defined as:

- anyone employed to work 'in or about a shop': this includes sales assistants, check-out operators, shelf-fillers, managers and supervisors; or
- a barber or hairdresser.

A 'shop', for this purpose, is defined as premises where goods are sold or hired. Thus, for employment law purposes, television rental businesses and auction rooms are 'shops' and so their staff have the benefit of the new right not to work on Sundays. However, service businesses (other than barbers and hairdressers) are not 'shops' for this purpose and so there is no protection for the staff of estate agents, betting shops, etc. Neither is there any protection for those employed by catering businesses – defined to include not only hotels, public houses, restaurants and cafes, but also take-aways where food is 'prepared to order for immediate consumption off the premises. Thus, this legislation leaves some questions open – for example, it is a debatable point whether security guards, maintenance staff, etc. employed to work in the common areas of a shopping mall work in or about a shop.

The new right in detail

The Act gives 'shop workers' – other than those employed to work only on Sundays – the right not to be dismissed, nor to suffer any other disadvantage such as being passed over for promotion, for refusing to work on a Sunday on which the shop is open to retail customers. Any such dismissal will automatically be unfair, regardless of the age of the employee, the hours worked or his length of service. It must be remembered that the protection exists only where the shop is open on Sunday: subject to the provisions of individual contracts of employment, a shop-keeper can still require his/her staff to attend on a Sunday to take stock for example, even if the shop is not open to serve the customers. Second, it is necessary to distinguish between two groups of workers:

1 Protected shop workers, namely those whose contracts of employment do not require them to work on Sundays or whose employment began before 26 August (whatever their contracts say about Sunday working).

2 Other shop workers, those whose employment began on or after 26 August and who are required by their contracts of employment to work on Sundays.

The terminology used by the Act is confusing, because even staff who are not protected shop workers are in fact able to refuse to work on Sundays. The difference is that protected shop workers cannot be required to work on Sundays unless they have given their employers written notice that they are willing to opt into Sunday working, wheras other staff can be required to work on the Sabbath unless they have given their employers three months' notice that they wish to opt out of Sunday working.

A shopkeeper engaging an employee on terms that he or she may be required to work on Sundays must give him/her written notice, in a specified form (see Sunday Trading Act 1994). It will automatically count as 'unfair' to dismiss an employee because he/she has given an opting-out notice. Finally, an employee who has opted out can opt back in again, and similarly, one who has opted in can opt back out – time without number.

Planning the service mix

The total assortment of services that a retailer may consider offering is almost without limit. Services range from the most basic, such as free parking or free carrier bags, to such specific services as engraving or gift-wrapping. The retailer can choose between offering free services, subsidising services or making them self-financing. The ideal service is obviously one that both offers an attraction to the store and is at least self-financing, although few meet these criteria. The value of the service must be set against the costs and possible effects on profit margin and prices (Parasuraman *et al.*, 1988).

Expectations of services appear to vary considerably between customer groups and between countries. It is probably true to say that most UK retailers are not high service providers, compared with their counterparts in the USA or some parts of Europe. Service expectation and priorities are obviously very different in the retail sectors where greater perceived risks are involved in the product purchases. A number of **service strategies** could be applied to reduce risks and assist the customer's purchase decision. Exhibit 12.9 discusses examples where service strategies are successful in encouraging customer confidence in this way.

Extended warranties (for example those offered by Comet, Dixons, major department stores) and electronic companies, may also reduce the risks of purchasing items where fears of expensive repairs may be experienced.

The examples offered above illustrate some of the range of services offered to enhance convenience and reduce purchase risks. However, a retailer must evaluate each service possibility with care and frequently re-evaluate those currently being offered.

Whereas some of the more basic services such as free car parking in certain areas have become accepted and could not easily be withdrawn by retailers, other supplementary services could easily be dropped depending on their importance in the retailer's marketing strategy. A matrix approach to the development of service

Exhibit 12.9 | **Encouraging sales by reducing customers' risk factors**

The liberal 'merchandise returns policy' operated by Marks & Spencer, for example, is more than just a substitute for providing changing room facilities. In an effort to encourage increased buying for relatives or friends a returns policy is offered in cases where the merchandise purchased is the wrong style, colour or size. Customers may return the purchased item undamaged. With the freedom to return items, shoppers feel less inhibited about buying clothes, either for themselves or for other members of their household. Once the items are tried at home, the chances that they will be retained are far greater. The considerable cost of operating the returns departments is, therefore, well justified. Special fast-service returns facilities are often provided for store card holders, which acts as an additional incentive to take up the offer of a store card facility.

The catalogue retailers also operate generous returns policies to overcome the perceived risks of off-the-page purchasing. Both Argos and Littlewoods catalogue shops offer 16-day money-back guarantees if the customer is not fully satisfied. The operation of such policies obviously has implications for staff training, in that returns must be handled courteously and efficiently, while checking that the product is undamaged.

strategies should be developed, with each service being evaluated according to whether its cost is high or low and whether its value to the customer is high or low. Low-cost, high-value services (patronage builders) are obviously attractive from the retailer's viewpoint; high-cost, low-value services, on the other hand, are clear candidates for elimination. The evaluation of service cost-effectiveness is not an easy task, however, as a wide range of direct and indirect costs and benefits must be carefully weighed in the balance. The retailer must also judge the competitive advantage that is achieved and the congruence of the service with overall strategy and positioning by the introduction of service innovations.

Retail service innovations

Retailing service innovations have usually entered the marketplace both from the prestige level, where new conceptions of service are usually emphasised, and from the minimum service level, where new cost-cutting concepts yielding ultimate price benefits to customers are emphasised. Credit plans, for example, were introduced at the upper-service levels and, as they proved acceptable to growing numbers of consumers, they were eventually added to the service components of many stores. Just as in the past when some stores hesitated to accept self-service, which they considered to be an unwanted service, some stores now hesitate to accept innovations that they consider to be of a service character. Self-service gained its acceptance as a price reducing innovation (Omar, 1995) and in the late 1990s is in the adaptive stage, where variations on the basic theme are being devised to make it more suitable for appropriate merchandise in stores on higher-service levels. This section briefly discusses the new services introduced by retailers for the benefit of increasing efficiency and reducing **waiting time** while shopping.

A store's atmosphere also depends on how efficiently the store allows customers to complete their transactions. Anyone who has stood in seemingly endless queues at banks, airports and retail checkout counters has experienced the frustration of dealing with inefficient transaction services. Queues or **waiting lines** at retail stores are by no means a new phenomenon, but two causes have increased their significance. In an effort to control costs, retailers have generally reduced the number of shop-floor employees. Moreover, many employees lack adequate training and motivation. As a result customers spend more and more time waiting in queues. In today's time-pressed society, customers are no longer willing to waste their scarce time waiting; people simply do not have the time to spare. Thus, while queues keep getting longer, customers become less tolerant of them.

Increasing transaction efficiency

Realising that long queues lead to customer complaints and ultimately to lost sales, many retailers are trying to improve the quality of their **transaction services** – such services as checkout, bagging, wrapping, cheque cashing, and so on. These are necessary to complete the retail transaction after the customer has selected the merchandise and to improve overall **transaction efficiency.** Indeed, some retailers have tried to differentiate themselves from competitors based on how quickly they complete sales transactions. One such company was Kwik Save, featured in the following mini-case.

MINI-CASE   **New checkout points at Kwik Save**

In early 1991 Kwik Save, a discount food chain, embarked on a mission to improve the quality of the transaction service at its outlets. Video cameras were installed at ceilings over checkout counters to record how customers passed through the checkout point. A store analyst was called in to analyse the video footage, to estimate the amount of time customers were spending in the queue, and to list the activities of customers and employees during the checkout process. The analyst discovered that the checkout process was slowed significantly because cashiers took a lot of time in bagging the merchandise for their customers. Also, due to the design of the checkout counter, cashiers had poor manoeuvrability within the checkout space. Retail designers were called in and new checkout points were designed for the firm.

In 1992 Kwik Save introduced these new style checkout points in all of its stores. The new design gave the cashiers more flexibility of movement. In addition, the cashier could face the customer throughout the process of checkout and loading the merchandise into the trolley. The new design also made it easier for customers to move the merchandise from the trolley to the checkout conveyer belt. Store managers at Kwik Save believe that the new checkout points have increased the rate of customers moving through the checkouts by at least 20 per cent.

Transaction efficiency is also important for service retailers such as banks, hotels, airlines, and restaurants. Efficient transaction service is an integral part of the benefit offered by any fast-food restaurant. If service at fast-food retailers is not quick, customers will have little reason to choose them over conventional restaurants. Realising the importance of efficient service to their retail marketing strategies, restaurants pay considerable attention to maintaining and improving service standards.

Reducing waiting times

To reduce customer waiting time, retailers are using improved technology, checkout personnel training and better workforce scheduling to improve transaction efficiency. Most major stores are adopting hand-held and fixed scanner technology to increase the speed of transactions at checkout counters. Scanners eliminate the need for the cashier to read and key in the price of each item. This speeds up the checkout process and also virtually eliminates mistakes by the cashier. Equally important, scanners allow stores to update prices automatically without physically changing the price tag on each item. They also allow the store to automatically update inventory and accounting records at the end of each day. Banks, too, are automating transaction services to increase efficiency. They are relying on automatic teller machines to reduce the number of customers requiring personal teller service. In addition, banks have increased teller efficiency with fast, computerised systems for recording customer deposits and withdrawals.

In order to shorten waiting times, retailers are paying closer attention to workforce scheduling. The level of activity in a store varies throughout the day and the week. Retailers can better synchronise workforce availability with demand patterns by:

■ shifting employees among departments;

■ reassigning lunch and break periods;

■ rescheduling working hours for part-time employees.

Another way to increase the efficiency of transaction services is to involve the customer directly in it. The automatic teller machines (ATM) or cash machines used by banks is one good example of this. Similarly, customers at fast-food restaurants typically have to collect their own utensils and hand cleaning tissues (Omar, 1995). There are pilot schemes to extend this concept to other areas of retailing such as supermarkets, as discussed in Exhibit 12.10.

The diversity in retail service patterns is certainly continuing and total standardisation does not appear to be imminent. Some merchandise may always need personalised sales attention and it is to be hoped that some stores will continue to serve this need. It seems clear, however, that the range of selling services applied to consumer goods generally has shifted perceptibly in the direction of increased self-service. Store management should continue to be alert to the significance of this shift. It is the retailer's action in tackling such a shift in consumer demand that occupies the central discussion of the next section.

| Exhibit 12.10 | Self-service moves towards self-checkout |

Some supermarkets are experimenting with self-checkouts by customers using scanner-equipped checkout counters. Supermarket chains such as Kroger, Safeway, and Dominick's have introduced self-scanning automated checkouts in some of their stores. Customers in these stores can scan their own purchases and then take the receipt to a centralised cash counter. The self-scanner design ensures that all items are scanned properly before they can be removed from the store. These self-checkout stands are designed to appeal to customers who want to save time. Due to lower labour cost the stores are able to keep more checkout counters operating at busy times.

The verdict on these self-checkouts is still mixed, with some customers feeling that they may actually slow down the transaction process instead of speeding it up. Other customers may view the process as a drop in service quality, which may have a negative impact on store image.

Retailer action in marketing services

Retailers who understand their customers, the nature of consumer purchase costs, and some marketing principles should have no difficulty in devising appropriate action. A retailer's approach to the kind of consumer behaviour in their market should not be generalised on the assumption that it is appropriate for any and every market. Here the utmost care must be exercised. Thus it may be imprudent to attempt specific recommendation of particular devices. Yet, the retailer may find useful some evidence that consumers do react to efforts to cut their shopping waiting time. Consider, for example, the appeal of the 'one stop' shopping trip to shopping centres, as well as the increase in automatic vending machine sales and telephone selling. Noticeable, too, is the increase in telephone banking and auto-banks. Market information (Omar, 1995) shows that congested shopping centres are losing business to less congested shopping centres where parking is easier and dress more casual.

Reducing consumer purchase cost

Several approaches may be adopted to reduce consumer purchase cost including, lowering the prices of merchandise, reducing purchase costs, and attending effectively to create a shift in purchase costs.

Lower prime prices

The retailer's action should aim at minimising customer total purchase cost. This should be done by manipulating the price of target products. The dangers of this kind of price competition are well known. The advantages lie in the store traffic building aspects and in the lower marginal 'secondary purchase cost' (cost of travel, waiting time, parking, etc.) where it is normal to purchase a number of target products. Also, the additive effect may produce a relatively large prime purchase dwarfing the total secondary purchase cost.

Reducing purchase costs

If, for instance, both price and parking expense are lowered for the consumer but searching time is increased because of lack of assortment; and if, for the consumer, the increase in the cost of searching time more than offsets the decrease in the cost of parking and price, purchase cost will represent an increase in the total purchase cost to the consumer. On the other hand, if the customer's cost of searching is increased less than the decrease in the cost of parking and price, his or her total purchase cost is decreased. What the customer thinks about this is crucial, and it should be clear that the retailer must know their customers' attitudes to this – and other key issues.

To the extent that shopping 'satisfactions' provide offsets to secondary purchase costs for some people, retailers may succeed in reducing purchase costs for their customers by employing satisfaction giving devices. Many stores have done this using trading stamps, premiums, give-aways, entertainment, and so-called 'attractions' and special promotions. Some of these, like most 'one-shot' efforts, have fleeting results. Some others, like trading stamps, have their effect dimmed by competitors' similar action.

Shift in purchase costs

Several important factors related to consumer purchase costs are worthy of retailers' consideration. The effect of shifting a secondary purchase cost from the consumer should also be analysed. It would be most helpful to retail managers to have at hand a continually updated checklist of secondary purchase cost elements, arranged on the basis of knowledge of the importance of each purchase cost element to each customer. Such a list is not usually available. But where certain costs are known to be heavily weighted by the customer, early action is demanded.

Secondary purchase costs, however, may be classified on the basis of the frequency with which they are likely to be encountered by the customer. Those of high frequency should command priority action to shift them away from the consumer (McGoldrick, 1990). In the high occurrence group are parking fees, travel time and expense, in-store waiting time, searching time, psychological costs due to problems with store personnel, **store layout**, lack of assortment of goods, store temperatures, store humidity, and so on. But other secondary purchase costs – such as correspondence costs related to ordering, paying, credit charges, installation charges, even delivery charges – are not likely to occur with every shopping trip or purchase event. Action on these may be deferred until after those with high priority have been dealt with.

Retailers may be well advised to proceed cautiously when a shift of service becomes a psychological cost to the customer. Suppose a store were to reduce its checkout cashier personnel causing an increase in customer aggravation and tension. This occurred at some Kwik Save stores and ultimately resulted in the closure of several stores in 1997. Such an increase in customers' 'psychological costs', even with a simultaneous decrease in prices, may be short-sighted on the retailer's part since many customers lay great store by their psychological purchase costs. Notable, also, is the increased impact on the consumer of additional increments of psychological cost, owing to the cumulative effects associated with pyramiding psychological factors.

Customer support services

Customer **support services** give retailers another important means through which to enhance the value of their offerings to customers and influence their behaviour within the store. Examples of such support services include acceptance of credit cards, cheque encashment, delivery and gift wrapping. These services are intended to support the sale of merchandise and are not consumed by themselves. They do, however, influence the store's atmosphere and consumer behaviour. There is almost no limit to the kinds of services a retailer can offer, but they all fall into one or more of the following categories:

1 Services that directly increase the utility of a merchandise item. Consider, for example, alteration services at a clothing store. A retailer that does not offer such a service may lose sales. Similarly, computer and major appliance retailers typically offer installation services.

2 Services that directly facilitate the retail exchange process. Some retailers, for example, grant credit, accept third-party credit cards such as Visa, Master Card, American Express, and personal cheques; and others deliver merchandise to make shopping easier for customers.

3 Services may be designed to make shopping more comfortable and pleasant for customers such as providing a waiting room at the airport. IKEA's approach, as outlined in Exhibit 12.11, falls within this category.

4 Some services are designed to create demand for particular lines of merchandise, and may include: cooking demonstrations, beauty counselling, and interior decorating advice.

5 Other services provide merchandise information to consumers; for instance, people with questions about home improvement may call the MFI Home Centre for free advice.

6 After-sales services provided to ensure customer satisfaction after completion of the transaction. These include repairs and servicing of appliances and judicious handling of merchandise returns and exchanges.

Exhibit 12.11	**IKEA – profiting from customer support services**

Managers at IKEA, a European furniture chain that now has a significant presence worldwide, have put considerable thought into designing support services. The firm realising that most of its customers are parents with young children and that furniture shopping is often time-consuming, equipped its stores with supervised playrooms where parents can leave young children while they shop for furniture. The stores also have restaurants and rest areas for customers. The restaurants serve baby food and gladly warm up milk bottles for children. IKEA's support services are uniformly praised by its customers.

Service cost

As in all service provision, there is a **service cost** to the retailer for these customer support services. In order to control these costs, many stores impose fees for some of their services. Furniture delivery is one example. While most furniture retailers offer delivery services, few offer them free. Some retailers may argue that this is a more equitable policy since those who use the service bear its costs. Free delivery, for example, would force all customers to pay more since the retailer would have to pass on the cost of delivery to customers through charging higher prices. Thus, customers who did not use the delivery service would bear part of the cost and subsidise those who have merchandise delivered. It is probably necessary for retailers not to charge fees for services like parking that benefit most of their customers or services – such as offering product information – that build retailers' positive images.

Some support services not only pay for themselves, but actually generate profits for the store. Retailers, for example, started offering their own credit cards as conveniences to their customers and as a means of building customer loyalty. These store credit cards are now integral parts of the service strategies of many retailers. The growing importance of credit sales has prompted stores increasingly to view credit card services as profit centres rather than merely support services. Many American retailers such as Sears and Dayton Hudson, for example, treat credit card operations as a profit centre, requiring it to generate the same return on investment as any other part of the firm. To calculate the revenue generated by its credit department, the firm estimates the incremental sales that result from the availability of credit and the revenue generated from interest payments. The profits generated in this way often exceed the profitability of some product lines in the store.

Responding to changing customer needs

Retail services can take a variety of forms, and the list of services changes continuously in response to changing consumer needs. Stores stay open late at night and for extended hours during weekends. Many offer the convenience of automatic cash machines to save the customer a trip to the bank. As customer lifestyles change, the stores have to change the type of support services they provide to meet customer expectations.

As retail competition intensifies, customer service is becoming an increasingly important weapon in the retailer's competitive marketing strategy. In fact, numerous studies have established that customer service is critical factor that affects where people choose to shop. The retailer can maximise the effectiveness of its support services by ensuring that they support its overall marketing effort. They must fulfil the needs of their target market and match their image.

SUMMARY

This chapter started by reviewing the concept of self-service retailing, noting that when a store is operated on a self-service basis merchandise is so displayed and arranged that the customer can make a selection without the aid of a store assistant. Self-service as a retailing concept has both advantages and drawbacks, and its application will depend largely on the nature and type of merchandise on offer. Merchandise such as car spare parts, electronic goods and expensive perfumes are generally not offered on a self-service basis; they and are more suited to personal selling.

Personal selling involves two-way communication between store employees and their customers to facilitate customer decision-making by providing relevant information about products and services, and by making shopping a pleasant experience. Personal selling proceeds through a sequence of five steps including: approaching the customer, determining customer needs, presenting merchandise, closing the sale, and follow-up.

One of the most important challenges to retail managers is matching supply and demand, especially in financial service provision. The ease with which customers can pay, both in terms of efficiency and availability of credit, has become a very important influence upon store choice and transaction size. Retailers introduce service innovation to aid the efficiency of such services and to reduce customer purchase costs. The concern of retailers about consumer reaction to purchase events requiring higher purchase costs is particularly noticeable in store location research efforts, in particular in relation to outlying shopping centres, in financing parking surveys, in city centre rehabilitation, and in attempts to improve store services. Obviously, it is believed that shoppers find no satisfaction in paying parking fees or travelling long rather than short distances to a store – in fact, they are averse to incurring any avoidable purchase costs. Retailers who are able to reduce or eliminate these cost elements benefit most from customer patronage.

KEY TERMS		
checkout point	quality service	support services
closing the sale	self-service	trading up
cross selling	service cost	transaction efficiency
follow-up	service provision	transaction service
perceived quality of service	service strategy	waiting lines/queues
personal selling	store layout	waiting time
personal service	suggestion selling	

ASSIGNMENT

Tesco Clubcard's greatest potential is in analysing customers and their purchases. Clubcard allows Tesco to establish customers' age spread, how many are single, how many have children and of what ages, how many are elderly, which are the highest and which the lowest spending. It produces maps showing where customers of each type are concentrated, how far they travel to the store, and where they are being tempted away by competing stores. A loyalty scheme not only gives much more complete information about store users, but also updates it constantly.

Task

Discuss the benefits of loyalty schemes such as Tesco's Clubcard and suggest its potential limitations, if any, for a retailer thinking of providing this service to its customers (1500 words).

REVISION QUESTIONS

1. Self-service operations are motivated by the store layout. What are the factors that determine the success and shortcomings of a self-service operational plan?

2. Each retail employee who comes into contact with customers plays an important role in the retailer's marketing effort. Discuss this statement in terms of personal selling.

3. Retail selling is a complex task and consists of four key processes. Discuss these selling processes with the aid of a simple diagram.

4. Store personnel use several approaches to close a sale. How could the salesperson decide on what approach to use in closing a sale?

5. What do you consider to be the main benefits of running a store card system both for the retailers and for the shoppers?

6. Apart from credit card provisions, retailers may provide several other forms of financial services. Discuss briefly what these services could be.

7. Extended opening hours and Sunday trading may help retailers increase sales revenue and retail patronage. Explain.

8. The service mix offered by the retailer must be planned the same as the physical product. How could these services be provided to meet with customers' expectations?

9. Innovation is the technological dimension of a retailer's marketing strategy. How could retailers use efficient transactions to improve store patronage?

10. How could retailers manipulate service costs in trying to meet the customer's needs?

CASE STUDY

UK shoppers are swamped by loyalty card schemes

There are an estimated 40 million loyalty cards in circulation in the UK and almost three-quarters of the shopping population probably have at least one card. It is a fair estimate that almost eighty-five per cent of those shopping at Tesco and Sainsbury (the two market leaders in UK grocery retailing) used a loyalty card for their purchases. Those who do not use loyalty cards tend to be causal and light shoppers, and, in the case of grocery shopping, may be 'singles' living alone.

The greatest potential of any credit card or loyalty card is in analysing customers and their purchasing patterns. This case study reviews the benefits and some drawbacks of store card schemes for both the retailers and customers, citing examples from the most popular store cards. The case evaluates the problems and opportunities for retailers considering the loyalty card scheme.

Tesco became the first supermarket to issue loyalty cards in February 1995, with the launch of its Clubcard. At the time the notion was dismissed by Sainsbury as a gimmick, calling them 'electronic green shield stamps'. But by June 1996 Sainsburys' had acknowledged their appeal and launched its own version: Reward Card. There are now several other cards including Safeway's ABC Card, Boots's Advantage Card, and W.H. Smith's Clubcard – each with varied rewards.

For retailers, the loyalty card's potential for database marketing is more important than the capacity to boost sales by offering discounts. By using computers to analyse information about card holders and their purchasing patterns, the loyalty card schemes help retailers to build a more complete picture of their customers than ever before and to develop a closer relationship with them. The shopping data generated are analysed and the results used to fine-tune the trading strategy of individual stores. In general, the most important feature of a loyalty card scheme is that it tells retailers who their customers are and what their spending patterns are. Many retailers only know how many transactions they conduct each week, and the individuals who make those transactions.

From the form that holders fill in on joining, retailers know the card holder's name, gender, address and postcode; the number and ages of people in their household; car ownership details; and the distance they travel to the store. This information may be used for demographic analysis of store catchment areas. One of the many advantages of this information is that it is up-to-date. It is, therefore, more suitable than the population census which, otherwise retailers have used to determine store locations and the composition of catchment areas. The census information maybe up to 10 years old and does not tell retailers which local residents use their stores.

A loyalty scheme gives a wide range of information about store users, and updates it constantly. Clubcard allows Tesco to establish customers' age spread, how many are single, how many have children and of what ages, how many are elderly, and which are high- and which are low-spending. It can produce maps showing where customers of each type are concentrated, how far they travel to

▶

the store, and where they are being tempted away by rivals. Retailers can already count hourly transactions, and identify peak and trough periods, through EPOS information and monitoring systems such as 'ShopperTrak' which count customers entering stores. A loyalty card, however, allows them to monitor which types of customers shop at which times of day. It may, for example, indicate the peak periods for mothers with children and those for the elderly.

Loyalty cards seem to create more enthusiasm among shoppers than their cash value would suggest. However, some shoppers are suspicious of retailers' motives and some are concerned about what retailers may do with the information they gain. Shoppers are also aware that retailers may well not have issued cards as an altruistic or benevolent act; they suspect the retailer is hoping that the card will encourage the shopper to spend more in the store. This attempt to lure customers into making additional purchases in one specific store has not been particularly successful as many customers hold more than one loyalty card.

Potentially the most powerful use for loyalty schemes – but also the most complex – is in targeting offers at specific customers through direct mailing. In theory, heavy buyers of particular product types can be identified and targeted with offers likely to appeal to them. Customers with high spending power could be offered more generous incentives, while those who stop shopping at a store – perhaps tempted away by a rival – can be targeted to win them back. Targeting may not involve discounts – it may simply mean making certain categories of customer aware of services or products relevant to them or inviting them to special promotions such as wine-tasting events.

Questions for discussion

1 Tesco's Clubcard has advantages for both Tesco and its customers. What in your opinion are the key advantages of any loyalty card to the shopper?

2 A loyalty scheme not only gives much more complete information about the store users, but updates it constantly. Discuss this statement.

REFERENCES

Conneran, E. and Lawlor, K. (1997) 'Customer perceptions of the superclub loyalty scheme and its influence on the store choice decisions', *Journal of Targeting, Measurement and Analysis for Marketing*, 5(3): 210–20.

Duncan, D.J. and Hollander, S.C. (1977) *Modern Retailing Management: Basic Concepts and Practices*. 9th edn. Homewood, IL: Richard D. Irwin.

Ghosh, A. (1994) *Retail Management*. 2nd edn. New York: The Dryden Press.

Hawkes, P. (1996) 'The customer loyalty challenge', *Admap*, (January), 47–8.

Hirschman, E.C. and Goldstucker, J.L. (1978) 'Bank credit card usage in department stores: an empirical investigation', *Journal of Retailing*, 54(2): 3–12, 93.

Lucas, G.H., Bush, R.P. and Gresham, L.G. (1994) *Retailing*. Boston, MA: Houghton Mifflin.

McGoldrick, P.J. (1990) *Retail Marketing*. London: McGraw-Hill.

Ogwo, O.E. (1981) 'Identifying the correlates of consumer credit behaviour', *The Quarterly Review of Marketing*, 6(4): 1–8.

Omar, O.E. (1995) 'Retail influence on food technology and innovation', *International Journal of Retail and Distribution Management*, 23(3): 11–16.

Parasuraman, A., Zeithaml, V.A. and Berry, L.L. (1988) 'SERVQUAL: a multiple-item scale for measuring consumer perceptions of service quality', *Journal of Retailing*, 64(1): 12–40.

Uncles, M. (1994) 'Do you or your customer need a loyalty scheme?', *Journal of Targeting, Measurement and Analysis for Marketing*, 2(4): 335–50.

13

Research and retail information management systems

LEARNING OBJECTIVES

After reading this chapter, you should:

■ understand the retailer's need for research information in making retail marketing decisions;

■ understand the definition and sources of retail information management systems (RIMS) in the context of retail marketing management;

■ be able to explain the method of retail marketing research and its organisation;

■ understand the retail marketing research planning process in the light of available information;

■ know how to report research findings and able to summarise the retail research coverage.

Research is one of the most important retail marketing tools used to coordinate activities. It may be defined as the organised search for, and the analysis of, facts related to problems in the field of retailing in order to produce useful recommendations for retail management improvement. In the past, many retailers failed to recognise the benefits that research can yield and consequently used it very little. This situation remains the case in some areas of retailing, and is especially acute among small and medium independent stores. The use of research by retailers in making retail marketing decisions has increased substantially, with successful results. One of the dominant reasons for the slow progress of many small stores and some larger ones is that their owners have been unable or unwilling to undertake research. Clearly, the large multiple's advantage is that it can employ qualified personnel to carry on the necessary research activities. These research activities include gathering and summarising the data, analysing and interpreting them (**data analysis**), preparing recommendations for improvement, and following up to see that the recommendations, when endorsed by the management, are actually put into effect. The final step is noting the results of the adoption of the recommendations. This is demonstrated in Exhibit 13.1 and Mercian's introduction of red wine into the Japanese market.

Retail research cannot be carried on effectively unless management is research-minded and recognises the importance of developing information to assist in

| Exhibit 13.1 | **Using research information to improve sales** |

Red wine has been known for years to contain polyphenol, an anti-oxidant that inhibits cholesterol from accumulating on blood vessel walls. Japanese consumers began to care about such things only recently but they are zealous converts. Mercian, one of Japan's wine suppliers which initially was selling only packets of polyphenol tablets made from raisin seeds and fruit skins, wished to introduce red wine into its stores.

The company was not sure of the suitable price to offer a bottle of red wine – a price that would be acceptable to its customers. Mercian therefore conducted in-store consumer research targeted at the 25–45 age group, deemed to be the major consumers of red wine. Analysis of the data suggested Y480 ($35) per bottle would be an appropriate price; Mercian, who was already selling a bottle at Y590, reduced the price accordingly. This action resulted in a 40 per cent increase in sales in the first three months of price reduction. Based on the research information, Mercian was able to adjust its retail marketing policies.

making decisions. Due to rapid changes in the retail environment (see Chapter 2), retailers must learn to develop and use an information system. Such a system should aim to provide the routine, recurrent and *ad hoc* information which is essential for retailers to enter the market, self-perpetuate and prosper. This particular system used should provide the necessary ingredients for management to allocate resources, use time, and make strategic decisions successfully. In a difficult business situation, the system must coordinate the total information-gathering efforts of the firm. This enables relevant and timely information to be captured, organised and delivered – to the decision maker who needs it, when it is needed.

This chapter is about research in retailing in its very widest sense – often now described as the retail information management system (RIMS). A general model of RIMS is presented in an effort to show its conceptual construct. Much of it, however, is about data which already exists in the organisation. Whatever the source of the data, the primary concern is looking for information about the customer. The first part of the chapter defines the role of **retail marketing research** and establishes how retailers might go about finding out what consumers want. This is followed by detailed analysis of how retailers could use research information for decision making.

Retail need for research information

The retailer is often faced with a degree of uncertainty, and can never be entirely sure that even the best laid plans will achieve their objectives in exactly the manner expected. Uncertainty is normally greater in retail markets which are changing due to new product innovations; it is greatest in those which are changing due to rapid technological developments. Unfortunately, a great many markets have been experiencing very rapid change over recent years. The 1980s and 1990s have seen the emergence of 'decline' as a factor to be managed. Even in mature markets, such as those of car production and car retailing, organisations have been caught out by developments. Exhibit 13.2 illustrates how Japanese car manufacturers were caught between falling sales and rising costs.

Exhibit 13.2 | **Japanese car manufacturers caught out by market changes**

Japan's top five vehicle manufacturers (Toyota, Nissan, Honda, Mitsubishi and Mazda) scaled back production in a desperate attempt to cope with declining sales and increased costs of inventory. Sales of new vehicles fell about 7.4 per cent in April 1998 as consumers continued to steer clear of high priced items in their annual budget. Simultaneously inventory costs had risen sharply – 27 per cent up on the 1997 figure. All five manufacturers reduced production by more than 10 per cent. Nissan, in particular, is struggling to cope with huge inventory costs in the USA, reducing exports by 14 per cent and, at the same time, cutting overseas production by 14.7 per cent. The group blamed poor demand for cars in Asia, Africa and the USA, which they admit could have been predicted by target research on consumer car demand in these markets. With forewarning, preventative action could have been taken.

To help reduce uncertainty in the marketplace, retail management needs a constant flow of information. This information is usually sought regarding the market, competitive activities, the impact of environmental factors, and the results of the retailer's own marketing activities.

Retailers operate in an environment whose characteristics make survival and profitability difficult goals to achieve. In general, retail life cycles are getting shorter and retail failure percentages are high. Technological innovations, evolving socio-economic trends, and the emergence of new lifestyles have accelerated the complexity and speed of change in the UK retail environment. The achievement of survival, growth and profitability goals are assisted by the increasing proficiency of the retail firm in terms of: retailers allocating limited resources effectively; management using time effectively, both in functional and planning areas; and strategic decisions being made successfully. In all of these cases, an effective decision-making process must take place. Such a decision-making process may consist of identifying goals, determining alternatives, deciding on the expected outcome of each alternative, and making a decision.

The process is common to both small and large retailers. In order to function properly, the above decision-making process requires information – a constantly updated stream of information. In essence, effective management is managing information well, and this principle is applicable to both large and small retailers. Thus, a retail information management system (RIMS) is essential in all retail marketing operations. Until recently the amount of research conducted in retailing in the UK and in other European countries has been very limited, with much of the research conducted in the field of retailing having been done in the United States. This is probably because, in the UK, retailing has traditionally been characterised by quick decisions, operating mainly on a day-to-day basis. The majority of major retail organisations grew to a considerable size largely as a result of the methods of their founders. These methods were entrepreneurial and favoured flair, speed of response and judgement. Analysis of problems and the testing of conclusions – characteristics of the approach of the researcher – were not typical of the entrepreneurial stage of the growth of retail organisations. Many retailers, therefore, sometimes was indulged in research, not because of direct benefits but because they had an ill-defined feeling that they had to do so and that research was 'a good thing to do'. To other retailers moving away from entrepreneurial beginnings, research and analysis were seen as integral elements of most decisions.

In the 1990s, however, a healthy growth of research in the field of retail marketing is taking place, covering some very interesting subjects – such as analysis of customers and the pattern of demand; store location; competitive strategies; shopping behaviour; attitudes and perceptions to products and/or stores; the use of human resources, and so on – with many retail organisations taking part. It is neither possible nor desirable to attempt here a comprehensive study of all this recent and current research; some of the recent studies have been cited throughout the chapter. In general, however, research in retail marketing involves the systematic design, collection, analysis and reporting of data and findings relevant to a specific retail marketing situation. In order to focus attention on the retail marketing situation, the term 'retail marketing research' is used throughout the chapter to mean marketing research within the retailing context.

Traditionally research has not been the forte of small retailers for a number of reasons: lack of resources to do research; lack of expertise to engage in research; a less than adequate understanding of what research can do; intense involvement in day-to-day activities, allowing no time to do anything else; inability to use research findings; and the view that research is a luxury activity few small retailers can indulge in. In addition, it has been suggested that the techniques are not fully developed, and that data collection and analysis are very complicated. Thus, it is safe to assert that, by the late 1990s small retailers had not been active in research areas, and remained woefully unaware of their need for information or how they could use it.

Retail information management systems (RIMS)

This section seeks to identify information sources, types of information, the **information flow** process, and the components of RIMS within the context of a five-stage development: idea planning and feasibility, definition of requirements, design, implementation, and evaluation. This five-stage development is necessary for RIMS to become functional and viable.

Origin and definitions

A RIMS can be viewed as a specialised marketing information system with a prime focus on the retailing industry. Its major objective is to create a better flow of the information needed to make retail management decisions. Thus, RIMS is considered a subsystem within a certain retailing institution with a basic function of optimum decision making through integration, feedback and control. Such a system may be defined as a 'system of people, equipment, procedures, documents, and communications that collects, retrieves, and presents data for use in planning, budgeting, accounting, controlling, and other management processes'. In specific terms, a marketing information system may be defined as a continuing and interacting structure of people, equipment and procedures to gather, sort, analyse, evaluate, and distribute pertinent, timely, and accurate information for use by marketing decision makers to improve their marketing planning, implementation, and control.

There may be many sources of data to be entered into such a system. As has already been explained, much of this information is already held in most retail organisations. On the other hand, without an organised RIMS it is often left in a fragmented and uncoordinated form. The supporters of RIMS, adopting a systems approach to information requirements (which does not have to be computer-based), considered that it can provide retail management with data which are oriented to its particular information needs. The RIMS is only valuable when it is there at the right time (the time of need). It is important to be able to control, and hence use, the system that has been created, particularly if the computer-oriented path has been chosen. RIMS may be computer based or **non-computer based**. In the following sections, a particular attempt is made to aid the retailer in establishing a computer-based system. However, a better understanding and appreciation of computer-based systems may be made possible by first providing a brief overview of non-computer-based systems.

Manual (non-computer-based) RIMS

Prior to the invention and use of the computer, both manual and mechanical means were employed to gather, process, store and retrieve information (see Exhibit 13.3).

A manual RIMS is likely to suffer from a lack of integration between functions, duplication of work, limitations in processing large amounts of data, and lack of precision. Perhaps the greatest deficiency of non-computerised RIMS is their inability to distinguish between the different types of information needed by management at different levels.

The above points support the preference – even the need for the use of computer-based RIMS. In addition, the introduction of several low-cost microprocessor computer-based RIMS has made the process relatively simple and inexpensive.

| Exhibit 13.3 | Human or machine based RIMS? |

A firm need not have a computer to have a RIMS. For instance, a newsagent could have a RIMS, using his or her own memory as a data storage and their personal logical and mathematical abilities as a means of processing the data. However, such simple manual information systems are rarely found, except in very small business organisations. Even in the smallest retail firms it is common to have cash registers and/or adding machines. It can, therefore, be stated that almost every RIMS combines both manual and mathematical techniques to accomplish its goals. Among the factors in the trade-offs between humans and machines within these systems are: size of organisation, amount of information, economies of processing, and value of speed.

There is no consensus among practitioners or in the academic literature regarding the number and types of stages involved in creating an information system. Regardless of the stages, it is important first to observe the nature and characteristics of a RIMS. Figure 13.1 illustrates a relatively simple RIMS model, indicating the process from data gathering to information formulation for retail marketing management decisions. The model displays the presence of the data-gathering component, the data-processing component, a management information base, and the feedback unit. These components generate and facilitate an overall information flow.

Fig. 13.1 RIMS FLOW PROCESS

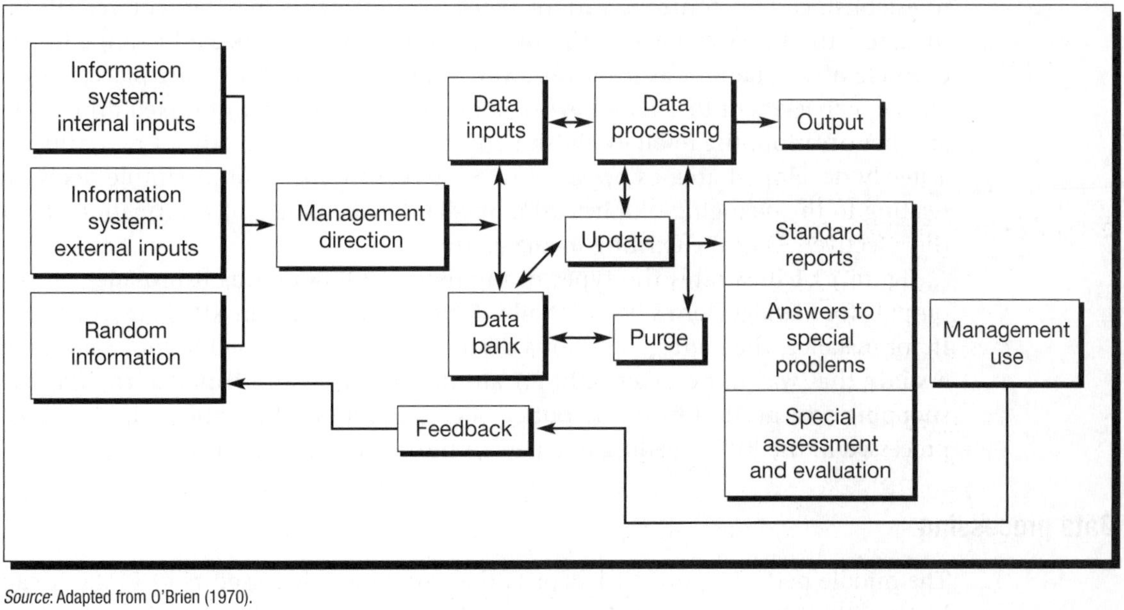

Source: Adapted from O'Brien (1970).

Information flow

RIMS is designed for retail management use and, in that capacity, it produces standard reports, provides answers to specific problems, and makes special assessments and evaluations.

Standard reports

These are generated by **internal information**. Reports on merchandising, operations, finances, personnel, and sales promotion are typical in retailing, irrespective of size. Information regarding the general operations of the retail establishment is the basis for evaluation, planning and control.

Answers to specific problems

Specific problems may vary from adding a new line or a new department to changing the internal layout or the image of the store. Adding new and more profitable merchandise lines and deleting those that are not being profitable are among the most important concerns of retail establishments. A strong and effectively functioning RIMS must cater to this type of need. Similarly, if the store needs to change its image, it is extremely important that RIMS facilitates such an activity by providing information on the strengths and weaknesses of the present image and on what the nature, characteristics and direction of the new image should be.

Special assessment

Not totally independent of the first two types of output, various types of evaluations are a very important output of RIMS. In order to make plans for the future or to establish certain controls, various types of assessments may be required. If, for instance, the RIMS can assess the market potential and expected change in the clientele of a restaurant as it moves away from being a family eating place, it may enable management to offer a new elaborate menu with a bar of mixed drinks. On another occasion, the retail establishment may consider the merits of relocating in a newly developed area as opposed to a city centre location. A simple decision relating to the changing of advertising media may be based on information about the effectiveness of the existing media used.

Figure 13.1 illustrates the types of inputs that RIMS uses as it provides proper outputs for management's use. Not all informational inputs in RIMS are deliberate. If, for instance, the management of a department store in a mall becomes aware of a study that was done externally for another purpose and if it reports that the shopping area needs a furniture outlet, such a random information input may be processed in the RIMS, leading to a new furniture department in the store.

Data processing

The middle part of Figure 13.1 depicts the data-processing aspects of RIMS. It can be seen that, in order for RIMS to provide proper information, it should have a data bank and a retrieval system. The nature of the data bank depends on the size and degree of sophistication of the retail establishment. The ideal system is fully computerised and is aided by marketing research as well as market intelligence services. The system can be totally computerised, partially computerised, or totally non-computerised. In all cases, not only the presence of a data bank but also its quality is important. The quality of the data bank is related to:

■ its scope – if the data bank does not have the width and breadth of data called for, it is not likely to be very functional;

■ the ability to update it – if the data are not updated so that new and fresh information is always available for the decision makers, the whole concept becomes self-defeating;

■ the ability to retrieve data – no matter how good the data bank may be in terms of its scope and its timeliness, if it does not have the versatility to provide management with any and all types of information generated through its retrieval system, the whole concept fails totally.

Figure 13.1 illustrates the presence of a feedback module. This module provides a built-in quality control and improvement mechanism that will be further discussed towards the end of this chapter.

Computer-based RIMS

The suggested five steps of a RIMS development cycle are presented in Table 13.1. The important thing to note is that this is a circular model, with Step 5, evaluation, feeding back into Step 1 – and thus restarting the process.

Table 13.1
RIMS DEVELOPMENT CYCLE

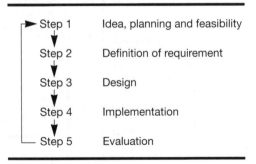

Step 1	Idea, planning and feasibility
Step 2	Definition of requirement
Step 3	Design
Step 4	Implementation
Step 5	Evaluation

Idea, planning and feasibility

Whenever the need to construct a RIMS arises, management should ascertain whether this need is a real one and if having such a system can be justified. Medium or large retail establishments may use a management team representing different managerial functions. The team should answer a series of questions including: What about existing information systems, if any? What about the proposed RIMS; can it be done? Is it practical? Is it economical? How should it be done?

The point to be emphasised is that managers tend to overlook existing systems in an attempt to acquire new ones. After any existing information system has been thoroughly investigated and the need to acquire a new system is certain, the team proceeds to examine available alternatives. A feasibility study of any proposed system is of crucial value since a considerable investment may be involved. The study helps management to identify potential problem areas and provides an objective basis for making the decision rather than acting solely on management wishes to have a new RIMS because it is fashionable. Figure 13.2 shows the complexities involved in this stage as exemplified by the number of steps needed.

As Figure 13.2 suggests, the team needs to compare existing and proposed systems based on costs and benefit analysis for each system. In addition, the management needs to know the relationship between the value of information and its determinant factors, since the cost of information is a function of accuracy, speed, time response, person–machine mix, and completeness.

Specifying the requirements

The main purpose of this stage is to define needed information. This will serve as a guide for the design of the central database which is a major component of the RIMS. The management is also required to make a decision regarding the equipment to be used. Normally, it will have a number of alternatives from which to select based on the firm's needs and capabilities. The success of the management

Fig. 13.2 RIMS FEASIBILITY STUDY PROCEDURE

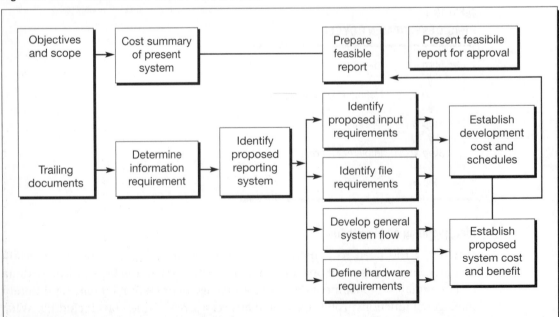

team is contingent on the inclusion of management representatives, users (middle management in medium and large retail organisations), and specialists in the decision-making process.

At this stage, it is necessary to decide how RIMS will be manned and where it will be located in the organisation. Many retailers that have some form of RIMS have made the mistake of putting the system within either the personnel or accounting department which limits its performance to a great extent. It is generally better to establish a separate department for RIMS which reports either to the directors or the board of governors. At this stage of development, performance criteria should also be established, to serve as a basis for control and evaluation.

Sources of information

In order to identify the information sources, both the internal and external environments of retailing have to be examined. Figure 13.3 presents some of the information sources a retailer might deal with. As can be seen, the sources are classified as internal and external. An information management system for retailers has to be both simple and sensitive to local changes. The simplicity and sensitivity become greater as the retail establishment becomes smaller; thus, the small retailer has to have a small and highly sensitive RIMS. Furthermore, RIMS must not be too costly. Small retail firms in particular do not have the means to develop an elaborate RIMS. On the basis of these criteria, the most important source of information is the internal one.

Internal sources and types of information

The first elements of the information available to retailers relate to the information held within retail organisations. In this book, these are dealt with in the context of the needs of retail marketing. It should become clear, however, that the same

Fig. 13.3 SOME RIMS INFORMATION SOURCES

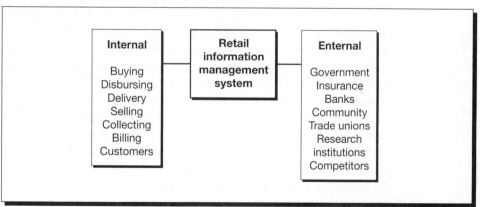

techniques can apply quite generally to most other areas of management. An engineer looking for historical information on product performance or an accountant trying to discover what lies behind a certain set of figures will face much the same task. For most retailers, finding and handling information is a key aspect of all management, and this also includes all the retail management functions.

Internal sources of information, particularly in small-scale retailing, are extremely valuable: they provide a vital set of facts; the information is easy to gather; and it is less costly to gather internal information than any other type of information.

Financial control may include the responsibility centre, budget data, cost data, revenue data, customer data if possible, schedule data, sales, receivable, purchases data, personnel and payroll, securities data (if any), data on debt, asset data, creditors data, and tax data. Data are gathered from books, transaction records, and management reports or plans. The transaction file may include receipts, payments, bank accounts, discounts, dates of transaction, amount of cash, description of securities, sales, purchases, and similar items. Sources of information are receipts, authorisation slips, vouchers payable, and other financial statements. These can be broken down by departments, product lines, and personnel. The human resources file may include names of employees, their social security numbers, departments, job classification, original employment data, seniority, and characteristics (such as sex, race and religion). This source yields additional information on different compensation programmes, scheduling, and staff requirements as well as personnel selection.

The sales file may include a breakdown by product, product line, customer class, cost centre, region or salesperson. The problem here is that most retailers deal in small quantities and with a large number of customers. It is, therefore, very difficult to include the name and address of each customer (an exception may be credit customers) as industrial firms do. However, it is possible to summarise the observations of salespeople regarding who shops at their store or to carry out marketing research frequently. In such a case, market research findings are added to the database for future use. Accounts receivable and customer file provide information about service charges, ageing analyses, collection performances, bill adjustments, and customer complaints. This is one of the most important information sources in determining performance effectiveness in the marketplace. A database sales file can be a vital tool with which to assist successful competition in the marketplace since it enables management to compare products and understand trends. It can also help management to carry out analyses of product life cycles and to make conclusions regarding the profitability of each product, salesperson and customer class. This also aids forecasting.

All of these information sources can be tapped by those who are involved in the types of activities to which these sources are related. The person, for instance, who is in charge of merchandising will be the most natural choice to provide the necessary information of the RIMS. Whether this information will be presented informally or formally will depend on the size of the organisation and its degree of sophistication. If it is a large multiple, and there are a number of layers between the top decision-making level and the accountant or the merchandising manager, then the information could take a formal report form. In such cases, the sophistication level of the specialists at different managerial levels is also high. This could further facilitate the presence of a formal information format. In addition to formal reports, the information system is likely to be computerised in these firms. In smaller and less sophisticated firms, a more informal approach is likely to be used, consisting primarily of semi-formal reports and word-of-mouth information flow.

External sources and types of information

Figure 13.3 illustrates some of the most important external sources of information. Table 13.2 identifies four more specific types of information – **population movements**; town planning requirements and legal requirements; competition; external support systems – based on the sources identified in Figure 13.3. As can be seen, neither the sources nor the types of information are difficult to gain access to. However, the simplistic nature of the sources and information does not imply that the information is not very important. On the contrary, this type of information is vital to the well-being of both small and large retailers. Lesser and Stearns (1986) have suggested more elaborate and complex **external information** systems based on shopping behaviour theory. Pessemier (1980) has suggested that such a system is necessary to develop an effective store image and to manipulate the position of the store accordingly. Mason and Mayer (1980) added that retail merchandise information systems are to be used for critical strategic decision making. Table 13.2 identifies four general types of information from four specific sources. As can be seen, the sources are not difficult to gain access to, and the types of information

Table 13.2
SPECIFIC TYPES OF EXTERNAL INFORMATION FOR SMALL BUSINESSES

Population movements	▪ Would the key institutions continue growing? ▪ What are the prospects for new business development in the area? ▪ What is the expected new housing development decisions by the government or local authority? e.g. newly expected residential areas, newly zoned commercial areas, road construction
Town planning regulations and legal requirements	▪ New licensing rulings ▪ New business permits ▪ Town planning and growth ▪ Attitudes of the local councils to supporting businesses
Competition	▪ Changing nature of competition ▪ Key changes expected in the near future
External support system	▪ Will there be a critical change in the money market? ▪ What is the sentiment of property owners?

obtained from them are rather simplistic. However, these types of information are vital, particularly to the well-being of small retailers.

In a small town, for instance, where a number of businesses thrive on the traffic passing through town on the main road, plans to build a bypass can be extremely important for the future of these businesses. Were the bypass to be built, many of these businesses would have to relocate or change their marketing strategy in an effort to appeal to the endogenous market segments of the town itself. Similarly if the town has changed the planning requirements for new businesses making it easier to open new retail stores, existing retailers will have to adjust or change their strategies in an effort to keep competition out.

The changing nature of competition has a significant impact on retail strategies. If competition has become keen, substantial differentiation or segmentation may take place on the part of the existing retailers so that additional competitive advantage is gained. **External support systems** in terms of finances, taxes, and landlords' attitudes all play decisive roles in retail marketing strategy. Numerous examples could be given for each item in Table 13.2. However, the types of information presented in Table 13.2 are self-explanatory in relation to their impact on retail marketing management.

Published data sources

Some other sources of data useful to retailers and which should be considered when searching for published information are the libraries, universal product code (UPC), electronic data interchange (EDI), news media, etc. There are several sources of published data; the appropriate one or ones may depend to a great extent on the nature and type of information being sought by the retail organisation.

Libraries

Libraries provide the most wide-ranging source of freely available published data. Most libraries have a broad selection of non-fiction books which will provide background reading on most subjects and should not be ignored as a source of data. Reference libraries, which are usually part of a central library, hold even more data. All the major cities in the UK and in other European countries have at least one major library, stocked with a vast array of books. Libraries, generally, will attempt to obtain books which are not on their shelves, typically having a catalogue of books held on computer which lists the stock of all their branches. In the UK, branch libraries also have access to the British Library lending section, which is located at Boston Spa. Books not available locally may be obtained on loan from the British Library on the behalf of the reader (though the process is not immediate and there may be a delay between the ordering and receiving of a requested book).

A number of abstracts are published regularly which list business articles, giving the details of where they have been published, etc. and a brief description of the contents. Probably the best known of these are provided by ANBAR covering most management and business subjects and ABI/INFOM – available on CD-ROM.

The design and operation of RIMS

Once the decisions have been made regarding data needs and data scope, the nature of the firm has to be considered for the RIMS design and operation. As noted earlier, the internal sources of data may include finance, selling, purchase, inventory, delivery, personnel, wholesale, etc. The external sources of data may be: research, customers, local authorities, banks, government (national and local), trade unions, shareholders, competitors, etc. These internal and external data have to be gathered for planning, control, risk avoidance and opportunity assessment. The preparation of internal and external data in the total RIMS is at least partially dependent on the level at which the managerial decision is made. Lower level managerial decisions are mostly programmed and routine and, hence, are mostly based on internal information. As the level at which decisions are made rises, the need for and dependency on external information become very real, emphasising once again the fact that a good RIMS gathers its information from both internal and external sources. Figure 13.4 illustrates these relationships. These interrelationships and the specific RIMS designs vary from one company to another. Some major retailers

Fig.13.4 RIMS DATABASE DEPENDENCIES

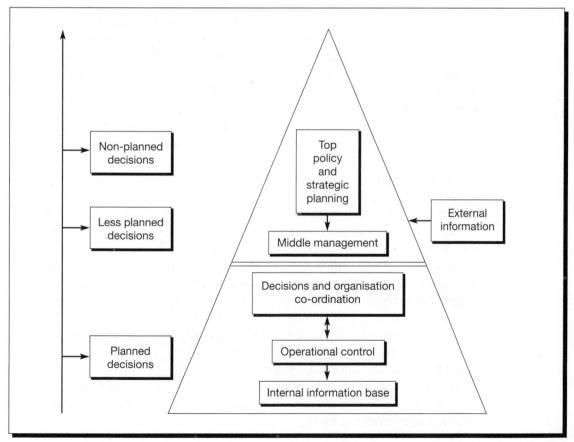

(Argos and other catalogue stores, for example) have devised RIMS systems that are unique to the store or types of store because of their particular needs.

In most major high street retail stores, **point of sale (POS)** registers are each linked to their main computer at head office. The POS devices 'report' to in-store computers that are linked to the head offices; the information is then reported to the main decision makers. Argos uses a RIMS to process orders, decide inventory, and plan its purchases. Many UK supermarkets and speciality stores have used RIMS primarily in inventory management and product line assortments; these stores are perhaps more likely to use electronic point of sale (EPOS).

One of the latest developments has been the extension of the use of the system to verify credit ratings. High street stores are now able to use NCR retail terminals which perform as cash registers to report information to their control office to verify credit worthiness. Thus credit decisions may be made in minutes.

Implementation and system support

Implementation of RIMS takes two separate paths simultaneously: information and personnel. One without the other is not effective. Hence, as the system is being operated in terms of information gathering, processing, and retrieval, the people responsible for the systems are trained.

Thus, the two components have to be developed and balanced alongside each other. Figure 13.5 illustrates the balance between the two. As the system is developed, all the procedures regarding personnel are also developed in the form of manuals. Implementation support for RIMS is related to the personnel who will be involved in its operation; the conversion of RIMS from an idea to a full-fledged system becomes a reality through the people responsible for its functioning. Information flow of the RIMS calls for special attention. RIMS is designed for management use, and in that capacity it produces a **standard report**, answers to specific problems, and special assessment and evaluative output.

Evaluation is the final step in the RIMS development cycle and the steps from file creation to implementation support are shown in Figure 13.5. If RIMS is to perform effectively, it has to be evaluated periodically and in terms of total performance. Evaluation is closely related to quality control and improvement mechanisms. This whole activity comes under the feedback component of RIMS. In order for RIMS to function as an effective system, it has to have a built-in quality control and improvement mechanism. This mechanism is represented by its feedback component. When management is using the output of RIMS, it has to keep track of how much output is used; whether it is in a proper form to be used; if the output needs to be changed, how and in what way; and finally, if additional output is needed, what kinds? All this information needs to be brought back to the information system level. If, for instance, rapidly changing prices require that a gift shop install an inventory control system based on units rather than on prices, management's needs are used as feedback to change that particular portion of the RIMS.

Fig. 13.5 RIMS IMPLEMENTATION ACTIVITY

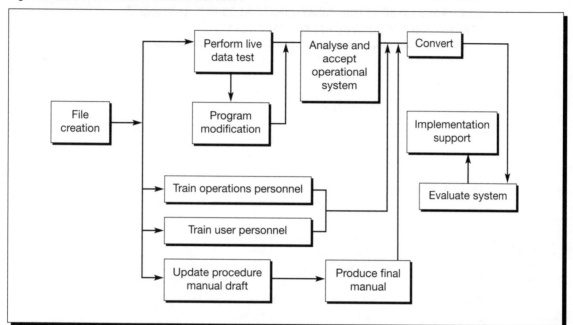

RIMS and retail life cycle

The life cycle of the retail organisation, just like that of a new product, has four distinct phases: introduction, growth, maturity, and decline. RIMS may have to provide some standard and some special types of information due to changing information needs relating to the stage of the **retail life cycle**. Table 13.3 illustrates some of these changing information needs, though the list is illustrative rather than exhaustive. As can be seen, many of the information needs are satisfied by standard reports but, in each stage, some particular problem areas and/or information needs arise. For example, consider the case outlined in Exhibit 13.4.

Exhibit 13.4	**The use of targeted reports on problem areas can yield rewards**

An organisation handled office supplies, both retail and wholesale. The company put most of its efforts into the retail aspects of the business. However, the business in general was not yielding a reasonable return. When the transactions and profits were analysed it was found that, whereas retail activity was losing substantial amounts of money, the wholesale activity – despite the lack of emphasis – appeared to be extremely profitable. The company discontinued the retail activity and became very successful.

Table 13.3
SOME RIMS INFORMATION COMPONENTS REQUIRED AT VARIOUS STAGES THROUGHOUT THE RETAIL LIFE CYCLE

Life cycle phase	Information component
Introduction	Market potential
	Feasibility
	Cash flow needs
	Promotional information
	Standard operational expenditures
Growth	Changes in the market
	Market segment information
	Image analysis
	Promotional information
	Operational expenditures
	Operational controls
Maturity	Changes in the market
	Market segment information
	Image analysis
	Promotional information
	Operation expenditures
	Operational controls
Decline	Changes in the market
	Market segment information
	Image analysis
	Promotional information
	Operational expenditures
	Operational controls
	Information for diversification
	New market feasibility information

Finally retailers, like manufacturers, continually face obstacles in their attempts to achieve success and they need to understand what these barriers are in order to overcome them. Basically, success depends on a retailer's ability to manage information. A major source of such information is retail marketing research. The research methodology used – the process used in the research – will generally determine the nature of information generated. The following sections, therefore, look at research organisation and the methods used for such research.

Research methods and organisation

Marketing research in retailing entails the collection and analysis of information relating to specific issues or problems facing the retail organisation, and involves the use of a variety of methods (Figure 13.6). Some of these methods include:

Qualitative research which explores attitudes, perceptions and ideas. It seeks to find out why people make choices and behave the way they do, and what they believe their future needs may be. As it asks for opinions which are hard to quantify or reduce to simple questions, it usually involves face to face interviews with individuals or groups with knowledge of the subject matter.

Quantitative research which seeks to measure or quantify factors for statistical analysis. It asks how many people buy certain products and in which ways. Since it tries to build up a statistical picture of the marketplace, it usually involves taking data from many people in order to draw general conclusions from a sufficiently large sample. It is conducted usually as large surveys and observations.

Desk research which evaluates the many types of existing data both within the retail organisation and in the public sector. A variety of sources exist for secondary marketing information. Primary research is usually a development from the secondary information gathered through desk research.

In some retail organisations, market research may be the only type of information gathering and processing that is done. The process embodies a series of activities including: problem definition, the examination of data, analysis and interpretation of data, making recommendation, and implementing the findings. It is, therefore, not a single act.

Fig. 13.6 METHODS USED IN RETAIL MARKETING RESEARCH

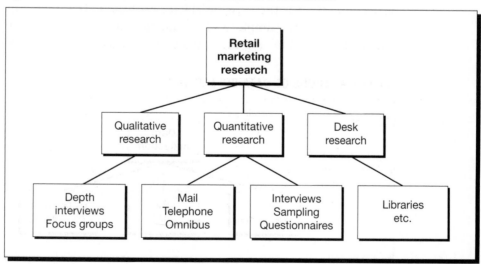

The use of the marketing research process will enable the retailer to conduct research systematically and to make better decisions. In such a process each activity is conducted sequentially. For instance, **secondary data** (data which already exists and can be collected by desk research. It is information relevant to the project which already exists somewhere else within the retail organisation or in the public domain) cannot be examined until after the problem is defined. The **primary data** stage (data specifically collected for the project through field research, and which generates information specifically for the project in hand) needs to be generated only when the secondary data search does not yield enough information to make an informed decision. These components of the research are described below.

Defining the objectives

Defining the objectives is the most important stage of almost all market research, and the one at which the research is most likely to be misdirected. Only the retailer knows what the firm wants the research to investigate. It is after the problem has been identified that the objectives may be established. The objectives need to be clear, and clearly stated, so that the researcher may understand them. On the other hand, they should not prejudge the issue.

Data collection methods

The methods of data collection focused on in this section include mail (fax, e-mail), and telephone and personal interviewing, as shown in Figure 13.7.

By mail

This is the cheapest solution, allowing large samples of the total market to be taken. Investigation of small market groups – especially in industrial markets – can be successfully carried out and remain within acceptable statistical levels. But in many respects it is the least satisfactory solution. The questions which can be asked are necessarily simpler and the questionnaire shorter; and it must be particularly well designed to keep the respondent interested and motivated to reply. More

Fig. 13.7 METHODS OF DATA COLLECTION

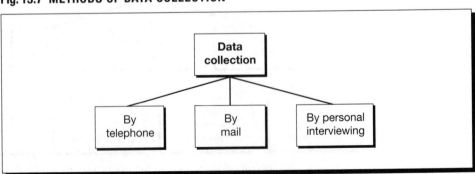

fundamentally, the response rates are usually so low that their statistical validity may be questioned; it is arguable that the majority, the non-respondents, may behave entirely differently from those who have responded.

Apart from making the material easy to complete and explaining the reason why the research is being conducted (in order to justify the time taken), this problem may be addressed in one of two main ways. The first is to increase the response rate by offering some form of reward (typically a 'free gift') in return for the competed questionnaire. The second is to follow up (typically by telephone) a subsample of those not completing the questionnaire, to see if their responses differ substantially from those of the sample who returned the questionnaire. If they are not different, the assumption is made (perhaps somewhat questionably) that those responding are representative of the sample as a whole.

By telephone

In this case the interviewer contacts interviewees by telephone. This limits the sample to those with a telephone, however, more than two-thirds of UK households had a telephone by the end of the twentieth century. This is a very fast survey technique, with results being available in a matter of hours if necessary. Its speed makes it an ideal technique for those opinion polls where time is of the essence. It is also relatively cheap and, thus, often affordable even in industrial markets.

The interview may last only a short time and the types of question are limited (particularly since the interviewer cannot check visually that the question is understood). Certainly a properly organised telephone survey can be a very cheap and efficient way of gathering information.

By personal interviewing

This is the traditional (face-to-face) approach to marketing research and it is still the most versatile. The interviewer is in full control of the interview and can take account of the respondent's body language as well as their words. It is, however, the most expensive and is dependent on the reliability of the interviewer; in the case of some of the more sophisticated techniques, it is also dependent on the interviewer's skill. This means that the quality of the supervision provided by the field research agency is critical, which may become a problem with so many organisations placing emphasis on cost-cutting. Horror stories are told of interviews being forged or made up by interviewers anxious to avoid going out on cold and rainy days. Fortunately, these instances are few and the reputable agencies do exert the necessary control over their personnel, usually by having a field manager conduct follow-ups of a subsample.

Data sampling

Another method of data collection is through **sampling**. The basic principle of sampling is that you can obtain a representative picture of a whole 'population' – the total group of people or objects being investigated – by looking at a 'sample' (usually, in this context, only a few hundred). This is a very cost-effective way of obtaining information. Samples are important in terms of understanding the accuracy which may be placed on the results which emerge and offer a good indication of the quality of the work being carried out. To guarantee a specified 'accuracy', respondents or objects should be chosen to offer a statistically valid sample, so that valid statistical analyses may be undertaken. There are a number of ways in which such a sample may be chosen. The two main approaches are **random sampling**, and **quota sampling**. Various other sampling methods exist and are available for use by researchers where necessary or appropriate.

Random samples

The classically correct method is to select a sample at random. The list of the total 'population' to be sampled is chosen. For consumer research, it is usually the electoral register; however, it must be noted that this is not necessarily comprehensive since it excludes those who have failed to register, for any reason, and those who have moved since the last time it was compiled. This list is then used as the basis for selecting the sample; most rigorously this selection is done by using tables of random numbers, most simply it is achieved by selecting every second, third, fourth, etc. name. A reasonable degree of accuracy may be achieved with samples as low as a few hundred.

An alternative and cheaper approach is **cluster sampling**, which may lose little accuracy if correctly employed. This consists of selecting the districts for interviewing on a random basis. Within these districts respondents may also be specified randomly (from the local register of electors, for example) or could be obtained 'quasi-randomly' by a 'random walk' (for instance, every fifth house on a given street).

In the case of **stratified sampling**, the original 'population' is grouped by some parameter – age, gender or income – and random samples are then drawn from each of these groups (strata). This ensures that there are adequate numbers in each of these subsamples to enable valid statistical analyses.

Advantages and disadvantages of random samples

The great advantage of random samples is that they are statistically predictable. Apart from any questions relating to how comprehensive the original lists are, they cannot be 'skewed' (that is, distorted). In some instances, however, results from poorly controlled research may be distorted or biased by poor sampling. This may be due to inadequate coverage, owing to incomplete lists of the overall population; it is, however, more generally due to a high proportion of non-response. It has to be assumed that the views of the members of the sample who did not respond would have been different to those who did, the result being that the views of particular groups of respondents are over-represented. Whatever the circumstances, however, the statistics – particularly those related to the degree of confidence which can be placed on the results – are easily applied. The major disadvantage is that this process is usually more expensive, and the necessary lists may not be available to the researcher. It is less frequently used for commercial work but it does usually offer a greater degree of guaranteed quality.

Quota samples

In this method of data collection, the interviewers recruit respondents to match an agreed quota of subsamples. This is supposed to guarantee that the overall sample is an approximately representative cross-section of the 'population' as a whole. The interviewer, by means of knocking on doors or standing in a busy street, is required to select predetermined numbers of respondents to match 'targets' within specified age and social categories. This technique clearly may be subject to biases or 'skew' – selecting only those who make a habit of visiting their local high street, for example, and excluding the more elusive elements of the population. It is also difficult to apply rigorous statistical tests to the data. Quota sampling is significantly cheaper than using random samples and so is the approach most frequently chosen for commercial research. Despite its obvious theoretical shortcomings, it often works well.

Analysing the results

After the collection of the required data, the data are analysed to assess and evaluate them for comparison with the defined problem. Possible alternative solutions are also anticipated and clearly outlined. Increasingly, analysts are using the massive computing power available to them to cut through the superficial results. The mathematics of these various techniques is beyond the scope of this book; the practical skill needed is that of finding the best expert to implement them and knowing how much reliance to put on their judgement. Some examples of the techniques used include multiple regression, factor analysis, cluster analysis, conjoint analysis, and so on. These are advanced statistical methods and are beyond the requirements of this book.

Reporting the findings

The final stage is to disseminate the results to all who need to know them. This process may initially appear to be a simple clerical task; however, it is a more complex and important process than is first obvious. The first task is to ascertain who would find the results useful and in what form. Important results may probably have relevance to managers throughout the organisation. It is equally important that the language of the report is appropriate and tailored to the different audiences within the retail organisation which the information must reach. Only few of the store managers will understand the terminology of market research. The favourite approach in presentation to top management seems to be that the dry statistics are considerably simplified and illustrated by verbatim quotes from individual respondents.

Instead of mysterious symbols and complicated tables, there are direct quotations in which people communicate their views at length and in their own words. The particular danger here is that senior management, unversed in market research skills, will merely use the quotes that reinforce their existing prejudices and ignore the rather boring statistics. Ideally, the results presented to each audience should be tailored to their particular needs.

Making recommendations

At this point, recommendations are made as to the strategy the retailer should follow to best address the problem. The last stage of this process is the implementation of the recommended strategy. If marketing research is to replace intuition in developing and enacting a retail marketing strategy, a decision maker must follow the recommendations from the research findings, even if they seem to contradict existing practice.

Syndicated research

Syndicated research is carried out by professional research organisations who generally offer the easiest and quickest market research service. Typically such organisations have ongoing or *ad hoc* research programmes, the results of which they sell to a number of retailers and other firms. Some of this may be standard research, such as the A.C. Nielsen store audits which provide information on retail purchases by consumers or the TGI (Target Group Index) of MRB, which has investigated the growth of some 5000 brands in the UK for more than 20 years. Shared cost is one advantage of the syndicated research approach, but the quality of the research itself is even more important. The main areas of syndicated research are **retail audits**, panel research, omnibus surveys, and consultants.

Retail audits

Retail audits are one of the most sophisticated of market research operations in terms of logistics; the concept, however, is simple. An 'auditor' regularly visits each retail outlet on a randomly preselected panel and carries out a physical stock check on the lines being surveyed. The change in stock from the previous visit, combined with the other stock movements, receipt of stock, and so on which are obtained from the store's records, gives the 'consumer sales'.

Panel research

Another approach to accurately measuring consumer behaviour (that is, their actions rather than opinions) is by panel. At its best this may approach the accuracy of retail audits (with the added, complementary, advantage that it is categorised in terms of consumer profiles). These panels adopt a variety of techniques and cover a range of subjects. The two main approaches are:

1 Home audit – the panel member is required to save used wrappers in a special receptacle (hence the alternative term 'dustbin audit' which is sometimes used). Once a week, say, an auditor checks the contents of the receptacle, as well as checking stocks of products in the house and asking the householder a short list of questions. This technique is particularly successful in terms of the recruitment and maintanence of a stable group of respondents which, in turn, helps to provide relatively accurate results.

2 Diary method – in this case the householder, say, records the required information in a diary, which is collected by the interviewer or (less successfully, but
more cheaply) returned by mail.

Omnibus surveys

These are very similar to *ad hoc* surveys, except that 'space' on the questionnaire is
'sublet' to different organisations and researchers; providing – in effect, a number
of 'mini-surveys' within the overall survey. Such omnibus surveys are often run
covering almost 2000 respondents per week on the back of ongoing research, such
as opinion polls. The cost benefits can be significant, since fieldwork forms the
major element of most market research costs. Such surveys may also provide a
faster turnaround of results, particularly if the survey is conducted by telephone.

Consultants

Some large scale surveys, such as the Taylor Nelson Monitor or Target Group Index
(TGI) in the UK), are run to provide data for the research organisation alone. The
analysed output, in the form of reports or computer-readable data, is sold to a variety of buyers, so recouping the cost of the survey plus profits for the organisation
providing this service. These surveys usually offer a very cost-effective way of
building a database of survey information.

Exhibit 13.5	**Buying in survey information may be most cost-effective**

The TGI usually monitors over 5000 brands, as well as over 300 attitude statements,
across 40 000 interviews each year. These data provide a profile of an individual brand
in terms of its consumer profile, including sophisticated lifestyle data derived from the
attitude statements; readership data; usage of complementary products; and the
same data on competitive products – for as little as £20 000 per annum.

Research planning

The design of the research is a complex process and demands the skills of specialist
staff. Clearly the amount of design time required will vary, depending upon what data
are required. A simple question of customer brand awareness may need little design
(which is not the same as little thought, as how a question is asked may skew the
answer), just a single question within an omnibus survey. On the other hand, a major
new piece of research may involve many important decisions. Ideally it will also incorporate a number of different approaches to the subject, so that the results can be
compared – to establish some indication of their likely accuracy rather like triangula-
tion is used in physical surveying. Thus the best research may employ not just one
method but a set of methods. There are many different types of research possible and
some of them are discussed below including: observation, experiment, **qualitative
research**, and group research.

Observation

This method involves watching participants as they undertake some activity, simply to see what happens. The pattern of customer flow in a supermarket could be observed by using sophisticated video recording and computer analysis to allow presentation of the data in a more accessible form.

Experiment

This exposes selected participants to different treatments. It may range from testing new products to viewing commercials and measuring responses to them. In theory, this approach may be used to establish experimentally the basic relationships involved. In practice it is more frequently used to select the best solution to presenting product or promoting store image from a range of marketing strategic alternatives.

Qualitative research

This category covers all research which does not produce rigorously validated numerical output including individual depth interviews semi-structured interviews and group interviews. Individual depth interviews (or 'intensive' interviews) and semi-structured interviews may last an hour or more, and can follow a variety of formats: from an almost totally free form (which is so specialised as to be outside normal market research practice) through the non-directive form (where the interviewer, while still in control, allows the respondent to answer in whatever form he or she wants) to the semi-structured (which is much closer to the conventional questionnaire interview, but which still allows the respondent some freedom of expression). The essence of all of these is that the answers are totally open, and have to be analysed by skilled personnel, but the freedom of expression often leads to a less constrained expression of their views, resulting in a clearer understanding of their true attitudes.

Group research

Group research is often also known as 'group discussion' or 'focus group research'. A selected and relatively homogeneous group (usually 6–10 members) of participants is encouraged to discuss the topics that researchers are investigating. The interviewer ('group leader' or 'moderator'), who has to be skilled in the technique and is often a trained psychologist, carefully leads the discussion, ensuring that all of the group members are able to put forward their views. The interviewer's role is then essentially a passive one, their prime concern being to foster group interaction and control of any one individual who is dominating the group.

The essence of such group discussions is that the participants may develop their own ideas in an unstructured fashion, interacting with and stimulating others. The whole session is usually captured on a tape recorder for later in-depth analysis. This often allows insights that are hidden by the preconceived questions posed in conventional surveys. The concept is based on the assumption that individuals who share a problem will be more willing to talk about it in the secure environment created by others sharing the problem. It is increasingly being used as a cheaper and faster alternative by retailers who cannot afford full-scale research. This is arguably better than nothing, but if such use is to be made of the information the 'researcher' should beware of attributing too much significance to it. The sample sizes are usually far too small to allow any statistical conclusions to be drawn and the conclusions are very dependent upon the researcher's interpretations.

Survey (questionnaire-based research)

The most widely used marketing research is survey or questionnaire-based research. Typically, this may be designed to find out, descriptively, what are the participants' habits, attitudes, wants and so on, simply by asking each respondent a number of questions. Though apparently straightforward, there are areas which need to be thought through carefully – issues relating to questionnaire design and the types of questions to be posed (open or closed).

Questionnaire design

The classic device used in surveys is the questionnaire: a printed form on which the interviewer or respondent fills in the answers to a series of questions. These questions are the key to the research. They must, therefore, be developed carefully and skillfully.

First, the questions must be comprehensive: if a key question is not asked it will not be answered. They need to be posed in a language that the respondent understands, so that the answers will be clear and unambiguous. They should not guide the respondent towards answering in a particular way – that is, they should not be leading questions. To ensure that the questions asked are valid and meaningful, it is good practice to test the questionnaire on a number of respondents. A questionnaire has to maintain the respondent's co-operation and involvement; communicate to the respondent; help the respondent to work out the answers; avoid bias; make the interviewer's task easier; and provide a basis for **data processing**. Clarity in the questionnaire and in the ideas behind it is amply rewarded by clarity in the results. The questions to be asked may be open or closed, as discussed below.

Open questions

This type of question allows respondents to answer in their own words. Although the question is fixed, respondents are not offered a preconceived set of 'expected' answers to choose from in reply. This means, however, that to be statistically useful the resulting answers later have to be 'coded' into groups which have something in common or share common interest. These 'open' questions may take simple forms such as: 'Why did you buy Brand A?'. Where there are barriers – such as psychological, language or social barriers – responses may be stimulated by a variety of devices, sometimes called 'projective techniques'.

Closed questions

Most questionnaires are based on 'closed' questions in which the respondent is asked to choose between a number of alternatives; or the interviewer is asked to listen to and then code the respondent's answer to an apparently 'open' question against a number of preconceived answers. The advantage of such closed questions is that the answers are easy to analyse and are unambiguous. The obvious disadvantage is that they preclude the respondent from giving an answer outside the prescribed limits.

Retail research coverage

Retail marketing research usually covers most of the areas of research with which most retail organisations are concerned when trying to make retail marketing decisions. The importance of each research area varies with the needs of the firm. In general, retail research requirements will normally cover all the elements of the retail marketing mix (discussed throughout this book). The key areas of research will usually cover consumer perception, habit, attitudes, store image, product/service, merchandising, advertising and promotion, retail operation, location, and many other areas of retail management. However, this list does not exhaust all of the subjects that are being studied by farsighted retailers.

As indicated so far in the discussion, most current retail research deals with day-by-day operating problems. Such research draws upon a reservoir of existing ideas and techniques from marketing, psychology, management and technology. It is directed at meeting current competition, but only through service innovation; it strives to increase sales, but only through customary inducements; and it looks to more efficient customer services, but only within the framework of traditional procedures.

SUMMARY

Retailers throughout the world continually face obstacles in their attempts to achieve success. To a great extent this success depends on the retailer's ability to manage information. Effective decisions cannot be made unless proficient information management takes place. This basic notion is the crux of this chapter. The retail management information system (RIMS) was introduced for that purpose. Five phases in the RIMS development cycle are discussed in this chapter: idea, planning and feasibility, definition of requirement, design, implementation, and evaluation. Each phase is discussed in detail in order to enable the student to understand the basics of developing a RIMS.

The key components of this chapter are: the retail marketing information system (RIMS) and retail marketing research – subdivided into its relevant components. Marketing research in retailing involves a process consisting of a series of activities: defining the issue or problem to be researched; examining secondary data; gathering primary data (if needed); analysing the data; making recommendations; and implementing findings. It is systematic in nature – a process not a single act. The steps involved in the process should be undertaken sequentially.

ASSIGNMENT

In recent years there has been considerable discussion concerning the application of marketing research in identifying retail marketing opportunities in international markets. Essentially, the application of marketing research techniques for identifying market segments opportunities for foreign retailers wishing to locate in the UK.

Task

You work for Mercian, a major Japanese retailer, as a retail marketing researcher. Mercian is determined to open a retail store in Britain in the next two years, but has no knowledge of British consumers. It is clearly advisable that some initial market research be conducted before the store is opened. Suggest, in not more than 2000 words, the nature of the desired research project and how it should be carried out.

REVISION QUESTIONS

1 Explain why you consider reliable information is necessary for effective decision making by retail management.

2 What do you consider to be the effective decision-making process for retailers, and what is the information requirement for decision making?

3 Suggest reasons why research is not traditionally the forte of small retailers.

4 Define the term 'retail information management' system (RIMS) and explain its relationship with the 'marketing information system' (MIS).

5 Whenever the need to construct a retail information management system arises, retailers should ascertain that this need is real and justified. How could retailers justify the need for RIMS?

6 It is suggested that finding and handling information is a key aspect of retail management. Do you agree?

7 Discuss the nature of internal sources of information available to a large multiple retailer.

8 How could retailers use internal and external data for planning, to avoid risks, and to assess market opportunities?

9 Effective retail management decisions are based on reliable information. What role does retail market research play in generating such reliable information?

10 In the data collection process, either personal (face-to-face) interviews, mail question-naires or telephone interviews could be used quite successfully. Discuss the nature of these methods.

CASE STUDY

A poor credit management at Ahmad's Food Store Ltd

Mr Yahaya Lye Ahmad, owner-manager of Ahmad's Food Store Ltd based in Kuala Lumpur, Malaysia, is evaluating his firm's credit policy. Ahmad's Food Store is an independent outlet with annual sales of slightly over £1.5 million. The firm is one of two grocery outlets offering its own charge account system in a residential area of Kuala Lumpur. The other store, offering a similar plan, is on the other side of town.

Ahmad's trade area is concentrated in the surrounding southern part of the town, but he draws around 25 per cent of his business from another area 2 miles away. Ahmad operated another store in the same area in Kuala Lumpur until it burned down nine months ago. Many of Ahmad's customers were then lost to competitive stores, but some remained loyal to Ahmad and drove to his remaining store. This store was built one year before his other store burned.

Ahmad operates his store on a 21 per cent gross margin; his net margin is 5 per cent, and his net sales to inventory ratio is 24 per cent. Credit sales currently amount to 80 per cent of Ahmad's total sales and last year he lost £1800 to bad debts. Last year's collection period varied from 30 to 36 days.

Mr Ahmad is concerned about his bad debt loss, and he is also concerned about the high cost of maintaining credit records for each customer. He is considering dropping his credit plan entirely but does not know what effect this move would have on his customers. Mr Ahmad does not know what his store's image is from his customers' point of view.

Questions for discussion

1 How would you design a research project that could help Ahmad make the correct decision on his credit problem and at the same time reveal his store's image?

2 What possible research methods could Ahmad use that may not cost him too much but achieve results to enable him to make reasonable and informed decisions?

REFERENCES

Cook, D. and Walters, D. (1991) *Retail Marketing: Theory and Practice*. London: Prentice-Hall.

Lesser, J.A. and Stearns, J.M. (1986) 'The development of retail information systems based on shopping behaviour theory', in Malhotra, Naresh (ed.) *Advances in Marketing Science*. Chicago: Academy of Marketing Science.

Marquardt, R.A., Makens, J.C. and Roe, R.G. (1975) *Retail Management: Satisfaction of Consumer Needs*. Illinois: The Dryden Press.

Mason, J.B. and Mayer, M. (1980) 'Retail merchandise information systems for the 1980s', *Journal of Retailing* (Spring): 56–76.

Mercer, D. (1996) *Marketing*. 2nd edn. Oxford: Blackwell.

O'Brien, J.J. (1970) *Management Information Systems*. New York: Van Nostrand.

Omar, O.E. (1992) 'Grocery shopping behaviour and retailers' own-label food brands', PhD thesis, Department of Marketing and Retailing, Manchester Metropolitan University.

Omar, O.E. (1994) 'Comparative product testing for own-label marketing', *IJRDM*, 22(2): 12–17.

Paliwoda, S. (1981) 'Using a mail questionnaire as a research tool', *The Quarterly Review of Marketing* (Summer), 9–14.

Pessemier, E.A. (1980) 'Store image and positioning', *Journal of Retailing* (Spring): 94–106.

Samli, A.C. (1980) 'Retail information management systems: an introduction to RIMS', in Proceedings of ESOMAR Seminar on Information Systems in Action, Amsterdam.

Schafer, E.A. (1972) 'Management control over the computer activity', *Data Management*, 10 (September): 45–55.

14

Retail marketing planning and control

LEARNING OBJECTIVES

After reading this chapter, you should be able to:

- explain the benefits and processes involved in retail marketing planning;
- define the corporate mission and know the strategic options available to retailers for developing their market segments;
- recognise the components of retail marketing audit and be aware that the audit is both a diagnostic and a prognostic tool;
- understand the application of portfolio planning in retailing;
- determine the retail marketing objectives and strategies for achieving the desired goals;
- recognise that the retail marketing control process and function are a necessary part of retail marketing planning.

Retail marketing planning is a logical sequence of activities leading to the setting of marketing objectives and the formulation of plans for achieving them. Most companies generally go through some kind of management process in developing marketing plans. The first step in planning effectively is to establish goals (Abell, 1980). A retailer's goals begin with the articulation of the retail objectives and positioning. Articulating retail objectives and positioning implies the unique ability to match external uncontrollable variables with internal controllable tools of management in such a way that the retailer achieves the competitive advantage. This is demonstrated in the Sears, Roebuck mini-case.

The development of effective retail market strategy begins with an adequate knowledge of external factors. In turn, this knowledge leads to the establishment of market opportunities which are based on total market potentials scaled down by the nature and intensity of competition. The retailer who is not able to approximate the market potentials and who is unfamiliar with local trends cannot possibly succeed in assessing external conditions (Mercer, 1996). Once the external conditions are assessed, the retailer must take a good hard look at the organisation. This implies an evaluation of the firm's inventory, including the existing image, financial resources, merchandise mix, administrative know-how, personnel,

MINI-CASE **Sears, Roebuck and Co.**

Sears retained its critical success factor in the distribution section of the 'value chain' by adapting to changing environmental conditions in the USA. They did so with such resounding success that it took them right through both world wars in the first half of the twentieth century. Until the mid-1920s success was based on providing quality goods by mail order to the isolated American farmers. 'Satisfaction guaranteed or your money back' remained critical to success. But the change in markets brought about by and an increased car ownership among farmers and other social factors made the company switch their emphasis from distribution by mail order to retail stores in cities. Thus, Sears served the car owners travelling from outside the city as well as those living in the city with limited purchasing power.

location of existing inventory, delivery system, and other physical facilities such as warehouse equipment.

Following the assessment of external conditions and an internal evaluation of the firm's resources, it is possible to establish goals (Kotler, 1997). For existing firms, instead of establishing goals, the revision of goals would be the next step. In either case, at this point the retailer knows where the store is going or wants to go. On this basis, it begins to formulate its retail marketing strategy. Clearly defined retail targets and specific positioning goals are necessary prerequisites for effective planning.

As the plan is put in place, control systems will be introduced to monitor the effectiveness of the plan. Due to the wide range of types of retailing organisation, control methods vary – from systems using calculated risks, to rigid and costly operations involving total control. Although this chapter makes some comments on the total control systems in retailing, the focus is on some specific key areas of control, in particular: inventory control, accounting control, budget control, and control of sales transactions with an electronic sales-recording system. The purpose of this chapter is to explain, in as simple terms as possible, what marketing planning is and how the process works, before going on to explain the key elements of retail marketing control.

The retail marketing plan

The need for planning is now almost universally accepted by managers. The use of such plans has a number of benefits, some of which are: consistency, responsibility, communication and commitment. These benefits are presented in summary form in Table 14.1.

The most important points to bear in mind are: there is not one system of planning but many systems; not one style but many styles; and a **planning process** must be tailor-made for a particular retailer in a specific set of circumstances.

Table 14.1
THE BENEFITS OF PLANNING

Benefit	Explanation
Consistency	The individual action plans need to be consistent with the overall corporate plan, and with the other departmental or functional plans which should be in place elsewhere in the organisation. The action plans should also be consistent with those of previous years, reducing mismanagement.
Responsibility	Those who have responsibility for implementing the individual parts of the marketing plan will know what their responsibilities are and their performance may be monitored against these responsibilities. It is unwise to load an individual with too much work. Monitoring devices put in place should be able to identify how individuals could be more effectively used.
Communication	All those involved in implementing the plans will also know what the overall objectives are, together with the assumptions which lie behind them, and what the context for each of the detailed activities is.
Commitment	Once the plans have been agreed with all those involved in their implementation, as well as with those who will provide the resources, group commitment to their implementation should be stimulated.

The planning process

The planning process can be divided into three discrete yet interlinked steps. The first step is a statement of the retail mission which answers the fundamental question: 'What business am I in?'. From this, objectives are established to answer the question: 'Where do I want to go?'. The statement of objectives will naturally lead to a series of strategies for achieving those objectives, thus answering the third question: 'How do I get there?' (Abell, 1980). These strategies will relate first to target markets. Once it has been decided who the target customer is, retail marketing mix strategies are developed to meet the needs of those customers in terms of merchandise, price, location, promotion, level of service, store atmosphere, and so on.

In most major retail organisations 'strategic planning' is an annual process, typically covering only the year immediately ahead. Occasionally, in a few large retail organisations, strategic planning may look at a practical plan which stretches three or more years ahead. To be most effective, the plan has to be formalised, usually in written form – presented as a formal retail marketing plan. This is a process which typically follows a number of distinct steps. The essence of the process is that it moves from the general to the specific; from the overall objectives of the organisation down to the individual action plan for a part of one retail marketing programme. It is also an iterative process so that the draft output of each stage is checked to see what impact it has on the earlier stages – and is amended accordingly (McDonald, 1989).

The corporate plan

The starting point for the retail marketing plan, and the context within which it is set, is the **corporate plan**. In most retail organisations the contents of the corporate plan will closely match those of the retail marketing plan itself, but will also include the plans for the disposition of the other internal resources of the retail organisation (McGoldrick, 1990).

The corporate plan will set out to answer the three questions posed earlier in the planning process laid out above: Where is the organisation now? Where does the organisation intend to go in the future? How will it organise its resources to get there? The first category is intimately involved with the customers. In retail marketing terms, although there are many other factors to take into account, the most important definition of where the firm is revolves around where the firm is in the market (and hence where it is with its consumers). The same is also largely true of the second stage. No matter how much its managers may wish otherwise, where the company can realistically expect to go is ultimately in the hands of its customers. There are many recommended approaches to such planning, but Figure 14.1 is a

Fig. 14.1 THE STEPS IN STRATEGIC RETAIL MARKETING PLANNING PROCESS

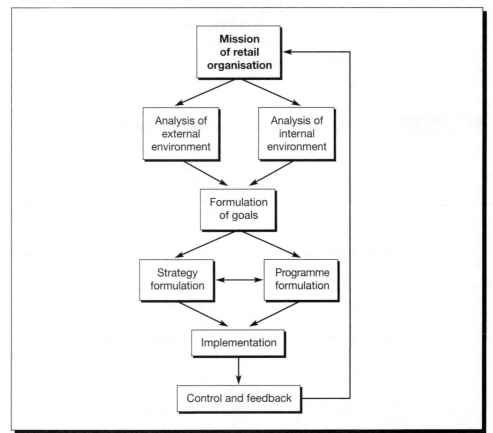

typical example of such a process. It is usual that corporate planning starts with the examination of the **corporate mission** and **strategic options** available to retailers in pursuing their mission.

Corporate mission and strategic options

Corporate missions

Behind the corporate objectives, which in themselves offer the main context for the retail marketing plan, lies the 'corporate mission'; which, in turn, provides the context for the corporate objectives. This corporate mission may be thought of as a definition of what the retail organisation is – a definition of what it does. The mission could be defined as 'what the firm plans to accomplish in the markets in which it will compete for the customers it wants to serve'.

The definition should not be narrow or it will constrain freedom and limit the development of the organisation; a too rigorous concentration on a mission such as 'We are in the business of making mens wear', for example, may restrain the business's development into other areas. On the other hand, it should not be too wide or it will become meaningless. The components of a mission statement are likely to include overall aspirations for sales growth, market share, net profit, return on investment, and/or cash flow. Although mission statements tend to be concerned mostly with economic aspects, increasing numbers of retailers are including social or moral elements – in terms of service either to their customers or to the wider community in which they operate.

Exhibit 14.1 | **Expanding corporate mission statements into ethical spheres**

Marks & Spencer have backed up this type of social/moral commitment with a range of community projects, and several retailers are now engaged in various forms of sponsorships both in the United Kingdom and worldwide. Some retail organisations are very guarded about revealing their corporate mission, whereas others such as J. Sainsbury, and Kwik Save, use it to inspire confidence, create share values, and generate goodwill.

The definition in the corporate mission statement should cover three dimensions: customer groups to be served, customer needs to be served, and technologies to be utilised. Thus, the definition of International Business Machines's (IBM's) corporate mission during the 1940s was: 'we are in the business of handling accounting information [customer need] for the larger US organisations [customer group] by means of punched cards [technology]'. Fortunately, as the name itself indicates, IBM already had a wider perspective and its corporate mission has since been modified to cover its worldwide operations.

Corporate vision

Perhaps the most important factor in successful retail marketing is the **corporate vision of the business**. If the retail organisation as a whole – and its chief executive in particular – has a strong vision of where its future lies, then there is a good chance that the organisation will achieve a strong position in its markets and attain that future (Mercer, 1996). This will be not least because its strategies will be consistent, and will be supported by its staff at all levels. In this context, the success of both Tesco and Sainsbury in the UK grocery market reflect the success all of their retail marketing activities, which are underpinned by their philosophy of customer service.

What a worthwhile vision consists of is open to debate but successful visions tend to be associated with strong, charismatic leaders. The vision must be relevant to the market if it is to be successful. The problem for some retailers is that their vision is often unrelated to their markets.

Exhibit 14.2 | **Corporate visions must match markets**

Alan Sugar's concentration on putting together cheap electronic packages and Clive Sinclair's flair for identifying innovative technologies, for example, had much too narrow a scope of vision. Such visions may be successful only while they approximate to market needs. Alan Sugar's vision moved from being a major advantage to being an overwhelming disadvantage because of the shift in market demand for personal computers.

A retail organisation usually begins with the customers and their needs, not with a selling skill. Given the customer's needs the firm develops backwards, first concerning itself with the physical delivery of customer satisfactions. Then it moves back further to creating the things by which these satisfactions are achieved. Adopting a wide business perspective has helped many organisations to appreciate better how they could develop (Levitt, 1986).

Exhibit 14.3 | **BMW's marketing plan and its success in a chosen market**

BMW is an example of a company with a well-formed strategy and a balanced marketing plan. BMW cars compete in the upper end of the executive car market and, in all aspects of their marketing approach, BMW promote the technical excellence, quality engineering and reliability of their product. By pitching their effort directly at a particular market sector which aspires to ownership of a BMW, price has become relatively insignificant in comparison to the product appeal and its promotion. The average lead time in 1990 for delivery of their 5-Series car was about three to four months, yet orders kept rolling in. The promoted features of the BMW product far outweighed any marginal price benefit so heavily featured in promotional campaigns by the other mainstream motor car manufacturers.

Some organisations have taken the process very literally, as is illustrated in Exhibit 14.4.

Exhibit 14.4   **Freddie Laker's short-term strategy**

Laker Airways, 'the people's airline', arrived with the spectacular low-priced, no frills, transatlantic fare and departed a few years later in 1982 in an equally spectacular liquidation. Laker's strategy was short term and based on low price. The undoubted weakness of such a strategy was the inevitable threat from the major international airlines.

The lesson to be learned from Laker is that any low-price dominated strategy, lacking insufficient product features on which a marketing plan can be based, is highly vulnerable to forces beyond its own control – such as well-resourced and determined competition.

Specifically in relation to retail marketing, the concept of product market strategy suggests various directions in which the company may consider moving in order to increase or sustain growth. Some of these 'growth vectors' are involved in the development or **diversification** of the product assortment, whereas others involve concentration upon the existing assortment. Whichever of the strategic alternatives the retailer decides to follow, the aim is usually to provide consumers with choice in breadth or in depth, unless the retailer is in the unusual position of being able to offer both. Retailers, of course, are not restricted to internal expansion or diversification; acquisitions and mergers have played a significant part in helping some retailers to accomplish their objectives.

Corporate strategic options

It is not possible for a retail organisation to stand still because it must adapt to changes with the environment if it is to thrive. In its simplest form, growth can be achieved by pursuing a number of different routes (as presented in Table 14.2) based on the company's aims and objectives. Growth may be described in terms of the merchandise offered and the customer chosen as the target market.

Market penetration strategy

This strategy is aimed at increasing market share. It has been pursued very successfully by Tesco and Sainsbury in the grocery retailing sector, where increase in market share has been won at the expense of direct competitors such as the discount stores and the regional Co-operative stores.

Merchandise development

There is a limit to the growth which can be achieved by a **market penetration strategy** and most retailers pursuing growth will look to add new merchandise to appeal to customers in order to generate extra sales. **Merchandise development** is a way of adding new products to the existing lines in order to generate extra sales. This

Table 14.2

PRODUCT-MARKET SCOPE AND GROWTH VECTOR ALTERNATIVES

Markets	Products				
	Present products	Improvement in present products	New products with related technology		New product with unrelated technology
			Assortment manipulation lines	Expansion of product	
Consumption markets: Same market	(1) Market penetration strategies	(3) Reformulating strategies	(5) Replacement strategies	(7) Product line extension strategies	(9) Horizontal diversification strategies
New markets	(2) Market development strategies	(4) Market extension strategies	(6) Market segmentation/ product differentiation strategies	(8) Concentric diversification strategies	(10) Conglomerate diversification strategies
Resource and distribution markets	(11) Forward and/ or backward integration strategies				

strategy has been pursued successfully by Marks & Spencer, who moved into food retailing, and Sainsbury, who moved into financial services (McGoldrick, 1990).

Market development

This strategy may be pursued in terms of new customers and in terms of **market development**. New customers may be sought in geographical areas not currently served by the company: for example, Marks & Spencer's move into Europe and Aldi's expansion into the UK. Market development, on the other hand, may involve attracting new customers in the same geographical area. This approach has been used by a number of retail organisations with varying degrees of success; Curry's, for example, have attempted to appeal to the discount-oriented customer with their out-of-town electrical discount stores.

The difficulty is that if the product remains the same but a new group of customers is being sought, some other element of the retail marketing mix has to be changed to appeal to them. As in the case of Curry's price may be the variable which changed. MFI, in an attempt to move upmarket, changed its location and modified its store image to reflect the nature of its new target customer segment.

Diversification

Many retail organisations rush headlong into diversification into new markets without fully exploiting the market for their existing products and services. Most retailers diversify because of domestic market saturation. In the UK, for example, the food multiple Sainsbury's has set up a chain of do-it-yourself stores called Homebase. Similarly, a number of French hypermarket groups have gone into fast-food retailing. Although potentially attractive, there are many pitfalls to look out for including: extension (even over-extension) of resources; less attention to the existing business; the necessity of making cultural changes; and the high cost of investment – usually followed by a slow return on capital employed (ROCE). Success is achieved by consistently promoting and developing existing and improved products in present and extended markets. Diversification should be carefully selected, planned, controlled and, in general, be a last resort – entered into when all other development options have been exhausted.

After the development of strategic options, the retailer should then embark upon developing a retail marketing plan by conducting the marketing audit.

The retail marketing planning audit

The first formal step in the retail marketing planning process is that of conducting the marketing audit. Ideally, at the time of producing the retail marketing plan, this should involve bringing together the source material which has already been collected throughout the year – as part of the normal work of the retail marketing department. The **retail marketing audit** may 'be defined as a systematic, critical and impartial review and appraisal of the total marketing operation of the basic objectives and policies of the operation and the assumptions which underlie them as well as of the methods, procedures, personnel, and organisation employed to implement the policies and achieve the objectives (Samli, 1989). Thus, a marketing audit is both a diagnostic and a prognostic tool. It differs from continuous control in that it takes a snapshot of the whole organisation together, along with all interrelationships, during the same period. In contrast continuous control, attempting to adjust both the **internal environment** and **the external environment** of the retail establishment, will appraise different segments of the marketing functions at different times. The retail manager who is involved in auditing needs a lot of experience to make the many required subjective judgements. These judgements are necessary because many aspects of retail marketing activities cannot be quantified as they are in a financial audit.

When a marketing system is being audited, the first item that needs to be reviewed is the basic organisation of the overall retailing entity. This would entail taking an opposite view of the retailing structure, which will point out how responsibilities are delegated compared with what should be involved in each job. After all responsibilities are properly assessed, each job is checked for general efficiency and effectiveness within the overall retail structure. The second component of the system audit is information. Chapter 13 discusses retail information management systems and so on in some depth so little needs be added here. Suffice it to say that the system must provide timely, accurate, and necessary information for the decision-making process. The information must be generated by a formal system which must also be tailored to the needs of the retailer.

The third component of the system audit is planning. This element, again, needs to be formalised with a structural schedule indicating the details of what is to take place and who is to be responsible during the time period when the events occur. This element is expected to provide proper evaluation and adjustments during the planning process, along with proper time constraints. Planning is, of course, related to the company's objectives and strategies. The marketing system audit in retailing must analyse and verify the previous objectives and strategies. Furthermore, it must examine the previous strategies to see whether or not they have been effective and are consistent with the company's objectives. This activity is particularly difficult since all of the audit components mentioned here have to be examined qualitatively.

The retail marketing audit as it is proposed in this chapter attempts to accomplish something else – to go a step further. It aims to provide a diagnostic and prognostic tool by bringing the critical variables together to assess the overall health of the organisation (Omar, 1994). Since the retailing process is multidimensional and complex, its multidimensionality must be taken into account so that the **control function** and related corrective action may eventually be facilitated. Table 14.3 shows the components of such a comprehensive marketing audit.

Table 14.3
SELECTED CHARACTERISTICS OF RETAIL MARKET AUDITS

Major areas of market knowledge	Technical aspects of the market	Product line characteristics
Economy	**Distribution**	**Product Lines**
Trading area	Trade associations	Special customer
Demographics	Government organisations	requirements
Political environment	Official regulations	Fashion trends
Historical factors and trends	Manufacturers' distribution	New product sources
Economic conditions	policies	Competitors' product mixes
	The wholesale system	
Market	Normal trade practices	**Product Features**
Size in units and value		Weights and measures
Growth trends	**Finance**	Quality and quantity
Scope of products	Availability of credit	Official regulation
Key factors influencing the	Attitude of lending firms	requirements
market	Status of consumer credit	Labelling
Market share	Availability of creative	Available materials
	financing	New technology
Customers		Substitute products
Who are the primary targets?	**Competition**	Replacement products
Who are the secondary	Major competitors	
groups?	Size of competition	
Who influences buying	Competitors' market images	
decisions?	Market coverage	
Store's image vs self-image	Market share	
	Marketing practices	
	Strong and weak points	

If the multidimensionality factor is to be used as a key source of understanding and assessing the store's status, then a carefully developed retail marketing audit may be extremely important, again for diagnostic and prognostic reasons (Omar, 1994). When the retailer's multiple dimensions are analysed simultaneously, certain types of irregularities or problem areas may be uncovered which would not necessarily be the case if these dimensions were not analysed simultaneously (Samli, 1989).

MINI-CASE **Periodic retail marketing audits may warn of dangers ahead**

Consider, for instance, the following cases which will be revealed only if multiple dimensions of the retail store are considered.

Store A has a well-recognised, well-respected, and well-frequented men's clothing store. The trading area within which it has been functioning is growing, competition has remained the same, and the store's marketing practices and volume have been steady. However, in terms of a growing market, further analysis indicates that while the store's marketing practices have remained the same, the store's customer profiles have changed radically. Both old customers and new additions to the market have been going out of town to shop because the present market – and particularly the store – do not satisfy the changed needs.

Store B has been in the central area of a small town for a long time. It is a discount department store. Although the town has been growing, Store B has not had its share of this growth. When its regular clientele is analysed against the changing population of the immediate area, it becomes obvious that the marketing practices of the store have been geared to the old clientele which, as a whole, is getting smaller. Examinations of the financial and sales situations are relatively reassuring in that they do not indicate that the problem is nearly as serious as it actually is. The change in the market, customer needs, and emerging competition in shopping centres at the edge of the town indicate a more drastic change than the financial and sales pictures have indicated. The impact is likely to be felt very soon and very drastically if the store management takes no action to reverse the trends highlighted by the audit.

The situations of Store A and Store B indicate that periodic retail marketing auditing is a must for retailers if diagnostic and prognostic planning, control and corrective action are to be facilitated.

Portfolio planning

The coordinated planning of the individual products and services – known as **portfolio planning** – may contribute towards a balanced portfolio being created and maintained. A classic form of such a planning approach is portfolio analysis which was an approach pioneered in the USA by the Boston Consulting Group (BCG). This form of analysis identifies the retailer's strategic business units (SBUs) and represents these on a matrix which considers market growth and related market share (Figure 14.2).

Fig. 14.2 THE BCG PORTFOLIO MATRIX

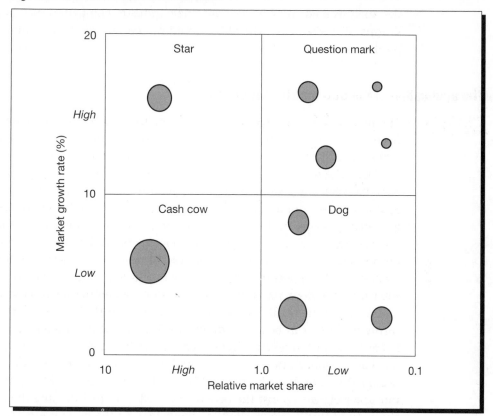

Four business types can be distinguished:

1 **Stars** are those SBUs that have a promising future. Significant investments of cash are necessary to develop their full potential. If managed correctly, they will develop into a valuable source of revenue as the market evolves.

2 **Cash cows** have achieved a high market share in a matured market. They deserve the company's fullest attention because the cash they generate can be invested in newer market areas with high growth potential.

3 **Question marks** (or problem children) pose a problem for management. While the market growth prospects are good, question mark SBUs have a low relative market share. If they are to be moved to the left (that is, if they are to increase their relative market share), substantial investment will be required. Based on the available marketing information, management must use its skill to decide whether such investment could be better employed in supporting other business units (that is, they must balance relative opportunity costs).

4 **Dogs** show no growth potential and their relative market share is low. Although they may not necessarily be a 'drain' on the company's resources, they are unable to make a positive contribution to profits.

The BCG model was originally designed for multi-industry organisations. However, the analysis made may be used by single industry companies such as retail organisations. In such a case, the SBUs would be represented by dominant products or product lines.

The application of the BCG matrix to retailing

The main difference between the Boston matrix and the portfolio matrix lies in the Boston Consulting Group's use of the experience curve (McDonald and Tideman, 1993). Manufacturing costs are reduced proportionately each time production is doubled. The retailer is, however, not in the business of manufacturing. The difference between the two matrices lies, therefore, in the star sector. Products in the Boston's star quadrant may be cash absorbers, as they are being financed in order to gain market share. In the retail Star sector, products are high generators of revenue. The cash generated may not be required for reinvestment but may be used for other purposes such as store expansion or general promotional activities. The cost of the retail star is the opportunity cost forgone in allocating the product to a prime display site within the store, plus the cost of the associated promotional activity.

The dog of the retail matrix similarly differs slightly. The dog from the manufacturing portfolio can be a cash drain in this sector when the reinvestment required is greater than the revenue generated. The retailing dog may not be a cash drain, but has an opportunity cost associated with it. This is the cost of the shelf space occupied by the dog which could be used by another product. This opportunity must be weighed against the benefits derived from maintaining the product in the store. All of this is summarised in Figure 14.3. In the description of the retail store model, only the product level has been discussed. The argument for product groups and departments is similar, but a product group or department in the dog sector is more serious than a product in this sector.

Every effort should be made to readjust the product mix of the products within these four categories so that their performance is improved. The retail matrix does not offer the ultimate solution to merchandise management. The matrix does, however, act as an indicator to the performance of a product, product groups and departments. Any final decision must be based on qualitative information. This matrix can be a most useful tool to buyers and merchandisers as they work together on the balance of the products within the store and on planning future policies. Retailers could use these basic concepts in their merchandising mix, and amend and apply the new analytical tools to help buying managers develop long-range marketing plans for different categories of merchandise, with extremely interesting results. Figure 14.2 shows the categories of merchandise used in the portfolios at their several levels of disaggregation; Figure 14.4 shows the data in graphical form at the highest level of merchandise aggregation at the national level.

This kind of application leads to a number of interesting questions, which arise automatically, depending on where the location of the circle representing the product positions is (*see* Figure 14.4). These questions include issues relating to the

Fig. 14.3 THE PORTFOLIO MATRIX FOR A RETAIL BUSINESS

Star High cash generators requiring a prime site in the store in order to attract custom. May be unstable especially if a fashion item.	**Wildcat** Product new to the store requires shelf space and promotion in order to become established. Small cash generator.
Cash cow A steady cash generator and occupies secondary shelf space. Little or no promotion required.	**Dog** Small cash generator. Possible candidate for deleation but may be supporting a product in the star or cash cow sectors. Occupying valuable shelf space.

positioning of merchandise in the store, pricing, promotion and range content. Of these, the most important relates to the future marketing policy – both for individual items of merchandise and for whole categories. Additionally, the three major considerations are: what customers expect from the store, what is happening in the external market, and what the level of profitability is.

Fig. 14.4 PRODUCT PORTFOLIO MATRIX – PRODUCT RANGE (NATIONAL LEVEL)

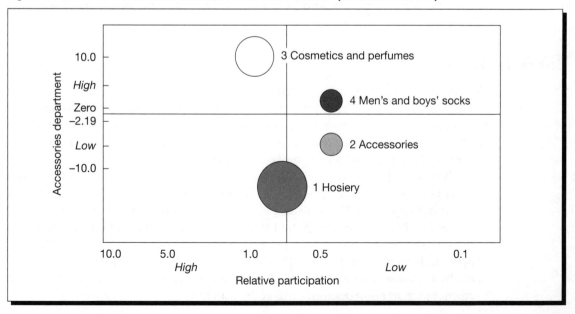

It is clear that such an approach provides little more than a visual representation of a retailer's statistics and – like all management aids – does not actually tell the alert management anything they do not already know. Its real value lies in the clarity and the analytical depth and creativity with which it is applied. Certainly the managers who have used it to develop retail marketing plans have found it to be an extremely valuable aid to marketing diagnosis and clarity of strategic thinking. There is much research still to be done, however, before any valid claims of validity as a management tool can be made with confidence. It may be regarded meanwhile as a form of strengths, weaknesses, opportunities, and threats **(SWOT) analysis**.

SWOT analysis

One technique not previously mentioned, but which is particularly useful in the analysis of the information contained in the retail marketing audit, is that of a SWOT (Strengths, Weaknesses, Opportunities, Threats) analysis. Typically seen by retail managers as being the most useful planning tool of all, it groups some of the key pieces of information into two main categories (internal factors and external factors), and then by their dual positive and negative aspects (strengths and opportunities, as the positive aspects; weaknesses and threats representing the negative ones).

Internal factors

Strengths and weaknesses internal to the retail organisation, its strategies and its position in relation to other competing retailers. The internal factors, which may be viewed as strengths or weaknesses depending upon their impact on each retailer's position (they may represent a strength for one organisation but a weakness, in relative terms, for another), may include all of the elements of the retail marketing mix, as well as personnel, finance, and so on.

External factors

These are the opportunities and threats presented by the external environment and the competition. The external factors, which again may be threats to one retail organisation while they offer opportunities to another, may include matters such as technological change, legislation, sociocultural changes and so on, as well as changes in the marketplace or competitive position.

It must be emphasised, however, that SWOT is just one aid to categorisation. It is not, as many retail organisations seem to think, the only technique. It also has weaknesses of its own. It tends to persuade retailers to compile lists rather than think about what is really important to their business. It also presents the resulting lists uncritically, without clear prioritisation; for example, weak opportunities may appear to balance strong threats. The aim of any SWOT analysis should be to isolate the key issues that will be important to the future of the organisation and that subsequent marketing planning will address.

In relation to SWOT analysis, it is essential to spell out assumptions. However, most retailers do not even realise that they make such assumptions. It may be wise to make as few assumptions as possible – and those that have been made should be very carefully explained. The most useful component of this part of the exercise may well be a 'sensitivity analysis' since this determines which factors have the most influence over the outcomes and hence which factors should be most carefully managed.

Retail marketing objectives and strategies

Theodore Levitt (1986) makes the very pertinent comment that 'if you don't know where you are going any road will take you there'. The main job of the chief executive is to know where their company is going. The answer to the question of where the organisation is and should be going depends on where the company has been, what its competences and strengths are, what the competition is doing, what is happening in society at large, and what is happening in the consumers' collective enigmatic mind. Only by considering the economic mission of the retail organisation and by having a full knowledge of the situation can the objectives be formulated, and only by formulating objectives can clear paths ahead be determined for the retailer.

Retail marketing objectives

Objectives and goals state the results that the retailer wishes to achieve. They translate the corporate mission into specific performance standards for retail managers. Retailers usually set their objectives in terms of financial performance (profit), market position (sales, market share), or productivity (stock turnover, sales per square foot). Retail organisations rarely have a single objective. The maximisation of profit is never the objective of any retailer, and exists only in the model of reality created by economists in order to create a situation which theoretically holds all other possibilities static. That there are a variety of shareholders in an organisation means the retailer will be almost certain to have objectives in relation to the vast majority of them, or at least the organisation will examine its objectives in relation to the effect of achievement upon the various shareholders.

Organisation versus personal objectives

Retail organisation consists of the people who are part of it, and individuals within the organisation will either be formed into groups (by the organisation structure created within the organisation) or form themselves into groups (often of an informal nature) determined by a congruence of interest created by their employment situation. In addition to group interests will exist the **personal objectives** of individuals: to seek promotion, to lead a quiet life, etc. All of these personal or group objectives will create aspirations or set goals, which may either conflict with, or be furthered by, the objectives established by the organisation.

The objectives of the organisation must, therefore, be motivational in character. An individual or a group are more likely to be motivated positively if the actions they are expected to perform in relation to company objectives are positively correlated to personal objectives: for example most efforts at creating a salesforce compensation plan – with commissions, bonuses, prizes, etc. – are an attempt to reconcile, and, if possible, integrate company and personal objectives.

Criteria and validity of objectives

Retail marketing objectives provide the basis for monitoring the retailer's actions and evaluating the firm's performance. The firm's actual results must be compared against its stated objectives (Omar, 1994). These objectives are the yardsticks for measuring how well the retailer is actually performing. For this reason, the retailer must translate the general objectives into specific goals that are measurable in terms of time, realistic in terms of resources, and consistent with each other.

Time

Retail marketing objectives are valid only if they are expressed in time terms since there is no pressure to achieve an objective which is stated without time limit. Similarly if there is an interlinking of objectives, where any one of them is stated without a time limit all may become unenforceable or unachievable. We must accept, therefore, that the need to establish time limits will act as a constraint upon the setting of objectives. An objective may be unattainable in the time available and, as a result, it may be necessary to establish intermediate objectives.

The extent to which time may act as a constraint on the setting of objectives may also be affected by the availability of resources. An organisation can often overcome the problem of reaching an objective in limited time by allocating more resources to its achievement. Here, however, a balance must be struck. To allocate additional resources to the achievement of an objective which has a relatively low priority could be unjustified, but it may be essential if achievement of that particular objective is essential to the achievement of the remainder of the plans.

Resources

Following on from the discussion on time limits, it is clear that objectives must be firmly linked to the resources available for their achievement. Thus we may see that objectives themselves are firmly linked to the plans formulated for their achievement or the plans which necessarily follow from the acceptance of an objective. No organisation could, for example, set itself the objective of ensuring that in one year's time its food products shall be on display in every grocery outlet in the UK if it does not have, or cannot obtain, the resources needed to establish a nationwide salesforce calling upon all food retail outlets. This is usually an area where companies fail in their planning. Objectives are set without regard to resources and the vain attempts to achieve the objective not only fail in this respect but also cause the whole operation to become twisted and distorted from the original intention. One of the major areas of failure here is to attempt to achieve objectives for which the managerial resources are unsuitable or lacking in competence.

Alternatives

The setting of objectives must always be accompanied by the setting of alternatives. There is always more than one way of achieving a goal, as is indicated in Exhibit 14.5.

Exhibit 14.5 | **Alternative approaches to achieving targeted increases**

An increase in the return on capital can be achieved either by selling more profitably or by reducing the level of investment. Similarly, an increase in sales turnover can be achieved either by selling more units at the same price or by selling the same number of units at a higher price.

In a competitive situation, action to achieve an objective is generally likely to provoke reaction from competitors. It is part of the analysis of the environment in which the objectives are established to attempt to forecast the possible or likely reaction of competitors. The extent to which such forecasts are possible will permit the selection of alternative strategies that will lead to achievement of the objective.

Objectives versus the retail structure

In establishing the objectives the existing retail structure must be examined to ensure that it is compatible with the attainment of the objectives. It may be necessary to amend the structure, or the responsibilities of individuals in it, to ensure that the objective can be reached. If such an amendment is not possible, it may be necessary to amend the objectives.

It is likely that the task of carrying out the retail marketing objectives will fall to people at the lowest level of the retailer's marketing hierarchy – as is usually the case, the fire is extinguished not by the chief fire officer but by the team of firemen who play a hose on the blazing house. The construction of an efficient retail marketing organisation, therefore, involves the setting up of an operative staff and superimposing on that staff a supervisory staff capable of influencing the operative group towards a pattern of coordinated effective behaviour. The executive who has the task of setting objectives must, therefore, take into account that the actions following from the objectives are to be executed by the retail organisation. If the objectives and their action needs are incompatible with the organisation their performance will fail.

Retail marketing strategies

A strategy may be described as a pattern or plan that integrates an organisation's major goals, policies and action sequences into a cohesive whole. Retail marketing strategies can be seen as the means by which retail marketing objectives may be achieved.

A strategy describes how the objectives will be achieved. The mixed elements are a useful framework for deciding how the retailer's resources will be manipulated (strategically) to achieve the objectives. The focus of the strategies must be the objectives to be achieved. The strategy statement may take the form of a purely verbal description of the strategic options which have been chosen. Alternatively, and perhaps more positively, it might include a structured list of the major options chosen. One aspect of strategy which is often overlooked is that of timing. Exactly when it is the best time for each element of the strategy to be implemented is often critical; taking the right action at the wrong time can sometimes be almost as bad as taking the wrong action at the right time. Timing is, therefore, an essential part of any plan and should normally appear as a schedule of planned activities. Having completed this crucial stage of the planning process, the feasibility of the objectives and strategies in terms of market share, sales, costs, profits and so on, which these demand in practice, will require re-evaluation and control action.

The retail marketing control process

Control is a vital aspect of implementing retail marketing plans, whether strategic or operational. It helps to ensure that activities happen as planned, with proper management. It also provides important feedback that enables managers to determine whether or not their decisions, actions and strategies are working appropriately in practice. The **retail marketing control process** is thus central to all marketing efforts.

Strategic control takes a broad, long-term view, considering whether the overall retail marketing strategy is actually driving the organisation in the desired direction. This is normally assessed through the retail marketing audit process and is often conducted on an annual basis, either as a special *ad hoc* process or as part of the retail marketing planning cycle. Operational control takes a shorter-term view, checking whether detailed, functional marketing programmes are actually working in practice. These checks may take place on a daily basis if necessary, and should certainly happen frequently enough to determine whether problem areas are developing. Operational control needs to pick up problems early, before too much damage is done, so that corrective action can be taken more easily. Designing an effective control system to suit the needs and characteristics of the organisation is a critical part of managing retail marketing effort.

Setting targets

When setting performance targets for retailing activities, however, it is important to ensure that they are realistic, that they can be measured and that the measurement criteria used are meaningful and relevant. This is especially important where managers' performance is, in part, judged by their achievement of the agreed targets. Typical measures might be sales volume or value, the number of new customers visiting the store, the number of enquiries generated, **stock turnover**, and relative market share. The retail information management systems (RIMS) considered in Chapter 13 should provide the essential flow of information that enables performance to be measured as well as highlighting emerging problem areas. This flow of data must, therefore, be timely and sufficiently detailed to allow deeper analysis.

As soon as the control mechanism shows that a gap is opening between proposed targets and actual achievement, managers should start to look for reasons why this is happening. Sometimes the reasons are obvious, for example, a stockout in a particular store or the loss of a major customer; in other situations, however, further research may have to be commissioned to support deeper analysis of the underlying causes. If, for example, a brand's market share continues to decline despite increased marketing effort, managers should start asking serious questions about customer responsiveness and the brand's competitive positioning.

Decision on corrective action

Unless managers can be sure why performance is missing the target, they cannot reliably define the right corrective actions. In some cases they might decide that no corrective action needs to be taken, in others they might devise a programme of major or minor changes to bring the retail marketing strategy back on track. Where the problem is that of stockout, the solution may be obvious; however, if brand share is declining unexpectedly, a fairly radical revision of the brand's marketing strategy may be called for. Failure to achieve targets does not, however, mean automatic condemnation of the marketing plan and its manager. It could be that targets were hopelessly optimistic, in the light of the emerging market conditions; alternatively, other departments within the organisations, for example buying or logistics, may have failed to achieve their targets.

Managers should, however, be wary of overreaction. A certain amount of deviation is to be expected since no forward plan can be absolutely right. Part of the planning process is to agree what the threshold is between tolerable and intolerable deviation. Real customers buying real products in a real competitive market do not necessarily behave predictably and therefore some flexibility and patience should be exercised. There is also sometimes a time lag between implementing marketing action and seeing the results of that action. Declaring a crisis and taking corrective action too soon may well be counterproductive (Mercer, 1996). If, however, a major event happens that represents discontinuous change, corrective action may have to be taken long before its effects start to show in the computer printouts.

Retail marketing control functions

The concept of control implies a process of taking steps to bring actual results and desired results closer together. Figure 14.5 illustrates this concept. As can be seen, analysis of retail functions is partially based on feedback of actual results. This analysis is used to formulate retail marketing plans (desired results). The desired results of

Fig. 14.5 THE CONTROL MECHANISM

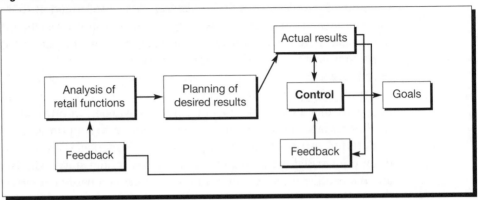

this plan are then measured against actual results through a control process which again obtains its information through the feedback mechanism. Thus, the control function attempts to bring the actual results closer to goals. To carry out this control function, systematic monitoring of both the internal and external environments of the store must be carried out and the necessary adjustments subsequently made. The general control function, therefore, has two major components: systematic monitoring and adjusting. Monitoring is achieved by the retail marketing audit (discussed above) whereas adjustment implies continuing efforts to bring actual and desired results closer together. The internal environment of the firm is controllable and includes all items within the retail establishment and its legal reach. On the other hand, the external environment is beyond the control of the organisation and includes historical, economic and political factors. Most retailers are concerned only with the monitoring and auditing of financial aspects, and turnover.

Financial analysis of product and product lines

In retailing, being able to determine the relative contribution of each product to the overall profit picture is essential. Only when the relative contributions are known is it possible to delete, revise, expand or combine product lines. Since on average there are too many individual products to be considered in the retailing situation, highly developed computerised record-keeping systems have facilitated the measurement of product contribution to sales and profit. The contribution approach is valuable because it enables the auditors to determine which products actually contribute to fixed costs, instead of allocating all costs and just looking at the net profit line.

Financial control

Purely financial concepts that are used for continuous audit and **financial control** include current assets, current debt, fixed assets, funded debt, net profit, net sales, net working capital, and tangible net worth. These criteria, both in isolation and in conjunction with others, provide information about the financial health of the retailer. Financial criteria used in conjunction with other retailing indicators include the collection period, inventory, net sales to inventory, turnover of new working capital, and turnover of tangible net worth. On the basis of these criteria, it is possible to develop a retail cash management programme that sets up the parameters for control and corrective action.

Gross margin return on merchandise investment (GMROMI)

The **GMROMI** is a relatively new technique that allows the retail manager to evaluate the profitability of numerous merchandise lines with different 'operating cycles' or investment requirements. Gross margin percentage is multiplied by a comprehensive turnover factor that incorporates accounts receivable in addition to inventory investment (Samli, 1989). The product of these two ratios is a measure of return on gross merchandise investment by a leverage factor, which is the ratio of (inventory plus accounts receivable) to (inventory plus accounts receivable) minus accounts payable (*see* Figure 14.6). This ratio indicates the extent of supplier financing received by the retailer. The denominator of this leverage ratio can be called the new merchandise investment of the retailer. The final product in this case is GMROMI. This particular measure clearly states that the principal financial objective in managing merchandise investments should be the gross margin return on owned merchandise assets, and it delineates three major paths in achieving this objective: increased gross margin, increased turnover in receivables and inventory, and increased leverage. Furthermore, this new measure underscores the need to focus on gross margin management of accounts payable. The GMROMI closely approximates the working capital investment of the retailer, and it provides a powerful framework for managing finances in retailing operations.

Fig. 14.6 GROSS MARGIN RETURN ON MERCHANDISE INVESTMENT (GMROMI)

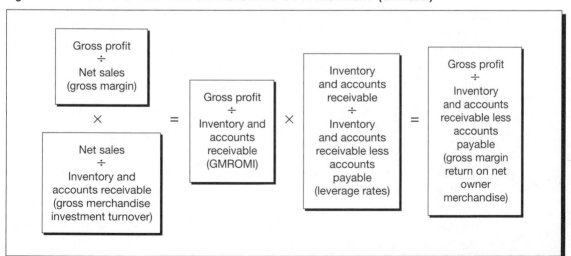

The concept of stock turnover

The concept of turnover rate is an approximation of the speed at which a given amount of merchandise is sold and replenished. Typically, an attempt is made to determine how many times the average inventory is turned over during a given year. Not all types of merchandise handled by the retailer have the same inventory turnover rates.

In general, pricing policies tend to follow a simple formula: products or product lines which have a high turnover rate are priced lower (a smaller mark-up is applied) than those with a low turnover rate, which are given a higher percentage mark-up. In this pricing process, those products with a low mark-up will have reduced profit margins, while those products with a high mark-up will have a higher profit margin. At some convenience stores and fast-food places, some across-the-board mark-up policy is practised. In these cases, adjusting the mark-up and the price to the turnover rate enhances the firm's overall profit structure.

Merchandise management audit

The merchandise management audit is another audit system in retail operation. Two sets of criteria are used in a merchandise management audit: qualitative criteria and quantitative criteria. Qualitative criteria explore at least three areas:

1 It must be decided if the product or products in question represent the image of the store. Here not only the past and present but also the future must be considered. Although a product or product line has been quite appropriate for the store image in the past, it may become inappropriate for the projected future image.

2 The merchandise management audit must ascertain whether the product or product line is in demand in all of the stores or whether there are variations in style and/or price points. Strategically, the answer to this question can substantially increase the efficiency of operations.

3 Even a product or product line is unprofitable, the decision to drop it is not automatic. It must first be checked whether competitors carry the products in question; if so, a decision must be made as to whether the store must also carry this product so that the store image will not be tarnished.

Quantitative criteria must also explore at least the following four areas:

1 Stability of demand for the product or product line must be determined.

2 The criteria to maximise the volume of sales must be established. The volumes needed and the frequency at which they should be purchased have to be decided.

3 In the case of seasonal products, the purchase date must be decided. When should the peak stocks be explored and when should elimination (if any) of stocks take place?

4 Space conditions must be examined to determine whether they allow adequate representation for each item of stock.

Much of a merchandise management audit is related to various types of ratios and merchandise lists. Since these lists provide basic constraints for a well-balanced merchandise offering for the store, they can serve as the chief criteria for planning the control function and particularly for taking corrective action. Among these lists, three are particularly common:

■ basic stock lists – these include the items that have stable sales or are fairly predictable;

■ model stock lists – these are constructed for certain shopping type goods and fashions;

■ never-out lists – these contain the key items and best-sellers. In most cases, these items become extremely important in the overall image of the store.

These pure merchandise management audit techniques combined with financial audit techniques provide a great depth of information that can be an effective part of a control and corrective action process. Certainly, each store will benefit from developing its own specific measures and using them periodically if not continuously.

Continuous controls for retailing

The continuous control function is illustrated in Figure 14.7. This illustration is a revised version of Figure 14.5, providing an overall perspective on where the control process fits into the retail scheme as a whole. As seen in Figure 14.7, continuous controls replace the feedback with actual adjustments in standards, actual retail functions, actual results and altered goals. This illustration, unlike Figure 14.5, demonstrates that the continuous control function is based on feedback and adjustment mechanisms which operate constantly to maintain control. Without capabilities to make adjustments, the total audit and feedback processes become an exercise in futility.

Fig. 14.7 CONTINUOUS CONTROL FOR RETAILERS

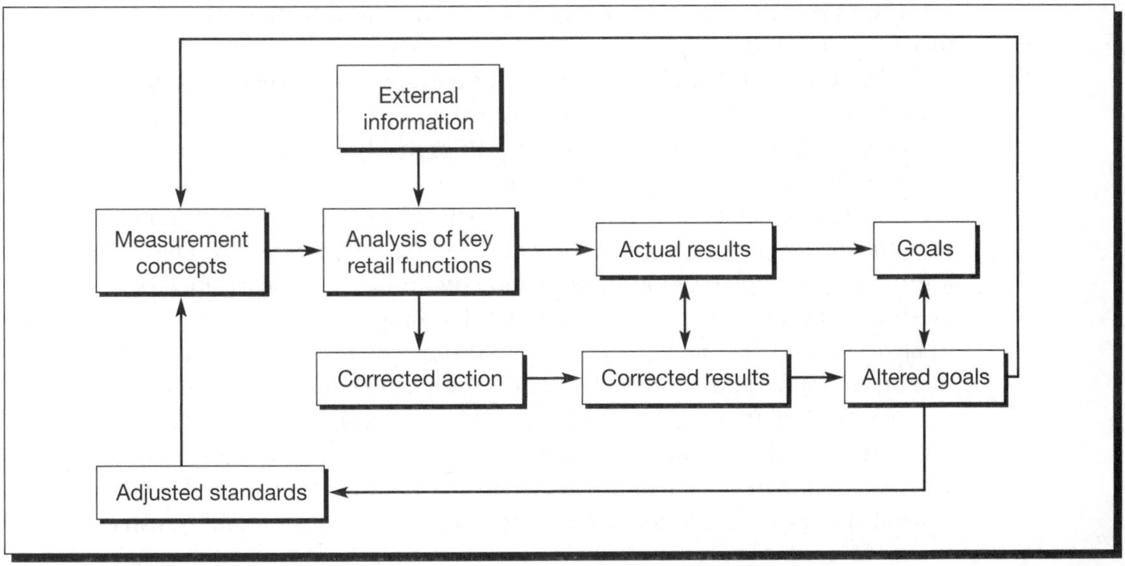

Adjusted standards

Standards state the optimum levels of various elements; they indicate the most desirable quality or quantity of particular aspects of the retail operations. Since the retailing environment is dynamic and continually changing, standards also need to be adjusted continually. Thus, we have the concept of adjusted standards. Two types of adjusted standards are particularly important in retailing. The first is operating standards which are basically quantitative and deal with the lower part of an organisation. The second is appraisal standards, which are basically qualitative and deal with the upper echelons of the organisation.

Standards may be expressed as both input and output data. Input data would include such items as commercials or other promotional methods, the subjective quality achieved in an advertisement, and so on. The output data would include such items as the number of orders placed, the amount of sales, the subjective feedback of compliments from customers, changes in traffic patterns, and so on. These inputs and outputs are usually derived components that are considered during the planning process and the chief findings of the marketing audit. Thus, in order to establish key standards, the basic marketing task along with all of its subcomponents needs to be determined. Research must then indicate how resources should be allocated to each task – that is, what proportion of available resources will be needed to achieve these standards, bearing in mind the relative priority applied to each one. Finally, as has been mentioned previously, the standards that have been establish must be reviewed regularly so that their value to the overall control system will remain the same.

SUMMARY

It is difficult to provide a concise summary of such a long chapter. Indeed, it is arguable that the practical strength of retail marketing comes from its wealth of detailed techniques for handling specific retailing situations. The one requirement is for the focus to be on the customer, and even that rule is, at least in part, broken by conviction marketing.

Defining the total product or service offering is the all-important decision, since almost all other decisions will be derived from it. Thus, techniques, such as segmentation and – in particular – positioning will probably be the most important for the majority of retail organisations. On the other hand, the more mechanistic models, such as the product life cycle and Boston matrix, may be less widely applicable.

In the longer term, changes in the wider external environment will probably be critical to the retail organisation's future and environmental analysis may be a skill that needs to be acquired. In the medium term, the competitive strategy will probably need to be developed. The buying and merchandising systems, and the organisation's messages (promotion and advertising), will be very dependent upon the exact nature of the retailer's activities. Again, however, in-depth knowledge of the exact retail marketing systems employed will be essential. Sales activities may well be more relevant to most retailers than those relating to advertising but the inner market, and quality in general, are important in almost all sectors of the European retail industry.

KEY TERMS	cash cows	GMROMI	retail marketing audit
	control function	internal environment	retail marketing control
	corporate mission	market development	process
	corporate plan	market penetration strategy	retail marketing objectives
	corporate vision	merchandise development	retail marketing planning
	diversification	personal objectives	stars
	dogs	planning process	stock turnover
	external environment	portfolio planning	strategic options
	financial control	question marks	SWOT analysis

ASSIGNMENT

The evaluation of the retailer's marketing and profit objectives consists of a determination of where the retailer should be heading in the future. A clear statement of the retailer's profit objectives is needed. Such a statement may establish a goal of obtaining an annual return on investment of x per cent. Explicit marketing objectives must also be established which will aim to satisfy consumers' needs at a profit. If this is not done, retail outlets can become obsolete quite rapidly as shopping patterns and preferences change.

Task

As a marketing specialist working for a large retailer, advise your organisation on how it could set its retail marketing objectives. These objectives should be measurable, taking time factors and the availability of resources into consideration. Your essay should not be more than 1800 words and should include appropriate examples from the retail industry.

REVISION QUESTIONS

1 The starting point for the retail marketing plan and the context within which it is set is the corporate plan. With the aid of a diagram, describe the contents of a corporate plan and the questions it will set out to answer.

2 The corporate mission may be thought of as a definition of what the retail organisation is, what it does, and so on. Define the term 'corporate mission' and explain the need for its clarity.

3 Several strategic options are open to a retailer who is determined to expand. Briefly discuss these options.

4 What do you consider to be the key characteristics of the retail market audit?

5 The need for retail marketing planning is now almost universally accepted by retail managers. What do you consider to be the benefits of such planning?

6 How would you adapt the BCG matrix to help a retailer to identify alternative strategies?

7 You have been called upon to advise a chain of not-for-profit organisations. How would you determine the target markets using a SWOT analytical method?

8 In the application of the BCG matrix to retailing, some differences between quadrants and product positions may be observed. Discuss these differences.

9 The concept of retail marketing control implies the process of taking steps to bring actual and desired results closer together. How may this process be achieved?

10 The GMROMI is a relatively new technique that allows the retail manager to evaluate the profitability of numerous merchandise lines with different operating cycles. Discuss the process of this method and state its advantages.

CASE STUDY

Gillette's plan to launch Mach3, a three-bladed razor

Gillette unveiled their plans for a new razor in early 1998 with a campaign designed to emphasise its determination to maintain domination of the global wet shave market. The Mach3 razor, according to its advertisements, is the stealth bomber of the shaving world, breaking the performance barrier to provide an optimum combination of shaving closeness, comfort and safety.

The parallel with military hardware was well to the fore in the presentation to the world's media – its launch to consumers is expected to be a major blitz. Gillette plans to launch Mach3 to US consumers in August 1998; western Europe will follow in the autumn, with the roll out in the top 100 markets to be completed by the end of 1999.

The video presentation by Gillette emphasised that aerodynamics and shaving are two technologies that have impacted on the lives of men for nearly half a century; and Gillette have brought them together for the first time.

The company is a long-established one and its products changed very little in the early decades of the twentieth century. Over the last 25 years of the twentieth century, however, it has adopted the mission statement: 'There is a better way to shave and we will find it'. This has meant innovations every nine years or so that have allowed Gillette to win 70 per cent of sales in North America and western Europe. In 1989 it launched the Sensor range – razors with a revolutionary two blades to give not just one but two cuts at those facial hairs. The Mach3 adds a third blade to the armoury, together with 35 new features the company believes competitors will struggle to emulate. These include a diamond-like carbon coating for the blades that means they are thinner than ever before, soft, flexible microfins that stretch the skin taut and a lubricating strip that moisturises the skin and changes colour when blades need replacing.

The company will have invested more than $1 billion – almost £600 million – on the new product by the time the launch is over. The price of a Mach3 and two cartridges will be between $6.50 and $7.00 (in the £4.00 range), 35 per cent more than the top of the Sensor range. To sell this to the consumer the company plans a set of ear-splitting advertisements which show a square-jawed fighter pilot breaking through the sound barrier three times, before enjoying the 'mother of all shaves'. The company regards the Mach3 as breaking shaving performance barriers – a quantum leap in shaving technology and performance.

Questions for discussion

1 Gillette's aim in launching the three-bladed razor (Mach3) is to maintain market domination in the global wet shave market. Would you consider the plan to be strategically feasible?

2 Basing your argument on the innovative aspects of the Mach3 (combination of aerodynamics and technology), what would you say is the likely market reaction to this product?

REFERENCES

Abell, D. (1980) *Defining the Business: The Starting Point of Strategic Planning*. Englewood Cliffs, NJ: Prentice-Hall.

Kotler, P. (1997) *Marketing Management*. 9th edn. Englewood Cliffs, NJ: Prentice-Hall.

Levitt, T. (1986) *The Marketing Imagination*. New York: Free Press.

McDonald, M.H.B. (1989) *Marketing Plans*. 2nd edn. London: Heinemann.

McDonald, M.H.B. and Tideman, C.C.S. (1993) *Retail Marketing Plans: How to Prepare Them, How to Use Them*. London: Butterworth/Heinemann.

McGoldrick, P. (1990) *Retail Marketing*. London: McGraw-Hill.

Mercer, D. (1996) *Marketing*. 2nd edn. Oxford: Blackwell.

Omar, O. E. (1994) 'Comparative product testing for own-label marketing,' *International Journal of Retail and Distribution Management*, 22(2): 12–17.

Samli, A.C. (1989) Retail Marketing Strategy: Planning, Implementation, and Control. New York: Quorum.

15

International retail marketing management

LEARNING OBJECTIVES

After reading this chapter, you should be able to:

- explain what international retailing means and distinguish between push and pull factors;

- identify the motives behind retail internationalisation and the theoretical framework (comparative advantage and economies of scale) on which the conduct of international retail marketing is based;

- explain the process of selecting markets, and eliminating unsuitable markets for an international retailer;

- understand the market entry strategies used by retailers when deciding to engage in international retail marketing process;

- identify the elements of international retail marketing mix and their modified application in the foreign markets;

- discuss international sourcing processes for UK retailers which are contemplating getting involved with international retail marketing.

One of the distinguishing features of retail competition is its local-market orientation. To generate sales, retailers – whether they are part of large chains or a small independent – must compete with other retailers in their sector located in the same market area. Retail managers are, therefore, more concerned about the nature of local competition in individual markets than competition at the national or international level. Since retailers cater to local markets with their own norms and expectations, they are said to be 'travelling slower' than manufacturers who sell their brands all over the world.

Although, when compared to manufacturers, retailers have been slow to expand internationally, this marketing situation changed dramatically during the 1980s and 1990s. Many retailers have expanded into international markets by starting their own branches or subsidiaries. Others have entered through direct investments in foreign companies or through **franchising** and licensing. In the globalisation of retail marketing, the expansion has been in both directions, with the European retailers entering world markets and non-European retailers coming into European markets (Alexander, 1997).

In the international retail environment, some retailers are very good at getting shoppers to visit and return to their stores, while many retailers, who have failed in the **international environment**, have been unable to persuade consumers to make even a first purchase. In part, this is a result of retailers failing to ask fundamental questions about what they are intending to achieve in international markets. In most cases, what retailers are looking for is the opportunity to achieve what they have accomplished in their domestic markets – international markets are seen as an extension of the domestic market. This is evident in the growth of international retailers. Markets which are considered to be appropriate are entered in the belief that they will not provide undue challenges; thus, there are groups of markets that appeal to retailers from particular markets of origin, as is discussed in Exhibit 15.1.

Exhibit 15.1	**Some markets have natural affinities with each other**

The British retailers often seek initial expansion in Ireland, Canadian retailers in the US; French retailers look to Belgium, Australian retailers to New Zealand, and German retailers to Austria; and retailers in the USA see the UK as an entry point into European markets. However, the very act of choosing such markets may be an abrogation of responsibility as far as market planning is concerned. Whether the market is psychologically close or not, retailers must analyse the international market on its own terms because the biggest difference is that between countries.

The thin red lines drawn upon maps may appear to be less significant than the geographical features they so often parallel. They are no less important in terms of the influences at work in the retail marketing environment that they encircle. This is despite the much reported emergence of globalisation, and country groupings and trading blocs such as the European Union. This chapter provides a general introduction to, and overview of, the various ways in which these differences affect retail marketing, and the special techniques which may be deployed to deal with these differences. A detailed examination is beyond the scope of this book and those retailers who aim to become involved in international retail marketing would be well advised to study one of the many books on the market dedicated to this topic, as it is a highly specialised form of retail marketing.

The internationalisation of retailing

Motivation for international development

A first consideration in the **internationalisation** of retailers must be their motivation for developing outside their own countries. There are various reasons for the influx of overseas retailers into the UK and other European markets. These can be divided into **push factors** emanating from the overseas markets and **pull factors** in the domestic market, as shown in Figure 15.1. The push factors include intense competitive pressures within the domestic marketplace; the prospect of saturation in the domestic marketplace, leaving little room for business development by retailers; sluggish performance in the domestic economy, resulting in flat home sales; and restrictive legislation on new store developments (McGoldrick and Davies, 1995). Many retailers usually opt for internationalisation by being reactive to the above push factors.

In contrast, other retailers take a proactive approach being attracted by opportunities in other countries. In this case there are a number of pull factors at work including the identification of fragmented, underdeveloped or niche marketing opportunities in other countries; the opportunity to establish a bridgehead for further expansion; and the presence of attractive **acquisition** targets. In addition, there are some important facilitating factors which come into play, including improved data communications, the international mobility of managers and the accumulation of company experience in international trading.

Fig. 15.1 PUSH AND PULL FACTORS ATTRACTING OVERSEAS RETAILERS TO THE DOMESTIC MARKET

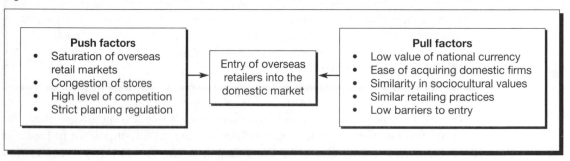

It may, of course, be argued that many of these factors have long been in existence; in themselves, they cannot be responsible for the wave of retail internationalisation that is particularly noticeable in the 1990s' international marketplace. The crucial difference seems to be that retailers began to become increasingly active in identifying and exploiting opportunities in other countries before opportunities for expansion at home were exhausted (Brown and Burt, 1992). Furthermore, this wave of internationalisation is unique in its scale, geographical orientation and motivations from earlier efforts to develop an international presence, as Table 15.1 shows.

A selection of retailers is identified in Table 15.1 which have established an international presence. While the selection is not exhaustive, it includes some of the principal competitors in **international retailing**, together with a number of companies which demonstrate particular approaches towards developing international retail business.

Table 15.1

SELECTED EXAMPLES OF RETAILERS WITH AN INTERNATIONAL PRESENCE

Name	Country of origin	Trading activity
Ahlod NV	The Netherlands	Food retailing
The Body Shop	UK	Cosmetics, skin care
Boots	UK	Dispensing chemists, variety stores
Carrefour	France	Food retailing
Dixons	UK	Domestic retailing, white goods
GUS	UK	Mail order, household furnishings, DIY
IKEA	Sweden	Flat-pack furniture
Laura Ashley	UK	Clothing, soft furnishings
Marks & Spencer	UK	Clothing, food, household
McDonald's	USA	Fast food
J. Sainsbury	UK	Food retailing
Sears Roebuck	USA	Department stores
W.H. Smith	UK	News, recorded music

Approaches to international retailing

There is no single path to developing an international presence in retailing. On a geographical basis (Treadgold, 1988), retailers can take one of the five following approaches to internationalisation:

- **concentrated internationalisation**;
- **dispersed internationalisation**;
- **multinational** organisation;
- **global** organisation;
- **international trade** approach.

Concentrated internationalisation

The retailers taking this approach form the largest number of retail organisations in any national market. They do not generally involve themselves in overseas markets – perhaps wisely so, as many small export operations are loss-makers. The formation of 'international' groupings such as the EU, however, may increasingly force them to face new **international retail marketing** issues. The type of overseas involvement of such organisations generally comprises 'border hopping' into adjacent countries with similar (and therefore familiar) conditions to those prevailing in the domestic market. Aldi, the German retailer which initially moved into Denmark (and since then the UK) is one example of concentrated internationalisation (Williams, 1992).

Dispersed internationalisation

In this instance, retailers may have developed a presence in a number of markets which are geographically remote and culturally diverse from their home market. A striking example of dispersed internationalism is that of Carrefour in Taiwan.

Multinationals

Multinationals are organisations which operate in many different countries; however, they also tend to have individual operating companies (subsidiaries) in each country, which market to (and 'manufacture' for) that market. Country organisations are, therefore, subsidiaries which control their own operations largely independently of the other country organisations. The marketing process is, thus, almost a national operation, with the parent company controlling the operations only at group level (and then typically in terms of the flow of funds). Retailers in this category have developed a more extensive presence than retailers in the two preceding categories. IKEA and Laura Ashley are two examples of multinational retailers.

Global

The truly global organisations, such as Coca Cola, IBM, BP or Shell, operate in most countries. They have marketing organisations in all the countries, and production units in a fair number. These organisations can afford to view national markets as one of the regional subsidiaries, with each region having its own marketing characteristics, but otherwise with no special marketing problems. Multinational retailers sometimes move into **global retailing**, developing a presence throughout the world and operating in a highly diverse range of trading environments. Current examples of global retailers are McDonald's and Benetton.

International traders

The **international trade** approach is practised by such organisations as Renault and Cinzano, which are typically based in one country and produce most of their output there. In other countries they have sales subsidiaries (and sometimes limited production – often assembly – operations). They are largely involved in the export business and sometimes do not have established subsidiary organisations in overseas markets. They may simply sell direct to the market. Different geographical approaches are also complemented by a range of methods for gaining entry to new markets.

Classifying international retailers

International retailers may be classified according to their geographical presence and their entry strategy for new markets. From this classification, four groups of companies may be identified:

- cautious internationalists
- emboldened internationalists
- aggressive internationalists
- world powers

Individual retail companies may change their membership of any one group as their business interests change over time. These four classifications are sumarised in Table 15.2.

Table 15.2
CLASSIFICATION OF INTERNATIONAL RETAILERS

Classification	Company
The cautious internationalists	This is the largest grouping of international retailers, which have chosen a high-cost strategy to develop a limited international presence. Companies from the UK are notably well represented in this group.
The emboldened internationalists	Retailers in this group usually have longer experience of international retailing than those in the cautious internationalists group. The uniting factor of retailers in the two groups is an unwillingness to loosen control over their overseas interests. Carrefour is, perhaps the archetypal emboldened internationalist.
The aggressive internationalists	Although few retailers are currently placed within this group, it appears that an increasing number of retailers aim for membership. Typically, the aggressive internationalists find a market niche which they exploit with an effective combination of product placement and brand promotion.
The world powers	Retailers in this group occupy a special place in international retailing. Above all, they are selling products and/or trading formats which have universal appeal, whatever the country.

In many cases, new markets are created where none previously existed. Typically, franchising is used to develop quickly on a global scale. The world powers usually exercise a high level of control over the supply chains. Benetton, an Italian retailer, for example, is probably the largest manufacturer of woollen garments in the world, as well as trading from more than 4000 shops. Although Benetton is one of the few retailers that can be classified as a world power, with around 4000 (mostly franchised) stores in 80 countries, Italian retailing in general remains largely undeveloped because of regulatory restrictions on store development.

Often there is an expectation that retailing in the northern half of the EC will be more advanced than in the south. Yet restrictions on large store development in Belgium have severely retarded the growth of multiple trading within Belgium. Leading retailers such as the GIB Group have had to look outside Belgium for worthwhile retail marketing opportunities.

There is a need to emphasise the importance of the process of retail internationalisation and the resulting need for excellence in marketing. Retailing in Europe is no longer self-contained, either for a member country within the EU or within the boundaries of the EU itself. Retailers from Europe are, in ever increasing numbers, exploring opportunities in other parts of the world. In turn, retailers from the USA and Japan are establishing a presence in Europe. The pace of internationalisation in retailing, particularly with respect to the EU, is therefore likely to quicken. A crucial consideration in the process of internationalisation will be retail marketing management, but success will depend on achieving a global concept and an understanding of market expansion factors.

Achieving a global concept

True globalisation can be achieved in only a few markets, where one or more of the following characteristics are present:

- technological development;
- innovation;
- concept-based characteristics;
- conviction marketing.

Technological development

A number of foreign markets are driven by highly developed and rapidly changing technology, and it is this technology which gives the cross-country and cross-cultural uniformity. At the same time the expense of developing the technology should also offer **economies of scale** to encourage the globalisation process.

Innovation

Some overseas markets have been conquered by retailers which first marketed an innovatory product or service, which they pulled out of their own national markets as competition became intensive.

Concept-based characteristics

Some brands have developed powerful concepts or images. These have, in some cases, been so strong as to verge on 'mini-cultures' in their own right and they have been able to overwhelm local cultures – at least in the field in which they hold sway.

Conviction marketing

The owners of most of these multinational brands have been so convincing in their marketing efforts that they have been able to overpower, and often obliterate, local differences.

Exhibit 15.2 **The overpowering of domestic manufacturers by Honda motorcycles**

The dramatic success of Honda in the motorcycle market was achieved by Honda turning market preference around to the characteristics of its own products and away from those of American and European competitors – even away from former 'cult' manufacturers such as Harley Davidson (USA) and BSA (UK).

It is also interesting that some of the most successful global brands seem to be able to embody a considerable element of what is best in their original national cultures – for example, Coca-Cola is quintessentially American.

Factors leading to international market expansion

A review of literature relating to international marketing (see Larsen and Rosenbloom, 1993; Simpson and Thorpe, 1995) may help to identify a number of factors which have led to the expansion of international retail marketing including:

1 The international monetary framework – the rapid development of the international financial markets which encourages trade between nations and makes easy **international trade** and payments.

2 The **world trading system** – in particular, the influence of the General Agreement on Trade and Tariffs (**GATT**) has helped to speed up international business transactions.

3 **Global peace** – reinforced by the demise of communism and the ending of the cold war – has improved the atmosphere among nations, though peace worldwide is still a sincere hope rather than a reality.

4 Domestic economic growth – this makes these markets more receptive to imports.

5 Communications and transportation technology has enabled business to be carried out on a global basis quickly and easily.

6 Global competition has transferred trading power between nations leading to retailer migration worldwide.

At its most basic level, a customer can walk into a supermarket, be it in Europe, Japan or the USA, and immediately be at home. The layout is much the same and the products are much the same. The store image and merchandise are promoted in much the same way. However, international marketing ventures will succeed or fail on the strength of a retailer's grasp of retail marketing theories in an expanded marketplace (Dawson, 1994).

Global marketing theories

While the motivations which lie behind internationalisation have received consideration in recent years, much work remains to be done on this issue. Treadgold (1988) has stated that 'for many retailers the principal motivation for expanding internationally has been the limited opportunities for sustained domestic growth'. Certainly, many retailers faced with 'saturation' in the domestic market may seek alternative growth opportunities in non-domestic markets, yet there are dangers in assuming that the primary reasons for internationalisation are push rather than pull factors. Indeed, empirical research has shown that push factors may not be the primary determinant of international development. Williams (1992) has suggested that 'the major motives behind the retail internationalisation of UK-based retailers originate from a perceived internationally appealing and innovative offering and growth oriented and proactive motives'.

The theoretical structure

McGoldrick and Davies (1995) identified a range of factors which explain the theory and concept of international retailing process, and grouped them under the trading theory of **comparative advantage** and economies of scale.

The theory of comparative advantage

Based on this theoretical framework, production can be located in those countries which have the most favourable cost advantage. This explains why the computer component industries have established plants mainly in Taiwan. One country has an 'absolute advantage' over another in terms of producing a specific product, because the factors of production (lower wage costs, material costs, capital costs, and so on) are more favourable. In bilateral trade, therefore, the country with the comparative advantage will export the product, in return for different products – ones for which the other country has a comparative advantage.

MINI-CASE   **Trade between Britain and Portugal in wool and wine**

Wool is produced from sheep, which do well in Britain; and wine is produced from grapes and vines which do very well in Portugal. The conditions and skills developed in Britain over centuries facilitate the production of wool which is of good quality and is an acceptable price. The conditions in Portugal are favourable for the growth of vines and grapes, and skills have been developed for the production of good quality wine at an acceptable price.

Although grapes and vines could be grown in Britain in green houses with artificial heating, the production per acre is small compared to that in Portugal and other warmer lands. Vine cultivation and wine making skills are not common in Britain. Similarly although sheep can and do live in Portugal, they do not thrive in the heat and tend to be reared for meat only. The conditions produce poor quality wool compared to that produced by sheep reared in the temperate British climate.

The trade between Portugal and Britain developed because each took advantage of its conditions and its local skills, and the mutual benefit to be gained from trading with each other. Each nation tends to maximise its supply of goods by concentrating on the production of those goods which it is best at producing with minimum effort (a comparative advantage).

As with most economic theories, this theory is then overlaid with additional levels of complexity, in an attempt to try to explain why real life diverges from the basic theory. In practice, the patterns which emerge in the developed world are very much more complex – particularly because the almost random fluctuations in the international money markets (often led or exacerbated by government intervention) make the scale of such 'absolute advantage' difficult to gauge. In any case, global retail organisations seem to carry this 'absolute advantage' with them. They base their country-by-country allocations of retail marketing functions on factors other than simple price advantage.

Economies of scale

This term refers to the advantages gained by the retail organisation through being larger rather than small. Large retail organisations, for example, are able to buy in bulk, and therefore obtain discounts and reduced cost elements. Both of these situations will result in economies of scale. In terms of international retailing, concentrating the total demands of a number of countries on a limited number of retail operations, and sharing the accumulated experience as well as engaging in joint purchasing across these operations, should lead to economies of scale.

Exhibit 15.3 **Economies of scale in the manufacturing sector**

In a manufacturing situation, for instance, Procter & Gamble successfully concentrated detergent production on fewer plants than Unilever, potentially gaining a cost advantage in the process (although this was possibly undermined by the shift to liquid detergents, which may have been less susceptible to economies of scale).

Similarly, there might be some economies to be achieved by global retailers sharing expensive advertising expenditure, or by the use of expensive commercials in several countries (Treadgold, 1988). What is interesting, in marketing terms, is how few truly global consumer brands there are. Coca-Cola, Heinz, Kellogg's, Marlboro and McDonald's spring immediately to mind, representing – at least to some – symbols of US economic domination. But, beyond these and a few other similar examples, there are fewer global brands than might be expected. Unilever has developed Lux soap as an international brand for decades, and has more recently promoted Timotei shampoo across a wide range of countries. But, like many other companies (including its main competitor, Procter & Gamble), most of its brands are purely national.

Many of the 'international brands' are national brands translated – often literally – into exports onto the world stage. Thus Johnny Walker scotch whisky, Volkswagen German cars, and Dole Hawaiian pineapples are firmly based on national identities. There is no doubt that many would argue for a different form of categorisation, and that the difference between transnational and international brands is not that significant. Even so, it should not be really surprising that there are so few genuinely global brands. Marketing theory assumes, correctly in most cases, that the product or service (and the whole marketing mix) has to be matched to customer needs and wants. The theory of global brands, on the other hand, assumes that 'global customers', with almost exactly the same 'global tastes', can be found (Williams, 1992).

The complication is that 'global marketing', in its purest sense, requires the differences between countries to be negligible, or at least so small that they can be ignored in practice. But this is not always so – indeed in many cases it is far from being the case. For example, to liken Japan to the USA, or Nigeria to Italy, would lead to marketing failure. Each national market has to be approached separately, and assessed in its own right and often in a very specific way.

> **MINI-CASE**   **Parker Pen's failure in global marketing**
>
> Perhaps the most dramatic example of the failure of 'global marketing' was that of the Parker Pen Company. In the mid-1980s it set out to bring its marketing across 154 countries under a 'global marketing' umbrella, with all major decisions and standards centralised. Unfortunately, as it soon found, the markets were very different in almost all respects. As a result the single, worldwide, campaign 'Make Your Mark With Parker' was a failure, and Parker Pen has apparently lost much of that worldwide business.

Differential advantage

Differential advantage refers to a benefit of a product or service that is perceived to make it more suitable and desirable to the customer than a competing product or service. Differential advantages are key elements which retailers can exploit in their pursuit of customers and profits for successful long-term performance. Differential advantage should be examined as a potential for distinctiveness that may offer business opportunities in an overseas market. However, how consumers view these distinctive differences or lack of differences would serve to guide retailers in the construction of a retail marketing mix leading to international marketing success.

The criteria for success include a proven, well-developed store concept, a commitment to expanding abroad, and financial resources to cover unexpected costs. Speciality chains of stores that focus on a single merchandise category and have brand-name recognition are the retail formats that meet this criteria (Simpson and Thorpe, 1995). These stores will succeed because they focus on a narrow group of products, which makes it easier to adjust to local tastes and fill gaps in international retail marketing (e.g. The Body Shop).

Differential advantage implies that retailers set themselves apart from their competitors, allowing an individual company to create the opportunity to develop a degree of monopolisation within its competitive environment. By focusing on specific elements such as product, image and niche, differential advantage can be more easily achieved. Elements appear to exist that are unique and inherently common to those speciality retailers who have successfully expanded into international markets, which they exploit for differential advantage. Thus these elements not only differentiate speciality retailers within the domestic market, but provide the basis upon which these retailers may employ international expansion as a viable growth strategy. In order to establish a successful differential advantage in the international marketplace, retailers must select feasible markets and jettision unsuitable ones.

Eliminating unsuitable markets

One approach to targeting international markets is to select, for consideration, just those countries where 'experience' or research has suggested there may be worthwhile business. This approach starts with a 'cluster' of countries which have characteristics similar to those that the retailer is familiar with. Another approach sometimes described as 'contractible', and one which might be worth pursuing, even if in parallel with the first one, is to start with all countries and then eliminate those which are proved to be unsuitable (Wagner *et al.*, 1989). The effect may ultimately be the same, but this approach has the virtue of not unnecessarily eliminating the potential markets which are less obvious. There are a number of methods which can be used to filter out unsuitable markets. However, a number of the factors which may be used to initially screen out the most obvious unstable markets are identified in Table 15.3.

Table 15.3
MARKET SELECTION AND ELIMINATION DETERMINANTS

No.	Determining factors	Evaluative analysis
1	**Common sense**	For some products or services, there may be groups of countries which are clearly unlikely to buy significant quantities. Strict Islamic countries are poor markets for alcoholic drinks, and the poorest of the Third World countries are unlikely to be large-scale purchasers of mainframe computers. Electrical goods will not sell well in a country with a poor electricity supply. Thus, electronic retailers such as Dixons or Tandy will not consider such markets.
2	**Size of population**	Some countries (for example, Belize or Ghutan) are so small that their markets for foreign goods may be smaller than some towns in the developed world. The 'infrastructure' which is needed to export to these countries may only be justified, therefore, by products with very large sales worldwide.
3	**State of development**	Even the larger Third World countries, such as Ethiopia or Bangladesh, may be so underdeveloped that a population the size of a European country will, once more, generate a market that is scarcely larger than a French or American town.
4	**Regulatory considerations**	There are a number of countries which have regulations or laws that can constrain the marketing of certain products or the activities of certain organisations. The main areas of concern will probably be: prohibition of certain categories of product; restrictions on foreign ownership; control of currency transfer between countries; official trade barriers such as tariffs may be imposed; and non-tariff barriers restricting imports/exports may also be imposed.
5	**Economic considerations**	GDP (Gross Domestic Product) in total, its growth rate and, in particular, GDP per capita can all say a lot about the potential spending power and patterns of a country's population. These figures are available in reference books, such as the OECD economic surveys or the United Nations' Yearbooks, which may often be found at the larger reference libraries. However, care should be exercised in using any such data comparatively since the bases for the different sets of data may not be strictly comparable.
6	**Social and business structures**	The culture can play a decisive role in deciding whether a product is to be accepted or not. The special problems of Islamic countries have already been cited, but there are many other cultural barriers. Business cultures also have their idiosyncrasies. In particular countries, it is a business way of life for 'access' to be 'purchased'. In US and European eyes this may be seen as bribery, but locally it is often seen simply as part of the normal costs of trading. Equally, in specific countries the structure of business may be very informal, so that it takes a deal of accumulated expertise to understand exactly what the

▶

Table 15.3 Continued

No.	Determining factors	Evaluative analysis
		deal that you have just struck actually means. In other countries still, the negotiation procedures are alien – ranging from the haggling of the bazaar (which is meant to be an entertainment in itself for both participants) to the sophisticated nuances of Japanese business (most of which are lost on Western business people). The state of development of the society can be gauged by the degree of literacy, and the employment levels as well as employment by sector service versus manufacturing versus primary agriculture, for example. The level of education may become a deciding factor in the use of any product which requires a degree of skill or the following of written instructions.
7	**Living standards**	Individual living standards may often be estimated by reference to a few simple measures, such as ownership of television sets or telephones or cars. Indications of the 'infrastructure' may be obtained from measurements such as the percentage of houses with mains drainage. Certain infrastructure elements may be very important to specific products or services. General Foods failed to make a success of selling packaged cake mixes in Japan, despite heavy promotion, because very few Japanese households own ovens in which to bake cakes. The 'skew' of living standards can be estimated from the distribution of income in general or by the extent of the 'luxury' industries
8	**Market accessibility**	The final set of questions to be asked relates to the ease of access to a given market. The potential that it offers may be placed on one side of the scale, but the costs of tapping that potential – of providing the necessary retail marketing infrastructure – must be put on the other side before any sensible decision can be made. The key factors may be the distance, the language and culture, and the general retail marketing infrastructure within the chosen markets.

For industrial goods the key factors favouring import demand are, in general terms, trade figures, consumption in general, energy production, and the monetary situation; those for consumer goods are income and stability of the currency. Having made the various decisions, having entered the market and having achieved an adequate level of sales, the retailer will then need to consider how its 'portfolio' of country operations is balanced, and how their different strengths and weaknesses complement the overall operation. As with any new venture, the next stage in the approach to an overseas market should be to conduct market research. In many respects this will follow the same paths as those of domestic market research, as described in Chapter 13. However, it must also be stated, any research overseas must follow a rigorous approach, with care being taken to avoid assumptions where possible.

Market entry decisions and strategies

Market entry decisions

Among retailers trading internationally, there is apparently no consensus on the most appropriate method for a particular market. Retailers have their own preferences, and what may work for one retailer may not work so well for another. On the whole, retailers with limited overseas experience appear to choose high control entry strategies, often involving acquisition. Mass merchandisers, in particular, seem to prefer acquisition. By contrast, speciality retailers appear to have a preference for organic growth, particularly through franchising, which represents a low-cost, but low-control, method of entry into overseas markets.

Once the screening process indicated in Table 15.3 has reduced the number of potential countries down to a relatively small number, these can be categorised and prioritised by the techniques that a retailer would use in judging any move into a new market. Such a move should be considered as a diversification, though the products or services involved may be the central ones from the home market. At the end of this process of prioritisation, retailers should have divided their potential overseas markets into a number of categories, each requiring different courses of action. Three of these categories may, for example, be: rejected markets; markets to be covered by agents or distributors; and markets for major development. Depending upon the strategies adopted (based on the portfolio planning discussed in Chapter 14, for instance), some of the major markets will be scheduled for development at some time in the future, whereas others will require immediate attention.

Country risk assessment

One of the factors which needs to be taken into account, particularly by multinational retailers, is the risk that their investments in a particular country will be nullified, either by 'investment recovery risk', resulting from government action, or by 'cash flow risk' due to radically reduced economic returns. This reviewing and forecasting process is generally known as **country risk** assessment. The risk assessment could be associated with the risk to the whole system of international trade; country specific risks; and project specific risks. The best advice is to include an assessment of such risks in the overall research and then to monitor developments (including political developments) closely.

Product decision

A further level of decision to be taken, even if the entry decision is made, is the product to be marketed in the chosen market. Many global retailers appear to use the same product worldwide – a simple extension of what is offered in the home market. It is the case, for example, that both McDonald's and Coca-Cola offer identical products worldwide.

On the other hand, many multinationals market offer very different products in diverse countries. These are often marketed as different brands. Sometimes the brand name is the same, but the formulation is different – to meet local needs.

Exhibit 15.4	**Tailoring the product or the promotional message to the local market**

General Foods (the manufacturer of Maxwell House coffee) blends different coffees for different markets: one for the UK, where it is mainly taken with milk; one for France, where it is often taken black; and yet another for Latin American, whose consumers like a taste of chicory in their coffee. Similarly, it may not be a matter of taste or culture but of physical needs. The Japanese, for instance, being physically small, demand smaller versions of almost everything – including some consumer durable items.

Even if the product or service is the same in all markets, the promotional vehicles and the promotional messages may be very different. The cultural constraints may mean that exactly the same basic message has to be told in different ways to be meaningful to different national audiences.

Price decision

Some global organisations, such as IBM, may choose to maintain much the same prices worldwide (although, typically, these will be higher than those in the domestic market of the parent company), always subject to the limitations imposed by varying currency exchange rates. Others, such as those in the pharmaceutical industry, may set prices by what each market will bear, leading to very different prices in each country.

The problem with significant variations in price between countries, particularly where the countries are close to each other, is that customers may indulge in 'cross-border shopping' (as is now the case between Britain and France) to take advantage of the lower prices for alcohol due to lower duties being levied in France. Even worse, wholesalers may do this too – thus creating a 'grey market' in the higher price country (which may have the effect of destabilising marketing operations in that country).

The price that the parent company charges for the product it ships into the country is called the 'transfer price'. This may be based upon actual or notional costs; IBM, for instance, is very careful to ensure that it reflects true costs. However, the price may occasionally be manipulated to avoid or minimise local taxes. Some marketers have been known to set very low prices in some overseas markets. They 'dump' the product, with the intention of undermining local suppliers, so that there will ultimately be less competition and prices can then be raised to a profitable level.

Market entry strategies

The objective of developing outlets in other countries may be pursued in several ways, and the choice of entry strategy is dependent on several factors, including the availability of capital, the availability of management skills in international operations, the level of understanding of market needs within the target country, and the compatibility of the domestic trading formats with those needs. The four main entry strategies which are mainly used by British retailers could be identified as:

- self-start entry
- acquisition
- franchising
- **joint venture**.

Self-start entry

In self-start entry the retailer builds the chain from scratch, as in the case of Woolworth within the UK market (many decades ago). A variation upon this approach is usually to make relatively modest acquisition to gain a foothold and local management expertise, then actively to pursue organic growth within the country concerned. This is broadly the approach adopted by Laura Ashley, which by 1988 had nearly 200 overseas outlets, over half of them in the USA.

Entry by acquisition

This is the approach used in the majority of instances of UK retailers developing abroad. Notable acquisitions include Kings supermarkets and the Brooks Brothers menswear chains in the USA by Marks & Spencer. In some cases the overseas retailing interests are largely unrelated to the company's activities at home. For example, BAT owns over 1600 department, variety and chemist stores mostly in North America, but at home now limits its retailing interests to Argos catalogue showrooms and the Jewellers Guild. A major problem of entry by acquisition is that the companies available for purchase are often in financial difficulty; considerable time and financial support is, therefore, required to restore such firms. The cost of buying into more successful companies with strong management teams can be extremely high.

Franchising

Where a retailing concept can be readily exported, franchising may avoid much of the risk and demands upon capital of direct acquisition. The Italian-based Benetton trades from over four thousand shops worldwide, as well as being the largest manufacturer of woollen garments in the world. The UK based The Body Shop has also largely followed this route, with around 200 outlets in many parts of the world. A major problem with this method is that many people with the capital to open a franchised outlet may lack retailing expertise. Many of the Tandy corporation's outlets in the UK reverted to company ownership for this reason.

Joint venture

The costs and risks of entry may be reduced by partnership developments with organisations already familiar with the country's market and trading conditions. This approach may also reduce the time-scale of overseas development. These have much in common with licensing. Both usually involve a local organisation handling the marketing (and typically retail operation function) in the foreign market. The difference is that the international partner has an equity holding in the local operation. The skills for setting up a local joint venture, and sharing the running with the local partner, are not those of conventional marketing and are, perhaps, more related to those of diplomacy. Differences in entry approaches, management styles and positioning strategies have led to some very different formats in international retailing.

Strategic (international) alliances

A much more positive approach to using 'third parties', used in particular by the larger corporations (who are often already multinationals in their own right), is very deliberately to build strong marketing links with other organisations. This method is known as a **strategic alliance**. To compete in the global environment, retailers must find a way to pay for immense fixed costs. Retailers need partners who can help them measure their fixed costs. Such strategic alliances are, therefore, created to engender monumental economies of scale in truly global undertakings. At the end of the day, when all the various selection procedures have been completed and international retail marketing has been put in place, things may still go wrong if care is not taken. It is necessary for retailers to watch out for any potential pitfalls when and before going into any new market where the external market environment may be strange.

Market positioning

Once the retailer has decided which segment or segments it wishes to target, it must communicate with the new market, informing consumers in that market what it stands for (Larsen and Rosenbloom, 1993). Positioning is the act of designing the retailer's image and value offer so that the segment's customers understand and appreciate what the retailer stands for in relation to the competing stores.

The incoming retailers must find a place in the minds of their potential customers, differentiating themselves from their competitors. Some retailers may begin with an advantage that the market already accurately perceives what it represents. Benetton is a global brand and its offering appeals to a global segment. On entering a new market, customers will be aware of what the company represents. In contrast, other stores may have less distinct images or images which are easily misinterpreted.

Retailers will have difficulty positioning themselves in non-domestic operations if they fail to understand the nature of their operation. It is very easy for retailers which have operated for some time in their domestic market to become complaisant about their operation and its market positioning. International retail marketing is often a shock to the collective company psyche. Non-domestic markets challenge assumptions built up in the domestic market. It is often, therefore, companies with a focused strategy and which are of relatively recent origin that are most successful in international market operation. A major challenge for the

| Exhibit 15.5 | **Establishing an image in a new market is vital** |

When Carrefour entered the UK market it did not have a distinct image other than it was a hypermarket operator – and hypermarkets were seen as challenging. The company, therefore, had to overcome negative perceptions associated with its format, as well as positioning itself in a market which was not familiar with its image. Carrefour eventually sold its stores.

Other retailers will find that they have an image that is different from their domestic image. The middle market Marks & Spencer's operation in the UK has had a more upmarket image in European markets when it has opened stores. In Spain, for example, the opening of the store was considered to be a fashion event.

'cross-border' retailer is to identify and adopt the most appropriate positioning in relation to other national markets. Some retail formats, especially in specialised niches, have been exported very successfully.

The incoming retailer may decide to address a single market segment, which is large enough to support a chain of stores and which is not currently served by the existing operators in the market. However, after opening stores in the market, the retailer may find that it has not positioned itself as far as the consumers in the market are concerned. While the retailer may have successfully positioned itself in its domestic market, in an overseas market it may be perceived as appealing to an older age group, or as being slightly more downmarket than it had intended. Its position in the new market may also bring the incoming retailers into closer competition with indigenous retailers. The retailer will, therefore, have to reposition itself through communicating with its customer group. This will entail various adjustments in the retail marketing mix.

The international retail marketing mix

Although, the retail marketing mix has been discussed in Chapter 1 and its components discussed in various chapters throughout this book, the international retail marketing mix concentrates on store image, product range, store format, shelf price, store location, distribution, and promotion. These elements are discussed in terms of their operational factors in the overseas markets selected for retail marketing development. The marketing mix elements discussed below recognise the need to adapt the marketing mix to both the retail and the international environment.

Store image

One interpretation of retail internationalisation is that based on the transfer of a product line, with its associated image for consumers, across national borders. Image is crucial to the successful internationalisation of a retail format. Many retailers have successfully built a consumer franchise by shifting loyalty away from manufacturer brands to their stores. Such retailers have built up their own brand products as rivals to manufacturers' products, on the basis of both price and quality. In consequence, these retailers have also built product ranges which appeal to their customers and which provide them with the ability to convey a distinct message to the market in which they operate. The image they have thus created has been an important tool in their international development.

The development of a strong image with international appeal may prove an important marketing advantage. Some retailers are able to internationalise their domestic operational format; however, others are not. Where their existing format will not possess a distinct image in the international market, retailers should consider either acquiring a local format or developing a new format for the international market as Boots attempted to (*see* Exhibit 15.6).

Exhibit 15.6

> Boots, the UK-based pharmaceuticals company and retailer, has divested itself of its once extensive international operations. However, the company also experimented with the Sephora chain in France which focused on a relatively narrow product range.

Product range

Product range will need to be adjusted slightly for any foreign market. However, most retailers will seek to retain their merchandise range as far as possible. Many UK retailers usually seek to retain at least a broadly similar merchandise offering to their UK operations. The domestic experience is usually influential in determining the international product range. Nevertheless, retailers must remain flexible and sensitive to local needs. As retailers extend their operation into new markets, they will find that they have to adjust their ranges for many different reasons. They may find that the styles acceptable in some markets would not be acceptable in other countries as is illustrated in Exhibit 15.7.

Exhibit 15.7   ### Matching the image to the market

> Laura Ashley has built its international operation on providing that 'quintessential English look'; but the quaint floral pattern image of the 1970s has become less relevant in the company's domestic market where clothes product ranges were adapted in the 1980s to encompass a working woman theme.
>
> Elsewhere, however, the softer image of country life and motherhood has allowed the company to retain its early image and sell products that would be unacceptable to many British customers. In the US, the company generates valuable sales volume from its matching mother and child clothing, a concept that the domestic British customer would not be attracted to. It must be remembered that what is fashionable in one market may not be fashionable in another.

Store format

The case with merchandise is mirrored in that of store format. Retailers will seek to retain those forms with which they are familiar when they enter an unfamiliar market. Only a small number of large UK companies would be primarily influenced by local conditions when introducing their format into the European market. Alexander (1997) observed that many large UK retailers would normally retain their UK format to a considerable degree.

The format that a retailer employs, and the operational advantage that it gives the retailer, may be the main determinant of international expansion. The international retailer may find that advantages which are derived from an innovative format may cause considerable problems when introducing a new format into the non-domestic market. In such circumstances, the retailer will have to be aware of the planning implications of introducing its store format and the possible opposition that will be generated in the new market.

Exhibit 15.8	Costco's format and operations generated opposition from competitors

When Costco entered the UK in the early 1990s, domestic retailers took legal action to stop the company operating from locations in which they were not able to locate and which offered a cost advantage to the Costco operation. The format that the company used was a major operational feature.

The format the retailer operates in the new market will require access to extraneous facilities. The in-store ambience and design of a store may be a distinguishing feature of the operation. The Gap maintains a distinctive image through the display of merchandise items. Other operators, such as The Body Shop with their refill service, create an atmosphere which helps to build and maintain a customer franchise. The format and in-store layout will be interpreted in the mind of the consumer. In the international market, retailers must be aware of the associations customers have and hence the messages that format design will convey. Customers will not wish to be unduly challenged by the operating procedures and format in the store, although they will want to be interested and in some cases involved in the service provision.

Shelf price

Price is not readily comparable on an international market level. Some companies are considered to charge higher prices outside their domestic markets. Marks & Spencer has been described in this way, although research has shown that at least in the French and Hong Kong markets perceptions of pricing levels are the same as in the domestic (UK) market.

MINI-CASE **McDonald's and Woolworth's – retailers which offer unchallenging formulaic exchange relationships**

The McDonald's format is very much on the edge of the retail and restaurant definitions. It is a place to consume food and in that sense is a restaurant, but the retail-like qualities of the dispensing of the food items is an example of the manipulation of the service experience which customers seek in many retail encounters. The success of the Woolworth operation and its international appeal was, to a large extent, built on the lack of social challenge which operating procedures set customers. Prices were set at limited points and merchandise was openly displayed. This contrasted with the more traditional shop atmosphere into which the Woolworth variety store operation was introduced.

In a similar fashion, McDonald's is built on retail, over the counter, formulaic exchange relationships, while providing a product which is usually associated with a more overt service provision – which, in turn, is often associated with the uncertainty of role playing. The McDonald's customer does not peruse a wine list evaluating the relative appropriateness of a white Burgundy or a red Bordeaux in the context of the social setting and culinary experience to follow. McDonald's provides a set of limited options, in a defined setting, where the host culture – for the most part – is left at the door and a limited range of responses are required from customers and staff alike. Luxury goods retailers may trade on the basis of greater customer service and customer–staff interaction, but as a basis for internationalisation it may be limited to only a few markets, customer groups and, thus, sites within those markets.

Comparisons of pricing arrangements must always be carefully qualified. Price, along with quality, is one determinant of value and arbitrary evaluations of price run the risk of ignoring the context in which prices are charged. Simple exchange rate calculations may seem a satisfactory way for tourists to calculate their expenditure, but indigenous consumers, because of relative standards of living, may make very different calculations.

Store location

In both the domestic and the international environment, location issues are crucial. Retailers entering a new market should be aware that the perceptions they have of their company's location needs may have to be altered in the new environment as is illustrated in Exhibit 15.9.

Retailers have usually built up a wealth of information on the locations they use in their domestic market by the time they move into the international environment. However, in the new environment they will face the prospect of the need for a relatively rapid store development programme in a market with which they are unfamiliar. There is a considerable danger that they will acquire inappropriate properties in this initial development phase which may lead to poor trading results, a loss of confidence, a reduction in the store development programme, and

The Canadian climate moved Marks & Spencer off the high street

Marks & Spencer has been, and remains, predominately a high street operation in the UK. When the company moved into Canada, however, the high street was not necessarily the best option. The climate of Canada, and hence the shopping habits which this has created, demands a more protected environment wherever possible. Marks & Spencer had to come to terms with this new reality..

often a growing disillusionment with international market. On the other hand, retailers may use experiences at home to prevent the same mistakes being repeated in the overseas market, as illustrated in Exhibit 15.10.

Habitat's improved and space-efficient French properly portfolio

It is possible for retailers to learn from the mistakes they made in their home market when they were developing a chain of outlets. The Habitat operation in France developed a far more space-efficient property portfolio than it had achieved in the UK. In the UK the financial pressures of early development had forced the company to make location decisions which were not entirely appropriate to the developing merchandise lines of the company. In France, with its established merchandise range, it was able to operate a balanced portfolio with, for example, larger merchandise items being located in its large out-of-town stores, where square footage prices were lower, and its town centre operations retaining a range of less space-hungry items.

Retail distribution

The problems associated with the movement of goods to a retail outlet in the international market have the potential to render the international operation ineffective and unsuccessful. The nature of the distribution will depend on the company, its level of vertical integration, and its product range. Grocery retailers are particularly prone to serious problems if the distribution system is not efficient. They depend on a very swift turnover of goods and cannot afford unnecessary delays in the system. Thus, grocery retailers are more likely than other retailers, such as clothing retailers, to acquire an operation in the international environment before growing organically. This is not to say, however, that clothing retailers are not vulnerable to distribution problems as Laura Ashley found, to its cost (Exhibit 15.11).

Retail promotion

Retailers have available to them vast amounts of information and many opportunities to promote their store and merchandise. They may favour major television campaigns promoting the store or a bundle of goods under the store's name.

Exhibit 15.11

Distribution of goods – a potential make or break factor

Laura Ashley encountered considerable distribution problems in the USA at the end of the 1980s when its autumn range arrived months late in the US outlets. As a result of such distribution problems, the company entered into a joint arrangement with Federal Express. Federal Express helped Laura Ashley develop an efficient distribution system based at Laura Ashley's centre in Newtown in mid-Wales. Similarly, much of Benetton's success is due to its ability to use its distribution system to react quickly to the needs of franchise stores as consumer demand dictates a reappraisal of styles and colours within the merchandise range.

Both Laura Ashley and Benetton are closely involved in the production of the goods which appear in their stores. Laura Ashley has produced more goods in-house than has Benetton, a company which depends on a system of subcontractors. Where such subcontractors are traditionally based in one market, tensions may appear when the operation becomes international. Marks & Spencer, for example, encountered problems in Canada when its suppliers in that market did not develop the same relationship with the company as its British suppliers had.

Equally, they may favour the targeting of particular groups in the locality in which they have an outlet. Retailers may achieve considerable recognition through their involvement with the local community and a vast amount of publicity which has the distinct advantage of being free. They are able to promote their products through the presence of their outlets on the high streets and in out-of-town locations. They also have the opportunity to promote products in-store with special signage, and service staff advice and recommendations. In the international environment, however, retailers will have to reconsider tried and tested methods of successful promotion.

On entering a new market, a retailer will be faced with relative ignorance of their organisation and its image. Some stores may be greeted with a barrage of publicity, as The Body Shop was when it entered the US market. This may, as was the case with The Body Shop, mean that the store does not have to engage in crippling advertising costs. However, many retailers may have to begin promotional campaigns of a type which they have not engaged in before. They will have to position themselves in the market and advertising is one means by which they may achieve this. If they do not communicate their message effectively, in-store customers may misinterpret low prices as poor quality rather than good value.

The international sourcing process

This section illustrates the diversity of approaches and contexts for **international sourcing**. A model of the sourcing process can offer, therefore, only an abstraction, as suggested in Figure 15.2. The main elements of this model are now explained.

Fig. 15.2 INTERNATIONAL PRODUCT SOURCING PROCESS

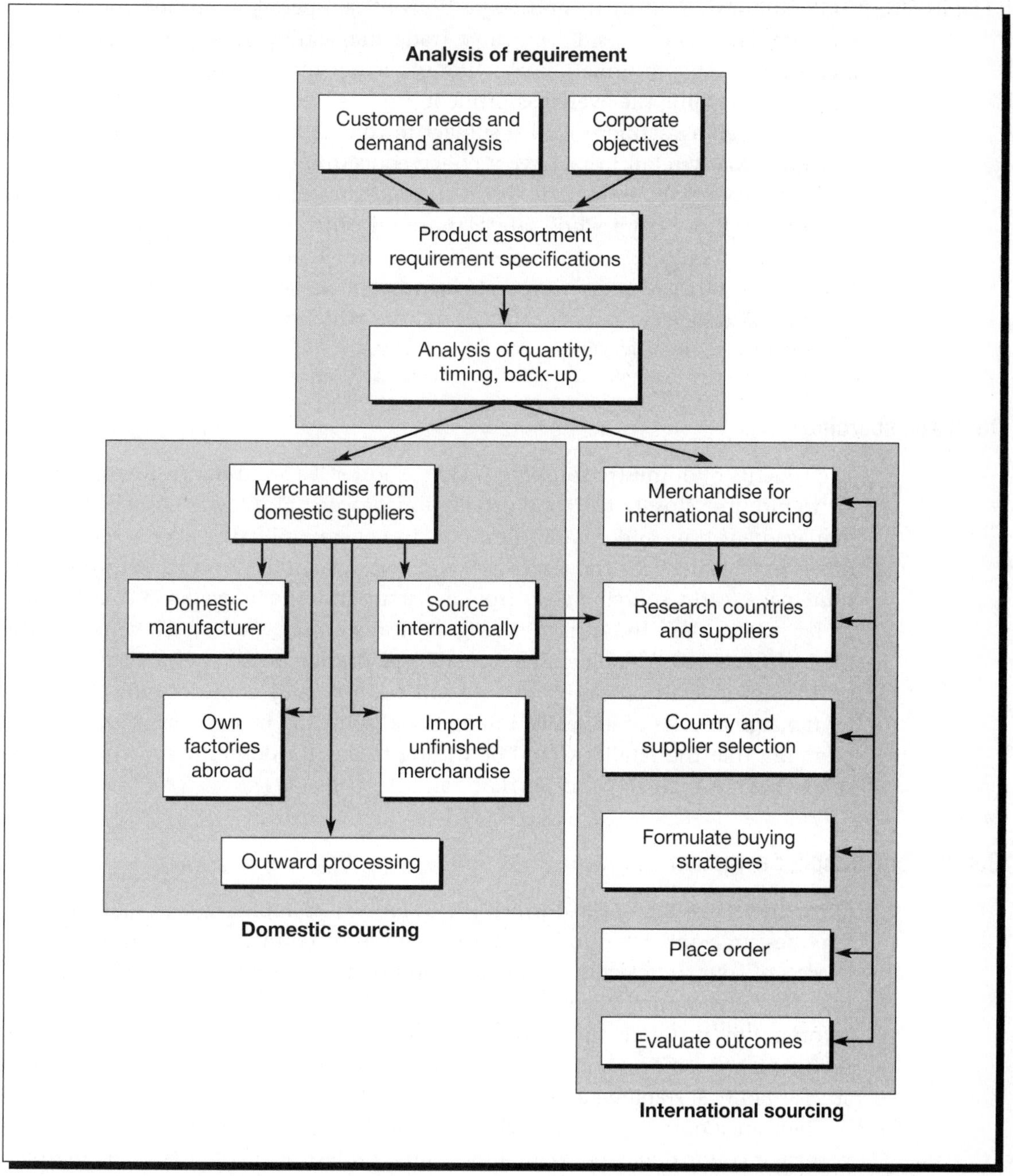

Analysis of needs

Increasingly intensifying competition in the marketplace requires retailers to be even more customer orientated, determining their store's overall assortment based on market requirements. Information about market requirements can be gathered from various sources, including: market research; EPOS data; customer complaints and enquiries; the insights and suggestions of salespeople; returned goods; overseas branches and subsidiaries; and trade magazines, newspapers and other publications. This information constitutes a major input to the retailer's decision making concerning the overall assortment.

The overall assortment is also subject to the retailer's objectives, policy and strategies. Many retail firms have a policy concerning the breadth of assortment. Other relevant policies include those on purchases direct from manufacturers as opposed to those from wholesalers; those on centralised buying as opposed to decentralised buying; and those on buying independently as opposed to joint buying with other retailers. Corporate buying policies and information about markets may also have an impact on the extent to which the retailer's merchandise is sourced internationally.

Domestic sourcing

The benefits of **domestic sourcing** include shorter lead and transit times, the ability to monitor closely the total production process, and lower costs in terms of management time and communications. In general, a retailer may accept higher prices in exchange for the lower risk and costs usually associated with domestic sourcing. Clearly, sourcing costs from a distant and underdeveloped country may be far greater than those from a geographically closer country. There is also the issue of fixed and variable costs. A retail organisation with an established buying office and/or retail operation in a distant country may consider only the short-term marginal costs of increased international sourcing. In such circumstances, the premium that the retailer would be willing to pay for domestic sourcing may be somewhat less than 15 per cent (Harris and Heppell, 1991).

Country and supplier selection

Once the retailer has decided which merchandise it is appropriate to sourcing overseas, research must be undertaken on potential countries and suppliers. The process of country selection involves scanning the economic environment, including the economic systems, economic structure, resources, demographic information, infrastructure and economic performance; the trade environment such as export control and bilateral trade relationships; the political environment such as political stability; and the legal system.

There are a number of channels through which information about suppliers in a particular country may be secured including: professional contacts, trade journals, directories, trading companies, import brokers, trade fairs, foreign trade offices, trade associations, and trade lists. Many firms have adopted a policy of sourcing in multiple countries. Nike, for instance, have its shoes manufactured in South Korea, Taiwan, Thailand and Hong Kong. Also, for different target markets, a firm may source the same product from different countries.

Selection of suppliers is one of the most important decisions a retailer makes in the process of international sourcing. Retailers must decide whether to source a product from a single supplier or from multiple suppliers. Considering the two options, the firm needs to balance the trade-off between operating costs and risks, particularly in the international context. Single sourcing has the benefit of cost reduction, but carries the risks of 'putting all the eggs in one basket'. Single sourcing has found favour among many manufacturing firms, for instance between 75 and 90 per cent of one leading UK retailer's total range of products is single-sourced.

Purchasing strategies

Having chosen a supplier, the retailer should develop a purchasing strategy concerning volume, frequency, target price, time of delivery, and trade channels. A retailer has a number of trade channels to choose from in order to organise the transaction. These options include: the use of an international trading firm, an overseas buying office, internal buyers, and/or a buying group. Many retailers may prefer the use of overseas buying offices in that a direct contact with suppliers can reduce the possibility of misunderstanding or poor communication between the two parties (Harris and Heppell, 1991). The choice of trade channel also depends on the expected volume and frequency of purchase. There are two main types of buying offices which buyers use for sourcing tasks affiliated buying offices and independent offices.

The majority of the largest retailing firms use their own (affiliated buying) offices to deal exclusively with purchasing. Independent buying offices act as buying agents for several independent retailers and are often a cooperative which encompasses a number of retailers. Having defined the purchasing strategy, the firm is involved in negotiating prices and terms with an overseas supplier, based on the chosen purchase strategy. In addition, a very important task is to manage the retailer–manufacturer relationship. Due to the importance of cooperation between retailer and manufacturer in the area of manufactured goods, a healthy and harmonious long-term business relationship is beneficial both to retailers and to manufacturers. The corporate buying committee should evaluate the strategy and performance of international sourcing over time. This will help the firm identify problem areas, learn from its mistakes, and revise strategies accordingly – including the balance between domestic and international sourcing.

SUMMARY

On entering a market, retailers must be aware of the competitive advantage that they believe they have. As, the operation is established, however, they must also be aware of the perceptions of the operation which are held by the consumers within that market. Many of the issues and problems discussed in this chapter imply that the internationalising retailer has adopted a global approach to its product development – that is, the retailer is attempting to replicate the same formula in a number of markets. This is only one option available to the retailer.

The retailer may wish to adopt a multinational approach. In such circumstances, where the retailer operates various distinct formats in different markets, an approach which tailors the marketing format to the specific market will be possible – something that the global approach does not permit. The multinational approach may have involved acquisition which, in itself, will mean that the existing operation already has a market position. The international organisation may wish to reposition the operation it has acquired, but many of the start-up issues will have been avoided.

The overall international strategy adopted by a retailer will have major implications for its marketing activities in individual markets.

KEY TERMS

acquisition	emboldened	international sourcing
aggressive internationalists	internationalists	international trade
cautious internationalists	franchising	joint venture
comparative advantage	GATT	multinational
concentrated	global	pull factors
internationalisation	global peace	push factors
country risk	global retailing	strategic alliances
differential advantage	internationalisation	world powers
dispersed	international environment	world trading system
internationalisation	international retail	
domestic sourcing	marketing	
economies of scale	international retailing	

ASSIGNMENT

Retailers will continue to expand overseas as many domestic markets become saturated. Within Europe, new markets such as those in central and eastern European countries are opening up. But many retailers have been looking further afield towards the Asia Pacific region, where during the mid-1990s economic growth, rising consumer spending, and development of a strong retail market have been attractions. Active retailers in the region include Mothercare, Bhs, and Marks & Spencer. Ventures by food retailers in the Asia Pacific region are being led by the French (Auchan in Korea and Carrefour in Taiwan, Malaysia and Thailand) and the Dutch (Ahold in Indonesia, Malaysia and Singapore).

Task

You work for one of the UK's leading electronic retailers contemplating market expansion into the Asia Pacific region. Write to your marketing manager suggesting a market entry strategy for your organisation and how it will decide on which market(s) to enter. Your essay should be no more than 2000 words.

REVISION QUESTIONS

1 Distinguish between push factors and pull factors, and examine their implications for international retail marketing operation.

2 There is no single 'correct' path for retailers to follow to develop an international presence. Briefly discuss the main approaches to retail internationalisation.

3 International retailers may be classified according to their geographical presence and their entry strategy for new markets. Discuss this suggestion.

4 In the theory of comparative advantage, retail marketing can be concentrated in those countries which have 'absolute advantage'. Explain.

5 Define what you understand by the term 'economies of scale', with specific reference to international retail marketing.

6 Differential advantage implies that retailers set themselves apart from their competitors in the international environment. Suggest how could retailers do this.

7 Discuss the key international market entry strategies for UK international retailers.

8 International retailers generally like to eliminate 'poor' markets during their market selection procedures. What do you consider to be the key determining factors in the market elimination process?

9 What impact is internationalisation likely to have on the way in which retailers manage the marketing mix?

10 Discuss briefly the international sourcing process and its implications for international retail marketing success.

CASE STUDY

Joint venture – a strategy for retail globalisation

There are several strategies for 'going global' in the retail sector including joint ventures, organic growth, franchises, and acquisitions. Retailers need to assess the degree of cultural distance that a market has and the severity of any entry barriers before deciding what strategy to pursue. Once globalisation is under way, retailers are faced with problems of format adaptation, and relationships with local suppliers and partners. This case study deals specifically with joint ventures and reviews how this strategy operates, with key references to its relevant and relative advantages and drawbacks.

Joint venture is the most appropriate entry strategy when the overseas country targeted is culturally distant and difficult to enter. It is not surprising that this is the strategy of choice for most European retailers entering Asia. The Dutch group Ahold, for example, has an equal partnership – a 50:50 joint venture – with Venturtech Investment Corporation in China and plans similar joint ventures in Malaysia, Singapore, Thailand and Indonesia. Ahold is trying to develop its retail brand 'Tops' across all of these countries. Other examples of joint ventures include Otto Versand of Germany entering China with the Shanghai Cheer group and Japan with the Sumitomo group.

▶

Often these joint ventures are undertaken with local partners which are at least partly retailers and/or importers of goods. Carrefour, for example, has a 60:40 joint venture with President Enterprise in Taiwan – a manufacturer and retailer with considerable experience in joint ventures with Budweiser, PepsiCo, Frito Lay and KFC. In some cases, own-label retailers form joint ventures with local partners to extend their brand. Joint ventures in which the overseas partner supplies an exclusive own-label line are more stable as it is difficult for the local partner to replace the own-label owner. An example of a company using own-label joint venture agreements is Cortefiel of Spain, which has an agreement with SB & Partners of Belgium to operate the Springfield chain. In this case Cortefiel uses its own-label merchandise to protect itself against imitation. Likewise, Cortefiel has a joint venture with Marks & Spencer in Spain covering five stores. In this case, Marks & Spencer is protected because without its St Michael brand the retail format will not work.

The choice of partner and the contract agreed are vital for the success of a joint venture. A basic rule is: there must be a long-term interest for both parties if they are to stay together. Usually the trade-off is for one partner to gain access to a new market by using the local partner's knowledge and network. In return, the local partner gets access to a new format, product range, management skills and the ability to create a new business. Joint venture partnerships are difficult to manage and have a high failure rate. The 50:50 joint venture set up in 1996 by Auchan, the French hypermarket group, and Commercial Mexicana failed in 1998 because of differences concerning the development strategy. Commercial Mexicana retained the hypermarket opened in 1997 and Auchan is currently planning to open around six of its own hypermarkets.

Questions for discussion

1 The joint venture strategic approach to entering an overseas market country is considered to be relatively safe. Why do you think some partners are still facing problems with this method?

2 What aspects of this strategy do you see as most advantageous for European retailers expanding into Asian countries?

REFERENCES

Akehurst, G. and Alexander, N. (1995) *The Internationalisation of Retailing*. London: Frank Cass & Co.

Alexander, N. (1997) *International Retailing*. Oxford: Blackwell.

Brown, S. and Burt, S. (1992) 'Conclusion – retail internationalisation: past imperfect, future imperative', *European Journal of Marketing*, 26(8/9): 80–4.

Dawson, J. (1994) 'The internationalisation of retailing operations', *Journal of Marketing Management*, 10: 267–82.

Harris, R.J. and Heppell, J. (1991) 'Apparel sourcing: a survey of retail buyers' attitudes in Canada, the USA, and Western Europe', *EIU Textile Outlook International*, 18 (November): 87–97.

Larsen, T.L. and Rosenbloom, B. (1993) 'A functional approach to international channel structure and the role of independent wholesalers', *Journal of Marketing Channels*, 1(2): 75–99.

McGoldrick, P. and Davies, G. (1995) *International Retailing: Trends and Strategies*. London: Financial Times Pitman Publishing.

Simpson, E.M. and Thorpe, D.I. (1995) 'A conceptual model of strategic considerations for international retailing', in Akehurst, G. and Alexander, N. (eds) *Internationalisation of Retailing*. London: Frank Cass & Co.

Treadgold, A. (1988) 'Retailing without frontiers', *Retail and Distribution Management*, 16(6): 8–12.

Wagner, J., Ettenson, R. and Parrish, J. (1989) 'Vendor selection among retail buyers: an analysis by merchandise division', *Journal of Retailing*, 65(1): 58–79.

Williams, D. (1992) 'Motives for retailer international: their impact, structure, and implications', *Journal of Marketing Management*, 8: 269–85.

16

Techno-marketing and electronic retailing

LEARNING OBJECTIVES

After reading this chapter, you should understand:

■ the meaning of 'technology' as it is defined and used in the retail marketing context;

■ the relationship between technology and marketing (techno-marketing) and the application of the application of technology as one of the retail marketing tools within the retail organisation;

■ the role of information technology (IT) as a tool for making retail marketing decisions;

■ the increasing importance of electronic retailing as a directing force driving retail marketing innovations worldwide;

■ what the Internet is, and how it is used for marketing products and services.

The centralisation of marketing and management control has been an important trend in retail organisation starting with buying, distribution, credit control, management services, accounting and payroll, and so on. Many of these services have resulted in economies of scale, which have been passed on to the consumer as lower prices in the stores. These economies of scale in service provision by retailers have been made possible by technological innovations. Changes in **technology** also create opportunities for retailers (Ghosh, 1994), both to provide new services and to improve their management systems (*see* Exhibit 16.1).

Exhibit 16.1

Retailing and technology – moving into the twenty-first century

The combination, for instance, of cable television and new satellite communication technology has fuelled the recent growth of electronic home shopping, one of the new forms of retailing. Improvements in satellite communication technology have also made possible and encouraged the use of electronic data interchange (EDI) between retailers and their suppliers, changing the way in which retailers manage their inventories.

Retailers are under extreme pressure, with overheads on the increase and profit margins under continual threat. The need for more accurate management of the technology and retail marketing interface (**techno-marketing**) is greater than it has ever been. Of course, the rapid advances of **retail technology** do not provide a panacea for all retail marketing problems; however, a solution to these problems will be quite unthinkable without technology (Omar, 1995). This chapter, therefore, looks at the relationship between technology and retail marketing in terms of the retailer's service provision and the management of the retail operation to meet increasing demands from consumers. The general areas of **electronic retailing**, including interactive home shopping and marketing via the Internet, will be reviewed.

The role of technology to involve competitiveness

The growth in retailing is generally accepted to be a major factor in improving living standards in a competitive market economy. It is in this environment that retail organisations, in free competition with each other, create and market useful products. The profits obtained from these operations may be used by retailers to expand and to make yet more new products. This, in turn, will satisfy their shoppers. As economists put it, 'sustained growth' is a goal for which nations and industries strive, despite recessions in the world economy (including that in the late 1990s). Everyone is agreed on this common aim, but how to achieve it is the subject of much heated economic and political debate around the world.

The role of technology as a motor that drives retail growth is a very important aspect of marketing development. Technology flows continuously from its sources and stocks, and the management of these stocks so that they meet retail market requirements is of prime importance. The current debate about the role of technology as a catalyst to all the elements of the retail marketing mix necessitates the discussion this chapter centres around.

Definition of technology and techno-marketing

There are several descriptions and definitions of technology, most of which are being constantly updated to reflect the widening use and rapid development of technology in general. The origin of the word **technology** comes from the Greek **tekhnologia**, which means a systematic approach to a craft or a technique. This encompasses a set of activities needed to obtain a specified result, usually in the form of a piece of equipment or something similar. Techniques are ways of making or creating things, whereas technology denotes the theory or logic of techniques. It could, therefore, be regarded as a science plus an art of 'how' and 'why' of doing things. From that point of view, and in terms of retail marketing, technology may be defined as 'the concept and the demonstration of a new ability to perform a specific retail marketing function using new and untried ideas, principles, techniques, or materials, for the development of new retail services, invention, or processing techniques'.

From the retailing point, it must be noted that by normal and usual marketing function, retailers do not manufacture or perform the art and science of fabrication. Retailers do, however, practise the art and science of marketing processes. It is the technology of these marketing processes used by retailers which concerns us in this chapter. This definition suggests that the physical sciences are the basis or the sources of technology, in line with the original meaning of the Greek word. However, it may be necessary in some cases to extend the definition to reflect the broad areas of purposeful application to include areas such as the physical, life and behavioural sciences, as well as those of the medical, agricultural, management and its related fields, whom retailers also serve as customers. It may be more appropriate simply to define technology from the retailer's point of view as the collection of knowledge, capabilities, and procedures used for developing, manufacturing, and marketing products and services to meet social needs (to satisfy the potential shoppers). This definition enables a review of the interface between technology and retail marketing (techno-marketing) within the retail organisation.

Retailers need to integrate technology with their retail marketing philosophy of customer orientation. Thus, techno-marketing is the combination of both these two functions (the functions of technology combined with and in relation to the functions of retail marketing). The effective and creative ability to manage the two functions, synchronisingly and unify their performance, will create a competitive advantage for the retailer. Techno-marketing is, therefore, used here to mean 'the relationship and application of technology, in conjunction with marketing within the retail organisation'.

The role of technology in satisfying market demand

Retailing is a fast moving and dynamic industry, and successful retailers have to keep their fingers very firmly on the pulse of their operations, reacting to changes as soon as they happen. The retailer who correctly anticipates the changing market is the one who prospers (Leeming, 1996). Retail marketing is surrounded by mystique and its definition vary from corporate planning to the preparation of new product promotion. Retail marketing simply means the process by which retailers satisfy the needs of their customers at a profit. Retail marketing is, therefore, seen as a function which organises and directs all those retailing activities involved in assessing and converting consumer purchasing power into effective market demand for specific products or services.

The relationship between technology and retail marketing is important to retailers because retail marketing is concerned with the means retailers use to direct their resources and capabilities to the satisfaction of consumer needs. Technology is one important determinant of a retailer's capability to meet the needs of consumers (Senker, 1986). That the difficulties of dealing with technologies are being overcome is illustrated by the signs of change which are evident in the retail industry. The efficient and imaginative use of technology in the retailing environment may reap rewards in profit terms as Wal-Mart has illustrated.

MINI-CASE ## Wal-Mart adopted technology successfully

In 1966, Sam Walton enrolled himself in an IBM school for retailers, having previously befriended the data processing manager of Franklin's Stores where he was then working. Walton obviously believed that technology could help retailers in the areas of distribution, relationships with suppliers, and the management information and internal retail communications.

In 1987 Walton established collaborative relationships with his suppliers. This aspect of his thinking capability was regarded as innovative. Today, Wal-Mart has over 400 000 employees, an estimated 41 million customers each week and a turnover in excess of $53 billion. Wal-Mart is a good example of a retail organisation which has successfully adopted technology into retail marketing.

Wal-Mart's control of the supply chain and quick response supply has pushed up its market share within its sectors of operation. Wal-Mart probably has the largest privately owned satellite system and civilian database in the world.

Retailers are employing technologists and scientists, and are generously funding their research and development projects to find revolutionary new technologies in such areas as food, fashion and general commodity retailing (Omar, 1995). Much of this work is intending to providing new ways for satisfying present needs. There is a significant increase in the proportion of well-educated, highly trained employees in retail organisations. This is because the employment in knowledge-producing occupations is growing very fast. New forms of retail organisations and methods of management are required to meet the needs of this proliferation of knowledge employees (O'Connor and Calvin, 1997). Retail marketing needs the application of new technology to satisfy present and future needs.

In the Asia Pacific region, for example, the socio-economic priorities are shifting from an emphasis on the size of gross national product (GNP) and the volume of output to an emphasis on the quality of life, the quality of outputs, and better business environment. This is a clear deviation from past experience. An additional shift from the previous retail marketing system, where individual retailers undertook to solve specific product development problems, is the introduction of a marketing system where large retail multiples work in a coordinated effort to solve complex problems relating to product innovation and marketing. In an era when complex social problems are a major challenge, there is a great need to apply this new technological management to a broader range of problems.

All of the above examples are given to emphasise that all retail organisations must anticipate, prepare for and use the opportunities which these technological changes provide. These indications of rapid change and discontinuous change suggest that the innovations of the future will require a serious and concerted effort if retailers are to appreciate the potential benefits of new developments and are going to be able to use technology fully in their marketing decisions.

Retail technology management

Retailers should normally measure their success by how quickly they can adapt to changes in the industry and the market. Revolutionary new methods of conducting business will bring significant change to the industry. One of the most innovative areas of retailing is the use of technology to drive retail marketing strategy. High-performance retailers are able to use their decision support system to achieve a competitive advantage through superior marketing strategy. Thus, technology plays a double role in retailing: marketing and strategy development.

Technological management

By managing technology, retailers may reach their universal goal of improving customer service. During a transaction, the decision support system gathers and manages information in a way that makes the transaction more efficient (*see* Figure 16.1). Five technologies – **bar coding**, **scanning**, automatic replenishment systems (**ARS**), electronic data interchange (**EDI**), and very small aperture terminals (**VSAT**) – ease the processes of credit approval, credit card verification, and merchandise receiving. The information gathered is then communicated to various departments. Customer service personnel use it for billing and mailing, buying for reordering merchandise, and accounting for recording the revenue from the sale. The data are stored and may be retrieved, as often as necessary, in a matter of seconds.

Fig. 16.1 THE USE OF TECHNOLOGY IN RETAIL TRANSACTIONS

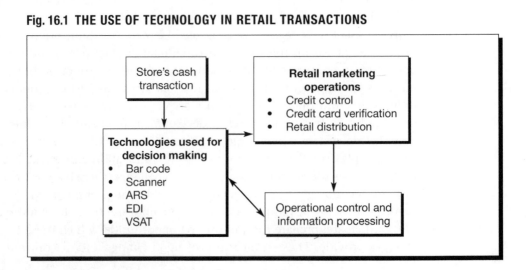

Bar codes and scanners

Bar coding is a technology that uses a printed bar and space pattern to represent numbers and letters. When decoded, the pattern yields important merchandise information, including brand name, style, size, colour, and price. Bar codes can be used to track inventory levels, indicate percentage mark-ups on items, and calculate stock turn rates and reorder quantities. Bar codes are decoded and their information entered into the decision support system with optical scanners.

Optical scanners are infra-red laser devices used to read computerised bar codes. Two scanning techniques are used in retailing. The more familiar method uses the universal product code (**UPC**), a 12-digit number used for item identification. The second technique, shipper container marking (**SCM**), facilitates the identification and shipping of containers among manufacturers, distributors, and retailers. The UPC and SCM can be read by a variety of optical scanners.

Exhibit 16.2

Infra-red laser scanners to suit the job – wands, guns or flatbeds

Most discount stores use hand-held laser guns, which read and record bar code information and offer speed and convenience. Department stores, on the other hand, tend to prefer optical scanning wands (a laser gun shaped like a wand), which work better with their loosely attached price tags. Supermarkets use flatbed scanners or in-line conveyors (infra-red laser devices used to read bar codes) to accommodate the enormous number of items and coupons they must scan.

Used in conjunction, the coding and scanning systems are used to collect information on product purchases. Every time a salesperson records a purchase using an optical scanner, the scanner notes what was bought, its manufacturer, size and price. The information is then recorded in the decision support system, where it can be combined with market intelligence and market research. As a result, retailers can find out the likes and dislikes of their customers. Such information helps retailers determine what kind of merchandise customers want and what factors may influence their purchase decisions.

Automatic replenishment systems (ARSs)

The automatic replenishment system (ARS) is used to analyse inventory levels and lead times for reordering; and to forecast sales and to generate purchase orders for items needing quick replenishment. The system is designed to carry the lowest possible inventory levels and still maintain sufficient quantities to avoid stockout. Since order quantities are smaller and ordering is more frequent when using an ARS, the system enables retailers to optimise their inventory levels. Merchandise availability is enhanced because reordering is automatic. Stock turn rates are higher, and the costs of spoilage and shrinkage decrease dramatically (Leeming, 1996).

Electronic data interchange (EDI)

Electronic data interchange (EDI) speeds the flow of information and merchandise from suppliers to retailers. EDI allows the electronic exchange of purchase orders, invoices, advance shipping notices, and product returns. In essence, it is the administrative arm of an automatic replenishment system. This technology increases sales, reduces markdowns, and lowers inventory carrying costs. It also reduces the clerical and administrative costs of merchandise ordering.

Exhibit 16.3	EDI and ARS – driving greater efficiency in retailing

Automatic replenishment systems and electronic data interchange are fuelling greater efficiency in retailing. Toys 'Я' Us, which has more than 450 stores in the US and about 100 stores in other countries, attributes its growth and profitability to its inventory and information systems. Almost 60 per cent of its sales occur during Christmas, and inventory control is the key to survival. To date, Toys 'Я' Us has networked with more than five hundred suppliers. Orders and shipment confirmations, as well as sales and inventory records, are all transmitted electronically, informing buyers and suppliers which toys were sold at which stores worldwide and alerting them when items need to be replenished. Since Toys 'Я' Us can monitor sales trends and communicate with suppliers automatically, some of its stores sell more 'trend' merchandise than other toy stores. EDI also allows buyers to balance the retailer's merchandise mix with less seasonal goods.

Very small aperture terminals (VSATs)

The VSATs provide many of the benefits associated with electronic data interchange, along with other, more far-reaching functions. Since it is based on satellite communications, the VSAT allows users to send messages to stores over a wide geographical area. Both, K-mart and Wal-Mart (American-based retailers), already use VSAT systems to send news of advance sales, new pricing plans, advertisements, and products to employees, as well as to deliver technical training to its staff.

Increasingly retailers are using these systems not only in information management and customer service but also as a strategic marketing tool. They recognise that a decision support system can give a company a competitive advantage. The next section, explores how these systems may improve a retailer's marketing capabilities, especially in decision making and problem solving. In some cases, the positive effects are of great benefit.

The use of information technology (IT) in retailing

The use of **information technology** in retailing is to enable the decision-making process to be carried out effectively by controlling stock and money more efficiently. With electronic data interchange (EDI), electronic point-of-sale (**EPOS**) and electronic fund transfer at point-of-sale (**EFTPOS**) in place, data and information distribution systems have speeded up considerably; but these are quickly being superseded by newer, more up-to-date technology. Further pressure on retailers comes from an increasingly competitive and fragmented marketplace (O'Connor and Calvin, 1997). The supply chain is having to become much quicker at responding to change. Retail information systems may include many subsidiary support systems such as space planning, store modelling and staff scheduling. Since the subject of retail information systems was dealt with extensively in Chapter 13, this section simply attempts to answer the question of how retailers may integrate the information gathered for decision-making purposes.

The role of IT as a marketing tool

Consumers all over the developed world have acquired wealth and, with it, discerning tastes. They are now more precise and demanding, and are rapidly segmenting into 'micro-markets' (small, highly targeted, lifestyle-specific, and possibly geographically specific, market segments), all requiring highly targeted new products and/or services. There are now fashion shops, brands and products to meet virtually any fashion taste.

Fashion customers are also becoming increasingly more volatile in their shopping habits (Leeming, 1996) tastes and loyalties. The penalty for retailers who fail to supply market demand may be severe – probably, resulting in market failure. So the need to keep in tune with customer demand has never been more critical. In such a fluid and competitive marketplace, most retailers may have to diversify into new products; develop internationally into new markets; or acquire market share from competitors. It is in the making such decisions that retail IT can play a significant role. Since stock, staff and space are the three most important resources for retailers, and their complete and accurate control is vital to retaining competitive edge, the gathering and usage of information in all these three key areas must be at the heart of any modern retail information system. Figure 16.1 illustrates how information may be effectively used to coordinate activities throughout the retail chain; Exhibit 16.4 focuses on the IT efforts of Japanese retailers.

Exhibit 16.4	**Japanese retailers focus on stock control**

A great deal of current IT expenditure and investment by Japanese retailers is being directed towards the effective control and management of stock levels and their contents. The highly complex multi-transactional nature of Japanese retailing, combined with its multiple locations, makes effective and efficient stock control high on the agenda. Many retailers are, therefore, trying to use their stock transaction systems in more creative and intelligent ways to maximise customer purchasing and loyalty.

Fashion retailers with complex inventory offers, often find it difficult to maintain high levels of line availability at all times and even argue, Pareto-style, that 80 per cent of sales come from 20 per cent of the stock.

Historically, too, retailers have always been more interested in the sales they have achieved rather than in the sales they have missed. At the most sophisticated level, using a combination of computer software systems may act as a multiple toolkit for merchandise planning, product range planning, and stock allocation and replenishment. Using industry standard databases (such as Informix and Oracle), the systems help to plan, control and support decision making for the complex stock flows experienced by retailers (O'Connor and Calvin, 1997). Such systems may, however, encourage a dependence upon forecasting at a time when forecasting may no longer be worthwhile. These systems usually create massive amounts of data – often too much for managerial staff to absorb, process and adequately act upon. To enable customer service to be a reality, retail IT systems must be suited to retail management structures.

Integrating business with technology

There is a need strongly to encourage retailers to use technology in more revolutionary ways; to move from identifying processes that can be automated to creating a new organisational structure fully interwoven with any new technology. This is particularly important in a climate when, so often, new retail systems fail to deliver as a result of a poor implementation process and a failure of management to break down historical organisational barriers and preconceptions. The complexity of retail marketing decision-making processes may be the root cause of the problem.

Exhibit 16.5	As retail technology expands and the demands for more integrated systems develop, the multi-disciplinary nature of the planning and control process within retailing will have to be broadened. At Bhs, for instance, functional barriers have been broken down; the hitherto seperate functions of finance, buying, and merchandising and retail operations have been fully integrated to enable decisions to be made uniformly and to be synchronised across the operation.

At the conventional front end of retailing, technology is improving customer service dramatically. Supermarket checkout queues are much shorter as a result of store traffic monitoring systems; stores are adequately staffed at key times as a result of staff scheduling information systems; and transaction speeds are getting faster. Levels of stock availability are improving, and the specific targeting of marketing communications to the right customers is becoming more precise. More technology – helped by parallel processing, data generation and the extensive use of data warehousing – enables retailers to know the shopping habits of individual customers. This can help speed up shopping time for essential goods, leaving customers more time to shop for the more exciting purchases.

420

Technology and retail marketing decision making

An up-to-date information system, coupled with decision support system technology, can yield powerful problem-solving and decision-making capabilities. The primary objective of a decision support system is to manage large volumes of information to enhance decision making. Such a system can handle questions relating to location for a new store, suppliers, and customer profiles. This section discusses how retailers may use technology as a decision support system to realise strategic advantages in stock management, marketing, and customer service. It also emphasises the importance of a retailer's technological capabilities to their overall competitive strategy.

Stock management

One major contribution of decision support systems is more efficient inventory management procedures. For most retailers, the cost of carrying and maintaining a high level of stock is very high in terms of both labour and warehousing costs. Since inventory is a major expense for all retailers, a reduction in the cost of inventory management benefits retailers and their customers.

Most of the savings in this area come from a customer service strategy called quick-response merchandising, which makes inventory decisions so flexible that what is forecast for sale today can be available for sale tomorrow. This process demands that the retailer has the right products in the store – on time, and in the appropriate quantities, styles, colours, and at the right price. Time management is at the heart of this strategy. Quick response reduces the forecasting period for product sales, increasing the retailer's ability to meet customer demand on time. It reduces the lead time needed to secure merchandise, decreasing the probability of stockout on popular merchandise. In general, quick response may allow retailers to order less merchandise but more frequently and at times when customer demand is highest.

Quick response is based on a business strategy called collaborative management (a mutually beneficial partnership among manufacturers, distributors, and retailers). Collaborative management is achieved through close communication, synergistic performance measures, and co-operation in pursuing common objectives. Implementation of this strategy requires a shared decision support system (Omar, 1998). The retailer must constantly monitor stock levels to be able to predict the demand for frequently ordered goods. It must share its information with manufacturers to increase the accuracy and timing of shipments. Manufacturers, for their part, must commit to and provide higher levels of service to the retailer. They must coordinate their operations with the retailer's ordering system and absorb the increased costs associated with shipping goods more frequently and in smaller volumes (Omar, 1998).

Buying functions

Retail technology can also reduce the complexity and increase the efficiency of traditional buying functions. Technology may be used to give buyers a better understanding of future demand and sales trends. Two critical buying functions that are directly affected by decision support systems are open-to-buy practices and inventory replenishment. Open-to-buy (OTB) is the difference between a retailer's merchandise needs for a particular period and any purchase commitments already made for that period (Lucas *et al.*, 1994). Retail technology, in the form of decision support systems, is changing many open-to-buy practices. Accurate information allows better planning of merchandise needs for a particular period (*see* Chapter 8). This result tends to reduce purchase commitments for the period, freeing funds for purchases of new, innovative merchandise.

Sale decisions

One basic assumption of any new technology is that more efficient business practices and enhanced customer service will increase sales. The introduction of new technology requires a substantial investment in marketing, education and training. Retailers must consider such systems on a cost–benefit, return-on-investment basis. Expected returns and incremental sales increases, therefore, should be quantified on a financial basis.

Marketing decisions

Retail technology can greatly enhance a retailer's ability to engage in relationship marketing. In the past, the goal of many retailers was to know their customers personally. Knowledge of customers' tastes, needs, and preferences forged a bond between retailer and customer that translated into strong store loyalty. However, during the 1980s, as retailers expanded geographically, much of the 'personal touch' in retailing was lost and store loyalty diminished. In the 1990s, retailers are attempting to re-establish their relationships with customers. Many are using technology to achieve that goal. By analysing the huge databases they have acquired through their decision support systems, retailers are better able to understand their customers and to adapt their merchandising strategies accordingly.

In order to get to know their customers, retailers collect information on demographics, customer lifestyles, how and where customers shop, and their reactions to advertisements and new product introductions. Then the retailer uses decision support system technology to match customer-specific information with data on buying trends. This knowledge of customers may have given retailers market dominating power over their suppliers.

Customer service

Using modern retail technology, customer service is now one way retailers differentiate themselves. Retail technology benefits the customer both directly, through interactive terminals and videos, and indirectly through specially trained retail salespeople. Already the availability of technology is beginning to eliminate many of the bureaucratic barriers that hindered customer service in the past. In the store, shared information systems are enabling salespeople to respond effectively to customers' needs. (The subject of customer service was discussed extensively in Chapter 12 of this book.) It is sufficient here to say that the introduction of new retail technology has allowed salespeople to process highly complicated transactions quickly and efficiently. These transactions, which may include multiple forms of payment, voids, returns, and gift coupons, can now be accomplished in a matter of seconds. Obviously, such capabilities not only increase the salesperson's and the store's productivity but provide high-quality customer service as well.

Retailers' technological capabilities

Technology is one element of a retailer's overall competitive strategy, designed to achieve cost leadership, overall differentiation or focus (Omar, 1995). Retailers who adopt a technological strategy can differentiate themselves from competitors by selling exclusive own-label products or offering higher quality goods than those generally available. This will enhance store reputation and increase the retailer's market share, especially if other forms of competition (such as price) produce diminishing returns.

Research evidence has indicated that retailers who have influenced technological innovation all have strong technology departments, providing a technological expertise capable of product innovation. Retailers become involved in innovation because they believe they can appropriate the benefits of technical innovation by controlling the quality of the products they offer to their shoppers (Senker, 1986). In addition to this wave of technological and economic growth, there is continuous technological progress in a wide variety of fields which results in a stream of improved and innovatory products. Provided that these innovative products can be used and sold at a profit, both the retailers' and consumers' prosperity will improve – as will the UK economy as a whole. It is, therefore, important to stimulate technological growth and retailing activities.

The structure and developments in electronic retailing

Electronic retailing was developed in the mid-1980s and is considered to be one of the major growth areas in the retail industry (Rowley, 1996). One reason for this dramatic growth is the diversity of approaches to electronic retailing. This retailing method can be subdivided into three broad categories: **one-way media**, **two-way media**, and **stand-alone media**.

One-way media

This category includes television, radio, and one-way cable systems. In one-way systems, the retailer controls the programming, the products or services offered, and the timing and method of presenting merchandise. The most common examples of one-way media are **home shopping clubs**, such as Home Shopping Network (HSN) and Quality Value Convenience Network (QVC).

Televised home shopping

Televised home shopping is a relatively new form of electronic retailing. It was introduced in around 1987 by the Home Shopping and Cable Value networks. In its early form, TV shopping was available only to cable TV subscribers, but competition from other networks such as SKY TV soon followed. Shop-by-TV retailers now broadcast over the air for limited periods of time. Presently retailers who offer televised home shopping vary from country to country and between geographical areas. In the US, seven major retailers of home shopping include: Home Shopping Network, Cable Value Network, QVC Network, Home Shopping Spree, Shop Television Network, The JC Penney Shopping Network, and Sky Merchant.

Exhibit 16.6 **Home shopping networks operate using differing retailing styles**

Some distinct differences in selling approaches and target markets exist among the competing networks. The Cable Value and Home Shopping networks, for example, are aggressive, fast-paced, hard-sell retailers. Specific products can be purchased only during specified time intervals, during which the price may be lowered to entice customers to place orders. These networks concentrate on jewellery, collectables, and low-priced home appliances (Assadi, 1998). QVC Network, on the other hand, uses a slow, soft sell and offers more national brand names. The network prides itself on the variety of its merchandise, which ranges from cosmetics to power tools, sporting goods, and home electronics. QVC provides extensive product demonstration and tends to depend on celebrity endorsements. The network offers easy payment plans, in-home credit, and direct-mail coupons. Rapid consumer acceptance of television shopping has prompted a major expansion among television shopping networks.

Two-way media

This category includes in-store and public access devices, **transactional kiosks**, videotext systems, and computer information systems such as Prodigy. Two-way systems allow the retailer to control informational content, but customers can select the amount and type of information they receive, when they receive it, and when they order the product.

In-store and in-home interactive systems

Two-way media retailing spans both in-store and in-home shopping. In-store access devices use videos to entertain and instruct. Customers can request information, view product demonstrations or, in some cases, order merchandise directly. Since a high proportion of customers' purchase decisions are still made in stores (Assadi, 1998), public access media are a logical investment for store-based retailers. These devices are likely to enhance in-store decision making by allowing customers to see how a wide range of products, such as power tools, sports equipment, and even cooking utensils, are used.

Several retailers, especially, multiple chains, have tested or presently use public access systems consisting of a product code scanner connected to a video screen. The customer scans the product code to get on-screen information on the merchandise and its price, filmed product demonstrations or, sometimes, coupon offers. A similar system at the checkout point may allow the customer to register a purchase and obtain discounts.

Transactional kiosks

A transactional kiosk is an electronic service station that allows customers to access information, order merchandise, or secure services by using a credit card or personal identification number. The proliferation and acceptance of the electronic kiosk is attributed to the success of 24-hour automatic teller machines (ATMs). For traditional retailers, electronic kiosks are one way to complement the in-store salesforce and increase customer service. Stores such as Woolworth's and Miss Selfridge use kiosks to advertise, to sell, and to enhance customer convenience and satisfaction. Kiosks also gather valuable demographic and psychographic information the retailer may use in making merchandising decisions. Interactive menus allow customers to view video demonstrations, compare product specifications and prices, and purchase merchandise without assistance.

Kiosks are particularly attractive to service retailers. Hotels, airlines, car rental agencies, and insurance firms use them in high-traffic areas like airports, railway stations and conference centres. Several airlines and credit card companies now have kiosks that show videos on holiday locations. At the end of the video, the customer can make airline or cruise reservations, book hotel accommodation or rent a car by inserting a credit card in the machine.

Videotex and computer technology

Videotex systems and home shopping through cable television are two examples of new forms of retailing made possible by advances in communications technology. Videotex is a generic name for **interactive electronic systems** in which data and graphics are transmitted over telephone lines or coaxial cables and displayed on a subscriber's television or personal computer monitor. A subscriber to a videotex system may gain access to information on the merchandise offerings of different retailers. The shopper first selects the product category of interest and then views on the screen the different brands, styles, colours, and sizes that are available; along with the price of each item. To make a purchase, the shopper may order direct through a home computer and charge the amount to a credit card. In addition to shopping information, videotex systems usually provide other services such as home banking, news, weather information, stock market quotes, and so on.

Videotex is an interactive information system that links in-home television sets, personal computers, and telephones to a remote host computer. For all practical purposes, the capacity of videotex systems to store and deliver information is unlimited. The systems are activated by a keyboard connected to a television set or by a keypad linked to a personal computer. Users can request on-screen messages in both textual and graphic form. This aspect of a videotex system is its interactive capability, which allows users to order and pay for merchandise without leaving their homes.

Prodigy

This system was first developed in a joint venture between Sears and IBM. Like videotex, Prodigy operates through commercial telephone lines. To receive the service, a subscriber must have an IBM-compatible or Macintosh computer with a graphic capability, a modem, and Prodigy software. Prodigy is positioned as an interactive shopping tool for the busy consumer who does not have time to shop. Customers receive immediate access to news, sports, stock market information, weather, and business information from more than 170 companies. Prodigy may well become one of the leaders in electronic retailing in the first decade of the twenty-first century (Leeming, 1996).

Stand-alone media

This category includes **video catalogues** and **electronic couponing** (often referred to as an electronic point-of-sale display). **Stand-alone media** are not interactive in the way that one-way and two-way media are; their primary purpose is to prompt immediate short-term sales. As such, some may consider them to be an in-store promotional technique.

Stand-alone media provide general information on a retail organisation and specific information on its products and services. Due to their interactive capability, they are usually classified as part of electronic retailing rather than a promotional device.

Video catalogues

Video catalogues are videotaped merchandise presentations, packaged as cassettes, that can be played in the customer's home on a video cassette recorder (VCR). They are similar in content to printed catalogues. The major difference between video catalogues and printed catalogues is the cost: video catalogues are approximately ten times more expensive to produce, develop, and distribute than printed catalogues. In addition, the customer must have a video cassette recorder to use a video catalogue. Although video catalogues currently account for only 3 per cent of total retail sales, their growth potential is high. The next generation of video catalogues will probably incorporate instant merchandise and service updates, as well as the kind of interactive capabilities now available through videotex

Electronic couponing

Electronic couponing is a process through which customers receive price-off coupons automatically at the checkout counter. This system is used mainly in supermarkets where the technology is tied to the electronic scanners that record customers' purchases at the checkout points. When a customer buys a certain brand, the machine instructs the register to print a coupon that can be used immediately. Since the coupons can be used only at the store where they are issued, many retailers see electronic couponing as an effective means of developing store loyalty. Electronic couponing is used in most supermarkets in the USA.

Besides developing store loyalty, electronic couponing may be an effective customer service vehicle. The couponing process gives retailers critical information about who is buying what products, at what price, and at what time. Such information allows managers to plan their merchandise and service offerings, price levels, and promotional appeals more effectively. As electronic technologies continue to develop, they will take on new forms and uses. In the long term, the obvious key to the success of electronic retailing will be customer acceptance. Not all customers are willing to abandon traditional approaches to shopping. However, as retail technologies improve and become more user friendly, greater numbers of customers are expected to become comfortable with interactive transactions.

Customer service in electronic retailing

Some customer service issues are particularly important in electronic retailing. Since the human element is usually absent from electronic retailing, the following tasks must receive special attention: facilitating information flow and facilitating the planning process (*see* below).

Facilitating information flow

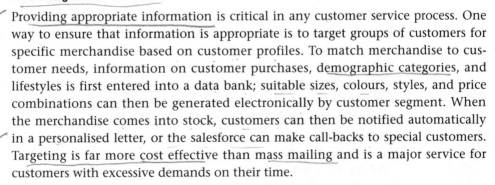

Providing appropriate information is critical in any customer service process. One way to ensure that information is appropriate is to target groups of customers for specific merchandise based on customer profiles. To match merchandise to customer needs, information on customer purchases, demographic categories, and lifestyles is first entered into a data bank; suitable sizes, colours, styles, and price combinations can then be generated electronically by customer segment. When the merchandise comes into stock, customers can then be notified automatically in a personalised letter, or the salesforce can make call-backs to special customers. Targeting is far more cost effective than mass mailing and is a major service for customers with excessive demands on their time.

Facilitating the planning process

Many customers plan their shopping to make the most of their money and time. Assisting customers in their planning is another way to improve customer service. For example, suggesting alternatives for out-of-stock items or complementary accessories for basic outfits may speed the shopping process, saving customers' time and increasing the retailer's sales. Answering customers' questions about transaction processes, and delivery and return procedures can also reduce the time needed to make a purchase decision. Being able to tell the customer when a delivery will be made and providing quick deliveries may greatly enhance a retailer's credibility.

Customer acceptance of electronic retailing

Electronic in-home shopping offers so many benefits that it already has gained considerable customer acceptance (Ghosh, 1994). In-home shopping reduces the amount of time customers spend on shopping, allowing them more time for leisure activities. This is a major benefit for working women, mothers and other time-pressed consumers. In-home shopping also provides greater flexibility in the timing of shopping. Purchases may be made 24 hours a day, 365 days a year, and whenever visiting a store is inconvenient (in bad weather, during roadworks, and so on). In-home shopping can save customers the physical effort of travelling to a fixed-site store, which is an extremely valuable benefit for elderly customers with mobility difficulties and customers with disabilities (Morgan, 1996).

One major obstacle exists to widespread customer acceptance of electronic retailing. The necessity of owning high-tech equipment like personal computers, modems, and interactive cable television links is a major stumbling block. Moreover, even minor flaws in the technology interrupted orders; overcrowded lines and software viruses may irritate customers and thus test their loyalty to the retailer.

Retail marketing via the Internet

The Internet is a collection of interlinked computer networks, or a 'network of networks'. In the late 1990s it connected over one million different computers and the rate of increase in use and subscribers was still growing, on a month-by-month basis. The Internet provides global connectivity via a mesh of networks. Historically, the Internet was essentially an academic network, but with growing business use the Internet is no longer an élite network for communication between eminent research centres; it is also accessible to small colleges, small businesses and libraries throughout the world (Morgan, 1996). The Internet offers a gateway to a myriad of on-line databases, library catalogues and collections, and software and document archives, in addition to such services as UserNet News and e-mail.

All the information that it is possible to access on the Internet is held on computers known as 'servers' which are attached to a network at points called 'nodes'. These servers are owned either by companies which want to distribute information on the network or by organisations that charge people for access to the network and for supporting services (Assadi, 1998). The number of people across the world who use the Internet on a regular basis is probably several million. From the retail marketing point of view, the Internet is a significant opportunity for retailers to extend their reach and their marketing communication strategy.

Resources available via the Internet

The resources available via the Internet are constantly changing, so any list is liable to date rapidly. However, it may be useful to summarise some of the categories of use of the Internet:

■ e-mail – allowing users to send messages or files to one another;

■ news – to inform users of available information;

■ remote log in – allows users to log in to remote sites;

■ file transfer protocol – allows users to access and retrieve files at remote sites.

Connecting to the Internet

There are five prerequisites for 'surfing' the Internet:

■ a PC;

■ a communications link (usually a phone and a modem);

■ an Internet service provider (ISP);

■ an Internet address;

■ access software.

Most individuals and small businesses will access the Internet via a PC and a standard telephone connection to an Internet service provider (ISP). The ISP's computer is attached to, and part of, the Internet. The ISP can provide a range of services from an account or address on its computer and the access software which allows access to the Internet, through to the provision of Web sites, dedicated high-speed telephone lines (ISDN) and other services.

Changing the marketplace and the product

Internet shopping has the potential to challenge the structure of the marketplace and the nature of the product. The Internet allows relatively easy and low-cost entry to retailers which are new entrants to a marketplace. The following are some of the advantages of retailing on the Internet:

■ small businesses can extend their reach;

■ it eliminates the prohibitive costs of entry to many industries;

■ hardware and software advances permit improved interfaces and functionality;

■ on-line information is current;

Exhibit 16.7 **Examples of shopping malls**

It is possible to venture into selling on the Internet using the relatively low-tech selling vehicle of e-mail, which facilitates communication between the retailer and the customer. Other, more established tools such as Telnet and Gopher have been used to support shopping activities, but by far the most interesting and fastest growing segment of the Internet is the World Wide Web. Here, cybermalls, virtual storefronts, interactive Web pages and on-line data entry forms are being established. Web presence can take the form of small advertisements or large virtual stores. Cybermalls are usually large Web sites that seek to emulate traditional shopping malls, offering stores, services and guides to information. Retailers rent a storefront (actually a Web page) and advertise using text, images or video. The following list gives examples of some of these malls:

1 Apollo Advertising in England offers worldwide ads for services and goods. Pages are arranged by geographical category, including Canada, Europe, the UK, the USA, and the rest of the world. Apollo offers on-line advertising services, ranging from plain text to multimedia commercials.

2 Branch Information Services is one of the largest and oldest shopping malls. It uses e-mail, FTP and Gopher to deliver information. It provides electronic store fronts; information booths; automatic e-mail responders; FTP, Gopher and Web space; on-line forms support; and a domain name registration service.

3 Marketplace Com is operated by Cyber-space Development Inc., and primarily offers electronic information such as newsletters, electronic books and software journals, and reports through its Internet Information Mall.

4 MarketNet is a UK-based electronic mall which offers a range of Net services including: Lawnet, Flowernet, Chocnet, Artnet, Craftnet and Banknet.

5 The Interactive Super Mall offers a broad variety of merchandise, including books, newsletters, software, collectables and employment services.

- interaction with customer representatives and immediate ordering are possible;
- it eliminates costs associated with the store, salespeople and possibly some warehousing costs;
- as compared with conventional catalogues there are no printing and mailing costs, and the information can be rapidly changed and updated;
- much more extensive advertising coverage can be achieved for a relatively small outlay.

Internet retailing also has the potential to change the nature of some products. Internet could also be seen as providing new possibilities for retailers. One possible future scenario has private television channels, and later the Internet, sponsored by multi-unit, multibrand concepts which will provide customers with the opportunity to order through the television or the Internet – though this is not around the corner. Customers, however, will indisputably benefit from more information.

Despite its advantages, however, Internet shopping presents challenges for both the retailer and the customer. There is widespread awareness of these issues and various developments that seek to eliminate the problems are under way. Although improvements in technology will minimise the effect of these issues, it will be a long time, if ever, before they are eliminated altogether. The stages in electronic shopping are search/browse, view/select, e-order, e-pay, e-delivery. The overall challenge is to ensure success at all stages in this process. In general, the Internet is a great technological marketing tool depending upon the audience that the retailer is trying to reach, although it is far less effective in generating direct sales.

Future of electronic retailing

Despite many experiments and the large amount of money that have been invested in it, electronic retailing is still in the early stages of its development. Many consumers consider shopping through mail, telephone or interactive devices to be risky (Assadi, 1998). Many resist buying products from non-store retailers (Lucas *et al.*, 1994). One reason for this reluctance is probably the consumer's inability physically to examine the quality of the products offered by non-store retailers. In contrast, consumers can actually touch and feel the product, at retail stores, and often get immediate delivery. The limited merchandise selection offered by many non-store retailers is also a drawback, since it limits the potential for comparison shopping. Moreover, many customers may value the store as an important part of the social and cultural landscape; some even consider shopping to be an important form of entertainment. Video catalogues, for example, cannot match the excitement of well-displayed merchandise, changing window displays, and the glitter of shining showcases. The future of electronic retailing is still unfolding and while it will grow in importance with time, the details of the end results are almost impossible to anticipate.

Efficient retail transactions

In addition to giving rise to new forms of retailing, technological advances are also making retail transactions more efficient. Devices such as optical scanners and voice synthesisers improve efficiency at retail checkout counters. Optical scanners can quickly read and interpret the Universal Product Code (UPC) on packages, retrieve the price of the product from a central computer, and calculate the total amount of sale. Voice synthesisers announce each item's price and the total amount to the customer.

These technological innovations are helping both consumers and retailers. For example, high-tech checkout counters speed up the check-out process and help eliminate the long queues at many supermarkets. Optical scanners also save labour by eliminating the need to mark prices on each item; instead, prices are displayed on large cards attached to shelves.

Control of retail operations

Computerised checkout counters (often called POS or point-of-sale systems) not only help to reduce queues and labour costs, but give retailers ready access to up-to-date information on sales and inventories. A large selection of computer software specifically designed for retailers is now available. Coupled with an electronic POS system, these software packages track sales and inventory levels and automate merchandise ordering, receiving, and pricing. They can also perform routine calculations of mark-up, margins, and other data necessary for merchandise valuation. Computers also help to prepare payrolls and maintain accounting records.

Computers are affecting large and small retailers alike. Stores of any size and type may use computers and an electronic point-of-sale unit to track inventory and sales. At the end of each day, a summary report displays the sales of each item and the amount of inventory on hand. The price at which each item was bought and sold, and the current wholesale price also appears on the summary. The summary sheet shows the direct product profit (DPP) of each item and its sales trend. Based on these data, the retailer then decides which items to order and which to mark down. Finally, the retailer places the order directly, through a computer link, with the supplier. Electronic data interchange (EDI) systems linking retailers to their suppliers enable retailers to manage their inventory more efficiently and thereby reduce inventory investments. EDI will be one of the most important technological trends in retail operations in the future. Computers are, therefore, revolutionising retail technology, information systems and merchandise control procedures for both large and small retailers. They are changing the way merchandise performance is evaluated and how it is controlled. Chapter 13 discusses in more detail the use of computerised retail information systems to control merchandise performance.

SUMMARY

This chapter looked at techno-retail marketing or the application of technology to retail marketing, and assessed how the development of techno-retail marketing is altering retailing methodology and creating dramatic shifts in consumer shopping behaviour. Retailers play a key role in advocating and introducing innovations. Technological innovations are of three forms: those that cause major shifts in accompanying consumer behaviour are labelled discontinuous innovations; dynamically continuous innovations are more moderate in the changes that they bring; and continuous innovations bring little changes in the way that customers use them.

As high-quality customer service becomes the new measure of retail productivity, decision support systems will become a key to success for retailers. As operations, the rewards will be better customer service, lower operating expenses, and increased productivity. Faster inventory turnover, lower inventory levels, and greater marketing efficiency will contribute to both productivity and profitability.

In general, regardless of the approach used, electronic retailing has unique characteristics that differentiate it from other non-store approaches. Perhaps the most obvious feature is a moving visual, which can be used for product and service demonstrations. Unlike traditional promotional materials, stand-alone electronic media allow customers to select the amount, type, and assortment of information they need; choose among competing brands; and even custom order merchandise and services – ranging from travel arrangements to home furnishings.

KEY TERMS

ARS	interactive electronic	technology
bar coding	systems	tekhnolgia
EDI	one-way media	televised home shopping
EFTPOS	OTB	transactional kiosks
electronic couponing	retail technology	two-way media
electronic retailing	scanning	UPC
EPOS	SCM	video catalogues
home shopping clubs	stand-alone media	videotex
information technology	techno-marketing	VSAT

ASSIGNMENT

The Internet is a global network of computers linked by high-speed data lines. Each computer contains pages and pages of information placed on it by local users – anyone, from individuals to major corporations. The pages are all indexed and classified, making it possible to search computers throughout the world for information on particular subjects or for sites containing particular words of interest.

Task

You work for an international retailer operating stores in the United States, Canada, South Africa, Japan, Hong Kong and Taiwan. Your organisation is considering marketing its store image through the Internet. Write a memo to your marketing manager indicating the benefits and implications of using the Internet for this purpose.

REVISION QUESTIONS

1 The role of technology as a motor that drives the growth of a retail organisation is a very important aspect of retail management for retailers worldwide. Discuss this statement with appropriate examples from the retail industry.

2 The strategic marketing approach is a way of thinking based on the philosophy that the goal of all retailers is to create value at a profit. Explain how retailers may operate based on this philosophy.

3 What do you consider to be the key technological impact on retail marketing?

4 There is a need to encourage retailers to use information technology (IT) in more revolutionary ways. Discuss the retailer's IT requirements in making retail marketing decisions.

5   Five technologies – including bar coding, scanning, automatic replenishment systems, electronic data interchange, and very small aperture terminals – could be used to ease retail operation processes. Briefly explain how they are used.

6   Discuss the role of technology as an aid to retail marketing decision making.

7   Explain how retailers could use technology to differentiate themselves from their competitors.

8   Electronic retailing may be subdivided into three broad categories of one-way media, two-way media, and stand-alone media. What similarities and differences exist between these categories?

9   What do you consider to be the main obstacle in customers' acceptance of electronic retailing?

10 Marketing via the Internet has some limitations in that only those with suitable computers may have access. What are the other possible limitations?

CASE STUDY

The cyberspace market

The term 'cybermarketing' is used to describe the type of marketing that operates through the use of computers and telecommunications, and is conducted via multimedia, the Internet and the World Wide Web, interactive television, virtual reality, and CD-ROM. Although there is no fixed store location for the cyberspace market, shopping via this medium is increasing rapidly, with sales running into £17.5 million in the first quarter of 1998. Amazon, one of the largest book stores in the world with 2.5 million titles, is featured in the cyberspace market.

The emergence of brands that are solely electronic is already a reality, and manufacturers and retailers are being encouraged to sell their brands through the electronic medium. The advantages of the Internet are that it can allow retailers to create new brands and experiment at very little cost. The Internet offers micro-marketing on global scale. In theory, it is now possible to present the same product in different ways, to appeal to very different customers, without duplicating the infrastructure cost.

In the financial services sector, for example, the same insurance product could be positioned as a conservative, middle-aged choice to one sector at the same time as being presented as an in-touch lifestyle product for the twenty-something age group. It is, of course, necessary to know that not all product sectors are suitable brand categories for the cyberspace market. It is probably true to say that while the technical and interface design issues are not insignificant, the logistical problem of home delivery is still the biggest challenge for on-line supermarket shopping. For grocery retailers, this does not mean that having an on-line service is not viable, rather that the Web could be better used for creating a new brand for just one product sector, which is suitable for selling on-line.

A typical example is the case for W.H. Smith. It is not known as a destination store for, say, acid jazz music but it has the database and infrastructure to sell it. So it could easily create an acid jazz brand and sell the product on-line. The idea is that by doing so, it would distance the WH Smith brand from the acid jazz brand and thus attract a different consumer base from that visiting its high street stores.

Three types of brand are most likely to benefit from cyberbranding: those with strong products but dull conventional images, such as banks; those that have tightly-targeted markets but international appeal, such as fashion and specialist retailers; and malleable brands, like Virgin and Marks & Spencer, because they will be able to stretch and endorse a wide range of products and services. However, whether or not a brand will succeed on the Internet is not always obvious. Just because one retailer has built a successful brand in cyberspace within a year does not mean that another retailer will be equally successful. All the marketing information must be explored to predetermine if success is a possibility.

Questions for discussion

1 The telecommunications barriers will have to be surmounted before the Internet moves forward. What other barriers are there for retailers selling through cyberspace?

2 The World Wide Web is one of the fastest growing technologies of all time. Discuss the advantages of marketing through the Internet.

REFERENCES

Assadi, D. (1998) 'Internet can offer more than a quick sale; try car-shopping', *Marketing News*, 32(2): 9.

Ghosh, A. (1994) *Retail Management.* 2nd edn. New York: The Dryden Press.

Leeming, A. (1996) 'Information technology and retailing' in Business News, City University Business School (Winter): 17–19.

Lucas, G., Bush, R. and Gresham, L. (1994) *Retailing*. Boston, MA: Houghton Mifflin.

Morgan, R.F. (1996) 'An Internet marketing framework for the Worldwide web', *Journal of Marketing*, (12): 757–75.

O'Connor, J. and Calvin, E. (1997) *Marketing and Information Technology: The Strategy, Application and Implementation of IT in Marketing*. London: Financial Times Pitman Publishing.

Omar, O. (1995) 'Retail influence on food technology and innovation', *International Journal of Retail and Distribution Management*, 23(3): 11–16.

Omar, O. (1998) 'Strategic collaboration: a beneficial retail marketing strategy for car manufacturers and dealers', *Journal of Strategic Marketing*, (6): 65–78.

Rowley, J. (1996) 'Retailing and shopping on the Internet', *International Journal of Retail and Distribution Management*, 24(3): 26–37.

Senker, J.M. (1986) 'Technological co-operation between manufacturers and retailers to meet market demand', *Food Marketing*, 2(3): 88–100.

Index